Penguin Books

MAN BITES MAN

'Ives himself has his share of mild eccentricities... melons, and he carried his gas-mask everywhere... over) and we are fortunate indeed that his treasu... plundered for our delight by Paul Sieveking with... Arthur Marshall in the *New Statesman*

'One wonders if today's headlines, large and small will have the same curiosity value in fifty years' time. Anyone with an eye for the enduring oddity might consider investing in scissors and a gum pot. Also, of course, in this book!' – David Sanders in *Now*

'It's a really strange collection, and a treat for a particularly odd relative' – *Time Out*

'This scrapbook of newspaper cuttings is a sample of the distinctly off-beat, fantastic, grim, strange and, in retrospect, funny' – *Oxford Evening Echo*

'A splendid cross between *Private Eye*'s "True Stories" column and Ripley at his quirkiest – with the added piquancy that they knew how to be odd-balls in those days and the press knew how to cover them to the public's satisfaction' – *Book Buyer*

George Ives (in cap) at a picnic in Nice in 1900

MAN BITES MAN

The Scrapbook of an Edwardian Eccentric

George Ives

EDITED BY PAUL SIEVEKING

PENGUIN BOOKS

CONTENTS

- 7 CALL OF THE WILD
- 12 DEPRAVITY AND MURDER
- 19 ECCENTRICS
- 27 FANATICS
- 34 FREAKS
- 43 HIGH ARCHIVES
- 51 LAW 'N' ORDER
- 59 MISCELLANEA
- 64 PHENOMENA
- 73 PUNISHMENT
- 80 RELIGIOUS MANIA
- 88 RICHES OR FAME
- 95 SPECTRES
- 102 STRANGE DEATH
- 109 SUPERSTITION
- 116 TABOO
- 123 TRANSVESTISM
- 130 TWISTS OF FATE
- 138 WAR AND PEACE
- 146 WEDLOCK
- 152 WOMEN
- 159 INDEX

Penguin Books Ltd, Harmondsworth, Middlesex, England
Penguin Books, 625 Madison Avenue, New York, New York 10022, U.S.A.
Penguin Books Australia Ltd, Ringwood, Victoria, Australia
Penguin Books Canada Ltd, 2801 John Street, Markham, Ontario, Canada L3R 1B4
Penguin Books (N.Z.) Ltd, 182–190 Wairau Road, Auckland 10, New Zealand

First published in Great Britain by Jay Landesman Limited 1980
Published in Penguin Books 1981

Copyright © Jay Landesman, 1980
All rights reserved

Made and printed in Great Britain by Butler & Tanner, Frome and London

Except in the United States of America, this book is sold subject to the condition that it shall not, by way of trade or otherwise, be lent, re-sold, hired out, or otherwise circulated without the publisher's prior consent in any form of binding or cover other than that in which it is published and without a similar condition including this condition being imposed on the subsequent purchaser

PREFACE
Paul Sieveking

In the Autumn of 1978, the publisher Jay Landesman showed writer Alan Brien the scrapbooks of George Ives, clipster-extraordinary. That evening, at his local pub, Brien overheard a woman at a nearby table, who had spent most of her life in service, saying to a friend: "That was the time when I used to go in next door and clean for George Ives . . ." It was indeed the same man. Brien tells the story in Punch:

> "Without a prompt or hint from me, except to ask what sort of a man he was, she said that he was very nice, very quiet, always sticking things into his black-and-gold books. 'I used to have to dust them. I peeked inside, and there were strange beasts, and tortures, and suicides, and ghosts, and the like.' She volunteered that he was 'queer', and lived with two men in a house just off the Camden Road. 'I think he kept them both. He was never short of money.'
> I asked if he were eccentric at all. 'Well, he had a passion for melons. He kept them everywhere. The whole house used to stink of melons. And he was very obstinate. He died in 1950, am I right? And to the end he still used to carry his gas mask in a cardboard box over his shoulder. He kept a silver tankard, with his initials and his crest on it, in the pub over the way, gone now. I think the family was Viscount Maynard, and he'd been brought up by the daughter, Emma Ives.'"

A few days after this, I got to hear of the Ives Archive through Robert Rickard, the editor of *Fortean Times*, and a connoisseur of coincidences. Jay Landesman commissioned me to read through the forty-five volumes, and the result is this book. I travelled through 50 years totally immersed in a procession of the naive and the pedantic and the bizarre and the grotesque and the sincere and the insincere, the profound and the puerile. It was as if I were seeing through the eyes of Ives, who pasted his last clipping as I was born. Like him, I am attracted to the anomalous and the anarchic.

Many of the clippings have mellowed into quaintness as they turned yellow—opinions that were obviously lethal at the time now give rise to hilarity. I hope, in reading them, that you will laugh as much as I did in getting them together; and that you will turn with a sharper vision towards the received opinions of our own time.

Paul Sieveking was born in London in 1949, the son of the writer and broadcaster Lance Sieveking. He read anthropology at Jesus College, Cambridge, graduating in 1971. With John Fullerton he translated *The Revolution of Everyday Life* by Raoul Vaneigem, published by Practical Paradise Publications in 1975. He is currently associate editor of the *Fortean Times*, the journal of strange phenomena.

INTRODUCTION
Jeremy Brooks

Queen Victoria was on the throne of England when the young George Ives, then an undergraduate at Cambridge, pasted his first press cutting into his first 123-page gold-tooled scrapbook. That was in 1892, and it took him nearly six years to fill that volume. After that, his snipping-and-pasting productivity speeded up. He took less than eighteen months to fill Volume II. Four kings and a queen later—nearly sixty years later—Ives had accumulated no less than forty-five fat volumes of cuttings, nearly six thousand pages. Dipping into them is like travelling in a time machine. Nothing can match the immediacy of journalism, nor its vulnerable transparency. The journalist reports what he has been told, what came over the wire or through the jungle in a cleft stick. Here is a baby with a wolf's head and the claws of a lobster; there the six-year-old mother of a fifteen-month-old baby boy. Here—in Virginia in 1909—are a white man and a black woman sentenced to 18 years' imprisonment for getting married; there, in Massachusetts in 1940, a woman is sent to gaol "for an indefinite term" for living with her ex-husband. And from Warwickshire, the heart of England, in 1933, a Mr Cornforth thunders: "All the best of England's youth are Fascist at heart, and only await the call and leadership. Nothing can stop us. The spirit of Fascism will sweep the world."

Not if George Ives could help it, it wouldn't. Like many intelligent men of his time, he was a "rational anarchist", as he made plain in a "Letter to the Editor" of January 1897:

> "Rational anarchy is but little understood, though a growing factor in our civilisation; its motto is, briefly, oppose power wherever it is found. But for the prevailing ignorance, I would omit stating that we do not wish to blow up anybody; we leave physical force to those who use it as their best argument, satisfied that it never yet ultimately prevailed, and never will. We reject as enemies those fanatics who deal death recklessly, destroying innocent and guilty alike; all outrages do but strengthen Governments, and tend to justify coercion. We hate the man who coerces, be he in patrician's robes or in a greasy black coat; we detest force; we despise the sordid rule of gold. Law and order! the old plea. The sins of law are as many as the stones on the sea beach, but the future shall sweep them away as the past has done the thumbscrew and the rack—both servants of the law and of the devil—and order!"

Old fashioned language, perhaps, but Ives was way out ahead of his time in his thinking. In his letters to newspapers, in his speeches to learned societies, his books about penal reform and related subjects, even in the many volumes of poetry that he published (often under a pseudonym) he hammered away at the blatant wickedness of the established order. These forty-five volumes of cuttings were both his evidence and his ammunition.

Ives hated cruelty, injustice and uninformed prejudice; at least half of his cuttings are on such subjects. They were not hard to find. In 1906 he notes a child of three being sentenced to 3½ months' imprisonment for stealing a toy "of little value". In 1910 a twelve-year-old gets seven years for stealing a lump of coal worth fivepence. In 1921 a child chess prodigy, by then an undergraduate at Cambridge with a good war record, got six months' imprisonment for making seditious (i.e. Communist) speeches—his brain, it was said, had been weakened by too much chess. In 1929 the police swoop on and impound some "obscene" paintings; they are by William Blake.

Apart from an occasional exclamation mark, or a note identifying a pseudonym, Ives seldom comments on his cuttings. Where he does—and it is seldom more than a line in the margin to indicate the passage that has most struck him—he most reveals himself. In a long (1933) article by Aldous Huxley on drugs, for instance, the two passages he marks are:

"The moral horror of drugs is a very modern invention. As recently as forty years ago a 'drug fiend' could still be the hero of a popular novel. Sherlock Holmes, for example, was a cocaine addict."
and
"All illness can be radically cured only by removing its cause. The cause of drunkenness and drug-taking is to be found in the general dissatisfaction with reality."

One has to have penetrated George Ives's world and mind to realise that he marked the first passage because he was a friend of Sherlock Holmes's creator, Arthur Conan Doyle—both were distinguished members, with J.M. Barrie and P.G. Wodehouse, of the Authors' Cricket Team of the day. He notes the second passage because he agrees with it. "Dissatisfaction with reality", Ives was convinced, was at the root of all mankind's problems. His collected scrapbook is a vast minefield of all the causes of dissatisfaction that surround us.

Ives was also fascinated by any evidence of things in the natural world which are "not right". In 1903 he notes a tree "with an alternating crop of apples and pears"; in 1904, a double-headed snake and a four-legged bird; in 1921 a woman who is an "animal magnet"—she has been attacked by weasels, horses and pigs ("With cries of 'Umratten-ratten' they charged her and nearly knocked her down"). Wild men of the woods, lost tribes, wolf boys, monsters of the deep, the vanished crews of undamaged ships, demons and monsters and ghosts of all sorts ("Facetious Ghost Hits a Policeman in the Eye with Half-a-Pound of Butter") all caught his attention, as if such phenomena were part of a pattern which, if only it could be unravelled, would free humanity from its chains.

And indeed this was exactly how Ives thought, as his poetry reveals. In 1896 he anonymously published a book of poems entitled *Book of Chains*, which on the whole was fairly savagely reviewed, probably because of an injudicious preface. But one reviewer saw through the aggressive, anti-State polemics:

"This is a book of short poems from the pen of a soul in revolt against slavery of all kinds. "Love Free" is the title of one of the poems—an appeal for a trial of Nature's plan as opposed to man's attempt to sever those whom she intended should meet in mutual love . . . there can be no mistaking the sadness and sense of wrong underlying all the poems."

This is perceptive. Ives's sense of wrong, his longing that people should meet in mutual love, underlies all his selections. On the subject of sexual love he is ambiguous. From the number of cuttings on the subject it might be inferred that he was homosexual; certainly he followed the Oscar Wilde case with close attention, and against an early cutting about an "indecent offence" which is never specified he has written "Taboo!" There are also many cuttings about transvestism, though more of these are about women masquerading as men than the reverse. He gives a lecture to the Malthusian Society on the effects of over-population, but makes no recommendations. On sexual relations he is largely silent.

But on sexual politics he is, as on so many issues, way out in front. "Science Proves Women Inferior" he notes with obvious disdain in 1909; in 1912 he finds a Professor of Pathology fuming about why women are constitutionally unfit for the vote—those who advocate it should be deported to join the convict classes in Australia—and in 1914 notes "a famous professor of Berlin University" opining that the "brain work" advocated by suffragism will cause women to go bald and "wear patriarchal beards and long moustaches". Clearly Ives regarded such attitudes as being as primitive as those behind the 1936 cutting: "Negro Shot to Give Week-End Party 'a Little Excitement'".

George Ives was an "original", but throughout his life a wholly consistent one. The kind of news items that sparked his interest after the Second World War were precisely the kind that grabbed him during the Boer War: the impediments to progress, man's inhumanities, nature's diversities. To read these cuttings is like pursuing the clues in an endless and unsolved detective story, in which the quarry is both the elusive personality of George Ives, and the mysterious nature of mankind. It is also to open a series of brilliantly lit windows on half a century of our immediate past.

CALL OF THE WILD

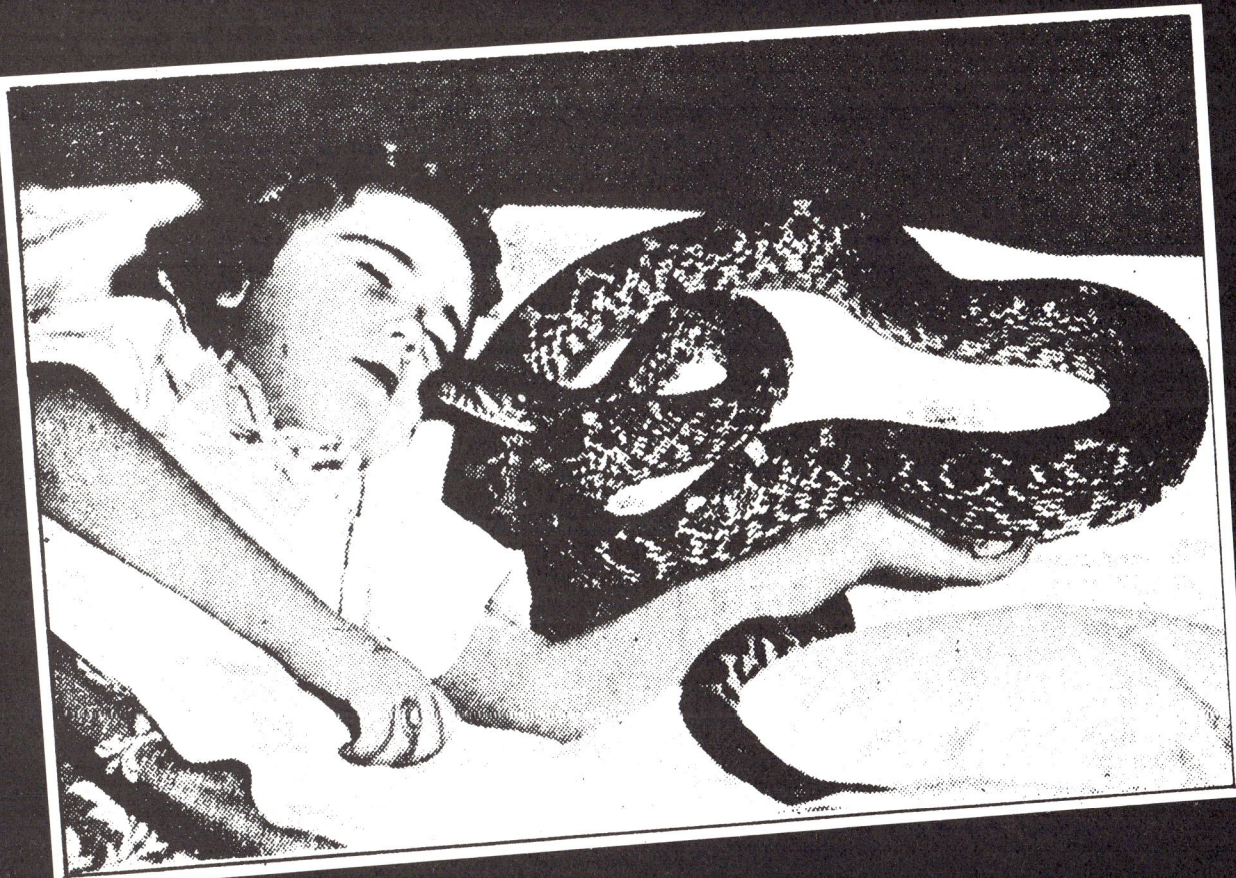

Here are the queerest bedfellows you ever saw—a little girl and a snake. She's Annette Avers, of Portage, Wisconsin, U.S., and the snake, a seven-footer, is her constant companion.
While Annette sleeps in orthodox fashion, between the sheets, the snake curls up on the pillow, sleeping, not with one eye open, but both—you see, snakes have no eyelids. 1938

8 Call of the Wild

1923

A BIRD WITH FOUR LEGS

Creature That Can Climb Like a Monkey.

The discovery in British Guiana of a bird with four legs was announced some time ago.

The crested hoatzin, opisthocomus cristatus, the only survivor of a race of birds, several of which are known as fossils, inhabit the most secluded parts of the forests of South America.

It is probable that it is owing to its retiring habits it has outlived the others of its kind, as well as to the fact that feeding as it does upon wild arum leaves, its flesh acquires so offensive a smell and flavour as to have gained it the name of stink bird, and to render it entirely unfit for food. It is a large bird, almost as large as a peacock, but it is very seldom seen.

The chief peculiarity of the hoatzin consists in the fact that when it is hatched it possesses four well-developed legs, the front pair being of a reptilian character.

Like Toads.

The young birds leave the nest and climb about like monkeys over the adjoining limbs and twigs, and act and look more like tree toads than birds. After hatching, the modification of the fore limbs begins, the claws of the digits falling off, and all of the claw-like hands, becoming flattened, change into wings.

After the modification has taken place feathers begin to grow, and in a short time not a vestige remains of its original character.

1905

SEA SERPENT'S RIVAL

The trawler Etrurian entered the port of Boston with a haul which startled the peaceful old-world fisher-folk, accustomed though they are to the wonders of the ocean.

That vessel's trawl beam had torn from their home at the bottom of the sea a score or so of crabs which recalled, by their appearance, the strange adventures of Sinbad. The largest weighed nearly 16lb., and measured a yard and a half across when its powerful claws were extended. The claws were 18in. in circumference.

1903

Fruit-breeders have produced many marvels, but nothing quite akin to the unaided performance of a tree in Forfarshire, which last year grew apples, and whose branches are this year reported to be laden with pears. There are more than five hundred different standard kinds of apples on the English market, and more than eight hundred different kinds of pears, but a tree with an alternating crop of apples and pears is an unaccountable oddity.

THE PICCADILLY GOAT

TO THE EDITOR OF THE MORNING POST

Sir,—With reference to Mr. Max Beerbohm's broadcast, maybe there are other readers of the "Morning Post" who, like the undersigned, can recall this celebrity of Piccadilly in the 'Eighties. My impression is that the billy-goat belonged to the Duke of Cambridge. Anyway, I saw it many a time in the stables at the rear of the Duke's residence, Gloucester House, which stood on the west corner of Park-lane.

The goat would wander around Piccadilly and its byways, and was a regular —and welcome—visitor at the bakers' and greengrocers' shops. Often it could be seen standing on the corner of Park-lane, being petted by the lads of the village, among whom was

CHARLES WHITE.

5, Airedale-avenue. W. 4

1931

VILLAGE OF THE BLIND

A MYSTERIOUS AFFLICTION

INFECTION FROM BATS

From Our Own Correspondent

BERLIN, Dec. 21.

Mr. H. G. Wells's famous tale of the Valley of the Blind has received remarkable confirmation by the discovery that in the village of Tiltepec, over four thousand feet above sea level, in the Mexican State of Oaxaca, all the inhabitants were blind from at least one year after birth. The village contained more than forty households.

That the general blindness has now been alleviated is principally due to the researches of a German doctor, Max Weihmann. This village of the blind had been the object of several scientific inquiries since it was first recorded in 1927, and a report upon the curious affliction of its inhabitants was issued by a Mexican doctor.

At first it was believed that the blindness was due to an infectious disease, or to abuse of methyl alcohol. There was, however, no evidence to support these theories. The inhabitants themselves attributed it to the wind-blown pollen of a flower called Verguenza, which has the peculiarity of blooming for half a day only.

The researches of the German doctor, however, led to the discovery of several other villages in the district in which blindness was also prevalent, and to the supposition that it was connected in some way with an infection carried by a midge. Upon examination of the sufferers they were found in almost every case to have large bumps or wens on their heads, in which the midge laid its eggs.

The correctness of Dr. Weihmann's supposition was borne out when the surgical removal of these bumps bestowed sight on the sufferers, sometimes after many years of blindness and within the space of a few days. The carriers of the infection having been found, the next question was where did the midges pick it up. It is supposed that the bats which hang in great quantities upon the beams of the village houses are the offenders.

1934

CAREER OF STANLEY STENSON

CAR GANGSTER WITH BLACK MASK

STANLEY STENSON, killed by the lions in their den at Whipsnade, was, it was revealed yesterday, a motor bandit.

He had served two terms of imprisonment, and had been lashed with the birch for carrying firearms.

Stenson was a young desperado who tried to emulate the exploits of American gangsters. When he turned criminal he obtained a revolver and fifty rounds of ammunition, and went about with a black mask.

1928

OWL ATTACKS MR. LINNETT.

MAN EXHAUSTED IN FIGHT.

While motor-cycling between Wollaston and Grendon, Northamptonshire, Mr. Louis Linnett, of Luton, was attacked by an owl and badly injured

The bird pulled out Mr. Linnett's hair and slashed with its beak and claws at both his cheeks. He left his machine and ran to a hedge, blinded by the blood which entered his eyes from wounds in the forehead.

Eventually Mr. Linnett had to throw himself face downwards in the grass for protection. Twice he beat off the owl, but it attacked again each time and bit his fingers.

When at length it flew away he was too exhausted to move. A passing motorist took him into Grendon, where he spent the night. He was removed to Luton yesterday by motor-car.

Call of the Wild

As you see in this picture, they're great pals. 1937
And they have another friend—the convict whose treasured pets they are. In his cell at a Californian prison, their quaint games lighten the drab and dreary days of a life sentence.

1921
PEOPLE WHO EXCITE ANIMALS.
By G. G. DESMOND.

Lizzie Thomas, of Pwllheli, was recently attacked by six weasels. Once now and then weasels do act in this way; it is a peculiarity, though a rare one, mentioned in every book of natural history. I expect that the person who plays the other role is what I would call an animal magnet, one who attracts other adventures of the same kind.

Sylvette is an animal magnet. When she was three years old she had a frightful adventure with little pigs. They waylaid her at a stile as she was bringing a pound of butter from the farm. With cries of "Umratten-ratten," they charged her and nearly knocked her down. She clung heroically to the butter, and just managed to get over the stile.

Then a very quiet horse that had been a most complacent playfellow suddenly turned on Sylvette, as though acknowledging the potency of dog days, knocked her down, and nearly bit a hole in her stomach. It was as great a shock to her as when a favourite dog of our landlady at the seaside jumped up and bit her face, for I know no one more good to animals that Sylvette.

When she was six or seven Sylvette was crossing the common with money in her hand when a jackdaw flew down to pass the time of day. Partly by force and partly by wile, he snatched her purse and flew away with it. She did not recover it for several days, when it was found in the garden of the cottager that the semi-tame jackdaw belonged to.

Sylvette has had pleasanter adventures. She stood under a tree in the wood once, and a squirrel descending the trunk used her whole body as a ladder to the ground. She has watched adders and lizards coiling in the sun as long as she would; they flash off very quickly from most of us, however quiet we think ourselves.

Then, last week an adventure of the old kind. Sylvette is a grown woman now, the equal of Oxford dons, and with big girls to teach. She was sitting near the wall of a field when a horse came up inside and snatched her coat away. Before she could get it back he had eaten most of the band and had torn holes in the rest. It comes expensive sometimes to be an animal magnet.

Cow 'Mothers' 1938
Deadly Snake

Queer story came in from Reuter yesterday. A farmer near Capetown, it said, sat up one night to watch one of his cows because he suspected that her milk was being stolen.

After some time a long ringhals (flat-headed, deadly snake, like a cobra) came from the scrub and started drinking from the cow. The animal made no attempt to deter it. And when the snake had finished the cow turned and licked its head.

The farmer considered there was something "unholy" in such a friendship. Next day he shot the cow

I have no reason to doubt this. When I was living in South Africa I heard two similar stories.

1904

"Ciro": Has any Aboriginalian ever seen a double-headed snake? I have. Near Werribee (Vic.), I was shooting one day, when the curious freak—about 2ft. long—was seen coiled up and asleep. I called my mate, and together we scrutinised the two distinct and evenly-shaped heads, set on necks about half an inch long. Sleeping.

1931
MULE FOALS TWICE
SOUTH AFRICAN SCIENTIST VERIFIES EVENT

(FROM OUR OWN CORRESPONDENT)
DURBAN.

A mule in Weenen, Natal, is reported to have given birth to two foals.

The first was born seven years ago, and the second this month. The authenticity of the births is vouched for by several witnesses. The first foal, which is now a grown stallion working on the owner's farm, was inspected by Dr. Ernest Warren, then Director of the Natal Government Museum, who wrote a scientific paper on the subject.

Dr. Warren stated that a fair number of reputed cases of mules breeding had been recorded from time to time, but doubt had been thrown on the authenticity of the majority. He was satisfied that the first foal was actually born of the Weenen mule and not adopted. He was also satisfied that the mare was actually a mule and not a horse resembling a mule. The sires of both foals have been horses running on the farm.

The second foal has every appearance of its sire.

1948
HARE SHOOTS MAN
And escapes from car window

JOHANNESBURG, Tuesday.—
A motorist from East London (South Africa) shot a hare and threw it into the back seat of his car.

The hare was only stunned and, regaining consciousness, touched off the trigger of the gun as it leapt out of the window.

The bullet wounded the motorist in the neck.—A.P.

1905
RABBIT BEATS FERRET.

On the sanded floor of an alehouse near Cheshunt a gamekeeper's most trusted ferret was lately matched against a rabbit, an old lop-eared buck, the property of the landlord.

Catching the rabbit's scent the ferret ran straight for the throat, but before his nose could sink in it the rabbit sprang over the ferret's head, delivering in his spring a kick which drove the enemy against the wainscot of the wall. A second and a third time the ferret attacked, to be worsted again and again with the same flying kick.

To the shame of his obstinate race the ferret could not be persuaded to face a fourth round.

1916
GUINEA PIGS AS "GAS GUIDES,"

How Soldiers' Pets Behave Under Poison Clouds.

A correspondent of the *Frankfurter Zeitung* on the Western Front supplies interesting details of the effect of gas attacks on animals kept by soldiers as trench pets.

The first to notice the approach of gas clouds are guinea-pigs, which leap up and look about scared, finally hiding their heads in dark corners. Cats act the same way, with incessant and mournful "meows."

An old cat carried six kittens, whose eyes were still shut, into one of the remotest corners of a dug-out, packed them together behind some wood, and stood by them. After the repulse of the attack she was found dead.

Dogs bark and howl pitifully at the first faint indication of chlorine gas, shutting their eyes tightly and attempting to hide, but seem to suffer the least from actual gas attacks, numbers remaining alive. Rats and mice almost always die. They come out of their holes and usually suffer frightened, speedy ends.

Several owls began to cry when gas came. One screech-owl, which was released, flew off at once in the direction of the wind—i.e., ahead of the gas cloud.

Several horses in front positions were asphyxiated and died, but most of the others galloped away to the nearest hill-tops. When the gas cloud was first noticed horses became very nervous, kept on sniffing the air, and could not be moved a step forward.

Fowls and ducks were extraordinarily excited. Fully a quarter of an hour before the approach of gas clouds they cackled and crowded together in corners. A number perished, mostly old hens.

Ants, caterpillars, cockchafers, butterflies, etc., die in gas attacks. The creatures which show the highest power of resistance against the effects of nitrogen gas are sparrows. They flock together and at first remain quiet, but soon afterwards reveal their characteristic cheerfulness, and twitter and sing as usual.

1928
PLAGUE RATS INVADE A TOWN.

SHOT-GUN VIGIL ON THE VELDT.

"Daily Express" Correspondent.
JOHANNESBURG,
Sunday, Nov. 11.

Great alarm has been caused at the important Cape railways junction of De Aar by an invasion of thousands of rats, which entered the town from the surrounding plains and are dying everywhere.

One De Aar householder alone swept out forty dead rats from his dwelling. The Government laboratories at Johannesburg announced that it is virtually certain that the rats are dying from plague, though final tests are still being made.

Medical authorities hurried to De Aar, where a great trek of rats is found to be in progress from west to east.

Travellers report passing through great droves of the rodents, numbering countless thousands, over a wide area. The municipality organised gangs of men, equipped with sticks, shot-guns and lanterns, who all day and all night long patrol the veldt west of De Aar, endeavouring to stem the tide of rat invaders before they enter the town.

1929
CAT SEVEN FEET IN LENGTH.

SMALLHOLDER HAS THE SHOCK OF HIS LIFE.

"Reynolds's" Correspondent.

PRESTON, Saturday.—When Mr. Tom Cartmell, a Freckleton (Preston) motor mechanic and poultry farmer, visited his hen houses the other night he got the shock of his life.

Out of seven hens in one cote six were lying dead on the floor, and in a corner there crouched a huge black cat seven feet long!

Hastily slamming the door, Mr. Cartmell returned to the house to think the matter out. Suddenly he remembered he had seen an advertisement offering a reward of £100 for information leading to the capture of a seven foot long cat that had escaped from captivity at Blackpool.

Mr. Cartmell got in touch with the advertiser, Mr. Albert Chapman, Church-street, Blackpool, who visited Freckleton, identified the beast, and took it away.

The animal, a Ginturong, is said to be the largest cat in the world. It was brought to this country from Sumatra by a sailor, who disposed of it to Mr. Chapman.

According to Mr. Cartmell, who declined to be interviewed about his "capture," the beast "looks like a cross between a cat and a bear." It has a huge body, a sharp, cruel-looking head, with fiery eyes and tufted ears. Its feet are widely splayed with terrible looking claws.

1934
TOWN INVADED BY— SPIDERS!

MANY PEOPLE IN HOSPITAL —THE DOCTORS POWERLESS

SANTIAGO, Chile, Thursday.

Huge, poisonous spiders are invading the town of Antofagasta, and are attacking the inhabitants. Their bite inflicts great wounds like the gash of a knife, and 20 people, including nine children, are already in hospital suffering from such wounds.

Nothing like these spiders has, apparently, ever been seen before. They are of an unknown species.

An SOS has been received by the public health authorities at Santiago, and the Antofagasta doctors have wired for help from the central Government, declaring themselves powerless in face of an invasion "of spiders of the most virulent kind."

Expert assistance has been promised, and the Antofagasta doctors are urged to "make a big effort" to capture a specimen of the spiders alive.—Reuter.

1927
'BLACK WIDOW' TERROR.

"WEEKLY DISPATCH" CABLE.
NEW YORK, Saturday.

"The Black Widow" has inaugurated a reign of terror in Southern California and Arizona.

Already her victims number twenty, all men. "The Black Widow," according to scientists in Los Angeles, is a small black spider, the most deadly that has ever appeared in North America.

Known to entomologists as *Latrodectus mactans*, the insect also has the more popular names of "Black Widow," "Shoebutton," and "Hourglass" spider

In some cases death followed within 24 hours of its bite. In addition to the known total of 20 victims in two months, scientists believe the spider responsible for other deaths attributed by hospitals to "blood poisoning."

Until recently it was believed that the spider did not exist in North America, but now it is considered certain that it was introduced from Oriental ports concealed in fruit or lumber. Specimens have been found near lumber yards, but in each instance, fearing the inevitable panic, scientists kept their presence secret until an intensive combing of the surrounding district convinced them that all the insects were captured.

Despite the scientists' reassuring statements against panic, persons with visions of sudden death and bodies bloated and discoloured by the insect's venom are shunning all spiders.

1931
MILLIONS OF MICE

ARMY ADVANCING OVER MILES

From Our Own Correspondent
MELBOURNE, Tuesday.

A plague of mice, numbering millions and coming from no one knows where, has invaded the Nullabor Plain, through which runs the Trans-Australian Railway.

While the stationmaster at Loongana was attending to a passenger's requirements a battalion broke away from the main army, entered his office and began to devour a roll of 100 £1 notes.

In an SOS to the head office in Melbourne, the stationmaster states that the mice have invaded houses all along the line, and the country for miles is infested.

Rest is impossible, he adds. "Everywhere one looks one sees thousands of mice, which seem to have come out of the sky. They are eating everything in their advance and are attacking furniture and bedding."

1931
PARROT TRAPS MURDERER.

DYING WOMAN'S CRY,

From Our Own Correspondent.
NEW YORK, Monday.

A parrot shrieking "Don't papa, don't," in the middle of the night, furnished a clue which led to the arrest of Frank Yitkos, a New York longshoreman, for the murder of his wife.

The bird's quickness in picking up new phrases was the wonder of the locality, and when neighbours were aroused from sleep by this unusual cry, they became alarmed and entered the Yitkos's apartment.

There they found that Mrs. Yitkos had been killed with an axe.

So impressed were they by the parrot's evidence, that the police sought for Yitkos, and to-day he confessed to the crime.

1934
BIRDS OF PREY TO BE SET FREE
MUNICH, Wednesday.

The Bavarian Home Minister has prohibited the keeping of birds of prey in small cages.

Only Zoological Gardens which possess cages in which the birds can fly may retain birds of this description in future. All others must be released. —Exchange.

1937
CHURKEYS

"Churkeys," bred from a cock turkey and a chicken, are being bred by Mrs. Cuckoo, of Southfleet, Kent.

A "churkey" has the body and legs of a chicken and the head and neck of a turkey. Its egg is larger than a chicken's egg and tastes better.

1929
COW THAT GOT DRUNK!
Farmer Finds Brook Running Whisky Instead of Water—Mayor Leads Raid!

FROM OUR SPECIAL CORRESPONDENT
NEW YORK, Sunday.

When a dairyman of Broadview Heights, near Cleveland, saw a milch cow zigzagging across a meadow it needed only her whisky-scented breath to confirm his suspicions.

He found that a brook in a nearby field was running whisky instead of water.

The dairyman hastened to confide this surprising discovery to the Mayor, who in dead of night led a raiding party to an upstream barn, which proved to contain two whisky stills.

1924
A BLIND RAT'S GUIDE.

Returning from work at an Ebbw Vale pit, a collier saw two rats, each with the end of a piece of straw in its mouth. He threw a piece of wood he was carrying and killed one rat. The other rat did not move.

On going closer, the collier found that the live rat was without eyes, and was being led by the other rat by means of the straw.

1920
DRUNK RATS CAUGHT STAGGERING HOME.
A Gay Night on Three Bottles of Wine.

Something new in the way of rat-catching is reported to The Evening News to-day by a correspondent who lives at Hendon.

Three bottles of wine had been broken. The wine was mopped up and thrown on a rubbish heap in the garden.

Next morning the householder was surprised to see a dozen intoxicated rats crawling round the heap.

"Several of them," he writes, "were unable even to walk straight; they repeatedly fell over on their sides. None had the slightest fear of me, but stared up with indifferent eyes."

The drunken rats were despatched with a crowbar.

"It is not generally known," said an authority, "that rats are attracted by alcohol. Bees, wasps and ants will also take it, especially if they can absorb it through sugar.

"Intoxicated ants always fall over on their right-side legs; wasps usually become quarrelsome and sting each other to death."

QUEER FOSTER-PARENT. — A chimpanzee which has taken pity on a litter of young leopards, is proving a most efficient foster-mother. The youngsters are thoroughly at home with their unusual "parent."

1940
ISLAND MONSTER SHOT

The "Isle of Wight monster" is dead. It was caught and shot by Mr. W. Clark in a copse near Bembridge yesterday after frightening for over six months women and children who had encountered it in the woods between Ryde and Osborne House.

The animal resembled a large fox about the head, but had a shaggy mane, and the rest of its body was practically hairless. Its paws were the size of a large fist.

Those who had seen it prowling stated that its movements were slow and deliberate.

1929
LAID 230 EGGS AND THEN CROWED!
Hen Mystifies Owner After Two Years' Good Behaviour

GREW A COMB
Gave Up Laying for a Noisier and Gayer Life

A brown Leghorn hen which has laid over 230 eggs in two years has mystified its owner by its transformation into a crowing cock.

This is the history of the bird, which was told to a Daily Mirror representative by Miss Hilda Bailey, of Christchurch-road, Winchester.

In 1927 a friend gave her three six-weeks-old brown Leghorn pullets, and in the following spring they began to lay. One, slightly larger than the other two, laid particularly well. Miss Bailey's notebook shows that it produced 119 eggs then, and the following summer it proved to be the best layer by producing a similar number.

Miss Bailey only keeps half a dozen hens, whose individual performances are recorded.

To her surprise, when two of the brown Leghorns began to lay again a week or two ago, the best layer—the big bird—failed to produce any eggs, and developed all the characteristics of a cockerel, with a fine tail and a loud crow, although it had a rather feminine head.

1921
THE ROAR OF THE OSTRICH.

Mr. F. Balfour-Browne, at the Zoological Society to-day, said very few people knew that an ostrich roared.

The roars of an ostrich and a lion were so alike that Dr. Livingstone could never distinguish the difference, save that the bird roared by day and the "man-eater" by night.

1928
A WHITE BLACKBIRD

A white blackbird has been seen several times during the past few days in the allotment gardens at Brancepeth Colliery, Willington, County Durham. About 30 years ago a white blackbird was shot by some sportsmen who were pheasant shooting near the same place.

1921
FIGHTING HEN-COCK.
Chanticleers Who Have Been Laid Low in the Ring.

Another "hen-cock" has made his—or her—appearance.

The Buff Orpington "hen," which was shown in London last week, had plumage resembling a cock, and also spurs. A rival bird was shown at the Cumberland Old England Game Club's show at Egremont on Saturday.

It was exhibited in the fighting class by Mr. T. Robinson, of Aspatria, and is described as a black "hen" cock.

The bird comes from a long line of fighting "hen" cocks who, equipped with formidable spurs, have proved game to the death.

Their appearance in the "ring" often deceived the opposing cock. The result was that many a proud and lusty cock has been laid low by the first spur-stroke of the formidable "hen."

DEPRAVITY AND MURDER

Negro Shot to Give Week-End Party "a Little Excitement"

FROM OUR OWN CORRESPONDENT

NEW YORK, Tuesday.

"To furnish a little excitement for a lagging party" of four men and their wives, a negro was shot to death.

This is the latest revelation of Dayton Dean Black Legion trigger man, who is being held at Detroit as the self-confessed murderer of Charles A. Poole.

Dean has now astonished the police by calmly telling how he and others murdered Silas Coleman, a negro war veteran, for the thrill of it.

He told the police how a week-end party was getting dull, so Coleman was lured to the cottage at Rush Lake, where the party was staying.

They hired Coleman as a wood carrier, telling him a contractor at the cottage wanted to meet him.

On marshland near the cottage Black Legionaries wounded him.

When he plunged madly through the marsh like a wild animal trying to escape, they hunted him down, shooting him to death.

Coleman's body was later found by fishermen. There were eighteen bullets in it.

1936

Depravity and Murder

1929
RIGHT TO KILL A WIFE —OR A HUSBAND.

REMARKABLE NEW MEXICAN PENAL CODE

NEW YORK, Thursday.

A husband will not be punished for killing an unfaithful wife, and a wife who kills her erring husband will be deemed not guilty of an offence also, under the new Mexican penal code drawn up by President Portes Gil.

This extraordinary code also gives a father the right to kill a daughter and her seducer where the daughter voluntarily sacrifices her honour.

Persons involved in differences calling for a duel will have to appear before a Court of Honour which will endeavour to bring about a reconciliation, but will have no power to sanction a duel.

Habitual drunkards must be sent to nursing homes. The transmission of certain diseases is made a punishable offence and medical treatment is obligatory.

The code, which comes into force on December 15 next, abolishes trial by jury and replaces it by trial before tribunals composed of alienists and other experts.—Reuter.

1920
WOMAN'S TWO "WIVES."

CHARGE OF MURDERING THE FIRST.

"Daily Express" Correspondent.
MELBOURNE.

Eugenie Fallini, a woman in male attire, who twice underwent marriage ceremonies with persons of her own sex, has been arrested and charged with having murdered Annie Burkett (or Crawford) at Chatswood in 1917.

The case possesses extraordinary features. Fallini, according to the story she told the police, married a man named Martelleo in Italy. The couple went to New Zealand and resided there for several years. Subsequently, with her daughter, the woman went to Sydney under her maiden name. She assumed male garb and worked as a man. In 1917 she went through the ceremony of marriage with a widow named Burkett. Some months later the charred remains of Burkett were found in the ashes of a fire in the bush at Chatswood. The supposition was that she had fallen into the fire in a fit or while drunk, and an open verdict was recorded.

Further evidence which came into the hands of the police led them to charge Fallini with murder. Fallini in November last went through the marriage ceremony with another woman.

1923
WOMEN'S STRANGE PACT

Plot to Kill Husbands and Live Together.

The trial was concluded at Berlin of two young women, Mrs. Klein and Mrs. Rebbe, aged twenty-three and twenty-five respectively, who were charged with having killed their husbands in order that they might live together.

Mrs. Klein was found guilty of the murder, but in view of extenuating circumstances was sentenced to four years' imprisonment. Mrs. Rebbe, who was found guilty of attempting to murder her husband, was sent to prison for eighteen months.

Mrs. Klein bought arsenic at a drug store on the pretence that her house was infested with rats, and shortly afterwards her husband died. She told the medical attendants that her husband was an habitual drunkard, and they gave her a death certificate that his death was due to alcoholic poisoning.

When the body was examined later, large quantities of arsenic were found. Mrs. Klein was arrested, and in her house were found 500 love letters from Mrs. Rebbe, disclosing an agreement between the two women to kill their husbands.

At the opening of the case the judge said it was the most amazing criminal case that had ever been brought before him.—Central News.

1924
To be Beheaded for Many Amazing Murders.
INCREDIBLE DEPRAVITY.

SPECIAL TO "REYNOLDS'S."

When the executioner severs the head of Fritz Haarman, the world will be rid of one of the most loathsome monsters in human history. After a trial without parallel, Haarman was sentenced to death at Hanover on Friday, and with him his accomplice, Hans Grans.

These two men will have their names and their deeds written in medical and scientific works as examples of how far human degeneracy may go, and what depths may be sounded when the plummet goes right down.

Twenty-four times in this court at Hanover was sentence of death pronounced on Haarman. It had been proved that twenty-four boys and young men had been done to death in the foulest manner imaginable.

It is believed that the total is really much greater; but these twenty-four cases have been proved. The charges concerned twenty-seven, though in three cases was the evidence deemed insufficient.

The details of these crimes are too dreadful to relate. Suffice it to say that Haarman was a sexual degenerate, that he lured the boys into his house, and after giving a sumptuous meal he would praise the looks of his young guest. Then, later, in a room upstairs, the crime was committed.

The end was always the same. Haarman held his victim down and killed him with a bite in the throat. The monster's teeth held tight until the young life was gone.

Hanover became alarmed at the disappearance of so many boys, but for a long time no suspicion fell upon Haarman. Yet the clothes of the victims were put on sale in the shop of an accomplice, while the bodies were cut into fragments, the skulls thrown into the river that ran at the back of Haarman's house, and the remainder disposed of in various ways.

For the first few days of the long trial the evidence was heard behind closed doors, being of too revolting a nature to find a place anywhere outside medical books. But in open court Haarman told day after day his grim narrative of how he cut up and disposed of the bodies of the boys.

Some of the risks of discovery taken were so great that it is astounding that detection did not come sooner. This led to the belief that Haarman was in league with the police.

He certainly had some connection with them. The fact that he was a recruiting agent for the "black police" kept him in the closest touch with influential persons who were at first alleged to be sheltering him.

Several of the members of the force admitted that they had received gifts from him, and the general testimony was that he showed himself to be an obliging, pleasant-mannered man.

Haarman did not deny the murders. He could not, for the evidence was too definite.

Yet he claimed that they were always done while he was in a state of trance. Not one of the crimes had, he asserted, been committed consciously.

Hundreds came in and out of his house, but it was only when he felt the irresistible impulse that he made his "tours" and brought in his victims. What followed he knew not.

The court refused to accept this "trance" theory. It was pointed out that the boys had to be held down in a special way before the fatal bite could be inflicted, and that both consciousness and diabolical cunning were combined with cruelty.

Time after time during the trial the principal prisoner appealed that the thing might be finished quickly that he might be put out of his torture. He was ready to confess anything and everything. But his ordeal was long.

Nearly 200 witnesses had to appear in the box, mostly parents and relatives of the unfortunate youths. There were scenes of painful intensity as a poor father or mother would recognise some fragment or other of the clothing or belongings of their murdered son.

Here it was a handkerchief, there a pair of braces, and again a greasy coat, soiled almost beyond recognition, that was shown to the relatives and to Haarman. And with the quivering nostrils of a hound snuffling his prey, as if he were scenting rather than seeing the things displayed, did he admit at once that he knew them.

If Haarman is a psycopathic monster, what is to be said of Grans, apparently normal, cynical, and with active brain missing no detail? He is an example of human callousness without parallel.

He it was who drove the victims into Haarman's gloomy room, and it is evident that he knew what happened there. He had looked after the belongings of the candidates for death; and when Haarman once was going to let a victim go, it was Grans who drove the boy back to slaughter.

The close of the trial was as sensational as its incidents. The news had spread that a well-known fanatic had sworn that he would shoot Haarman as soon as sentence was pronounced, lest any prerogative of mercy should be exercised.

Every member of the public who came into court was carefully searched for arms, and when the judges returned to court to deliver their sentence a row of policemen separated the public from the members of the court.

Well may one say that this trial has been unique. And it certainly must be without precedent that a human vampire, whose abnormality was known, and who had been repeatedly sentenced for loathsome offences, should have been allowed so long to scour a town for victims and do them to death without challenge.

No wonder that it was a common belief that this great criminal, before whom the deeds of Jack the Ripper pale almost into insignificance, enjoyed the favour and the protection of those whose duty it should have been to bring him to justice.

Sketches in Court of HAARMAN and (inset) GRANS.

1924
MASS MURDERER SENTENCED.

Found Guilty Of 26 Crimes.

A TOMBSTONE WISH.

The 44-year-old pervert, Fritz Haarmann, was yesterday found guilty of 26 murders during the last six years (says a Reuter telegram from Hanover).

The trial had lasted ten days, and had been followed with the keenest interest by students of criminology.

The details of these atrocious crimes, all the victims being between 12 and 18 years of age, were extremely revolting. It was proved that the accused actually sold the flesh of his victims for human consumption.

He once made sausages in his kitchen, where, together with the purchaser, he cooked them and ate them. The medical witnesses declared the murderer was not insane.

"One Merry Evening."

After his conviction, Haarmann asked that the following inscription should be inscribed on his tombstone: "Here rests the mass murderer, Haarmann." He also expressed a desire to "pass one merry evening in his cell, and also that his last meal should consist of coffee, hard cheese, and cigars, after which he would curse his father and regard his execution as his wedding."

Haarmann on several occasions prayed that his trial should be expedited so that he might "Go to Heaven before Christmas."

Extreme hatred of his father seems to have been a dominant passion with him, apparently for the reason that his parent had made strenuous efforts to persuade him to give up his immoral life.

Death Sentence.

Berlin, Friday.—Sentence of death by beheading has been imposed on Haarman, the mass murderer of Hanover, and his accomplice Granz.

Depravity and Murder 15

DEATH CHAIR FOR "NICE OLD MAN"

HIS COUNTRY HOME A CHARNEL HOUSE

100 CHILDREN KILLED IN 20 YEARS

(FROM OUR OWN CORRESPONDENT)

NEW YORK, Saturday.
Albert H. Fish, America's most terrible child killer of the century, was found guilty last night of the fiendish murder of ten-year-old Grace Budd in a lonely Westchester "haunted" house on June 3, 1928.

The jury in the County Court-house of Westchester, at Whiteplains, 20 miles from New York, pronounced their verdict after five hours' deliberations.

Fish will be sentenced on Monday by Justice Frederick Close to die on the "hot seat" in Sing-Sing Prison.

Fish, 65, white-haired and frail, had been assisted to and from the court-room during the trial, and twice tried to commit suicide in gaol.

Grace Budd disappeared from her home after being invited to attend a children's party by a "nice old man," who was known as Howard to the girl's parents, but who was afterwards proved to be Fish.

In his confession to the police Fish related that six years before he had become interested in cannibalism, and longed to kill a boy for a thrill.

Then he described how he took the girl to his dilapidated mansion, and sent her to pick flowers in the garden while he got a cleaver and carving-knife to dismember the body.

Fish also admitted that he had once lured two boys to the house with the intention of killing them and drinking their blood. The boys became frightened and escaped.

On the witness-stand itself Fish confessed to the practice of weird rites and self-torture and perversion, and confessed that he had murdered a hundred children during the last 20 years.

His lawyer, James Dempsey, eloquently attempted to convince the jury that Fish had given way so long to strange and perverted instincts that he had no self-control left, and turned from a benevolent old gentleman into a homicidal maniac whenever the impulse to kill for the thrill of it seized him.

CELLAR BONES

The house he tenanted outside White Plains is known as Wisteria Cottage, and was found to be a veritable charnel house when the police dug up the cellar and uncovered piles of bones of children and adults.

Fish's eldest son Albert told the Court how he had seen his father stick pins into himself, and X-ray photographs of the elder Fish's stomach showed 29 needles now embedded in the flesh.

Born in Washington, Fish became a house painter and carpenter, and then developed artistic tastes. He painted murals and cherubs in churches.

Six of his grown-up children were in the court-room to hear the verdict, and only one son, Eugene, aged 27, showed any emotion.

The parents of the murdered Grace Budd heard the judgment with stony faces.

"Fish is an unfortunate maniac, and I bear him no animosity, but I am glad justice has been done," said the father, Edward Budd.

Fish slumped in his chair, his shoulders shaken with sobs, after the conviction, for which all the credit belongs to Det. William King, who made a vow to solve the mystery of Grace Budd before he retired from the force.

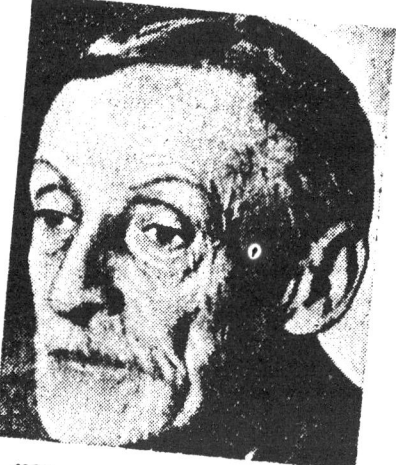

1935

1934
HE ATE HIS VICTIMS

Teheran, Persia, Saturday.—A murderer who ate his victims has just been executed in Teheran.

Regarded as the most bloodthirsty criminal in the Orient, Ali Zafer Ali Mirza was "credited" with no fewer than 33 murders. He was a Persian subject, but "practised" for many years in Irak before making the country too hot to hold him.

Then he fled to Persia, where he continued his life of crime. Most of his victims were young men.—Reuter.

1925
GERMAN CANNIBAL

MURDERER FOR 20 YEARS

HUMAN FLESH AS 'GOAT-MEAT'

FROM OUR OWN CORRESPONDENT.
BERLIN, Sunday.

The bonfire made by the police of the effects of the Muensterberg cannibal, Karl Denke, apparently marks the close of the official investigation of the career of this ghoulish monster. The object of the holocaust was to prevent gruesome relics from finding their way into the hands of showmen or morbid collectors. Following the case of the Hanover vampire, Haarmann, that of Denke has left in the public mind an uncomfortable sense that human life is very insecure in this country. Muensterberg has only 8,000 inhabitants, and in a town of that size people generally know all about their neighbours' goings and comings. Yet, living in a small jerry-built tenement house, of which he was the owner, Denke murdered his fellow-creatures in his flat with as much unconcern as if he had been wringing the necks of hens or drowning mice caught in a trap. In broad daylight, apparently without any attempt at concealment, he poured their blood down the sink in the courtyard, and carried trays of their flesh to and from the shed in his garden, where he kept it in a pickling vat. No one seems to have been particularly curious as to the errands he undertook to the surrounding woods in the evenings, laden with bulky sacks and other parcels.

Possibly his long immunity was due to his church connections. Some years ago he filled the office of cross-bearer at Evangelical funerals, and he was also for some time organ-blower in the Lutheran Church. These occupations doubtless gave him access to the Evangelical hostel, where he made the acquaintance of travelling journeymen, from amongst whom most of his victims were selected. How many persons he murdered is not likely to become even approximately known. Among his possessions were found fifteen sets of identification papers, in three of which the names had been rendered illegible. The last entry on one of these documents is dated 1905, from which it is inferred that Denke must have commenced his human butchery nearly a score of years ago—he was 58 when his crimes were discovered. On the other hand, evidence indicated that he had killed three men in the last five or six weeks of his life.

It is not surprising to hear that many people in Muensterberg are suffering from "neurasthenic abdominal pains." Practically no doubt has been left that Denke not only devoured human flesh himself, but also sold it in considerable quantities as "goat-meat," which came largely into use in Germany during the war. A particularly horrible detail of his enormities is that, as concluded from the information collected, he usually struck down his victims when they were consuming a dish of the flesh of their predecessors in this grisly fate. Only last autumn a whole wedding party partook of meat which had been supplied by Denke. Thongs of human skin were found put to many different uses in his rooms.

Depravity and Murder

1928
SHOT GIRL TO SAVE HER.
ACQUITTAL FOLLOWS DESPERATE ACT

Rouen, Saturday.

Making a tragic figure in the dock, Mme. Blot, a native of Rouen, was acquitted of the murder of her daughter, aged 21.

She related that her daughter wished to go to Paris and intended to lead an immoral life, and that she shot the girl rather than let her be ruined.

The girl was said to have told her mother that she was old enough to choose her own way of life, and that she intended to go to Paris despite all her mother's pleadings.

Failing to move the girl from her resolve, Mme. Blot got a revolver and shot her daughter.—British United Press.

1906
HUNG TO THE CEILING BY HIS THUMBS.

Although agreeing that the woman had been guilty of "very great and very unnecessary cruelty," the Cranborne (Dorset) Bench yesterday passed the lenient sentence of six weeks' hard labour on Sarah Jane Selwood, the wife of a farm labourer, of Blagdon, for having subjected her stepson, an intelligent little fellow of nine, to brutal and systematic ill-treatment extending over a lengthy period.

The woman (who pleaded guilty) had peppered the child's eyes, put a red-hot poker on his hands, hung him up to the ceiling by his thumbs, and cut his eye with a knife. A neighbour stated that the woman had told her she had cut the boy's nails down to the quick "to make them bleed."

The lad had also been unmercifully beaten with a stick which her husband used to drive a bull. The child's body was a mass of bruises, whilst one of the legs had become deformed owing to the repeated beating. The child—the only one by the first wife—had also been sent to school without food, whilst at his meals he was given dry bread to eat, the woman's four children having bread-and-butter and tea. He also slept alone in a bed, the scanty clothing of which was rotten.

The woman's husband said he had beaten his wife for her treatment of the child.

1923
STOLE CORPSE'S GOLD TEETH

Cologne, Saturday.

A woman at Wiesbaden, notified that her sister had died in hospital, called at the institution and the authorities left her alone in the death chamber. When the attendants subsequently entered the compartment they found that the visitor had forced open the mouth of the corpse and wrenched all the gold teeth from the jaw bones with a pair of pliers.

She coolly admitted the deed, declaring she was entitled to do as she pleased with her own property, being her sister's only relative.—Reuter.

1942
KEPT DAUGHTER CHAINED TO BED 20 YEARS

FROM JOHN WALTERS
New York, Wednesday.

A WOMAN of 38 was freed by the police in Denver, U.S., today after being kept in chains by her mother for twenty years.

Mrs. Mae Adams, 65, said she had chained up her daughter, Verna, in 1922 "because she was unbalanced."

Sister Raised Alarm

But a specialist described the girl as sane, and Verna told him that as a girl she was fettered to her bed.

The discovery was made when Mrs. Adams's other daughter, Amy, was seen screaming from a window with chains about her body.

Police entered the house, where Mrs. Adams explained she had put Amy in chains last Friday because she became violent.

Verna, in twenty years, had seen only her mother and sister.

1925
SERIAL MURDERS.

Woman Killed Children As They Were Born.

A single woman, aged 37, a cook at an hotel in a town near Copenhagen, is alleged to have confessed to the police, says the Exchange, that of her six children she had killed five.

Her first, born in 1914, died in hospital in 1915. Her second, born in February, 1916 was taken to Fredericia, killed in a public garden, and thrown into the Little Belt.

A third child born in December, 1918, she is said to have strangled and buried in a garden.

She gave birth to a fourth in February, 1920, and a fifth in March, 1921, both of which, she said, she immediately strangled and buried in the forests.

A sixth child, born last month, appeared to be unable to breathe when it was born, and she killed it with a knife in the back.

1925
JAZZMANIA AS MURDER COMPLEX.

STARTLING DEFENCE BY DANCE-MAD FLAPPER.

EXPERT THEORIES.

JEALOUS RIVAL FOR FATHER'S LOVE.

DOROTHY ELLINGSON, the sixteen-year-old girl who killed her mother in Los Angeles because she had been told to "give up night life," has had entered on her behalf the defence that she was suffering from "Jazzmania," or the dancing craze, a "new mental ailment."

1908
CRUEL STEPMOTHER.

MIDNIGHT TORTURES OF A NERVOUS CHILD

(From Our Own Correspondent.)
Berlin, Sunday.

All Berlin is applauding the sentence of four months' imprisonment imposed yesterday upon Frau Bergmann, wife of a physician, for inhuman treatment of her thirteen-year-old stepdaughter. The woman's cruelties, which extended over two or three years, shattered the child's health, and almost unbalanced her mind.

Former servants and neighbours of Frau Bergmann related in court stories of diabolical torture which made both the court and the public shudder. One of the stepmother's favourite practices was to compel the girl to take "electric-light baths" at an insufferable temperature. While the child was beseeching release from the agonising heat the woman would belabour her with a walking-stick until her whole body was disfigured. On several of these occasions the beating continued until the child swooned.

The child was frequently so starved that the cook would secretly give her pennies to buy food. The stepmother used to compel the girl to go up and downstairs with heavily laden coal scuttles and to wear inadequate clothing in the coldest weather. As another method of chatisement the stepmother used to terrorise the child by impersonating a ghost at her bedside in the dead of night.

The girl's father excused his wife's conduct by giving the child a bad reputation, which was in no way borne out by other witnesses. The stepmother's plea was that the girl "ruined her matrimonial happiness." The Bergmanns were married in London in 1905.

1905
MONK'S DREADFUL SECRET.

[From Our Correspondent.]

BUCHAREST, Monday.

A murder mystery of thirty years' standing has been cleared up.

In Moldavia an old man and his three sons, all grown up, were discovered one morning murdered. Suspicion fell immediately on the wife of the man, who was missing, and who was known to have lived on exceedingly bad terms with her husband and sons, who were in the habit of beating her very cruelly and otherwise ill-using her. Though a hue and cry was raised, she was never found.

Two or three days ago there died in the monastery of Tibucani an aged monk called Vasile Popovich. When the body was being prepared for burial it was found that the supposed monk was a woman. The "monk" had been thirty years in the monastery and all this time had preserved the secret. The authorities had to be informed of the fact, in order to, if possible, establish the identity of this strange being; on inquiry it was confirmed that she was no other than the missing murderess, it being found she entered the monastery as a man the very morning of the murder, which took place only a few hours' journey

1905
LIKE A NOVEL.

JEALOUS LOVER STABS HIS SWEETHEART'S BROTHER

A romantic and tragic story was told at the police-station of the Vilette quarter of Paris. A young girl, Pauline Grandjean, employed in a dressmaking establishment, made the acquaintance of a young man named Drouant, to whom she became engaged.

She told her fiancé, however, that the name she went under was not her real name, and that there were secret reasons for this fact, which she refused to divulge. Drouant apparently accepted this, but seemed suspicious.

Yesterday, calling unexpectedly upon the girl he found in her flat a postcard bearing these words: "I shall come and see you this morning. You have my love in spite of all that has happened, and we will try and forget the past."

Hid in the Flat.

Mad with jealousy Drouant determined to be avenged on what he regarded as the treachery of his fiancé. He hid himself in the flat and waited for the arrival of the author of the postcard.

An hour or two afterwards the girl returned, and was soon followed by a man who immediately upon seeing her fell into her arms. Drouant sprang from his hiding place, and tearing the man from the girl's embraces, plunged a knife into his back.

The man fell down in a dying condition. "Murderer!" screamed the girl, "You have killed my brother!"

The Girl's Secret.

The mystery to which the girl had referred was this: Her brother had been condemned to two years' imprisonment and had been released the day that he wrote the postcard.

The two had changed their name in order to start life afresh, and the man had come to see his sister for an hour before going out into the world to search for work.

The injured man was taken to the hospital in a dying condition, though at the last reports he still lingers on. He refused to formally charge his aggressor.

—"Morning Leader." Telegram.

1910
20 YEARS IN GAOL BY ERROR

"MURDERED" MAN ALIVE AND WELL.

(From Our Own Correspondent.)

NEW YORK, Wednesday.

Sentenced to forty years' imprisonment for murder, Roger Williams, a cattle dealer, after serving half his sentence has just been released from the Texas penitentiary as a result of the startling discovery that Bernard Carter, the man whom he was supposed to have murdered, is alive, wealthy, and well.

Williams and Carter quarrelled in the spring of 1890. Meeting on a cattle trail, Williams stabbed Carter and flung the body into the Pecos River. A few weeks later a decomposed body was discovered in the river and identified as that of Carter. The identification, it now turns out, was erroneous, for Carter, by a miracle, was rescued in an unconscious condition from the river and sent to hospital at El Paso.

After his recovery he drifted into Central America, whence he returned with a large fortune ten years ago, settling in Seattle. A few days ago Carter was reading an account of cruelties practised in the gaols of Texas, when he noticed the name of Williams among those of other prisoners who had made statements on the subject. His curiosity was aroused, and he learned that Williams, who he supposed had fled the country and escaped arrest, was actually serving a forty years' sentence for murdering him.

Carter has now secured a pardon for Williams, whom he is providing with a good home for the rest of his life. Williams, who was thirty-three when he was arrested, is now a bent and prematurely aged man. He burst into tears when informed that he was free and was not a murderer.

Depravity and Murder 17

1922
NEGRO BOY BURNED.

Terrible Lynching Atrocity in America.

DAVISBORO (Georgia), Friday.

A 15-year-old negro, named Charles Atkins, who had been arrested in connection with the murder of a rural mail carrier, named Mrs. Kitchens, was to-day burned at the stake under horrible conditions.

In the first place he was tortured over a slow fire for 15 minutes, and then, whilst shrieking with pain, was questioned concerning his accomplices, as a result of which he implicated another youth.

The ringleaders of the mob, which consisted of some 2,000 people, then proceeded to chain Atkins to a pine tree and relit the fire. While the tortured boy was burning some 200 shots were fired at his body. The mob are now searching for the other lad.—Reuter.

1908
DOUBLE MURDER BY MISTAKE.

JEALOUS HUSBAND KILLS HIS WIFE AND SON.

FRENZY OF REMORSE.

"Express" Correspondent.

NEW YORK, Tuesday, June 30.

A pitiful tragedy due to mistaken jealousy took place in Southern Illinois last night, when Julius Turner, one of the wealthiest business men in the district, shot and killed his wife and his sixteen-years-old son, mistaking the latter for his wife's lover.

Mrs. Turner was twenty-five years younger than her husband, and a woman of striking beauty. Her husband's groundless jealousy had caused several separations, but the couple were always reconciled after Turner had promised not to suspect her again.

He had often threatened his wife, who was not afraid, however, and she ignored his warnings that he would kill her if he ever caught her in the company of another man.

Last night Mrs. Turner attended a church bazaar at Clay City, a village near her home, and her son, who was six feet tall, went there in order to escort her home.

Turner, who did not know of this arrangement, awaited his wife in a thick grove near the church. When Mrs. Turner passed, accompanied by a tall man, Turner shot her three times and the man twice. Then he shouted to the people who were leaving the church, "Come over here, all of you, and see how I have done justice."

The people crowded about the bodies, but it was too dark to see the faces, so Turner dragged the body of the man face down to the edge of the grove, where the church lights shone clearly, saying "We will see who he is."

He turned over the body, and as he recognised his son, he groaned, and then shot himself in the body. The wound did not prove fatal, however, and he was disarmed before he could fire again.

Turner is now a prisoner in the county gaol, where he refuses all food, saying he will starve himself to death by way of punishment for his terrible mistake.

1920
A LOBSTER SALAD BEFORE EXECUTION.

Murderer Goes to Death After 10 Hours' Sound Sleep.

"SMILE! DOCTOR, SMILE!"

How Gordon Fawcett Hamby went to his death in Sing Sing prison for the murder of some bank clerks is told by the New York correspondent of the Central News.

Hamby awoke at noon on the morning of his execution after sleeping soundly nearly ten hours. He handed the warder three letters to post after he was dead, one to a girl, the others to his parents.

The condemned man had been wearing the death suit of black, with a black shirt. "Can't I have a light-coloured shirt, warder?" he pleaded. The guards brought him a white shirt, and Hamby then asked if he could have a stiff collar and a coloured tie, but this was refused.

He made a big breakfast. For dinner he selected steak, mushrooms, strawberries, and coffee. Frank Flannigan, another "hold-up" man under sentence of death, asked permission to "stand Hamby treat," and it was granted.

Flannigan ordered a box of cigars, a box of bonbons, and ice-cream, which Hamby divided among his twenty-nine death-house companions after taking his own portion. For supper he ordered lobster salad.

"I need not worry about indigestion," he explained.

The Gloomy Guard.

He ate the salad, all the while conversing with the warder and his guards. "Smile! doctor, smile!" he said as the surgeon looked through the bars of his cell.

He protested about the "gloomy looks" of one of the guard. "He is taking his duty too seriously," said Hamby. "He hasn't a smile in him. Bring me a more cheerful fellow."

He declined to accept spiritual consolation, and calmly lit a cigarette as he walked to his death. Beaming all over, Hamby raised his cigarette, and, filling his lungs with smoke, said, bowing, "Warder, may I say a word?"

He was then standing in front of the chair. He looked half apologetic and wholly unconcerned.

"Certainly," said the warder.

"I want to thank you for the wonderful treatment I have received here," said Hamby. "You have been very kind to me. Nobody ever died in front of John B. Allen's (probably his real name) gun unless he had a chance."

Then he added: "I don't wish to appear in the light of a moralist, but you can tell all young men from me not to ever start doing wrong; for once you start a career of crime you can never stop."

Then he flicked the stub of his cigarette on the mat in front of the death chair and stamped on it. He seated himself, still smiling. The keepers bound, helmeted, and masked him.

A sigh went up from the witnesses. The amazing murderer was dead.

1923
SENTENCED FOR LIFE.

Maximum for Man Who Cut Off Stepdaughter's Hands.

"No punishment I can inflict on you is adequate.... Penal servitude for life."

Speaking with emotion with these words passed sentence at Manchester Assizes yesterday on John Whalley, thirty-two, a fitter, of Accrington, who cut off his little step-daughter's hands and dangerously wounded his landlady, Miss Sarah Anne Horbury, on September 18.

"The story of your offence," said the Judge, "is the most horrible to which I have ever listened—a cold and calculated and fiendish attempt to be avenged on your wife through this unfortunate little girl."

Several jurymen appeared to be much affected by the evidence.

1928
KILLING FOR REWARDS.

CHICAGO OUTDONE BY TEXAS.

From Our Own Correspondent.

NEW YORK, Sunday.

Murder for money on a system which makes even Chicago seem an Arcadian resort is reported from Texas.

Driven desperate by the robbing of their banks with impunity, the Texas Bankers' Association offered rewards to the police and others who should kill bank robbers—£1,000 in daylight and £4,000 at night. Some protests were made, but the offers remained.

Captain Frank Hamer, of the State Police Force—known as the Texas Rangers—has now presented a signed affidavit to the Governor, who has instructed him to take it to the county grand juries. Captain Hamer declares that a syndicate has been formed to shoot innocent men in order to claim the rewards. Already several people have been killed and rewards granted.

Two men who were killed by the police were alleged to be concerned in an attempt to rob a bank, but they had no instruments with them for opening safes or vaults. Repeatedly men shot in this way have been proved by their fingerprints to be not only not professional bank robbers, but men with no crime record of any kind.

Captain Hamer says the scandal is a revival of the days when the Mexican Government, worried by the Indians, offered a scalp bounty for criminal Indians and groups from Texas went into the business of wholesale murder of Indians for £20 a head. He says he is prepared to give the name of the man at the head of the syndicate for securing the blood money.

1925
PRISON CAMP HORRORS.

GUARDS FLOG MEN TO DEATH.

ORGANISED "HELL."

From Our Own Correspondent.

NEW YORK, Monday.

Disclosures recalling the slave days are made by a special commission which has been inquiring into conditions in two North Carolina prison camps, where convicts are hired out as roadmakers, a custom not uncommon in the South.

Following sentences on two guards of 20 years' imprisonment for beating a prisoner to death, a commission was appointed, and it is now declared that deplorable conditions existed at Rockymount camp, which are without a single redeeming feature.

The guards maintained a reign of mental terror by threats, disregarded all the laws, consumed unlimited quantities of illegal liquor, received nightly visits from associates and distributed State goods wholesale to friends.

Floggings with heavy leather straps were a regular part of the routine. Even boys received 20 and 30 lashes without regard to their physical condition. Floggings were often administered by powerful guards mad with drink.

A negro youth was flogged, then burning liniment was poured on to his wounds, and he was brutally kicked as he writhed on the ground. The negro confessed that he had prayed for death for two years.

When working on the roads gangs of men were spurred on by sharpened nails in the end of staves. Other punishments were stringing men up by the hands and holding them under water.

The revelation of this organised "hell" has led the commission to demand the complete abolition of corporal punishment, and, now that the prisoners' mouths are open, cases will be begun against various guards for murders and assaults.

ECCENTRICS

THE MAN WITH £1,500,000

HAGGLED OVER COST OF HIS DEATH

From A Special Correspondent
PARIS, Saturday.

Samuel Tapon, a millionaire miser, has committed suicide because he lost £50,000 in unlucky speculations.

He owned thousands of acres of vineyards in the Cognac district, and had several castles.

His sole interest in life was money.

He left more than £1,500,000, yet the comparatively small loss of £50,000 upset him so much that death seemed preferable.

Even till his last moments he could not abandon his miser's habits.

He went to the village shop to buy the rope with which he hanged himself.

He haggled over the price, and succeeded in having a few centimes knocked off!

1934

PRISONER OF DEAD BROTHER

ELEVENTH HOUR NIGHT CLUB VISIT

NEW YORK, Sunday.

1931

THIS city's strangest house, the old Wendel mansion on Fifth-avenue, has lost its mistress, Miss Ella Wendel, the last of six sisters and heiress to £30,000,000, being found dead in bed.

Since her last sister died a year ago, Miss Wendel, who was 80, had lived alone with a maid in this gloomy early Victorian house, in which nothing had been altered in decades.

The shuttered mansion, standing in the heart of a fashionable shopping district and dwarfed by skyscrapers, was a weird anachronism and aroused more curiosity than any other private residence in the city.

The family had lived with the single object of keeping their immense fortune intact, and now that the last one has gone their millions will probably be split up among charities.

For many years the six sisters lived as virtual prisoners of their cruelly tyrannical elder bachelor brother John, who forbade them to marry or to leave his sight.

BROTHER'S EDICTS

He ordered that to the end of their lives they must :
  Wear the trailing skirts and high necks fashionable in the sixties ;
  Not alter the early Victorian furniture or appointments of the house ;
  Not instal a telephone or electric light or other new-fangled devices ;
  Never encourage friendship ;
  Enjoy no change except a summer visit to his country house.

Two of them rebelled, but one returned penitently, the second marrying a professor and dying last year at the age of 87. The others sacrificed themselves to the brother's obsession and even after his death, 15 years ago, religiously followed his stern edicts, which resembled those in the play "The Barretts of Wimpole Street."

TOO LATE TO DISCOVER LIFE

Two of them became mentally unbalanced as a result of this repressed existence, and Ella, in her last lonely years, conducted the house as though her brother and sisters were still living, their beds being made each day.

As death closed about her she began to yearn for all she had missed in life, and a fortnight ago she left her prison for a secret visit to a Broadway night club. She sat at a table for an hour, a strange figure from the past in a rusty frock that had gone out of fashion 50 years ago.

Death came to her at the moment of her first attempt to discover life.

1908
DR ZAHARIN

Dr. Zaharin, who has just died in Moscow and left a fortune of over £200,000, was one of the most famous as he was also the most eccentric physician in Russia. Even when he was summoned to attend Tsar Alexander III. in his last illness, Dr. Zaharin required the same preparation for his visit to the Palace as to any of his patients' homes. That is to say, all dogs had to be kept out of the way, all clocks stopped, and every door thrown wide open. Following a process of gradual undressing, he left his furs in the hall, his overcoat in the next room, his goloshes in the third, and, continuing, arrived at the bedside in ordinary indoor-costume.

This was only one phase of Dr. Zaharin's golden theory that "you should take a rest before you are tired." Accordingly he sat down after walking every few yards, and every eight steps in going up stairs. From the patient's relatives, and everyone else in the house, he required absolute silence until he spoke to them, when his questions had to be answered by "Yes" or "No," and nothing more. To the actual patient, however, he was courtesy and consideration itself.

1934
Bearded Men's Rights

TEST CASE IN SWISS COURTS

Eccentric Wins the Day

RAILWAY STATION SCENE

From a Special Correspondent
GENEVA.

A Geneva eccentric who believes, among other things, that men have as much right to grow their hair long as women have to cut theirs short, has vindicated the honour of all hairy beings by creating a valuable precedent in Swiss law.

Charged with causing a grave scandal by wearing a beard some eighteen inches long with hair to match, and thus contravening Article 233b, paragraph 3 of the regulations for the control of locomotives and the maintenance of public security, the gentleman concerned defended himself with vigour before the Bench, who discharged him without a stain on his character.

Undeterred by the dictates of fashion and the jeers of his neighbours, the old gentleman has for years cultivated a magnificent flowing growth. Not satisfied with the full effect of this, he took to wearing a voluminous blue blouse, wellington boots, and a sweeping black sombrero.

The ensemble was so startling that when he took a stroll to the railway station recently he was surrounded by a large crowd consisting largely of unbearded youths. Not the slightest bit worried, the old gentleman continued his dignified way, but officialdom in the form of an over-zealous stationmaster intervened.

"CAUSING A SCANDAL"

"You are causing a scandal within the meaning of the Act, and thus menacing the security of my trains," declared the official, "and I order you to leave the station premises."

But the hirsute gentleman was a believer in personal as well as civic rights.

"The station is State property and I have just as much right to be here as you," he retorted with considerable dignity. "What is more, I have a perfect right to grow my hair as I like, and in any case it is not hurting your railway."

So the stationmaster called a policeman and the King of Beavers was arrested.

Whether it was because they admired his beard or his courage, or whether it was because he had committed no offence against the Swiss State railways, the magistrates acquitted the old gentleman, and he left the court amid the cheers of the assembled populace, a justifiably proud upholder of the rights of man.

Eccentrics

The Rev. John Gwyon, late rector of Bisley, left all his £9,976 estate for a fund to provide knickers for boys. He was found hanged a few months ago.

1929

1942

DENTIST ROBS WOMEN OF TEETH TO SATISFY A 'CRAVING'

A FANTASTIC "dentist," who has been going round Nottingham offering to examine women's teeth, suddenly extracting one and running away with it, is regarded by psychologists as a "mental case."

The mystery man was first heard of when, posing as a representative of a Mansfield dental firm, he called on Mrs. Mabel Foulkes, of Lowtham-street, Nottingham, extracting a good tooth while examining her mouth.

NEARLY FAINTED

He had previously put her into a chair, opened her mouth and told her that one of the back molars needed attention. She then saw a shining instrument in his hand—and the tooth was jerked out.

Mrs. Foulkes said: "I screamed. The man, holding up the tooth, called out, 'Isn' it a beauty?' and dashed out of the house. My sister came in directly afterwards and found me nearly fainting."

She said he was of medium build, aged about 40, very persuasive, well dressed, and impressive.

He also called on Mrs. Edith Haywood, who lives a few houses away. She refused to have her teeth examined and ordered him out of the house.

He is believed to have called on a number of other women, without finding a victim.

1906

FATAL DIET OF NAILS AND HATPINS.

The "human ostrich," Robert Naysmith, who for years amazed crowds of people at fairs and fêtes held at different places in England by swallowing nails, hatpins, and stones, and eating glass, has paid the penalty of his extraordinary diet.

He died in the Islington Workhouse Infirmary on Wednesday last and the inquest on his body was held on Saturday by Mr. Walter Schröder, the deputy-coroner for Central London.

It was stated that Naysmith, who was thirty-four years old, was a member of a highly respectable Scotch family, his relatives living at Montrose. He lost touch with them some years ago, and earned a livelihood by exhibiting himself as a "human ostrich." He chewed glass, swallowed needles, hatpins, hairpins, and nails; but the inevitable result followed.

He became ill, and had to give up his "profession." Afterwards he earned a few pence a day by selling bootlaces, but he became worse, and at last he had to seek admission to the parish infirmary, which he entered last April. He informed the doctors that he had been swallowing nails and hatpins, but they did not believe him at first.

Shortly after his admission he told one of the nurses that he had been swallowing nails, and asked for a knife to relieve himself of them. This was reported to the doctors, who thought that the man was mad, and ordered that a watch should be kept on him. A few weeks ago an abscess formed on his body, and when it was opened a brass-headed nail was found in it. The doctors then questioned him closely, and discovered that his story was true, and that he had been made the subject of several magazine articles, describing him as a "human ostrich."

It was decided, however, that he was too weak to stand an operation, and he gradually sank and died. A post-mortem examination was made, and more than thirty nails and hatpins were found in the body. Some of them were in the liver, some of them in the kidneys, but the larger number were in the intestines. The actual cause of his death was gastritis and peritonitis.

The jury returned a verdict of "Death by Misadventure."

1903

VICAR'S SON CHARGED.

Before the Cannock (Staffordshire) Magistrates on Wednesday, George Edward Thomas Edalji, a young Birmingham solicitor, was charged with unlawfully wounding a horse, the property of the Great Wyrley Colliery Company. It is stated that during the past two years, Wyrley, a village lying between Walsall and Rugeley, has been from time to time the scene of some extraordinary outrages on cattle and horses. Occasionally animals were found lying dead or dying from shocking abdominal wounds. Animals to the value of at least £200 have been destroyed. The last victim was a horse belonging to a local colliery company, which was found on Monday—mutilated in the same diabolical manner as previous victims—in a field adjoining that in which one of the earlier occurrences had taken place. The deed was carried out with great daring. There were men at work in the vicinity, but the culprit, as in the previous cases, succeeded in escaping without leaving any clue behind him.

Subsequently, however, the police arrested Edalji on suspicion of being the perpetrator. Edalji is the son of the Vicar of Great Wyrley, and resides with his parents at the Vicarage. He is a medallist of the Birmingham Law Society, and the author of a hand book on railway law. His father is of Oriental origin.

A peculiar circumstance of the case is that soon after one of the preceding outrages a reward of £25 was offered for information as to the originator of a supposed rumour connecting young Edalji with the mysterious slaughter of animals.

Inspector Campbell stated that he had found reddish stains and hairs, apparently from a horse, on the clothing worn by the prisoner on the night of the last outrage, and in a pocket was a blood-stained handkerchief. On the way to the station the accused remarked, "I am not surprised at this. I have been expecting it for some time."

The Prisoner's Father, called for the defence, said they occupied the same bedroom, and he was positive that his son was in bed until seven on the Tuesday morning.

A remand was ordered.

1903

A MANIA FOR SPECIAL TRAINS.

A curious case was that of James Wolstencroft, aged twenty-four, lately clerk in the service of the Crompton Urban District Council, who pleaded guilty to having forged a number of cheques for £1,434, and was sentenced to three years' penal servitude at Manchester Assizes yesterday.

On the prisoner's behalf it was stated that part of the money had gone in betting, and part—most unaccountably—in special trains. Prisoner would turn up at a railway station five minutes before an ordinary train was due, and without the slightest reason order a special train, say, for Liverpool or somewhere else.

1901

A PORTSMOUTH SCARE.

Mothers Frightened by Stories of a Man who Slashes at Children's Boots.

The Portsmouth police are searching for a man, believed to be a lunatic, who is going about the town slashing children's boots with a knife or some other sharp instrument. In the first instance reported, this individual stopped a girl, aged 14, who was accompanied by a little boy, in the street, and told her that her bootlace was undone. She stooped to look at her foot, and the man quickly drew something across her boot, cutting through the leather. The girl was not injured, but both children were frightened. They state that the man, who carried a bag, hurried away, and was joined by a woman. Five other occurrences of a similar character have since been reported to the police, the latest happening on Tuesday evening. A little girl was with her mother in a busy thoroughfare when her shoe was cut. She complained that a man had hurt her foot, but thinking that it had been merely accidentally trodden upon, the parent took no particular notice until they reached home. Then it was seen that the shoe had been cut right through across the toe, and the child's stocking was stained with blood from a wound in the foot.

Eccentrics

1904
HARES HIS RUIN.

In sentencing a man at Marylebone yesterday for stealing a hare, Mr. Plowden said to the prisoner, who had previously been bound over for a similar offence:

"You are an honest man, I believe, except when you see hares. Then your honesty completely breaks down. It's a good thing you don't live where hares are abundant."

1906
MIDDLESEX.

LIVING UNDERGROUND.—In the village of Heston there is a man named Ives, known as "The Hermit," who lives in a large hole, the result of his excavations on an allotment ground which he has rented. He descends to his curious abode by means of a ladder, and at night he protects himself with a glass roof. The place contains a small bedstead, an oil stove, and a few pots and kettles. The authorities are in doubt as to whether he can be removed, in view of the fact that he pays rent for the ground.

1900
HIS PASSION FOR BOOKS.

A well-dressed man, brought up before the Commissary, says a Paris telegram, for having attempted to steal a volume in a bookseller's shop, pleaded that he was the victim of uncontrollable monomania.

"Ordinarily," he said, "books never enter my head; but once in sight of a bookseller's shop an irresistible impulse to steal them takes possession of me.

"I never read the books nor sell them. My passion is simply to amass them."

When the police visited the man's residence they found that the place was literally crowded out with books, of all sorts, sizes, and prices, and without a single leaf cut. The man was released.

1913
THE SLIPPER SNATCHER.

"Express" Correspondent.
NEW YORK, April 12.

Slipper snatching is the amusement of an amiable lunatic who is causing some inconvenience to young women.

He follows girls up the stairs from subways and, reaching forward, catches hold of their slippers as they lift one foot, and runs away with the trophy.

Several cases have happened in the last few days, and one of the victims had to be carried across the road by a policeman to a boot shop, surrounded by a bodyguard of young men.

1921
MANIA FOR PRAMS.

"This woman has a perfect mania for stealing perambulators," said Detective-Sergeant Porter at West London Police-court yesterday, respecting May King, 26, married, of Rackham-street, North Kensington, who pleaded guilty to three charges of stealing perambulators, two from Shepherd's Bush, and one from North Kensington.

The detective-sergeant stated that lately King had stolen 14 perambulators, 11 of which had been recovered by the police, and in each case she sold the pram for 20s. or 25s.

Sentence, six months' imprisonment.

1932
ATTEMPT TO DRUG A GIRL?

Stabbed In Arm While Getting Out Of A Bus.

Miss Ivy Franklang, of Eswyn-road, Tooting, has reported to the local police that when alighting from a bus at the Mitcham tram terminus she was stabbed with a sharp instrument in the left arm.

"I felt a sharp pricking sensation in the arm," she said. "It went right through my coat. On looking round I saw a woman standing behind me. She hurried away in a suspicious manner. The next moment I felt faint."

Miss Franklang, accompanied by her mother, went to a doctor's to have the wound cauterised, and later, went to the police.

1908
THE TROUBLES OF CYRANO

MAN SHOT BECAUSE HE HAS A LONG NOSE.

"Express" Correspondent.
PARIS, Sunday, May 24.

Charles Bertrand, a mechanic, aged twenty-five years, yesterday lost an eye, and is now lying in hospital because nature has bestowed on him a nose of phenomenal dimensions.

He was walking along the Rue Croix-Nivert when a man approached him, and, walking by his side, continued to take an offensive interest in his facial appearance. Bertrand is accustomed to annoyance of this sort, but in this case it was so pronounced that he turned into a café to escape it.

But the man followed him, and, accosting him peremptorily, demanded what he meant by going about with such a monument on his face. The owner replied sadly that he was irresponsible, but the man declared that he was an artist, and would not stand it.

He thereupon drew a revolver and fired at the object of his hatred, but aimed so badly that he shot the unfortunate Bertrand through the left eye. He was at once arrested, and his victim was removed to hospital.

1930
EPIDEMIC OF ROOSTING.

HEIGHT OF MADNESS.

From Our Own Correspondent.
NEW YORK, Sunday.

Many hundreds of boys are now perched in trees throughout the United States, and this mania for endurance sitting is ravaging some towns. At Camden, New Jersey, for example, no fewer than 104 of the town's boy population are living in tree tops, some declaring their intention not to descend until winter.

A number of boys in various parts of the country have injured themselves falling from boughs, but the local authorities have been unable to stamp out the practice by making by-laws against it. William Kearney, aged ten, of Kansas City, has been sitting in a tree for 230 hours.

Stuart Brehm, aged 11, at New Orleans, arranged for a priest to conduct a special tree-sitting Mass for him to-day, but crashed and was hurt before this could be done.

There is no explanation why this craze should seize boys simultaneously in all parts of the country.

1938
THE TROUSERS THIEF

HE HAS STOLEN NOTHING ELSE FOR 33 YEARS

A man who stole nothing but trousers has just been sentenced to two months' imprisonment in Toronto for stealing a pair from a shop.

The prosecution described the man, John Easson, as a "specialist in trousers."

"His record goes back to 1905, and only once, in 1907, did he lapse from his standard and steal anything but a pair of trousers," it was stated.

"On that occasion it was a shirt."—B.U.P.

Ripperism

1927

STABBED BY "PHANTOM."

TOWN TERRORISED FOR THREE YEARS.

"WEEKLY DISPATCH" CABLE.
BRIDGEPORT (CONN.), Saturday.

The "phantom stabber" of Bridgeport made his twenty-sixth attack last night when he stabbed a young married woman above the right breast. He again escaped.

The first attack on Bridgeport women was made in 1925, since when the man has worked with almost clock-like regularity, every three months sinking a sharp-pointed weapon into the breast of the woman he attacked. The scenes of his activities vary. Sometimes it is a public library, sometimes a church, or a store, or a crowded street.

His twenty-fifth attack was made only three weeks ago. Four days later Police-Superintendent Patrick Flanagan died, his death being attributed to overwork in search of the phantom stabber who has terrorised women for nearly three years.

1921

HAIR-CUTTING MANIACS.

Prison for One, Asylum for Another.

The owner of a quantity of human hair and 72 hair ribbons was charged at West London with being a suspected person. His name is Albert Mannix, of Delaford-street, Fulham.

With a pair of scissors in his hand he was seen by a constable to approach two little girls, who ran away. When arrested, he had pieces of hair, with tape attached, protruding from his pocket.

Mr. Melville, for the police, said there was reason to believe that the hair found at the man's house was connected with cases of plait-cutting in the streets, which had been rife of late. This has been particularly the case in the West-End, a police witness explained.

Mannix, who said the hair was brought home in his kit-bag from Asia Minor, and belonged to Armenians, was sentenced to three months' hard labour. "I wish I could have given you more," added the magistrate.

Albert John Adams, of Seven Kings, who had been charged with cutting off a girl's hair at an Ilford cinema theatre, was reported at Stratford to be an imbecile, and was sent to a mental home.

1938

"MEDIEVAL outbreaks of witchcraft epidemics must have been something like it. When one woman thought she had been looked at by the evil eye, many of her neighbours found their milk went sour and their cattle went lame."

Professor J. C. Flugel, of London University, yesterday suggested this parallel to the "slasher" scare which, in the last few days, has spread from Halifax to Bradford, and from there to Wigan, London (Brentford), Settle, Sale and Glasgow.

Police are now of the opinion that, apart from the original "Slasher" and his 13 victims, " an accumulation of incidents which have no association with any such person" have been attributed to a bogy man.

Where there is any real core to the innumerable tales of slashings, Professor Flugel thinks there may be found "a sexual pervert troubled with a milder form of Jack-the-Ripperism, with all the elusiveness of some of the mass-murderers."

"Compulsive Acts"

Dr. Edward Glover, Director of the Institute of Psycho-Analysis, said yesterday: "Slashing should be classed among what psychologists know as 'compulsive acts,' which may not have more than a superficial sexual significance.

"From time to time, they don't know why, some individuals suffer from powerful compulsions to commit irrational offences against persons or propery—including ink and vitriol throwing, cutting little girls' pigtails, slashing, cattle maiming, burning haystacks, etc.

"Naturally news of such outbreaks as this leads to a certain amount of imitation, both actual and hysterical."

Under hysterical types Dr. Glover places the individuals who accuse themselves of having been slashers, or those, frequently unmarried women, who invent tales of having been attacked by men, or who will actually slash themselves to bear this out.

"This type of fantastic imitation is commonly observed in children, who gratify unconscious wishes and inflate their self-importance with tales of attacking or being attacked by animals, strange men, etc."

(Boys in a Sheffield school took to "slashing" girls in the school playground at the height of an "epidemic.")

Like A Wolf

Dr. Stekel, the internationally famous psycho-analyst, who came to London from Vienna when Hitler marched, quoted the case of a man who, under a different sort of impulse, bit his victims, tearing them with his teeth.

His obsession, known as leukanthropia, or identification with a wolf, spread to others, and for a time there was an epidemic of such attacks all over Switzerland.

1921

JACK THE CUSHION RIPPER.

Hunt for Man Who Slashes Omnibus Seats.

ALWAYS THE "K" AND "S" LINES.

Some mysterious Jack the Ripper is at work these nights in the London omnibuses.

He is not really dangerous.

All he rips is—*the cushion seats*!

But in a month he has hacked and practically ruined 40 of the comfortable seats in the big new 'buses.

Strangely, he only attacks seats in the K and S type vehicles. Stranger still, no one has ever seen him do it, not even a conductor.

"Most of these cushion-maiming outrages have been in omnibuses going out West," said an official of the L.G.O.C. to *The Evening News* to-day.

Favoured Victims.

"The routes most affected are No. 9 and No. 11.

"Sometimes we are having three outrages reported on one night: then there will be a pause of a few nights: then more cutting.

"The cuts are always about the same—very deep, long (some have been about 10 inches long) and always starting at one corner of the cushion seat.

"The knife or razor or whatever the fellow uses goes down nearly to the bottom of the cushion, which is deep, so that the fibre padding of it bursts out.

"Then whoever is doing this absurd thing nearly always tears the rip wider open!

All the conductors have been specially watching for the ripper for the past week or two. So have plainclothes inspectors on the omnibuses. None of them has seen anything suspicious.

Now the omnibus-using public is asked to look out for this curiously methodical vandal—or it may be a little gang of vandals—and report any suspicions they may have. A reward of £10 is offered for information leading to a conviction.

1935

SLASHING MANIA

Women's Clothes Cut And Smeared

Lack of "emotional reaction," solitary habits and "a kink in his make-up for which no one had so far suggested a corrective" were pleaded in defence of Sidney Albert Eastbury, aged 28, who was sentenced at Birmingham to-day to two months' hard labour on three separate charges, the sentences to run consecutively, for slashing women's clothing and throwing a fluid composed of chocolate and oil on them.

Mr. Hatwell said Eastbury was happily married, but latterly had been on short time, which apparently led him into this aberration.

1927

BARONET'S ACTS OF IRRESPONSIBILITY.

GRAVE WARNING BY JUDGE.

BLACKED GIRL CASE SENTENCE.

Sir Gerard Arthur Maxwell Willshire (36), of Hindhead, was sent to prison for six months in the second division at the Kent Assizes at Maidstone yesterday on an indictment charging him with assaulting Miss Jean Olds, a 22-year-old girl of West Kensington.

It was alleged by the prosecution that in the early hours of the morning of May 10 Sir Gerard, who had taken Miss Olds for a drive in his car from London, stopped at a wood near Maidstone, ordered her to undress, and when she was clad only in her shoes and stockings tied her hands behind her and blackened her body with some polish.

Sir Travers Humphreys, K.C., with Mr. Paul Bennett, V.C., prosecuted, and Mr. Norman Birkett, K.C., and Mr. H. D. Roome appeared for the defence.

WOMEN IN THE QUEUE.

Mr. Justice Rowlatt expressed the opinion, when charging the Grand Jury, that "refined people" would not wish to listen to the case. Women, both old and young, however, were early arrivals in the queue which was headed by a woman.

Sir Gerard Willshire entered the court by the public door and sat in front of counsel with his solicitor.

Miss Olds was outside the court with a companion. She was dressed in a dark blue hat, dark blue coat trimmed with fur, and light, flesh-coloured stockings and shoes. Under her coat she had a dark blue dress with a pink collar. She carried a handbag and

Miss Jean Olds.   Sir G. Willshire.

talked frequently to her companion. Miss Olds is a girl of striking appearance with jet black hair.

When the Clerk asked if he pleaded guilty or not guilty, Sir Gerard replied in a firm tone, "Guilty."

Sir Travers Humphreys, addressing the Court, said additional evidence had been taken with regard to other acts. These statements had been taken with a view to throwing some light upon the matter.

They indicated that Sir Gerard was very far from being a normal person. He did things at times which were certainly the actions of a person of abnormal mentality, possibly of abnormal sexual ideas.

HAPPY HOME LIFE.

Mr. Birkett said there were matters contained in the additional evidence which it was right to consider.

"On the other hand, there would be much which one could say in favour of the defendant in every other part of his life," said Mr. Birkett. "His home life, for example. He has been most happily married to Lady Willshire for four years, and Lady Willshire told me that that life had been one of continuous happiness without any blot. They have a child, and their home life, she says, has been one of perfect happiness.

"Defendant, during his war service, contracted rather a virulent type of trench fever, which still has recurrent effects upon him at the present time. I have a doctor here who will speak to the effect that the trench fever causes a mental disturbance, and in these circumstances the slightest quantity of drink taken by defendant has a very pronounced effect.

"There can be no doubt that during the days immediately preceding the offence defendant had been drinking heavily and was at the same time suffering from trench fever."

Dr. Beckett Overy said that during the last 12 months Sir Gerard had suffered from neurasthenia.

"During the winter," said the doctor, "Lady Willshire and Sir Gerard told me he had on one occasion disappeared for some days and could give no account at all of what happened except that he had been drinking. He came to me by himself afterwards and said the same thing had happened again. I am perfectly satisfied that he had no recollection of either occasion."

JUDGE'S WARNING.

Mr. Justice Rowlatt, passing sentence, said:

"It comes to this, that in your special circumstances this shocking outrage was committed owing to drink.

"You seem to fall under the influence of some curious tendencies when you have got this drink, and you know, if you yield to it again, let me tell you quite frankly, one of these days it may be that you will handle some woman in some way and you will be charged with murder.

"Now you must go to prison—I cannot possibly, in the face of an outrage of this kind, yield to the plea that you might be put under medical supervision. If I could commit you to an inebriates' hospital or something of that kind I would do it, but I cannot. Prison will be an inebriates' home for you. You will have medical attention, and let me urge you when you come out to take the advice of your doctor and absolutely quit the drink, or I do not know what your future may be."

1906

BELIEVED HE WAS A WOMAN.

At the Essex Quarter Sessions yesterday a man was indicted in the name of Beatrice Alger, aged 24, for felony at Chingford.

He was dressed as a woman when apprehended but now wore male attire. Counsel for the defence said prisoner was brought up as a girl and always wore women's clothes. He had always believed, until this affair happened, that he was a woman.

The Bench believed that he had no intention of disguising himself, and ordered him to be imprisoned for one day—meaning immediate release.

1916

PRINCESS CHARLOTTE

It is stated that Princess Charlotte, the insane widow of the Emperor Maximilian of Mexico, who was assassinated in 1867, is still living undisturbed at the Castle of Bouchout, near Brussels. The castle and park have not been touched by the Germans, and soldiers are forbidden to enter the grounds. The Princess has never been informed of the war, but often asks why King Albert and Queen Elizabeth no longer visit her.

The unfortunate lady, daughter of Leopold I., of Belgium and cousin of Queen Victoria, is 76, and she has been mad ever since her husband's assassination. He was an Austrian archduke, elected Emperor of Mexico in 1863. The Princess was married at 17, an Empress at 23, and widowed and insane at 27; and for nearly half a century she has hardly once left her palatial asylum.

For years after her retreat to Belgium she believed she was still Empress of Mexico, and awaited the return of her husband from an expedition to quell the revolt of his Mexican subjects. Her father, Leopold I., left her an ample fortune, and every year she would hold a mimic Court, the 300 odd members of her household being "presented" to her with all royal ceremony.

1932

YOUTH FASCINATED BY HANDKERCHIEFS

DETECTIVE AND "THIS MORMON BUSINESS"

Reference was made by a detective to "this Mormon business" when Frederick Clifton Haley Green, a 19-year-old clerk, of Gladstone-road, Sparkbrook, Birmingham, was placed on probation for 12 months at Birmingham yesterday on a charge of stealing handkerchiefs, ties, &c., from a shop.

The Chairman—What has Mormonism to do with stealing handkerchiefs? It is not a weeping society, is it?

The Officer—I do not know. I only know that he has made a statement that all these articles have been given to him by elders and others in the Mormon Church when, in fact, they were stolen.

It was stated for the defence that the only explanation was that Green was fascinated by handkerchiefs and ties.

Green's father said that his son had belonged to the Mormon Church for twelve months. He thought it was better than having his son on the streets.

The Chairman—It depends on the weather.

Green was ordered to pay costs.

1914
75 YEARS IN THE DARK.

Jilted Bride Who Shut the World and Daylight Out of Her Life.

(From Our Own Correspondent.)

STOCKHOLM, Jan. 31 (by mail).—Miss Christina Witlund, an eccentric and wealthy woman, has just died here at the age of ninety-three.

Seventy-five years ago Miss Witlund, then a handsome young girl of eighteen, was engaged to be married to a dashing officer of the Royal Guards, and everything was ready for the wedding, when the bridegroom suddenly broke off the engagement and eventually married another.

Miss Witlund, it is said, nearly lost her reason from the effects of the shock, and when she finally recovered made a solemn vow never to look upon treacherous man again.

Her parents being dead, she had sole control of her own affairs, and she shut herself up in the house, where she remained for the whole of her life without ever going out.

For seventy-five years she saw no other human beings than her servant girls.

Living as one dead in the midst of the bustle of modern civilisation, she had never seen trains, steamships, tramway-cars, taxicabs, airships or aeroplanes.

Even daylight was strictly tabooed in her house, all the blinds being carefully drawn

1921
BE-DECKED BATHER.

IN THE WATER FULLY DRESSED AND WEARING JEWELS.

A DEAUVILLE SCENE.

The greatest sensation of the Deauville season was caused by a woman walking down to the beach from a bathing tent and entering the sea fully dressed.

The fair bather, whose auburn hair was bobbed, had a perfect figure. She was attired in an ankle-length skirt of white adorned with gold fleurs-de-lys, a sailor hat, silk stockings and high-heeled shoes, the heels of which were studded with diamonds and an occasional ruby.

A ring with a great diamond the size of a halfpenny was on the third finger of her right hand, while her left arm was resplendent with diamond and sapphire-studded bracelets three inches in width.

The Crowd's Greeting.

An enormous crowd collected to watch the woman, who made no attempt to swim, but held the bathers' rope and contented herself with bobbing up and down.

The other bathers looked on amazed. As she emerged from the water five minutes later (says the "Daily Express" correspondent) she was almost mobbed by the crowd, who greeted her with ironical cheers. Finally half a dozen gendarmes cleared a way for her, and she regained her tent in safety.

Half an hour afterwards she emerged, smiling, in a gown of white silk stockinette with a large picture hat, and drove off in her motorcar.

1917
72 YEARS SPENT IN BED.

Extraordinary Love Tragedy Recalled.

An old lady's death in Scarborough recalls a remarkable tragedy of disappointed love.

When she was 21 years of age she contracted an engagement which did not meet with the approval of her father, who forbade it. The young lady in her disappointment took to her bed, where she remained until her death, except that on one occasion she rose to leave Cambridge for Scarborough.

She never suffered from any complaint until the end, when she was ill for only two days.

She died at the age of 94, and had therefore been in bed for seventy-two years.

1926
THREE DELUDED DAUGHTERS.

MOTHER'S SKELETON IN KITCHEN.

TABLE SPREAD WITH FOOD FOR HER.

From Our Own Correspondent.

NANTWICH, Friday.

Acting under an order in bankruptcy, Mr. H. Hughes, auctioneer, of Crewe, entered a house in Nantwich to-day occupied by a family named Nixon.

The house had been barricaded, and the door had to be broken in with iron bars.

Mr. Hughes was met by three sisters with hands uplifted. One of them exclaimed

"We are in God's hands. This is God's house. There is fire and brimstone in every room. Mother must not be touched: she is in God's hands."

Close to a couch in the kitchen was the skeleton, wrapped in a sheet, of the person believed to be the mother. Near by was a table spread with fruit, nuts, bread, butter and a bowl of tea.

Pointing to this one of the daughters said to Mr. Hughes: "That is God's table. It is for mother. Don't touch it."

Another daughter said they had not been to bed for five years and had lived in the kitchen with the body.

The youngest daughter, a pathetic figure in rags, ran from the house weeping and gesticulating. She was a despairing figure seated on the garden wall at whom crowds gazed.

The daughters have been certified for removal to an asylum.

The Nixons have some independent means, but have lived in poverty. The mother is believed to have been dead for a long period.

1926
STRANGE WEST-END INCIDENT.

Unknown Man And Boy's Poisonous "Insect Bite."

A strange outrage on a London schoolboy in the West-end is engaging the attention of the police.

The boy was standing outside a shop in Oxford-street, when an irritant matter was squirted on his neck by a man, who told him he had been bitten by a poisonous insect.

The man induced the boy to accompany him in a bus to Victoria, where he called at a chemist's shop and obtained an ointment, which he said would kill the poison.

Afterwards the man engaged a taxicab and offered to drive the boy home.

During the journey the man left the taxi on the pretext that he wanted to buy some cigars, and was not seen again.

The boy informed the police and gave a full description of the man, who was about 40 years of age, fresh complexion, grey moustache, and wearing a grey suit and trilby hat.

1908
HORRIBLE OCCUPATION

A man named Malone, who was fined at Northampton yesterday for breaking hotel windows was said to earn his living by going from place to place exhibiting freshly-caught rats. These he tethered to a table with string, giving them a certain latitude, and then, with his hands tied tightly behind him, he fought and killed a rat with his teeth. Nine times out of ten he was said to succeed, but frequently the rat bit him severely.

1927
DISGUISE ESCAPADE OF PASTOR.

ROAMED AT NIGHT IN FEMININE ATTIRE.

'TO TEST MORALS.'

FROM OUR OWN CORRESPONDENT.
TAUNTON, Saturday.

THE identity of the mysterious "woman" six feet high, wearing white shoes, white stockings to the knee, a black skirt hemmed with white, a red hat, and a veil, who frightened the women and children in Curry Rivel, Somerset, last winter, and who reappeared recently, has been discovered.

At ten o'clock last night a villager, seeing the "woman" in a lane, jumped from his bicycle and grasped "her" wrists.

"Now," he said, "who are you?"

There was no answer.

A leading member of the Congregational chapel arrived, lifted "her" veil, and shone a light in "her" face. The mystery was solved.

It was the Rev. A. Harold Read, the Congregational minister at Curry Rivel, a married man of advancing years with several grown-up children.

Asked why he had gone about in a woman's clothes, the Rev. Mr. Read said he had been looking for material for a novel.

AN EXPLANATION

This discovery was followed by two public meetings at Drayton where Mr. Read gave his explanation for the action.

"I was drawn to this venture," he said, "because of what appeared to me, as reflected in the Press, a gross degeneration of manners and morals. I wondered whether the world was as bad as it was painted.

"My idea was to discover what was the attitude of the ordinary man to an ordinary woman going alone on country roads rather late at night.

"To my surprise and to my intense satisfaction, though I walked many miles on various occasions, there was not any one who became at all troublesome.

"Some will say that it was no engaging female. My only reply to that criticism is not a few opportunities would have opened out if I had given any sign.

"After having proved again and again in all the local districts as far as I could, and to my entire satisfaction (in various disguises, and also by riding a woman's cycle for a whole week) that men were far more chivalrous to women than I had imagined, I resolved to confirm and establish my convictions by visiting other and more populous areas.

ONLY ONE BAD MAN.

"My experience was just the same, with one exception—a town at some distance—where, as I sat on the sea front, all at once I felt a man leering at me. It was a terrible feeling, and I moved away very quickly.

"I am sure any woman, whose moral intuition must be keener than that of a man, would have been pained most deeply.

"Men, I raise my hat to you. I can truly say that you never had so high a place in my esteem as now. The lurid Press, the daily journals that give much space in their columns to sensation, are not fair to you. The heart of English manhood seems as sound as ever.

MANY A SMILE.

"These doings and goings have not been (happily for me) without their humorous side. Many a silent chuckle have I had when I have passed the people of the place all unknown to them.

I calculated, however, that my position as a minister would lend added weight to the evidence, the testimony, I could give.

At the conclusion of the meeting a member of the audience rose and asked if he could ask a question.

"No questions allowed," said Mr. Read.

In an interview he said: "I do not see that any harm has been done. I have travelled in many places so disguised, and have never been detected. No one, not even my family, knew anything about my adventures."

1927
ROGUE IN PULPIT.

BOGUS ARCHBISHOP.
From Our Own Correspondent.

PARIS, Friday.

One of Europe's biggest rogues, a Pole named Tarlowski, was sent to gaol at Caen yesterday for three years.

Tarlowski, who appeared on a charge of posing as a bishop, astonished the judges by delivering a long address to them in fluent Latin, in which he pleaded for an acquittal which would enable him to continue his "divinely inspired work."

"Not a bishop, but a notorious international swindler," was the police description of him. His career, the court was told, had been an astounding one.

LOVE AFFAIRS.

Expelled during the war from a Hungarian Jesuit house, he wandered through Europe and the Near East, imposing on pious, simple people. Love affairs which he had in Vienna and Warsaw led to his hasty flight from those towns to Cracow, where he entered a monastery, having given a pledge to reform.

A theft committed in the monastery led to his expulsion and flight to Radoff, in Russia. Here, posing as an ordained priest, his habit of saying Mass at uncanonical hours led to his arrest as a lunatic, and his detention in a madhouse.

The revolution in Russia incidentally procured his release, and he hastily left for Italy. In Florence, suspected of spying, he was once more sent to gaol.

After leaving Italy he next appeared in the North of Spain, where he posed as the exiled Catholic Bishop of Odessa. Pious Spaniards listened to his eloquent sermons, delivered from cathedral pulpits, and furnished sums for destitute Russian Catholics, which he said he represented.

"ARCHBISHOP."

Bordeaux was the next scene of his exploits. Here he appeared in the guise of an Army chaplain, wearing the war cross and the Legion of Honour ribbon. Then he turned up at Paris, where he won the confidence of the Cardinal and other leading ecclesiastics.

Caen was the next field of his roguery. Here he posed as an archbishop, and, showing stolen letters of recommendation, he was able to borrow large sums from the faithful. Then he moved on to Lisieux, where he gave himself out as a fugitive "Bishop of Petrograd." Here his astonishing career ended in his arrest.

"I am the son of a Russian grand duke," he exclaimed when arrested. But police inquiries reveal him to have started life as an agricultural labourer in Poland.

FANATICS

MONUMENT TO SATAN.

[THROUGH LAFFAN'S AGENCY.]
NEW YORK, Thursday.

The people of Detroit are greatly indignant over the action of Mr. Mend, a contractor, who has put up a monument to Satan.

The work, which was unveiled yesterday, is 14ft. high, and represents the devil crouching in a pulpit.

It hears the inscription, "Man is not created, but developed. God did not make man, but man has made gods."

1905

1947

DEATH BEATING

JOHANNESBURG, Saturday. — After reports that two Europeans killed a native because he was "too well dressed," Mr. James Gray, mayor of Johannesburg, called for a meeting to form a Race Relations Committee.

The native, before he died yesterday, said that he was standing at a bus stop when two men referred to his gloves and said he was too well dressed. They then knocked him down and beat him with a large stone.—Reuter.

1930

THE LAST POST!

Sergeant Enters His Own Suicide in Record Book.

From Our Own Correspondent.

POTSDAM (Received yesterday). With the old stern Prussian discipline and sense of duty, strong in face of death, Paul Falck, 27, Sergeant of the Reichswahr, before committing suicide, reported his own tragedy in the company record book. The entry read:—

"At ten minutes after midnight Sergeant Falck committed suicide by shooting himself. Corporal Junker has been instructed to take over the reveille."

1904

HALF-HOLIDAYS A "CURSE."

In fining a number of working men for being drunk on Saturday afternoon and evening, Alderman Dr. Crosby, at the Guildhall yesterday, remarked that the Saturday half-holiday was a curse to working people instead of a blessing.

The men, directly they drew their earnings, went to the public-house with them instead of taking them home to their wives. It would be much better for them to stick to their work instead of taking a half-holiday.

1905

MR. G. BERNARD SHAW & THE CHILD

In an address at Clifford's Inn Mr. G. Bernard Shaw said:—

"A child is a savage, cruel, noisy, dirty, frightful, inquisitive being, indiscreet to the point of telling the truth on all occasions, and regardless of the feelings of others."

Persons who lived with their children, added the lecturer, did so because they could not afford to do otherwise.

1903

WHAT A PARSON SAYS.

Mr. Luke White, the Member for the Buckrose Division of Yorkshire, who has been prominent in the opposition to the Motor-Cars Bill, received yesterday the following communication on a postcard:—

29, Bedford-square, Brighton, Aug. 5.
Motor-Cars.

It is my full intention to decline in future to vote for any candidate for Parliament unless he pledges himself to go in for the total abolition of all motors. There is no language of any sort half strong enough to express my detestation of these damnable engines of Satan.

F. T. WETHERED, Vicar of Hurley, Berks.

1935

"GOOD TO SUFFER, SAYS BISHOP

DR. P. Amigo, Bishop of Southwark, speaking to a gathering of men at Lambeth last night, condemned the principle which, he said, seemed to be growing in this country to put an end to the lives of people suffering from incurable ailments.

It was contrary, he said, to the teaching of the Catholic Church, and, in his opinion, it was a very wicked suggestion.

"We have no right to take other people's lives," he said. "In my view it is good to suffer purgatory on this earth."

People did not realise the value of suffering in the world.

1903

1,000 Years' Imprisonment.

At Houston, Texas, on Saturday, Allen Brown, a negro, was sentenced to 1,000 years' imprisonment for an assault. It is not stated if this is the maximum term, or if good conduct will entitle the prisoner to release after 800 years.

1924

SERMONS BY FIRE.

Fire was discovered during the week-end at the Baptist Tabernacle, Swindon, and on the charred door was found written:

This is an attempt to burn down the church, as is the Third Sermon By Fire, as a warning to all people to abstain from frivolity and amusements.

It was also discovered that an attempt had been made to burn down a chapel at Coate. In both cases only the doors were burned.

A man of 72, said to be a Londoner, was arrested and certified as insane. He has been sent to an asylum. In a diary in his pocket was mention of another church for destruction. Finally, the man's intention was to saturate his clothes with oil and set fire to himself in a place of amusement

1927

THE "Sunday Express" regularly publishes articles in which representative writers express opinions it cannot and does not endorse. It does not censor its distinguished contributors. If they were so foolish as to submit to our censorship, their articles would be worthless. We allow Mr. Wells to say what he thinks about marriage, because we believe in free discussion as vigorously as we disbelieve in birth-control and its inevitable by-product, free love.

BIRTH-CONTROL is a proved quackery, and its advocates are quacks masquerading as social reformers. Its general adoption would destroy marriage, disintegrate the family, and weaken the vitality of the nation. Civilisation, after centuries of struggle, has been built on marriage. The family is the foundation of patriotism and citizenship. Trial, or "companionate" marriage, based on birth-control, would be reactionary. It would be a reversion to an inferior type and a lower ideal. Experimental marriages would tend to displace the nobler and higher state.

Fanatics 29

1912
JOHN THOMAS HANCELL

HANCELL'S SON.

1939
Fed Son Like a Bird

A MOTHER'S devotion to her 17-year-old son who had never spoken since birth and for whom she masticated food so that she could feed him like a bird, was described at Hull coroner's court yesterday.

The inquest was on John William Bibby, who died from asphyxia in hospital. "He was my heart and soul," declared Mrs. Emily Bibby, wife of a lighterman.

Her son had never been able to chew his food, she added, and she had partly to masticate it for him and transfer it to his mouth. He simply swallowed it.

The boy died in the hospital to which he was taken when his mother was ill and could not attend to him.

"Death by misadventure," was the verdict.

A medical authority commented last night: "It is not unique for a boy of the type mentioned to be kept alive under hospital conditions, where there are special means of feeding the patient, but it is unusual for such a case to reach the age of 17.

"It is certainly very unusual for a mother, presumably untrained, to keep her child alive by her devotion as in the present instance"

1927
LYNCHINGS.

"The Negro in American Life." By Jerome Dowd. Cape. 21s.

Professor Dowd has written an almost too comprehensive book on all aspects of negro life. He writes of the negro as a criminal, the negro as a soldier, the negro as a preacher, and the negro as a poet. He tells us that nearly all the negro poets are mulattos, and that in crimes against women the negroes are at least proportionately less guilty than the Italians, Frenchmen and Russians.

In his chapter on lynchings he shows how the number of victims has decreased in the last 40 years, during which period more than 3,000 negroes and more than 1,000 white men were lynched. The author quotes another writer who attributes lynchings to the fact that in the South the white townspeople are starved emotionally and crave some excitement. He confesses with something like shame that after many years' attendance in Southern churches, though he has heard denunciations of nearly every sin to which human nature is susceptible, he has never heard from the pulpit one utterance against lynching. "To judge Southern clergymen by the themes for their sermons," he writes, "one would suppose that they did not regard lynching as comparable to the sin of dancing, playing cards, or going to the theatre."

TERROR AGED SEVEN

COMPELLED FATHER TO FETCH BEER AND CIGARETTES.

Amazing admissions were made by a father, at Macclesfield, when application was made under the Children's Act (by Mr. H. E. Smale, on behalf of the N.S.P.C.C.), for a boy aged seven years and nine months to be committed to an industrial school, he being entirely beyond his father's control. "This is a most extraordinary case, and a very sad one," said Mr. Smale. This boy of seven years and nine months is a child over whom the father has lost all control. The boy had only to say to his father, "Go and fetch me some beer and some cigarettes, or if you don't I will give you a jolly good thrashing, or something worse." When in bed the boy had repeatedly kicked his father to such an extent that dry abscesses had formed on his body.—John Thomas Hancell, cotton operative, Bollington, said he had had to fetch beer when requested, because the boy had led him such a life, and threatened him with the brush, tongs, and dolly peg. The lad would not let him get into bed until he had gone to sleep; sometimes he had pushed him out of bed.—Alice Forrest, one of the neighbours, said she had repeatedly heard the boy ill-using his father. When anyone went to the father's assistance the boy locked the door, took the key out of the lock, and so prevented anyone getting into the house. The language the boy used was so bad that she would not like to repeat it.—Another neighbour, Ellen Wood, said the boy used awful and fearful language, and he was not fit to be at large. His father dare not do anything other than fetch the beer and cigarettes when the boy demanded them.—The boy was committed to the Macclesfield Industrial School until he is 16.

1943
"RUSSIA MORE CHRISTIAN THAN BRITAIN"

BISHOP'S BLESSING FOR STALIN

The Bishop of Chelmsford, Dr. H. A. Wilson, presiding last night at a meeting in the Albert Hall, London, to mark the second anniversary of the German invasion of Russia, said:

"I speak as a Christian bishop to the Christian bishops and Christian people in Russia—a far larger number and percentage of the general population than is the case in this country.

"I sent to that great multitude of my fellow-Christians in Russia my greetings, and I say to the Christian bishops, priests, and people of Russia, 'We greet you, we salute you, we thank you, we remember you in our prayers, and we say God bless and God guide the people of Russia and their great leader, Joseph Stalin.'"

1935
ANGELIC SOULS TO ORDER

A DOCTOR'S SIMPLE OPERATION

"Sunday Dispatch" Cable

CHICAGO, Saturday.

MOROSE, irritable, and unbearable people are being transformed into sweet-tempered, angelic souls by the surgeon's knife of Dr. George Crile, of Cleveland, Ohio.

A simple operation on the glands above the kidneys, he explained to an international assembly of physicians at Chicago to-day, worked this wonder.

It is also a beauty operation, for he finds that all signs of worry, fretfulness, and fatigue have disappeared from the faces of his patients.

Fanatics

1931
1,000,000 FEEBLE-MINDED IN SCOTLAND

"Over one million of the population of Scotland are permanently dull or feeble-minded, not including the mentally or physically defective or insane. It will be a long and slow process to effect an improvement."

This statement was made by Dr. John Harvey yesterday, in an address to the conference of the Educational Institute of Scotland at Clydebank.

1938
If Guilty They Would Be Gassed While In Court

SPECIAL TO "REYNOLDS"

DR. H. M. STEPHENSON, a Dorset country doctor who thinks brutal crime should be punished with brutality or even death, declared in an astonishing speech, at Dorchester, that lethal chambers should adjoin all Assize Courts.

The chambers would be installed to execute persons of continuous criminal habits or guilty of sex crime.

Dr. Stephenson, who was debating that "The leniency with which crime is treated nowadays is becoming a menace to law-abiding citizens," attacked "people who think that soppiness with a criminal pays."

There seemed to be a growing idea, he said, that if one were sweet and gentle enough to a thug, he would shed a few tears and cease to be a thug. A greater mistake could hardly be made.

He spoke of the hopelessly depraved class of criminal, one of whom he knew has spent 13 years in prison, though he was only 23.

This man, guilty of a crime of violence, was perfectly sane but found great difficulty in controlling his impulses.

He was last sent to gaol for 18 months. "You might as well give a tiger 18 months and expect it to cease to be a tiger when it came out," said the doctor.

"CRUEL BUT EFFECTIVE"

"To deal with such cases by prison is wrong." For crimes of violence there should be flogging, which was cruel but effective

Dr. Stephenson said he would not punish recidivists and sex perverts. He would say to them, "I am sorry. I hope you will have a better time in another world, but we cannot keep you in this." He would then put them in a lethal chamber. That was the only sane thing to do. The lethal chamber was immeasurably kinder to such people than to shut them up in gaol for life.

If he had his way, there would be a lethal chamber attached to every assize court. When the oxygen in a chamber was exhausted without increasing the carbon dioxide, the person inside just dropped to the floor.

He would have prisoners sitting in the lethal chamber, and if they were found guilty of such crimes of violence as he indicated, the oxygen in the chamber would be exhausted without their being told the verdict.

1933
"WHAT IS FASCISM?"
The Threefold Aim

TO THE EDITOR OF THE MORNING POST

Sir,—Signor Mussolini, in his wonderful article in your columns, described the Fascist State as: "Unitarian, authoritarian, and totalitarian." One wonders how many of your readers realise vividly the full implication of these words.

UNITARIAN.—The troubles of the world to-day can all be traced to a lack of unity in thought and action, both in the field of politics and in religion. Without entire unity of thought there can be no advance—only internecine conflict. All lines of action meander like a river that has entered a bog, diverging into numerous streamlets and becoming lost in final stagnation.

AUTHORITARIAN.—All the best of England's youth are Fascist at heart, and only await the call and leadership. We are weary of the muddled "democracy" that has produced Communism and other ridiculous and perverted growths of the human mind.

TOTALITARIAN.—Fascism is not a new form of party politics—it is an *inspiration*. We believe that all personal aims and petty diversities of opinion in the community must be merged in one splendid Unity of idealism, of faith in national glory and patriotism, in religion and prosperity and peace. Thus, united in one grand adventure, we may march forward towards the rising sun.

We believe in Idealism, but we believe also in the Strength and Action that makes dreams come true.

Nothing can stop us. The spirit of Fascism will sweep the world.

E. CORNFORTH.

Binorie, The Fordrough, Four Oaks, Warwickshire.

1934
"BLOOD AND HONOUR"

The demand made of Storm troopers that those possessing "daggers of honour" inscribed with Capt. Roehm's name should return them to headquarters, has a peculiar significance. The daggers also bore the words, "Blood and honour," and were only awarded to those who could prove beyond dispute that they had Communist blood on their hands.

1905
THE STUPID DIE YOUNG.

Judges and Others Who Think Outlive the Rural Labourer.

Brain-work lengthens life, was the effect of some remarkable statements made in Mr. Justice Swinfen Eady's Court yesterday.

The case arose out of a driving accident, the victim of which developed softening of the brain.

A Dr. Duke stated that softening of the brain was a very common occurrence in the country, one-third of the labourers in rural districts dying from it. The cause of the disease was the lack of brain exercise.

The intellect of a rural labourer, said the witness, rusted rather than wore out, and when he attained the age of sixty-five or seventy-five he usually went off in an apoplectic fit or something of the kind.

In support of his theory the doctor referred to the cases of Judges and others whose thinking capacity was continuously employed, and who, he said, invariably lived longer than the average labourer.

1931

SUICIDE TO TEST DEATH THEORY

ATHEIST'S VIEW ON THE AFTER-LIFE

"A RETURN TO THE NEGATIVE"

A remarkable letter, written by a man who, according to the Coroner, probably killed himself to justify his obsession that there was no life after death, was read at the Yeovil inquest yesterday on the unknown man who was found shot in a compartment of the Channel Islands boat train on Thursday.

The man, who appeared to be a foreigner, left a seven-page manuscript on the question of life and death. His final note read:

"As before life, so after life, a return to the negative. The conditions of pre-life have become desirable. Therefore, I will commit suicide. I am an atheist. Therefore, I desire no service.

"My body is fundamentally a mass of cells; because it is so, respect towards it is unplaced. I desire that my remains shall be cremated, and the ashes mingled with those of the furnace. In other words, I do not wish to be disposed of in any manner which indicates that universal folly 'corpse worship.'—Yours sincerely, F. W. Bentron—no fixed address.

"P.S.—You will find sufficient money in my possession to make a payment of five guineas to the Cremation Society, and this sum will ensure cremation."

An electric pistol firing a steel bullet was found in the compartment, and a pathologist said it was evident that the projectile, which was about the size of a lead pencil, had passed through the brain, and that the weapon had been placed in an upright position on the top of the head and discharged downwards.

A verdict that an unknown man who gave his name as Frank W. Bentron committed suicide while insane was returned.

The Coroner said he should not allow cremation without identification, adding that it was rather curious that a man who believed there was no life after death should worry about whether his body was buried or cremated.

1927

IS JAZZ SAVAGE?

"NATURAL MUSIC" is evidently not musical. Does he know that to see girls dancing to many of these jazz "tunes" (particularly during the war) was a real shock to many, particularly so to those who had seen native dances practically identical so far as rhythm is concerned?

Savages are presumably as near nature as any. Jazz is nothing more than the music of savages. When there is any tune in it, it is usually borrowed from so-called "highbrow" music.

For anyone who can listen to, or even hear, jazz without a shudder, to give himself a nom-de-plume which includes the word "music" is ridiculous—jazz is *not* music. M. SAVILE.

1945

Kill off useless at sixty, said shot major

Major Corbett-Smith.

A LETTER written before his suicide by **Major Arthur Corbett-Smith**, 65-year-old author and former B.B.C. official, advocated "the lethal chamber" for all sixty-year-old people whose "continued existence does not in some measure benefit the community."

Major Corbett-Smith covered his head with a Union Jack and shot himself on Margate Promenade on Wednesday after having posted the letter to the Chief Inspector of Police.

It was headed "Corbett-Smith on his self-dispatch," and was read at the inquest at Margate yesterday.

1931

SIR HARRY WANTS A FIGHT

KILLING AND DISABLING IS SUCH GOOD SPORT

ADVICE TO LEGION

This story is presented to readers for their edification and, maybe, entertainment, without comment

"Reynolds's" Correspondent

MINEHEAD, Saturday.—Many comments are being made in West Somerset to-day about the remarkable speech made last night by Sir Harry Malet, Bart., when proposing the toast of "Sport" at Stogursey British Legion dinner

Sir Harry began by attacking the criticisms of hunting by anti-blood sport societies, and then declared that

the highest form of sport people could possibly get is war.

In war both sides set out to kill or disable as many of their enemies as possible, he said.

Both had equal chances and had to play for their side when fighting.

Admiral Sir Percy Green, who spoke later, declared that the League of Nations was run by politicians, fanatics and cranks.

If the British Legion went fooling about with the League of Nations, he said, they would undermine their constitution.

Fanatics

SIR ALMROTH WRIGHT, F.R.S.,
Who recently Denounced Woman's Suffrage in a letter to the "Times."

1909
WOMAN—THE SAVAGE.

UNGALLANT CRITICISMS BY A PROFESSOR.

"Express" Correspondent

NEW YORK, Thursday, June 24.

Professor Starr, of the University of Chicago, who occasionally startles the world with unexpected and sensational criticisms, has made another bitter attack on womankind, in which he says:

"It is impossible to civilise woman, for her fundamental nature is barbaric, and the continuance of the race depends on the rigid assertion of this difference between man and woman.

"I challenge any one to show a single first-class achievement by woman in literature, science, or art.

"Her religion is also notably that of lower culture. She is always seeing signs everywhere. She is the chief supporter of spiritualistic mediums. She founds new sects in which the religious attitude of savagery is given new names.

"The twentieth century woman shows herself no farther advanced than her jungle sister by her love of bright colours and by decorating herself with birds and the furs of animals, also by her love of jewels and perfumes.

"In the fundamental principles of her character and in her instincts woman has passed through the ages unchanged. Her savage ingenuity in gaining her ends through deception and treachery has become proverbial.

"When it would be equally easy for her to gain her end by straightforward and direct methods, she delights to resort to duplicity and sinuous means.

"Woman lives in the old, old world, she thinks old thoughts, she feels old emotions, is moved by old impulses, dresses in old gewgaws, and is thrilled by world-old hopes and fears.

"Her fondness for evidence of bloodshed and slaughter shows in the most pronounced way her utter savagery.

"Woman is an eternal savage, whose only salvation lies in the fact that she always has been and always will be barbarian."

1914
BEARDED SUFFRAGETTES.
"Express" Correspondent.

BERLIN, Sunday, July 12.

Dr. Hans Friedenthal, a famous professor of Berlin University, writing in the "Berliner Tageblatt," describes the new woman as he thinks she will be evolved by suffragism and the higher education.

He declares that brain work will cause her to become bald, while increasing masculinity and contempt for beauty will induce the growth of hair on the face.

In the near future, therefore, Dr. Friedenthal declares, women will be bald, and will wear patriarchal beards and long moustaches.

1912
WOMEN UNFITTED FOR THE VOTE
Medical Expert's Remarkable Letter on Militant Hysteria.

There is likely to be much controversy over a remarkable letter on what is called "militant hysteria," from the pen of Sir Almroth Wright, the well-known medical authority, which has appeared in the "Times." Sir Almroth, who has made numerous contributions to scientific literature, is a former Demonstrator of Pathology at Cambridge University, of physiology at Sydney University, and for ten years was professor of pathology at the Army Medical School, Netley. In his letter, which occupies three columns, he advanced many reasons why women are both mentally and physically unfitted for the franchise.

MILITANT'S RECRUITING FIELD.

Emigration to the Colonies is suggested by the expert:—

The recruiting field for the militant suffragists is the half-million of our excess female population—that half-million which had better long ago have gone out to mate with its complement of men beyond the seas.

Sir Almroth divides into types the women in the militant movement:—

(1) First come a class of women who hold, with minds otherwise unwarped, that they may, whenever it is to their advantage, lawfully resort to physical violence.

(2) A class of women who have all their life long been strangers to joy, women in whom instincts long suppressed have in the end broken into flame.

These are "the sexually embittered women, in whom everything has turned into gall and bitterness of heart and hatred of men. Their legislative programme is licence for themselves, or else restrictions for man.

(3) The incomplete. One side of their nature has undergone atrophy, with the result that they have lost touch with their living fellow men and women.

"Their programme is to convert the whole world into an epicene institution (says the writer)—an epicene institution in which man and woman shall everywhere work side by side at the self-same tasks and for the self-same pay. These wishes can never by any possibility be realized. And even then woman, though she protests that she does not require it, and that she does not receive it, practically always does receive differential treatment at the hands of man."

(4) The woman who is poisoned by her misplaced self-esteem, and who flies out at every man who does not pay homage to her intellect.

In an eloquent passage, Sir Almroth says:—

Up to the present in the whole civilized world there has ruled a truce of God as between man and woman. That truce is based upon the solemn covenant that within the frontiers of civilization the weapon of physical force may not be applied by man against woman nor by woman against man.

Under this covenant a full half of the programme of Christianity has been realized; and a foundation has been laid upon which it may be possible to build higher, and perhaps finally in the ideal future to achieve the abolition of physical violence and war.

And it is this solemn covenant, the covenant so faithfully kept by man, which has been violated by the militant suffragist in the interest of her morbid, stupid, ugly, and dishonest programmes.

"Peace will come again," predicts the writer of this letter. "It will come when woman ceases to believe and to teach all manner of evil of man despitefully. It will come when she ceases to impute to him as a crime her own natural disabilities, when she ceases to resent the fact that man cannot and does not wish to work side by side with her."

1910
WOMAN AS THE DESTROYER.

Futurist Leader's Fierce Denunciation.

POISON OF LOVE.

Signor Marinetti, the leader of the Futurist movement in Italy, with whom an interview was published in this paper on Thursday last, was in his most audacious mood yesterday when he gave an address at the Lyceum Club. It was in many ways a remarkable scene—remarkable as showing the extraordinary tolerance of opinion among women of to-day, and the absolute candour with which they are prepared to face the problems of their sex and life.

If Signor Marinetti had been speaking to Early Victorian women they would have swooned in horror at his words or fallen into violent hysterics. If he had spoken to Mid-Victorian women they would have risen in righteous indignation and left the room as a protest against this blasphemy. But yesterday the ladies of the Lyceum Club sat very still, smiled at the most daring utterances of this young Italian philosopher, and actually applauded some of his most violent phrases.

He did not mince his words. It was well indeed that he spoke in French, for in that language one may utter phrases which could not be tolerated in hard plain English.

A NEW BRUTALITY.

He stood before these refined women of the intellectual class—these literary and artistic ladies—as the champion of a new brutality, and as the enemy of their sex. Swiftly and vividly he began by describing the spirit of the Futurist movement and its active warfare against classical ideas in art and life, against the beauty of old dead things, against philosophers, archæologists, professors, and antiquaries who live in the old traditions, against old ideals and old conventions. He told them how the new movement is sweeping the young men of Italy into its ranks, he described the free fights which have taken place in Venice, Florence, and Rome between the "Antiquists" and the Futurists—fights in which some heads and many canes have been broken—and he gloried in the awakening of the modern industrial spirit in Italy, where he alleges that the old-world cities are stagnant with the worm-eaten grandeur of a dead and decadent past.

Then Signor Marinetti came to the influence of women on life, and his voice rose with passion as he denounced the place of woman in history, and the evil blight of that "romantic love" of which she has been the object throughout the centuries.

This romantic love, he says, has been a poison in which all the vice of men has been bred. The woman of beauty with her amorous desires, her erotic nature, her utter selfishness, her cruelty, her greed, her frailty, has been like the infamous woman of the Bible, of whom young men were bidden to beware.

THE SERPENT'S POWER.

Her snake-like coils have crushed and choked the noblest ideals of manhood. By this infamous and romantic love men have lost their virility and their moral health. Poets and painters and artists of every kind have been seduced by its evil spell, and modern life in all its aspects is made foul by this romanticism.

"We must get free of this infamous womanhood," cried Signor Marinetti, gazing fiercely at the amiable ladies of the Lyceum Club, who smiled at him.

The Futurist, he declared, will put the love of woman away from him. His machine will be his mistress. The grand ideals of mechanical progress will influence his heart. He will become more like a machine himself, as regards order, perfect adaptability to the object to be obtained, in power, and single purpose. Perhaps the time will come when men may do without women altogether, and when the human races may be continued by mechanical means. To the Futurist this is the one grand hope.

PRAISE FOR SUFFRAGETTES.

With apparent inconsistency Signor Marinetti praised the Suffragettes. He admired them for adopting violent methods, for braving ridicule, for breaking down that snobbishness which is the curse of the English people, and for destroying that Parliamentary system, which, he says, he willingly delivers over to the claws of the Suffragettes. But let them make no mistake. The men of the future will not tolerate the equality of women. They are going to assert their greatest strength of manhood and liberate themselves from the debasing and debilitating influence of the old romantic love.

There was much more of this passionate defiance of womanhood and the old idealism, but enough has been given to show that Signor Marinetti has peculiar views which he expresses in the most forcible language.

1909
SCIENCE PROVES WOMAN INFERIOR.

Many Arguments Put Forward by Objectors Answered.

"NO FEMALE GENIUS."

By CHARLES H. HEYDEMANN, Ph.D.

In his article published in *The Daily Mirror* yesterday on the question whether women are equal to men, Dr. Heydemann pointed out that the result of frequent experiments had been to show that women are inferior to men in the senses of smell, taste, and sight and hearing. This is the reason, he contends, that piano tuners, tea and wine tasters, and great dressmakers are men. Woman may be able to assimilate knowledge quickly, but this assimilation faculty is sponge-like and "turns out knowledge like Birmingham buttons."

1928
LONE WOMAN EXPLORER.

EVENING DRESSES IN THE JUNGLE.

An American woman will be the only white person accompanying 20 negroes on an expedition to the heart of Darkest Africa.

She is Mrs. John Inglis Fletcher, of San Francisco, who arrived at Liverpool yesterday in the White Star liner Baltic. She sails for Capetown on Friday.

"The real purpose of the expedition," she told the Liverpool correspondent of the "Daily News and Westminster," "is to study native folk lore. I want to find out all I can about the origin of Voodoos, witchcraft, devil and python worship, and trace the sources of the many superstitious beliefs of the American negro.

"I have lived in Alaskan mining camps and explored the Canadian and American North-West on horseback. I'm a fairly good shot, and hope to do some shooting on the trip."

She is taking evening dresses, khaki trousers, table linen, a silver dinner service, and Army mess kits—"because," she said, "that's the whole secret of keeping the natives under control and impressing them with the superiority of the white race.

"Although I'll be dining in the forest with nobody but natives present," she added, "my table will be set with damask and silver, and I'll wear an evening gown."

FREAKS

Lina Medina, six-year-old mother of a fifteen-month-old baby boy, arriving in Chicago. The astonishing case of the world's youngest mother is arousing interest in youthful mothers among doctors.

1940
GROWN UP AT FIVE

NEW YORK, Saturday.

A CORPS of physicians led by the famous specialist, Doctor Karl John Karnaky, of Houston, Texas, are bringing all their knowledge to bear in an effort to save two little girls of five from dying of "old age" before they reach the age of twenty.

The cases are unprecedented in medical history.

Both girls have reached full adulthood and one of them, Linda Medina, of Peru, is already the mother of a normal child.

She will be flown to Houston to receive treatment by Dr. Karnaky because of his apparent success in treating the case of Ruby Franklin, five-year-old daughter of a Houston farmer, who has been mature since the age of two.

On the question of who is the father of her baby son there is still profound mystery.

Lina's mother, Donna Loza, a stolid peasant of the Andes, said at the time that she believed that Lina was bitten by a snake called "Tiracha," which, according to Indian legend, holds strange power over women, sometimes creeping up on them and sinking its fangs into them as they sleep in the open air.

Lina often slept in the open air in her mountain village.

Her father also has a theory. He says that there is a pool up in the mountains called "the pool of birth." Those who bathe in it find the power to create new life.

Lina used to bathe in this pool.

The doctors in Chicago, who have been waiting to see Lina Medina for a year, will try to solve the mystery of a birth that has baffled the medical world.

AFTER WHICH POOR LITTLE LINA MAY GO ON TOUR IN A SIDE-SHOW.

Freaks

1937
She Has Two Tongues Too!

Moscow, Saturday.

A girl with two heads and four arms is puzzling Soviet scientists at the All-Union Institute of Experimental Medicine.

Only one similar case, they say, has ever been recorded before.

From the shoulders down the child is one normal individual, but from the shoulders up it is twins. Born six weeks ago in a Moscow nursing home, the child is thriving, eating with both mouths and gaining weight.—B.U.P.

1941
He Had Two Hearts

A man who lived 73 years with two hearts of normal size has died at Medford, Oregon, says British United Press.

His doctor said that one heart was in a normal position, while the other—the one that failed—was just below the left lung.

1913
WOMAN WHO LIVED TWICE.

AMAZING KNOWLEDGE OF A FORMER EXISTENCE

"Express" Correspondent.

Paris, Monday, Dec. 15.

The death is reported this evening of Mme. Laure Raynaud, who created some excitement in Paris a few years ago by her extraordinary knowledge of a former life.

Mme. Raynaud, who was forty-five years old, was a nurse in a private hospital in Passy. A few years ago she told the doctor that she knew she had died at the age of nineteen many years before. She described the town and the house in which she had lived. It was a foreign town, although Mme. Raynaud had never been out of France.

The doctor thought the town might be Siena, in Italy, so he wrote to the mayor of that place and procured a collection of photographs. In one of them he recognised a house and a church exactly like those Mme. Raynaud described. She gave many details, among others that she died in 1840, and that her death was due to consumption.

Without telling her where she was going, the doctor took her to Siena. The first day she arrived she walked straight to the house she had described, and from there to the church. There she went to the tombstone of a girl who died of consumption in 1840 at the age of nineteen, and fell on it in a fainting fit.

Mme. Raynaud refused to make any money out of her peculiar gift, and though she had a strange magnetism which enabled her to effect cures of certain nervous maladies, she always refused payment. Her death was due to cancer.

1940
BLACK AND WHITE TWINS

Mrs. Herbert Strong, a negress of Hokerton, North Carolina, has given birth to twins, one of which is white and the other black.

The twins, a white son and a black daughter, were born last September but they have been concealed indoors until now because their Negro father simple, coal-black Herbert Strong feared that the "world would talk."

But now the secret is out, the parents are being besieged for film and vaudeville offers amounting to many thousands of dollars.

The father told John Walters, "Daily Mirror" New York correspondent: "We are tickled to death at having twins, but, gosh, how folk will gossip when they hear one is white."

Scientists believe that either Mrs. Strong or her husband had a white ancestor.

1940
Twins Born Four Days Apart

FOUR days, two and a half hours, separated the birth of twin boys born to Mrs. Walker, aged 33, of Chalgrove Road, Tottenham, N.

Mrs. Walker is living at a holiday camp at Heacham, Norfolk, to which she was evacuated with her three other children. The births took place at King's Lynn Infirmary, and mother and babies are making good progress. The first twin is to be named James Edward, the other Brian Richard.

["Four days apart" twins were born to the wife of a Walthamstow baker in 1936. About a year later a coloured woman gave birth to two children within three months in Africa.]

1939
Twins With Different Fathers

IN a court case brought by the mother of twins, medical experts established that each twin had a different father, says a Reuter Berlin message.

Blood tests revealed without any doubt that the children belonged to different blood groups, and that they were, therefore, only half-brothers.

1921
CHILD WITH WOLF'S HEAD.

A child who had a head exactly like a wolf and feet resembling lobster's claws has just died in the foundling ward of a hospital at Avignon, says the Central News.

The child had no arms, and lived less than six weeks.

It has been decided to preserve its body as an anatomical curiosity.

1922
THE SIAMESE TWINS

Rosa and Josefa Blazek were Czecho-Slovaks. They were forty-two years of age. They were joined together by a broad bony union of the lower part of the back and pelvis. They had two hearts, two pairs of lungs, but only one stomach. Rosa was married, and her husband, a German officer, was killed in the war in 1915. She had a son of twelve called Frantz. He is in every respect normal. Josefa was attacked by jaundice, but Rosa refused to allow the surgeons to separate her from her sister. She was told that her sister might die. "If Josefa dies," she said, "I want to die too." Her love for her sister was stronger than her love for her son. Even when the doctors begged her for the sake of her son to consent to an operation she was obdurate. And Frantz, after Josefa's death, said he would rather be an orphan than allow his mother and his aunt to be separated. It is said that the jaundice was caused by overeating. Each sister ate several pounds of meat per day. We are not told whether both sisters ate too much or whether one ate more than the other. Rosa died fifteen minutes after Josefa.

Two, Yet One.

Although Rosa and Josefa had only one digestive system, they had two distinct personalities. Their brains functioned separately, and they had different idiosyncrasies and tastes. They were fond of each other, but at times they quarrelled over their food and drink. Rosa drank wine, but Josefa drank beer, and the mixture disagreed with their one stomach. They were able to share each other's sensations. While Josefa was lying ill, Rosa ate to keep up Josefa's strength. The fact that they were indissolubly bound to each other might have made their union one of hate rather than one of affection, but they appear to have mastered the art of give and take. Otherwise their life would have been unendurable. During their tours of Europe they amassed a great deal of money, but they neglected to make either a joint or separate will, and died intestate.

The supreme mystery of these strange sisters is the fact that one was married and the other was unmarried. Josefa, we are told, was a spinster. What a triangle!

The Boy with Two Mothers.

Even in death they have enriched the Chicago lawyers with an unanswerable riddle. It is claimed, on behalf of Frantz, that they were his joint mothers, and that therefore he ought to inherit their joint fortune, some £45,000. But the doctors are in a dilemma. Some doctors hold that it is impossible for any child to have two mothers. But other doctors contend that it is possible. Although the child was borne by one sister, both sisters nursed him. Is nursing the test of motherhood? Romulus and Remus were nursed by a she-wolf. Perhaps, after hundreds of years, the story of Rosa and Josefa will ripen into a legend or a fairy tale. There is nothing in folk-lore more marvellous than this Chicago miracle of the boy with two mothers. They called him " our son "!

1929

HUSBAND FOR ONE OF THE SIAMESE TWINS.

SISTERS WHO CAN NEVER BE PARTED.

DEATH RISK DRAMA.

"Sunday Chronicle" Correspondent.
New York, Saturday.

ROMANCE has come to one of the Siamese twins, Margaret Gibbs, who is joined to her sister, Mary. In a few weeks' time she is to marry Carlos Josefe, a young man of 21, said to be a graduate of the University of Mexico.

The couple have just applied for a marriage licence at Newark, New Jersey. The date and place of the wedding are being kept secret.

This extraordinary romance follows an attempt by the twins to have an operation performed to separate them, so that Margaret might marry in a normal way.

WILLING TO RISK DEATH.

Behind it is the drama of the other sister's willingness to risk death in order that her twin sister might have a chance of happiness.

The twins had reconciled themselves to the thought that fate had decreed they should always be one and that they would never be able to marry.

"We are joined together and we must live and die that way," Margaret said some time ago. "We can never marry, for we can never be separated."

And then came romance to upset their resolve. Margaret, who is 18, fell in love with Mr. Josefe.

THE ONLY WAY OUT.

"I told my sister what had happened, and how I felt about him," she told me to-day. "It seemed impossible that I could ever marry, even if he were willing to marry me. It was then my sister suggested a possible way out of the dilemma.

"Despite the risk of death she urged that we should undergo a separation operation, so that I might be married in a normal way.

"We agreed to see what could be done, and sought the advice of an eminent surgeon. He pronounced the operation impossible, as it would certainly result in the death of one, if not of both, of us.

"We therefore decided that I should get married as I am rather than lose my great chance of happiness."

The "Siamese" twins, Mary and Margaret Gibb, with Carlos Josefe, whom Margaret is soon to be married. See story in adjoining column

DIFFERENT MINDS.

The twins are joined together by a cartilaginous bond at the base of the spine. The difficulty of performing an operation to separate them lies in the fact that they have arterial and nerve systems common to each.

Despite her physical misfortune Margaret is an attractive girl, with fresh complexion and a mass of dark hair.

Although their bodies are one their minds are distinctly individualistic. "My sister likes a lot of life," Margaret said. "Her favourite occupation is doing embroidery, while mine is reading. I like mystery stories best. We can do nearly everything in the household, including baking and making pies.

"We can also dance, sing, play the piano and the ukulele."

1936
SURPRISE IN THE RUXTON TRIAL

DEFENCE K.C. REVEALS WHAT DOCTORS FOUND

Professor Glaister, Regius Professor of Forensic Medicine at Glasgow University, one of the medical experts for the Crown, was cross-examined by Mr. Norman Birkett, K.C. (for the defence), when the trial of Dr. Buck Ruxton was resumed to-day at Manchester Assizes.

Dr. Ruxton, of Dalton-square, Lancaster, is charged before Mr. Justice Singleton with the murder of Mrs. Isabella Ruxton between September 14 and 29 of last year.

Human remains found in a ravine at Moffat are alleged to be those of Mrs. Ruxton and of Mary Jane Rogerson, aged 20, who was employed at the house as nursemaid for the Ruxton children.

"Startling"

Professor Glaister said he first saw the remains at the mortuary at Moffat on October 1.

Mr. Birkett: In these remains, I understand, there were 43 parts which remained unassigned to either body?—That is the position.

Included in those 43 unassigned soft parts was there a cyclops eye?—There was a portion which he thought was a cyclops eye.

That was a very remarkable and startling discovery?—A most unusual find in the circumstances.

A cyclops eye is the product of a monstrous birth, is it not?—It is.

By some irregular process of nature there is one eye in the forehead?—Yes, or close together.

When they approximate to one eye in the centre of the forehead that is called a cyclops eye?—Yes.

"Not as Human"

That cyclops eye in those remains is undoubtedly the product of a monstrous birth?—That is our view.

For all that you know to the contrary it may be the sole remaining portion of a human foetus?—We did not regard it as human.

In the case of a cyclops eye being animal, it is usually a grazing animal?—It is commonly associated with the pig.

1921
THE DENTIST'S DILEMMA.
Woman with Extra Row of Teeth.

Dr. de Lapersonne has informed the Academy of Medicine of the curious case of a young woman who at the back of one eye (at the base of the socket) has a row of teeth perfectly formed which are pressing against the ball of the eye, says an Exchange message from Paris.

The discovery was made by means of an X-ray photograph. Such an anomaly has never previously been reported.

As the presence of the teeth is threatening the sight of the eye, it will be necessary to extract them. The dentist's task will not be an easy one.

1942
EYES IN BACK OF HIS HEAD

A DUCKLING hatched at Molesworth, Northamptonshire has two eyes in the back of its head and two in front.

It also has fore and aft beaks, four legs and four wings.

1932
PIG WITH TWO HEADS.

A pig with two heads has been born at the village of Hegyhatszentpeter (St. Peter's Ridge) near the Austrian frontier, says Reuter's Budapest correspondent.

The heads are perfect in all respects, except that there are only three ears, one on the outer side of each head and one in the middle, between the two heads.

The little pig is being specially fed and nursed, as its legs are as yet too weak to support the two heads.

1904
A CALF AND A HALF.

A heifer belonging to a farmer at Hallow, near Worcester, has given birth to a curious freak in the shape of two calves in one.

The heads, necks, and hindquarters are separate, but the bodies are in one skin.

An extraordinary feature of the freak is that there are two forelegs and six hindlegs. The calf expired immediately after birth.

1936
LAMB WITH CYCLOPS EYE

A lamb with a cyclops eye—a single eye in the middle of the forehead—has been born at Woodlands Farm, Apperley Dene, near Stocksfield, Northumberland. It lived for only an hour and a half.

1927
HEART ON WRONG SIDE.
MAN'S ORGANS VICE VERSA TO THOSE OF NORMAL FOLK.
(From Our Own Correspondent.)

Following every day the strenuous occupation of a ripper in the Cortonwood colliery, near Sheffield, is a man named Joseph Johnson, of Oaks Green, Sheffield, whose internal organs are engaging the attention of well-known medical men. Johnson is one of a large family of brothers and sisters who are normal and healthy people, but he, it has been declared by doctors, has his heart on the wrong side, and all his other organs are vice versa to those of normal people. Nevertheless Johnson does not feel any ill effects from his peculiarity. On the contrary, he declares that he is as strong and as healthy as any man, and he certainly looks it.

1931
TWO-HEADED GOAT
It was Greedy, Ate with Both—and Died

BOIZANO, Italy, Saturday.

A two-headed kid goat has died here from greed.

The animal was born with two heads, and insisted on eating with both. It died of over-eating.—B.U.P.

1936
AND NOW "DECUPLETS"!
TEN BABIES SAID TO HAVE BEEN BORN TO CHINESE MOTHER

Tokyo, Saturday.—Ten babies—nine boys and a girl—have been born at one birth to the wife of Chao Wang a peasant of Kalgan, according to the Peking correspondent of a Tokyo newspaper.

The "decuplets" are stated to have been born on Nov. 16. Five of the boys and the girl died the following day, but the mother and the other four boys are doing well.—Reuter.

1938
One-Eyed Pig Has Trunk

A one-eyed pig with a short trunk resembling that of an elephant has been born on a farm near Lille. The eye is in the middle of the pig's forehead, says Exchange, while the trunk is just above the eye. The freak pig's sixteen brothers and sisters are all quite normal.

Freaks

EVEN A CAT CAN FLY!—At least this one can a little, for it has what appears to be two fur-covered wings on its back. It was found in an Oxford garden and is now one of the curiosities of the Oxford Zoo.

CAT WITH WINGS!

ZOO EXPERTS PUZZLED BY FREAK THAT CAN "FLY"

FROM OUR SPECIAL CORRESPONDENT

OXFORD, Thursday.

I have just seen a cat that has on its back fully-developed fur-covered wings, with which, it is stated, it can fly.

It is now housed in the Oxford Zoo, and it is one of the strangest of Nature's freaks—and the most pathetic.

All the time it seems to be ashamed of its unusual appearance and tries to be as like a normal domestic cat as possible.

When I approached him, the winged cat rolled over on his back and then frisked round an enclosed paddock.

Here is the strange history of the animal, which is puzzling eminent zoologists.

LEAP TO BEAM

A few days ago neighbours of Mrs. Hughes Griffiths, of Summerstown, Oxford, saw a strange black and white cat prowling round their gardens.

Last evening Mrs. Hughes Griffiths saw the animal in a room of her stables.

"I saw it move from the ground to a beam—a considerable distance, which I do not think it could have leaped—using its wings in a manner similar to that of a bird," she said to me.

Mrs. Hughes Griffiths at once telephoned to the Oxford Zoo, and Mr. Frank Owen, the managing director, and Mr. W. E. Sawyer, the curator, went to her house and captured the animal in a net.

I carefully examined the cat to-night, and there is no doubt about the wings. They grow just in front of its hindquarters.

Tate's Brilliant Catch.

"I DON'T BELIEVE THERE IS SUCH A FISH."

From Our Special Correspondent with the M.C.C. Team.

AUCKLAND, N.Z., Monday.

Try to imagine a fish that groans when caught, has big yellow wings, has lots of pink spots, several legs, and stares at you with huge blue eyes.

You can't! And Maurice Tate couldn't, and that was why he very nearly fell overboard when he made this brilliant catch.

We were fishing from a motor launch 15 miles out of Auckland, when the Sussex bowler hooked this queer thing.

"I Don't Believe it."

He took one look, staggered back, and said, "I don't believe it."

None of us quite trusted our eyes till a yell from Wally Hammond told us that he had got another.

The pair of fish groaned their lives away while G. O. Allen, Hammond, Voce, Tate, Ames, Leyland and I just stared.

BABY'S THREE-INCH TAIL

Second Case of the Kind in London— Operation a Success

The second case of a baby born with a tail has occurred in a London hospital.

It weighed 6lb. 4oz. and was normal, except for the tail, which was 3in. long and which, according to a report in the current issue of the "British Medical Journal," resembled a pig's tail. An X-ray examination showed no evidence of bone.

When the child was five weeks old the "tail" was removed.

MOTHER'S PATHETIC STORY.

Magistrate Unable to Advise in a Painful Physiological Case.

To Mr. Paul Taylor at Marylebone to-day Mr. Alfred Kirby, the missionary, introduced a diminutive woman, who sought advice concerning her baby.

She was a poor woman with a large family, and, having a weak husband, she had been compelled to go out charing in order to maintain the family.

She had been employed at the house of a lady who kept a parrot, which was allowed to fly free about the rooms.

One day the bird flew upon the applicant's shoulder. This gave her a terrible fright.

Later her baby was born with feet and hands almost identical with the claws of a parrot, while its head was also similar in shape to a parrot's.

"Really," exclaimed the magistrate, "would you mind me looking at it?"

The mother uncovered the baby's "hands" and "feet."

"Oh! poor little child," said Mr. Paul Taylor.

Mr. Kirby explained that the formation of the baby's head was such that it would probably grow up an imbecile. The mother wished to know whether she could recover compensation from the owner of the parrot.

Mr. Paul Taylor replied that he was very very sorry for her, but he could not express any opinion upon the matter. This was one of those terrible things which he supposed no one could guard against. He wished he could do something for her; but he did not feel in a position to give her any advice.

The poor woman left the court crying.

"PSYCHIC LIGHTS."

American Medium's Strange Manifestations.

NEW YORK, Tuesday.

The "Scientific American," the foremost scientific journal in America, which has been offering a prize for those able to prove psychical manifestations, announced to-day that they were unable to find the slightest evidences of fraud in the manifestations of the medium, "Margery," of Boston.

This medium, it is stated, produced psychic lights and tore a cabinet to pieces among other manifestations of her psychical influence.

Among the judges in the "Scientific American" competition are Houdini, the well-known conjurer, and members of the American Psychical Research Committee.— British United Press. Copyright in U.S.A.

Freaks

1908
HUMAN SALAMANDER.
MAN WHO CAN HANDLE RED-HOT IRON.

The best man in London for a snapdragon party, or for snatching Christmas pies from the oven, is undoubtedly Mr. Anthony Ryder, of New Cross-road.

Mr. Ryder, who describes himself as a "genuine English Human Fire Freak," is able to handle fire and grasp red-hot irons —and does so for pleasure.

Several doctors have seen him playing with fire and suffering no harm, and they have given certificates that it is "a natural gift," and not in any way a trick.

An "Express" representative last night saw the Human Salamander in his natural element. Mr. Ryder was seated in front of a blazing fire, cheerfully juggling with the red-hot coals.

"Medical men have taken the greatest interest in me," said Mr. Ryder, at the same time applying a blazing torch to the bare soles of his feet. "They cannot explain why it is I am not affected by heat. I was born like it.

"I take this red-hot steel bar from the fire," he continued, drawing a poker from the coals. "You see I draw it across my tongue— so. I feel nothing unusual.

"Now I draw my hands tightly clenched along the bar, and nothing happens. The palms of my hands are not even scorched.

"This steel bar is so hot that few men could even hold the other end, but I enjoy it.

"I have a certificate here from Dr. Sydney Williams. He writes:—'There seems a general impression that Mr. Anthony Ryder is a case of deception, or, in other words, that he anoints or otherwise prepares his body.

"'I, as a medical man, have taken great interest in his case, and have washed his skin and tongue on frequent occasions previous to his applying the heated irons.

"'I can consequently state that his body is in no way prepared, and that the ability to stand such astonishing degrees of heat is in no sense a fraud, neither due to any known medical condition.'

"I hope to have a blistering New Year," Mr. Ryder said genially. "Cold weather is too oppressive."

1934
PAIN PROOF PEOPLE

HERE is the story of the man who had all his teeth out without an anæsthetic —and enjoyed it.

The story was told to-day by Dr. Macdonald Critchley, of London, at the British Medical Association Conference at Bournemouth.

He was talking of the curious cases of people who are unable to experience pain.

The man who went to have his teeth out —"he was a small, weedy, miserable undersized man"—declined to have an anæsthetic.

The dentist pulled out one tooth. The man came through without a twinge.

He pulled out more teeth. Still the patient enjoyed the performance. Eventually the dentist removed all the teeth. The man seemed to regard it as a pleasurable operation.

FINGER SEVERED

There was a man who, in the course of a heated political argument, was struck violently on the head with an umbrella. The umbrella was broken, but the politician went on with his harangue without knowing that he had been struck.

During a fierce argument a man of 54 had his finger trodden on so severely that it was almost severed from the hand.

"He did not feel any pain," said Dr. Critchley, "but the dangling of the finger so annoyed him that he bit it off."

This man never experienced pain throughout his life. On his deathbed he merely complained of a little discomfort.

THE AUDIENCE COLLAPSED

There was an American music-hall artist who had had 60 pins stuck into him without feeling pain. Then he staged a crucifixion.

"They pierced his hands with nails," said Dr. Critchley. "But the performance had to be brought to an end because most of the people in the music-hall had collapsed."

1922
RED-HOT IRON TEST.
MAN CARRIES GLOWING BAR IN HAND WITHOUT BURNING.

While on a visit to his native village, Southam, Warwick, Mr. Thomas Smith, of Wigmore, Hereford, has just performed a remarkable feat of endurance, it was reported yesterday.

At the village blacksmith's he said he could carry a red-hot iron in his bare hand, and was at once put to the test. A 16in. file was made red-hot and placed on two bricks.

Dipping his hand in cold water, Mr. Smith, who is 71 years old, seized the iron, carried it three yards to a bath of cold water, and held it there until it was cold. Marks of the file were printed on the palm of the hand, which, however, was not burnt.

"I have done this many times in my younger days," he said to the spectators. "Nerve is the chief thing that is required."

1943
WERE ONCE SISTERS
DEATH BRINGS STRANGE FACT TO LIGHT
From Our Own Correspondent

Tragedy brought to light the strange fact that two members of the same family, who for years lived as sisters, changed their sex.

The first member of the family to do so was Mark Weston, who became a man in 1936. Up to that time he had been known as Mary Weston, British woman champion javelin thrower. Mary Weston won this title in 1927, while in 1934 she won the women's international shot-putting title.

Mary Weston also took part with the British team in the Olympic Games on the Continent.

Within a year of changing sex Mark Weston married 20-year-old blonde Alberta Bray, who had been his girl friend for years.

The second member of the Weston family concerned in a sex change was Harry Maurice Weston, 26, of Oreston, near Plymouth.

The other day a man walking across a field at Plymouth found Harry Weston hanging from a tree.

At the inquest evidence showed that the dead man had been a victim of depression following operations performed at Charing Cross Hospital, and the coroner, Mr. A. K. Johnstone, returned a verdict of "Suicide while the balance of mind was disturbed."

Harry Weston was brought up as a girl, being known as Hilda Margaret Weston and, as a child, attended the village girls' school. For years while named Hilda he always wore girl's clothes.

The subject of an operation was only considered when the question arose of Hilda's registration for National Service. Then it was deemed advisable for the operation to be performed.

For some years Harry Weston had been employed at the house of a butcher in Oreston.

The Westons' case is the second one of its kind recently in Britain of two sisters becoming brothers.

In August, 1939, Mark and David Ferrow returned to their home in Middlegate-street, Great Yarmouth, which they had left as Marjorie and Daisy Ferrow.

1936
SHE CAN'T DROWN
This Woman Puzzles the Doctors

Mrs. Rebecca Parker, of Sydney, is a woman who cannot drown. She is puzzling Australian doctors.

Her amazing buoyancy is believed to be due to the low specific gravity of her body.

In a demonstration at a swimming pool she reclined on the surface of the water, resting on her hand with arm crooked comfortably. She read a magazine, and lay basking in the sunlight, her head protected by an umbrella she held. She rolled over on top of the water like a cork.

Freaks 41

Beatrice Maud Hoe—as she was. FAREWELL TO FROCKS. Arthur Hoe—as he is. 1924

1939
Two Sisters Turn Into Brothers

From Our Own Correspondent
GT. YARMOUTH, Friday.

GREAT YARMOUTH schoolgirls who had missed their two school friends, Marjory and Daisy Ferrow, for some months, have been astonished to meet them again wearing men's clothes and known as Mark and David.

At 13, both the children developed characteristics that made them hold themselves aloof from other schoolchildren, and eventually forced them to sacrifice scholarships which they had won to Yarmouth Central School and Yarmouth High School for Girls.

STAYED INDOORS FOR A YEAR

For more than a year Marjory, the elder, remained indoors. Then both left the town for a time.

While away they accustomed themselves to wearing men's clothes, and Marjory had hospital treatment.

This week they have come back to live in the town, no longer as girls but as young men.

It is believed unique for a change of sex to occur twice in one family.

NOW SMOKES A PIPE

Yet other members of the family, who live in Middlegate-street, Yarmouth, are entirely normal, and one older sister who is married is a mother.

Mark Ferrow at 17 is now 5ft. 10in. in height, and has to shave.

He smokes a pipe.

His brother David is a well-built youngster of 15.

1936
NINE-POUND CHILD BORN TO EX-SOLDIER A YEAR AFTER "HE" CHANGED "HIS" SEX

FROM OUR OWN CORRESPONDENT
WARSAW, Thursday.

A YEAR after "his" sex had changed from male to female, ex-soldier Nochmen, Tenenbaum, aged twenty-five, has given birth to a perfectly formed 9lb. baby.

An artist is the father of the child, and he says that he intends to marry the mother.

Tenenbaum, up to the age of twenty-four, was a man. He served in the army and was promoted to the rank of sergeant.

Several military distinctions have been conferred upon him, and he won medals for exceptional bravery in rescuing people from drowning.

After serving in the army his sex gradually changed, but he continued to wear men's clothing.

Some days ago doctors and nurses in a Warsaw maternity home were surprised when a nurse announced that a man had asked to book a room, stating he was going to have a child.

A room was taken. Doctors and nurses attended, and a child was born.

This is believed to be the first time in history that a person who has changed his sex has given birth to a child.

1908
MYSTERY OF DUAL PERSONALITY.

GIRL WHO CROCHETS, WRITES AND READS WHILE ASLEEP.

PUZZLING CASE.

A remarkable case of a somnambulist who can work and write in the darkness is told in this week's "British Medical Journal" by Dr. James Russell, M.A., assistant physician to the Birmingham General Hospital.

The case came under his notice in July 1907, when a girl, aged twenty-one years, was sent to the hospital complaining of sleep-walking. She was a typist, a teacher, and a student of music. Both her parents are dead.

Her father shot himself in her presence when she was a child. This made a lasting impression on her, and in one of her sleep-walking periods she said: "Take it away—don't let him do it." When she is sleep-walking she does many things. She gets out of bed at about 1.30 or two in the morning. She does not seem to be asleep, but she has no sense of her surroundings, nor does she recognise any one.

In this condition she writes letters and postcards in German, does crochet work, reads a book, and studies harmony. She does all this in absolute darkness. If there is a faint glimmer from the gas she takes her work away to the darkest corner of the room. After a few hours she goes back to bed, and beats her head against the bedstead, or with her hands.

SUBCONSCIOUS WORK.

On August 17, 1907, says Dr. Hincks, the house physician at the Birmingham Hospital, she sat up in bed and did crochet work. She did not talk. The ward was dark, except for two single and well-shaded electric lights far away from the bed. Then she got out of bed and wrote a postcard, addressing it to a relation in Canada. The next night she did more crochet work, and wrote a letter in German, put it in an envelope, and enclosed a sovereign.

When she awoke the letter was shown her. She did not remember writing it, but recognised the address as correct. Dr. Hincks asked her while she was awake to write the same address under the same conditions of light. This she could not do properly. The lines all ran into each other.

A few days later, while in a somnambulistic state she wrote a short letter to her music teacher, and a short essay on "The Sonata Form," which was perfectly accurate and intelligent.

She has now left the hospital and earns her living as a typist, but she still has occasional night wanderings. Her eyes have been examined, but the doctors have been unable to find out why she can read and write in the darkness, when in her normal condition it is impossible for her to do so.

42 Freaks

1928
ELECTRIC BOY.

FREAKS IN A LONE KENTISH FARM.

WIRELESS CLUE.

From OUR SPECIAL CORRESPONDENT.

BETHERSDEN, near Ashford, Kent, Saturday.

WILFRED BATT, the shy 18-years-old son of a Kentish farmer, is amazing his relatives by the manifestations of an uncanny and mysterious " power."

I have just had a long talk with this remarkable boy. He lives at Wissenden Lodge, a lonely farmhouse which has been the scene of many amazing occurrences, so weird that they have baffled even those familiar with psychical phenomena.

A point which may throw light on the mystery is that the happenings did not commence until the installation of a wireless set in his home. It has been suggested that the electricity in Wilfred's body has been intensified through the medium of wireless.

Wilfred is an intelligent-looking, perfectly normal and healthy lad, though said to be nervous and highly strung. Here are some of the strange happenings which he has told me himself:

Iron bars which he has held in his hand have suddenly bent almost double. One bar was attracted so violently towards the earth that it pulled him flat on the ground.

Going up to bed, he saw a candlestick come jumping downstairs to meet him, and then follow him about the bedroom.

A silver tray almost leaped at him when he passed it.

Without anyone touching it a dining-room gong began to sound loudly.

"I don't understand what happens at all," said the boy simply. "All I know is that I feel a kind of electric shock go through me, and I have the sensation that it is something inside me which causes the queer things to come about, in spite of myself."

He added that when he put on his wrist-watch it immediately stopped.

Lumps of coal and wood had "flown about" when he was near, and the furniture "danced."

Keeping watch while he lay in bed one night, said his aunt, Mrs. Dan Batt, the chairs "hurled themselves across the room," and ornaments "jumped about the dressing-table."

She declared, too, that a wire-spring mattress on which she sat suddenly began to undulate and quiver "as though a powerful current of electricity was passing through the springs."

Mr. Edgar Batt, another relative, told me that he was standing beside Wilfred in the coal shed the other day when a heavy crowbar which the boy could scarcely lift leaped from his hands when he touched it and drove through the thick galvanised-iron roof of the shed.

The family are hoping that Sir Conan Doyle or some other authorities on occult and psychic subjects will study the matter and provide a solution of the mystery.

Standing only 23in. high and weighing no more than 24lb., forty-five-year-old Harold Pyott, of Stockport, is the world's smallest man. No bigger than a large doll, he would have the appearance of a dwarf even at the side of Tom Thumb. He was called up for the Army three times during the Great War, and each time the authorities had a shock when he appeared before them. He sits quite comfortably in a top hat in the same manner as a normal person can recline in an armchair. One of his favourite tricks is to stand on the palm of someone's hand.

1933

1907
HYPNOTISED JURYMEN.

CHICAGO, Tuesday, July 2.

The physicians of Chicago are baffled by the extraordinary illness which has attacked a number of men summoned as jurymen in the trial of Herman Billik for the murder of the Vzral family.

One expert who examined the jurors on behalf of the prosecution declares that Billik, who was a professional fortune-teller and "voodoo" doctor, exercised an extraordinary psychic influence over them. Whenever a juror was summoned whom Billik thought was adverse to him he hypnotised him from the dock.

When the trial opened on Friday, two jurymen were prostrated after being accepted by the Public Prosecutor.

When the court opened yesterday morning two other accepted jurymen rushed into the jury box in a condition bordering on hysteria, and begged to be released from the case. A third, who appeared to be very ill, was unable to answer questions put by the judge. He eventually said that he felt giddy.

The puzzled judge finally told the juryman that he was excused, and as he attempted to leave the jury box he fell on the floor, and lay at full length in front of the dock.

Billik smiled grimly. He smiled again when the two following talesmen betrayed great agitation, and begged to be excused.

The Public Prosecutor declares that Billik is able to exert powerful influence over all persons subject to hypnotism. The belief is general that he is hypnotising all the talesmen possible in order to prevent the impanelling of a jury.

1924
PRIESTESS IN PRISON

GIRL LION-TAMER WHO BECAME A SPY.

AMAZING MASQUERADE AND MIRACLE CURE.

(FROM OUR OWN CORRESPONDENT.)

Brussels, Saturday.—The police here have arrested Berthe Mrazek, alias Georges Maresco, whose life story is one of the most extraordinary on record. She has been lion-tamer, faith-healer, spy, priestess, young man about town, and soothsayer. Born in 1890 in Brussels of a Bohemian father and a Belgian mother, Berthe Mrazek early displayed unusual psychic powers, and obtained complete ascendancy over her parents. At 13 she joined a circus as lion-tamer, and never had any trouble with the lion Brutus, which later killed a male tamer. During the war she was employed as a nurse for political prisoners at the St. Gilles Prison in Brussels. She escaped from the Germans and reached Belgian headquarters in male attire. She took the name of Georges Maresco, and executed several dangerous missions for the Belgian Intelligence Service. Although she had come direct from serving the Germans, to whom she is believed to have given information about the political prisoners under her care, she had no difficulty in convincing the Intelligence Service at Belgian G.H.Q. of her bona fides, and she certainly rendered great service to the Allied cause during the closing months of the war. After the armistice Berthe kept to her male attire, and was a well-known and popular figure at dancing resorts and night cafes, always faultlessly attired in a dinner jacket. She had countless lady friends. Early in 1920 she fell sick, and despite all the doctors could do for her wasted away and was soon almost a living skeleton. As she grew weaker

PARTIAL PARALYSIS AND BLINDNESS

supervened. Despite her former life she became profoundly religious, and expressed the belief that if she could go on a pilgrimage to Lourdes she would be healed. A priest, learning that she could not afford the journey to the South of France, advised her to go and pray at the shrine of Our Lady of Hal, where there is a miraculous statue of the Virgin Mary. So Berthe Mrazek, or rather Georges Maresco, for she was still in male attire, was carried on a stretcher to the shrine. She was barely in the presence of the statue for a minute before she rose from her stretcher, and, after kneeling at the altar, proclaimed herself cured. She was able to walk and could see. But on her side and through her hands and feet there appeared stigmates of the wounds of Christ. These have been photographed, and doctors are as unable to account for them as they are for her sudden recovery. The Church made an investigation of the alleged miracle, and, although accepting it as a fact, forbade the administration of the Sacraments to Berthe Mrazek until such time as she should have given up all pretence of being a man. This she refused to do, and, proclaiming herself of the male sex—although she is the mother of a child—she asserted that she had been sent by Christ as an apostle to heal the sick. Exhibiting her stigmates, she withdrew to a chapel of her own, and soon had a large following of worshippers, amongst them many wealthy society women, who paid liberally to be initiated into her rites. Although no specific charge has been lodged against her, the authorities have decided to have her sanity inquired into. Meanwhile the keeper of the gaol in which she is lodged does not know what to do with the numerous floral tributes that come pouring in from his prisoner's female admirers.

HIGH ARCHIVES

Hour of Illusion in Cocaine Test 1936

DRUG THAT LEADS TO INSANITY 1929

Schoolchildren Victims of a Deadly Weed.

SMOKED IN CIGARETTES.

DRUG MAD GIRLS BREAK INTO CHEMIST'S SHOP

Startling Sequel to Biggest Blow Yet Made at European Dope Traffic: Eighteen Doctors on Trial. 1928

Hashish Distorts Time—Space 1938

OFFICERS of Scotland Yard's dope squad and Home Office experts start this week-end their investigations into the peddling in Britain of marihuana, the vicious drug which causes men to lose all sense of responsibility and perform the most reckless acts.

The use of the drug was dramatically revealed at the Old Bailey when an addict, Andrew Vanderberg, 37-year-old soldier-gunman, was sentenced to 10 years' penal servitude. Under the influence of marihuana, it was disclosed, he carried out a series of crimes of violence, culminating in a gun battle with police officers. 1938

SLEEPLESS MAN.

"A NEW WORLD BY MEANS OF DRUGS."

MAKING CHARACTER TO ORDER.

1926

1903
"CURSE" OF TOBACCO.

BLINDNESS AND CANCER DUE TO SMOKING.

Probably more panegyrics have been written on tobacco than on any other article of common consumption. It has been a "solace," a "comfort," a "friend," an "inspiration," a thousand and one other things according to successive generations of writers.

Yesterday a well-known specialist in the treatment of eye diseases, who is consulted on an average by nearly a hundred patients daily from different parts of the kingdom and from abroad, expressed the opinion that tobacco was a national curse, and that the Government should take steps to prevent its use.

Dr. C. Bell Taylor, M.D., F.R.C.S.E., of Nottingham, the authority in question, declared that every man and woman who smoked half an ounce of tobacco a day—a very moderate allowance—was smoking himself or herself blind. In addition, he attributed the increase of cancer in this country mainly to indulgence in tobacco by both sexes.

"Scarcely a day passes," the doctor proceeded, "without persons consulting me who owe the impairment or loss of their sight to smoking tobacco. I have had as many as five such patients in one day. The eye diseases caused by tobacco are white atrophy of the optic nerve and tobacco amblyopia.

OPTIC NERVE DESTROYED.

"The first indication of trouble observed by the patient is a difficulty in reading. The last thing he blames for his failing sight is tobacco, and so he keeps on smoking. He finds that spectacles are of little if any use. Then he consults an ophthalmic surgeon and discovers to his surprise and alarm that the tobacco which has 'solaced' him has also destroyed his optic nerve. One of my patients smoked himself absolutely blind."

Mr. Bell Taylor further pointed out that colour blindness is frequently caused by smoking. Many of his patients are railway men who find that they cannot distinguish the colours of the signal lamps. "In nine cases out of ten the defect is due to smoking."

1915
'SNOW SNUFF' DANGER

Soldiers' "Fear-Banisher" a Compound of Morphine

"Snow Snuff," the poisonous preparation of heroin which caused the death of a Canadian soldier at Shorncliffe, and is said to be taken by soldiers to "banish fear," is apparently unknown in this country, though it was said at the inquest on Saturday to be obtainable in France.

Heroin is the trade name of the well-known drug diacetyl-morphine or acetomorphine, described as a soluble white crystalline powder, and it is sometimes prescribed in cases of asthma, bronchitis, and irritable cough.

Soothing the Nerves.

"It has a soothing effect on the nervous system," said a druggist to a "Star" representative to-day, "but it has a very serious effect. I have never heard of it being taken as snuff, but the powder could be taken in that way. It is as easy to become addicted to the habit of taking heroin as morphine.

"Heroin has nothing at all to do with heroism; and although it might steady a man's nerves for a time, it would only do so by its sedative effect."

"Many Canadians and Americans use various forms of snuff and, indeed; all kinds of preparations for the relief of the nasal catarrh which is so prevalent amongst them in consequence of the excessive heating of private and public buildings.

"The French pharmacists are men of standing and responsibility, and it is difficult to believe that they would be parties to the promiscuous sale of a dangerous preparation such as this among the armies in France.

"I am quite sure that if it is being sold there a request from the military authorities would be sufficient to prevent it being sold to soldiers.

Scheduled as Poison.

"In this country it is scheduled as a poison and can only be obtained either upon a doctor's prescription or when the purchaser is known to the chemist personally, or through a third person. It must be signed for in the poisons' book.

"Most of these drugs had their origin in Germany, but heroin was, I believe, first made in London a few years ago."

Snuff containing morphine is not unknown in this country, and there are several preparation of it in the British Pharmacopœia. One of them contains bismuth and morphine hydrochloride, but it is very rarely prescribed nowadays.

1919
DRINKING DENS OF LONDON

DARING TRAFFICKERS IN COCAINE.

Mr. Harold Begbie, writing in "Lloyd's News" on "The Dangers of London," referring to drinking dens, says:—

There is a public-house in the very centre of London which is a meeting place of very vile women, and which is used almost as a club by some of the worst crooks in the town. It is always crowded at night, and much public love-making takes place in the midst of a press of people which might suggest a crowd at a booking office. But here and there you will see two men holding a conversation in whispers, while their eyes are marking down a well-dressed man, who is getting gradually more drunk in the company of a clever woman of the streets, and if you open the door of a little compartment, which is reserved for women only, you will get a view of some of the most daring traffickers in cocaine known to the police. Why this house should be allowed to conduct its business in this manner at the very heart of London civilisation I cannot for the life of me imagine.

1938
NEW FORM OF DRUG SMUGGLING

SENT BY LETTER POST

The report of the British Government to the League of Nations on traffic in dangerous drugs during 1937, issued yesterday, states that several attempts to import small quantities by letter post were discovered.

"All the channels through which dangerous drugs circulate legitimately," adds the report, "are open to frequent inspection, and the addict or would-be trafficker has little chance of obtaining drugs from such sources without the fact of excessive supplies coming to light and proper investigations being speedily undertaken."

The drugs principally imported during the year were:

Raw opium 211,969lb,
Coca leaves 91,954lb,
Indian hemp 8,057lb,
Crude morphine 16,059oz, and
Crude methymorphine 2,673oz.

The number of known drug addicts in the country was 620, made up of 300 men and 320 women. Of these 13 were members of the medical profession, one a dentist, five pharmacists and two veterinary surgeons.

The percentages of addiction to different drugs in relation to the total was: Morphine 72, diacetylmorphine 17, cocaine 8½, medicinal opium one, dihydromorphinone one, codeine half.

During the year seven members of the medical profession and seven pharmacists were convicted of offences against the Dangerous Drugs Acts.

1938
GANG FLOG WEST-END CROOKS

BY A SPECIAL CORRESPONDENT

BULLDOG DRUMMOND has stepped from the pages of fiction to clean up London's West End.

Dog whips wielded by stalwart members of his Black Gang, punishing dope pedlers and other crooks, are making Mayfair a cleaner place in which to live.

SAPPER (MAJOR CYRIL McNEIL), CREATOR OF BULLDOG DRUMMOND, IS RESPONSIBLE FOR THE FORMATION OF THIS REAL-LIFE BLACK GANG TO WAR ON VICE.

Disgusted by the degenerate parasites of the West End, against whom the police were powerless, he suggested, half humorously, in an Army mess not long before he died that any young man of energy should take a tip from Bulldog Drummond.

A band of young officers, many of them bearing distinguished names, have taken him at his word.

Masked Kidnappers

This is how they work.

Their quarry is marked down. The gang satisfy themselves that he deserves punishment.

When a suitable opportunity offers, he is kidnapped by a body of sturdy, masked men. His struggles are fruitless.

Into a car he is bundled and driven to a garage attached to a large, isolated house off the Great West-road.

There the "executioners" wait with dog whips. He is flogged until he promises not to offend again.

Then the victim is turned loose. He limps back abjectly to the West End.

Never does he go to the police. They are the last people to whom he wants to make explanations.

Dope-cigarettes have become a West End menace.

Wrecked Lives

Society girls started to smoke them as a mild adventure, but now they are wrecking their lives.

A young officer told me yesterday: "A friend of mine was very upset when his charming fiancee was taken ill and her mother told him the engagement had better be considered off. She had been going to these cigarette orgies. It will be years before she is well.

"Then someone remembered Sapper's joke. So the real life Black Gang was formed."

Final sidelight—from a hospital casualty report:—

Man treated for laceration on the back and shoulders. Refused to have the police informed.

When this patient left the hospital he was presented with a dog-whip. On the label was: "Souvenir 1938."

1903
"MAD DRUNK" WITH CORDITE.

TERRIBLE HABIT OF SOLDIERS IN SOUTH AFRICA.

The South African war and the weariness of life on the "illimitable veldt" are responsible for the discovery of a new and extraordinary form of intoxication.

Some British soldiers discovered that by eating cordite they could get all the excitement of the most powerful narcotic—and all the terrible after-effects, too. Cordite consists roughly of about 58 parts of nitroglycerine, 37 parts gun cotton, and five parts of mineral jelly.

Each cartridge contains 60 cylindrical strands of cordite, and when Major Jennings, D.S.O., learned that the men were eating these (says the "British Medical Journal") he experimented on himself by sucking a strand. He found that it tasted sweet, pleasant, and pungent, but it resulted in giving him the most racking, splitting headache he ever had in his life, and it lasted for 36 hours.

Dissolved in tea, cordite produces an almost immediately exhilarating effect "inciting to almost demoniacal actions." If many persons have partaken of the beverage all begin talking at once, each seemingly anxious to inform the other of everything that has happened to him since his birth.

This condition is followed by heavy sleep and stupor, lasting five to twelve hours, according to the quantity taken. To awaken the subject it is often necessary to slap his face, punch or shake him, and awakening is accompanied by severe dull, boring headache, muscular twitchings, and protrusion of the eyes.

It is as an addition to beer that cordite appears to produce its worst effects. It then excites a quarrelsome, destructive mania in an otherwise peacefully disposed individual, and produces immediate intoxication in a man who can commonly consume as much as four or five pints of beer without exhibiting a trace of having done so. If taken in quantity insufficient to produce sleep it makes him not only quarrelsome, but brings out the worst traits in his character.

A possible clue to the inception of this habit is given by the fact that a large number of the men seem to have used cordite as a means of lighting pipes in default of matches.

1905
A Day in Society.

The lady novelist's idea of society has been fiercely challenged, but the following picture of the society lady, from the "World," is not much more favourable:—

"What is the daily life-history of a woman in society? Too jaded by selfish indulgences, after a night of morbid sleep born of some favourite drug, she rises to face a day's racing with its concomitant betting. Her breakfast inadequate, probably supplemented by brandy or whisky and soda; luncheon indigestible, savoury but unhealthy bonnes bouches, liberal potations of champagne, or more likely recourse to familiar brandy or whisky peg; a rush home, further pandering to a morbid appetite, more champagne, later perhaps a dance, or many hours devoted to inevitable Bridge—a game equal, at any rate in its intrinsic interest, to the old-fashioned whist, but prostituted by the facility with which it provides added excitement in the form of gambling; again brandy or whisky and soda; then bed, with sulphonal, trional, morphia, or some equally noxious drug."

1929
DRUNKEN ORGIES BY GIRLS & BOYS.

PARENTS ARRESTED FOR LAXITY

From Our Own Correspondent, R. J. CRUIKSHANK.

NEW YORK, Wednesday.

Fifty-six parents were arrested in Chicago to-day and charged with being lax in the discipline of their children. Twenty-two of them were fined, and two who refused to pay were sent to prison.

The arrests, which were ordered by Chicago's Superintendent of Education, followed revelations of drunken orgies indulged in by grammar and high-school girls and boys.

Two years ago all the saloons and "speakeasies" were padlocked, but a section of the youngest generation has continued to drink, and an inquest on a young man who was killed in a motor smash last Sunday, after an all-night party of dancing and drinking with schoolgirls, has cast a bright light on the ideals of modern youth.

The jury was made up of eminent University professors, sociologists and psychologists, and it was summoned to inquire into the moral outlook of the young as much as into the cause of this particular death.

BOOZE PARTIES.

Schoolgirls of 15 and 17 described quite candidly their "booze parties," and suggested that young men were only interested in them when they could provide a bottle.

Virginia Graf, aged 19, summed up for her colleagues when she said to the jury:

"If a girl doesn't drink she isn't wanted at a party nowadays. They think she's foolish or old-fashioned and never ask her again. When you go visiting you have to take a bottle."

A girl of sixteen said:

"I carry my own key. My parents don't know when I get in." And another testified to drinking "highballs" till two o'clock in the morning.

Nine youths, some of them only schoolboys, and six girls took part in the road-house drinking orgy which culminated in the motor accident death. Asked if she were not impressed by death overtaking her companion, Virginia Graf said:

"It was just George's time to die, and he was killed."

1913

More delightful even than the overthrow of his prosecutors by challenging them to say "truly rural," was the defence of a man arrested for drunkenness some years ago. With quiet assurance he pleaded (unsuccessfully) a Scriptural authority for his offence. In fact, a Scriptural command to offend. And you will find the command in Proverbs, where it says "Give strong drink unto him that is ready to perish, and wine unto those that be of heavy hearts. Let him drink and forget his poverty, and remember his misery no more."

1929
PUNISHING THE "WETS."

Some Bright Ideas For Enforcing Prohibition.

The administration of castor oil, the "sea-sick machine," the electric chair and exile on St. Helena were among suggestions submitted by competitors for the W. C. Durant prize of 25,000 dollars for the most practical plan for enforcing prohibition in the United States, says the Central News New York correspondent.

Another bright suggestion made was that an offender should "hang by the tongue from an airplane and be carried over the United States."

One thought that the "torture collar" would be very effective, while another advocated a "big black cross on the window of the living room."

A not particularly benevolent suggestion was that policemen failing to report "speakeasies" (illicit bars) should "get 30 years."

1931
£200,000,000 A YEAR ON DRUGS

NEW YORK, March 17.

A billion dollars a year (about £200,000,000) is the price the United States pays for narcotic addiction, according to Mr. C. K. Crane, of Los Angeles.

Mr. Crane, nationally known as an expert on the narcotic evil, urges international action to cope with the trade.—Reuter.

1903

The adherents of the Semi-Teetotal League may be interested to hear how our forefathers managed in a time when tea and coffee were unknown, and beer was the common beverage of the Englishman. In the "Northumberland Household Book," commenced in 1512, we have an exhaustive account of the domestic economy of the great Percy family; and from it we learn that at breakfast, which was served at seven in the morning, the earl and countess had a quart of beer and a quart of wine between them; two sons, "My Lorde Percy and Maister Percy," a pottle (two quarts) of beer; and two children in the "Nurcy" (nursery) a quart of beer. For dinner, at ten o'clock, my lord and lady had a gallon of beer and a pottle of wine; the two boys a quart of beer; and the younger children a pottle of beer. At supper, at four o'clock, the earl and countess shared a pottle of beer and a pottle of wine; the children also had their allowance. For "livery," which was served in the bedroom between eight and nine in the evening, the parents were supplied with a gallon of beer and a quart of wine, and each pair of children with a pottle of beer. Surely there could in this case have been no "drinking between meals."

1929
"DRY" LAW AT ITS WORST.

30 DAYS' SENTENCE ON GIRL OF 12.

£1 FOR INFORMER.

"SUNDAY DISPATCH" CABLE.

NEW YORK, Saturday.

Sentence of 30 days' imprisonment has been passed at Greenville (South Carolina) upon a twelve-years-old girl, May Johnson, because she carried some liquor across a street for a woman and was arrested on the way.

Recorder Aiken, who had the privilege of passing this sentence, said that he had no alternative under the prohibition law.

Two Congressmen, both well-known "drys," are charged with breaking the prohibition law. A warrant has been issued for the arrest of Mr. Michaelson (Illinois), a member of the House of Representatives, on a charge of attempted smuggling. He is expected to surrender at Chicago immediately.

Mr. Michaelson voted for the new Jones Law, with its maximum penalty of a £2,000 fine and five years' imprisonment, but he cannot be tried under that law because the offence alleged against him was before that Act was passed.

CONGRESSMAN'S DENIAL.

Congressman Morgan (Ohio), who has been five times elected on the "dry" platform, is accused of having brought liquor into the country this week under the free entry permit granted to a member of the House of Representatives travelling on official business.

Mr. Morgan denies that he carried liquor, but if an official investigation proves the charge he could be prosecuted under the Jones Law, which he assisted to place on the Statute Book about two months ago.

The Chicago police are inquiring into the city's most expensive party, given by a rich young Chicagoan, who says it cost him £12,000 in drinks for a three-days entertainment.

THE "SNOOPER'S" REWARD.

An inquiry into the death of Mrs. Lillian de King, of Aurora, Illinois, who was shot dead during a raid by prohibition agents on her home has revealed the fact that the "snooper" who gave the agents the tip that he had bought a drink at de King's home received £1 for his services.

Michigan State has just repealed its "Life for a pint" law which sent offenders against the Dry laws to life imprisonment. One person who will benefit by the repeal is the mother of ten children recently sent to prison for the sale of liquor.

This medley of contrasting incidents is stirring the country to renewed grave thoughts of the value of the prohibition laws.

1928
JURY TESTS THE LIQUOR.

LOS ANGELES, Saturday.—Nine jurors, five of them women, drank up the "evidence" in a liquor law prosecution yesterday and then proceeded to acquit the liquor dealer.

The judge promptly discharged them from further jury duty, adding a few remarks on the duties of citizenship. He is now considering reinstating them, as they subsequently humbly confessed their fault and sought forgiveness.

What moved the judge most yesterday was the fact that they had taken an unusually long time to reach their decision, and that there was no apparent need to "test" the evidence, as its alcoholic character had been admitted by the accused himself.—Reuter.

1926
92,888 ARRESTS FOR INTOXICATION IN CHICAGO.

500 LIQUOR DEATHS.

SURPRISING FACTS FROM THE LAND OF PROHIBITION.

"Sunday Express" Correspondent.
NEW YORK, Saturday, April 17.

RETURNS of the arrests for intoxication in American cities for 1925 show that Chicago was the "wettest" city in the country with 92,888 arrests.

1930
TEN YEARS OF LIQUOR BAN.

CRIME DECREASE
—The "Drys."
CRIME INCREASE
—The "Wets."

MUFFLED BELLS IN U.S. CITIES.

From Our Own Correspondent.

NEW YORK, Thursday.

The tenth anniversary of prohibition was celebrated throughout the United States to-day with gay chimes of bells in "Dry" strongholds and muffled tolling in "Wet" cities.

The day was marked by bitter debates in and out of Congress.

FOR.

"Dry" leaders, in speeches and manifestoes, claimed that the decade of Prohibition had:

Increased from 10,000,000 to 50,000,000 the number of persons with savings bank accounts.
Added £3,000,000,000 to the spending power of the nation.
Saved 2,000,000 lives.
Reduced crime.
Increased health.
Diminished insanity.
Improved social conditions.
Raised wages.

AGAINST.

"Wet" leaders, in their counterblasts, declared that ten years of Prohibition had:

Cost the Federal Government alone £80,000,000 in half-hearted enforcement, not counting the cost to State Governments.
Brought a loss of £600,000,000 in revenue.
Led to 200 persons being killed by law enforcement agents.
Caused the arrest of 500,000 persons for offences against the enforcement laws.
Increased drunkenness.
Promoted debauchery among young persons.
Led to 34,000 deaths through alcoholic poisoning.
Created widespread crime and corruption.
Encouraged the growth of bootleg rings, which lay whole cities under their toll.

It is interesting to record that Prohibition's tenth anniversary coincides with President Hoover's remission to Congress of fresh plans for better enforcement of the law.

1926
PRINCE IN PETTICOATS.
SENSATIONAL ARREST OF A KING'S COUSIN.
COCAINE EPISODE IN LIFE OF ADVENTURE.
(FROM OUR OWN CORRESPONDENT.)

Paris, Saturday.—Attired as a woman, and accompanied by three men friends, Prince Louis Orleans de Bourbon, son of the Infanta Eulalia of Spain, and cousin of King Alfonso, has just been arrested in a room at the Hotel Villa Real, Santo Antonio, near the Spanish frontier. The reason for his masquerade in this amazing fashion is not yet clear, but the suspicious element of the whole case is that among luggage which he had, and which consisted of numerous dresses, all in the latest fashion, were discovered 20 pounds of cocaine, which, it is alleged, he was about to smuggle into Spain. He had been living at the hotel for several days as the "wife" of one of his companions, and two of the prince's friends were also arrested for alleged conspiracy. Prince Louis immediately telegraphed to Queen Victoria of Spain protesting against the treatment he had received, and asking her to intervene to obtain his release. Prince Louis is one of the best-known men in Bohemian circles on the Continent, and this is by no means the first escapade which has brought him into the glare of publicity. It is only a little over a year ago that, as a result of a certain wild adventure in one of those unconventional haunts which lie around Montmartre, he was ordered to be expelled from France, on a special warrant issued by the Minister of the Interior. The prince was apprehended at a house in the Rue des Tournelles, where he and others had taken a room with two young sailors. The story was that these latter had been promised money on certain conditions, and that they thrashed the prince when he refused to pay. It was his cries that attracted the police, who found over a dozen men in the place. The prince,

1916
THE CHINESE PERIL.

Earlier in the sitting the employment of Chinese on British ships was the subject of some vigorous speeches of protest. Mr. J. Cotter, of Liverpool, told an extraordinary story of Chinese life in this country.

"I have been," he said, "in one of their houses, and directly I got in I saw Fan-Tan gambling tables bearing three or four hundred pounds. Forty Chinese were round the tables. I went upstairs, and in the first room I saw four beds side by side, with two men on each bed in a comatose condition through opium. I saw opium actually being made, the preparations of the poppy heads. On one occasion we found twelve hundred pounds of opium on one ship."

Mr. Cotter explained that Chinese were filtering from the ports to the inland towns. Chinese laundries were being set up, and some of these places were of an immoral character. He asserted that at Chinese houses in the East End of London girls of from 14 years of age upwards were visitors up to two o'clock in the morning.

There were cries of "Shame!" at this, and Mr. March, a delegate who comes from Poplar, said that the Borough Council would certainly take steps to clearing out many of these places in Poplar, if definite addresses were given the Congress to a resolution in favour of a Bill to repatriate Chinese who are not of British nationality, and to ensure that in future no Chinese shall be signed on for service in British ships west of Suez.

1921
HEROIC AIRMAN A SLAVE TO DRUGS.
Man Who Bombed Germany Fifty Times.
A PHYSICAL WRECK.

A distressing story of an airman who took part in no fewer than fifty-three bombing raids on German industrial centres, and who resorted to drugs as a stimulant, was told at Marylebone police-court, when John Dudley Edward Dudley, 28, formerly an officer in the R.A.F., and now a general merchant, married, and living in a boarding-house in Leinster-square, Bayswater, was charged with forging and uttering prescriptions for cocaine, having eighteen grains of the drug in his possession, and attempting to procure a further eighteen grains.

IN A STATE OF STUPOR.

On March 23, said Mr. Muskett, Detective-inspector Burmby went to a boarding-house in Leinster-square, and there found the accused in bed in such a state of stupor as to satisfy the inspector that he was suffering from the effects of a drug. In the room were phials containing morphia, heroin, atropin, and chloroform. When the accused awoke he admitted writing the two prescriptions (produced), and begged that he might have a hypodermic injection before being removed, as he said he was quite unable to get out of bed without it. He then admitted having used the names of medical men and obtained cocaine and other drugs from a number of chemists.

Mr. Henry Stewart-Moore urged in defence that the accused was a public school boy with highly artistic temperament, and said that immediately on the outbreak of the war he sacrificed a good job with good pay and enlisted as a private in the Royal Fusiliers. He afterwards obtained a commission in the Durham Light Infantry, took part in a great many engagements, and was ultimately wounded at the battle of the Somme and sent home. On recovery he joined the R.A.F. Having obtained his wings he undertook what was perhaps the most perilous task of the war—the bombing by day of the big German industrial centres, including Metz, Strasburg, and Mulheim. Altogether he had to his credit no fewer than fifty-three of these air raids. The nervous strain, however, of flying eight hours a day surrounded by German aeroplanes and bullets proved too much for him, and feeling that he could not continue unless he fortified himself he eventually resorted to the pernicious habit of taking drugs. At first he took only sufficient to enable him to drop his bombs over the towns; but the terrible habit grew, and now he stood before the Court one of the worst victims of the drug habit, a mental and physical wreck.

RESTRAINT NEEDED.

In view of all the pathetic circumstances the solicitor appealed to the magistrate not to send this hero to prison, but to allow him to go to a home, that he might be cured of his terrible craving and restored to society.

Mr. d'Eyncourt said it was clear that the accused had distinguished himself immensely, and that he had developed the habit as a result of a very natural collapse of his nervous system. In that he had every sympathy with him. But it was also clear that at this stage he needed to be restrained, by force if necessary, and in his own interest, therefore, he sentenced him to six months' imprisonment in the second division, in the hope that it would effect his cure. The magistrate added that the accused was perfectly free from anything criminal.

1930
DRUG DREAM TESTS.
WHIZZING CHAIRS VISION.

A new drug which possesses in unequalled measure the property of causing hallucinations and evoking amazing visions has been tested by two London doctors upon themselves.

The doctors were Dr. Macdonald Critchley, junior neurologist, of King's College Hospital, and a friend. The drug was mescal, the increasing use of which has been perturbing the police authorities of Paris and elsewhere.

Dr. Critchley, describing the effect of the drug in the "British Medical Journal," states:

"The hallucinatory images were at first simple in pattern and colour, and only visible when the eyes were closed. Later they became more complicated, and no longer comprised simple geometrical designs as at first, but took a three-dimensional form, and were most brilliantly illuminated and coloured.

WITH EYES OPEN.

"The hallucinations now became apparent with the eyes open, though never to the same extent as when the eyes were closed. This bewildering state reached its maximum in 90 minutes, and persisted at this level for several hours."

A note dictated during the test describes a stream and bridge, and continues:

"The water now dries up, and a rocky bed becomes visible, and is gradually transformed into a stone road in a moorland scene, and still later into a meadow with buttercups and daisies, at length changing into a bandstand in a park, with chairs, each of which is whizzing round rapidly on its own axis.

Analysing the hallucinations Dr. Critchley observes: "A change in the appearance of external objects frequently occurred. Newspapers and carpets looked like relief maps, stationary objects appeared to move, and regularly moving objects appeared to move jerkily."

1948
DRUGGED LABOUR

A fine of £10 was imposed on Chan Sui San, a Chinese seaman, at Grays, for being in possession of one and a half pounds of raw opium. Through an interpreter, he said he gave £3 for the opium at Liverpool, and could not do his work without it. The opium was confiscated.

Hour of Illusion in Cocaine Test

1936

PROFESSOR Gilbert Murray once took cocaine.

"It was lovely," he told an audience at University College, London, last night. "All pain went.... I was in a sort of celestial calm; I scarcely thought, but such thoughts as I had were beautiful."

Professor Murray was addressing the British Institute of Philosophy.

He told how he was once recommended to spray his nostrils when suffering from hay fever. He diluted the mixture with a solution of cocaine and took the remedy freely.

"All worry and depression, all sense of disappointment and fear of the future melted away," he said. "In the course of the morning a visitor came in and talked to me. This I felt to be tiresome. I resented the effort of having to attend to what he said, especially since it did not, and could not matter in the least.... Whatever words or noises he might make could not matter to me...."

That brief hour of illusion had made him realise as never before the state of mind of the drug-addict or the drunkard.

1937

ONLY 616 DRUG ADDICTS IN BRITAIN

There are only 616 drug addicts in Britain according to a Government report to the League of Nations just published. During 1936, the report says, there was no evidence of any organised illicit drug traffic in Great Britain, Northern Ireland, the Isle of Man or the Channel Islands.

Addiction to narcotic drugs is not prevalent in the United Kingdom.

Among known addicts there are 313 men and 303 women.

Of these, 137 are doctors, three dentists, five chemists and two veterinary surgeons.

1903

KISSING A PILLAR-BOX.

"I do not recollect what happened," pleaded a man who was fined for drunkenness at Clerkenwell Police Court yesterday.

It was stated that when discovered the prisoner was tenderly kissing a pillar letter-box and entreating it to go home.

1930

As regards addiction to drugs, Professor Dixon stated, it is rare in Great Britain and is not common in France except among artists, demi-mondaines, and the idle rich but large quantities of narcotic drugs are manufactured in France and exported. In Germany addicts are increasing in number. Egypt has become the happy dumping ground for narcotics, and nearly 25 per cent. of those confined to prison are charged with drug offences. In the United States the Commissioner of the Treasury in 1921 estimated that there were at least one million addicts, but since then the number has steadily diminished.—Reuter.

1935

A DRASTIC CURE

China Proposes Death to Drug Addicts – After 1937

The Chinese Government proposes to execute all uncured drug addicts in China after 1937!

This fact was revealed yesterday by Mr. Victor Hoo, the Chinese delegate to the Advisory Opium Commission of the League of Nations, says Reuter.

He said that 263 drug traffickers were executed in China last year, and figures of drug addicts and opium smokers still run into millions.

The Commission was reluctant to endorse China's drastic proposal.

1929

DRUG THAT LEADS TO INSANITY

Schoolchildren Victims of a Deadly Weed.

SMOKED IN CIGARETTES.

CAPETOWN, Monday.

Disclosures of the deadly peril of a South African drug have been made here.

The drug, known as dagga, is taken by natives and Europeans, and even by schoolchildren. Victims eventually become insane.

The Pretoria Mental Hospital reveals that during the five years 1908 to 1912, 17.8 per cent. of all men and boys admitted became insane through smoking dagga.

Dagga resembles dried weeds, and is in reality Indian hemp. When an inch or two high it can easily be mistaken for a young tomato plant.

It is grown in many small places in the Veldt and sent to the towns and cities where, among the natives at least, it is almost as great a curse as opium is to the Chinaman.

1926

SLEEPLESS MAN.

"A NEW WORLD BY MEANS OF DRUGS."

MAKING CHARACTER TO ORDER.

From Our Own Correspondent.

NEW YORK, Tuesday.

A new world by means of drugs was the startling suggestion made by Mr. Irénée Dupont, the head of the biggest munition chemical works in America, which bears his name, to the convention of the American Chemical Society at Philadelphia.

Poppy & Mandragora

By ALDOUS HUXLEY

THE League of Nations is a courageous institution; it has undertaken to investigate and ultimately to control the traffic in drugs.

A report of its most recent deliberations on the subject is now before me—and a most depressing document it is: depressing in its description of the world in which we live, and depressing in its revelation of the official philanthropic mind.

What are the facts? The police are everywhere active; but the illicit traffic still goes on. No amount of vigilance can check the smuggling of substances so highly concentrated, and, therefore, so portable and concealable, as morphia and cocaine.

The logic of these facts imposes upon the official mind an inevitable conclusion. All that has been done up to date is only

An Inevitable Conclusion.

"a first step towards the limitation of the production of the raw material." The sources of supply must be closed down.

But opium constitutes a quarter of the total exports of Persia. What compensations are to be offered to the Persian agriculturist in return for a self-imposed limitation of production? And by whom? And if the Persian trade *were* stopped, what then? The poppy will flourish almost anywhere.

Experiments carried out in the nineteenth century proved that it is possible to grow bumper crops of opium in the neighbourhood of Edinburgh.

Why, then, did Persia remain the world's opium granary? The reasons were purely economic, not ethical. The moral horror of drugs is a very modern invention.

* * *

As recently as forty years ago a "drug fiend" could still be the hero of a popular novel. Sherlock

"Drug Fiend" as Hero.

Holmes, for example, was a cocaine addict. The reasons, I repeat, were economic. Labour costs more in Edinburgh than in Teheran, and the harvesting of opium requires a good deal of labour.

The Scotch were unable to compete with the Persians. But suppose that the Persians were now prevented from cultivating poppies. The price of opium would rise, just as the price of alcohol rose in the United States after Prohibition. Bootlegging would at once and automatically become profitable. Poppies will grow all over the temperate zone; there are millions of poor farmers only too anxious to earn a bit of money.

And the League talks about cutting off the sources of supply! Even with cocaine, derived as it is from a plant of far more limited growth than the poppy, the difficulty of limiting production would be very great. Moreover, it is highly probable that the drug will soon be made synthetically.

* * *

At a stroke the whole world will become a potential source of supply. But where money is to be made, potential sources

Ineffective Prohibition.

inevitably become actual sources. Prohibition, as the American observer attached to the League should surely have known, is not effective.

And yet this same observer seriously proposed total prohibition as the only solution to the problem. The official philanthropic mind is a most mysterious object.

An illness can be radically cured only by removing its cause. The cause of drunkenness and drug-taking is to be found in the general dissatisfaction with reality. More or less frequently and more or less intensely, men and women dislike the world in which they live and the personality with which nature and upbringing have endowed them.

* * *

Alcohol and drugs offer means of escape from the prison of the world and the personality. Better and securer conditions of

Monotony of Happiness.

life, better health, better upbringing, resulting in a more harmoniously balanced character, would do much to make reality seem generally tolerable and even delightful. But it may be doubted whether, even in Utopia, reality would be universally satisfying all the time. Even in Utopia people would pine for an occasional escape, if only from the radiant monotony of happiness.

The League of Nations advocates prohibition, which is like advocating the surgical excision of the pustules as a cure for smallpox. The only rational way of dealing with the drug and drink problem is, first, to make reality so decent that human beings will not be perpetually desiring to escape from it; and, second, to provide them, whenever they *should* feel the imperious need of taking a holiday, with a physiologically harmless method of escape.

The money which is spent in trying, quite vainly, to enforce prohibition ought to be spent on bio-chemical researches for the purpose of discovering the ideal substitute for alcohol, cocaine, and opium.

A century or so too late the official philanthropic mind may perhaps come to realise this; but for the present it seems to be committed to the absurd and mischievous policy of prohibition.

LAW 'N' ORDER

LOVE-MAKING, GAMBLING AND GAIETY IN THIS "MODEL" PRISON

FROM JOHN WALTERS
NEW YORK, Sunday

PETTING parties, gambling tables and narcotics were among relaxations of Tattnall "the model prison" of Georgia from which twenty-two convicts escaped recently.

Georgia citizens were shocked when they learned that the prison's thousand convicts had three whisky stills

But today the citizens were astounded by a new report of investigators which revealed that the prison has been a resort of love-making and gaiety.

Intimacies Revealed

Thick walls and stout doors divide the male and female sections of the prison. But when any woman convict was lonely she had only to ask for an electrician or plumber and a male convict was immediately sent to her cell.

"It seemed that most of the men prisoners were either electricians or plumbers," stated the investigators' report, which revealed intimacies between men and women prisoners.

Some convicts did a lucrative business by the operation of gaming tables

1943

Law 'n' Order

1924
SENTENCED TO CHEW.

Fate Of A Negro Who Stole An Automatic Machine.

Samuel Curtis, a negro, who had been captured with a stolen automatic machine containing 250 pieces of chewing gum, was (says the Philadelphia correspondent of the Central News) sentenced to chew every piece of gum in the mechanism, dropping pennies in the slot for every piece taken out.

When he had completed his task the judge allowed him to go, and gave the machine, with the pennies in it, back to its owner.

1913
DETECTIVE AS A "STATUE."

Few detectives have had such an exciting and successful career as that which stands to the credit of Detective Inspector Eustace, of the Brixton Division, who has just retired from the Metropolitan Force after twenty-seven years' service.

On one occasion, while keeping observation inside a London nunnery to discover the author of a number of mysterious thefts, he jumped on a pedestal and posed as a statue so that he could secure the thief, whom he heard approaching.

His make-up as a Jewish receiver of stolen property has long been the admiration of the detective service.

1937
NO FREEDOM HERE
German Householders Under New Search Threat

One of the German householder's last links with freedom has been severed. Under an order issued by the Ministry of the Interior—the German Home Office—every householder must deliver a duplicate set of the keys of his home to the local police authorities.

He is given a receipt, the set is numbered, labelled, and carefully docketed.

The reason? Spread of "underground" propaganda aimed at the Nazi regime.

Activities of the German Freedom Party and the secret radio stations have stirred the police to action.

Armed with the keys of every home, the police can enter without formality, and conduct a cellar-to-attic search.

1903
QUAINT TRIALS.
ANIMALS AND THE LAW.

Almost up to the very beginning of the last century the lower animals in all the continental countries were considered amenable to the laws. Domestic animals were tried in the common criminal courts, and their punishment on conviction was death; wild animals fell under the jurisdiction of the ecclesiastical courts, and their punishment was banishment and death by exorcism and excommunication. An account of some of the most noted of these trials appears in some musty old volumes published a century ago, and a brief mention of a few of these quaint and extraordinary causes célèbre may be of interest to the readers of "The People." Some of the trials it should first be mentioned

LASTED FOR YEARS,

and cost hundreds of pounds. A law suit between the inhabitants of the commune of St. Julien, and a certain insect lasted for more than 42 years. The summonses against animals, insects, and birds, were served by an officer of the court, who read the charges at the places frequented by the offenders. Thus, in a process against rats in the diocese of Autun, the defendants were described as "dirty animals in the form of rats, of a greyish colour, living in holes." In the annals of the French law this particular trial is famous, for it was at it that Chassance—the Coke of France—won his first laurels. The rats not appearing on the first citation, Chassence, who appeared as their counsel, argued that the summons was of a too local and individual character; that as all the

RATS IN THE DIOCESE

were interested, all the rats should be summoned in all parts of the diocese. This plea being admitted, the curate of every parish in the diocese was instructed to summon every rat for a future day. The day arrived, but no rats appeared. Chassance then objected to the legality of the summons. A summons from that court, he said, implied full protection to the parties summoned, but his clients, the rats, though most anxious to appear in obedience to the court, did not dare to stir out of their holes on account of the number of evil-disposed cats kept by the plaintiffs. With this argument Chassance gained the day, and laid the foundation of his great legal reputation. Such a trial was not regarded as

A TRAVESTY OR A BURLESQUE,

but was conducted with all seriousness by the law officers of the times, and even more curious legal battles than this are recorded. In a process against leeches, tried at Lausanne in 1451, a number of leeches were brought into court "to hear the indictment read," and at Laveguy, six years later, a sow and her six young ones were "placed in the dock" on a charge of having murdered and partly eaten a child. The sow was found guilty and condemned to death; but the young ones were acquitted on account of their youth, the bad example of their mother, and the absence of direct proof as to their having been concerned in the eating of the child. In one remarkable trial which took place at Basle in 1474.

A COCK WAS THE CULPRIT.

This unfortunate bird had committed the extraordinary offence of laying an egg. The account of this trial states, "For the prosecution it was proved that cock's eggs were of inestimable value for mixing in certain magical preparations; that a sorcerer would rather possess a cock's egg than be master of the philosopher's stone, and that in Pagan lands Satan employed witches to hatch such eggs, from which proceeded animals most injurious to all of the Christian faith and race. The advocate for the defence admitted the facts of the case, but asked what evil animus had been proved against his client; what injury to man or beast had it effected? Besides, the laying of an egg was an involuntary act, and as such,

NOT PUNISHABLE BY LAW."

The pleadings of this case, as recorded by Hammerlein, are most voluminous, and after a lengthy trial the cock was condemned to die, "not as a cock, but as a sorcerer or devil in the form of a cock." It is recorded that the bird with its egg was "burned at the stake with all the due form and solemnity of a judicial punishment."

1934
CRIMINALS' REGISTER
All Convicted People Must "Sign On'

TRENTON (New Jersey), Monday.

The authorities of Camden, New Jersey, which has a population of 120,000, have drafted a new law which requires all people, resident or transient, who have been convicted of crimes within the last ten years, to register at the police headquarters immediately.

Their names, addresses, occupations, aliases, fingerprints and photographs will be taken and kept on file as a permanent record.

Heavy penalties will be imposed upon those failing to obey these regulations, and anybody with a known record failing to register will be arrested on sight.—Central News.

1911
PRISON FOR SUNDAY TENNIS PLAYING.
Mr. Upton Sinclair Made a Convict for One Day.

[From our Correspondent.]
NEW YORK, Wednesday.

The "blue laws" of the State of Delaware have been responsible for an amusing state of affairs in the little Socialist colony at Arden, near Wilmington. To-day Mr. Upton Sinclair, celebrated as the author of "The Jungle" and other advanced works, was compelled to start stone-breaking in convict garb.

Mr. Sinclair and nine other leaders of the Socialist colony were arrested at the instance of an English shoemaker, named George Brown, on the charge of playing lawn tennis and baseball last Sunday.

Law 'n' Order 53

1922

1905
SILENCE IN COURT.

Justice Without Words by Mr. Denman.

The superfluity of words was notably demonstrated at Marlborough-street Police-court yesterday.

A deaf and dumb little woman occupied the dock; most of the witnesses were deaf and dumb; deaf and dumb relatives and friends were ranked at the back of the court.

A vocal policeman announced briefly that the prisoner's sister would interpret for her. The sister advanced to the dock and stood silent, while the friends at the rear of the court gesticulated eloquently.

After waiting a few minutes Mr. Denman, the magistrate, discovered that the "interpreter" was also deaf and dumb, and that no one in the court was able to interpret the deaf-and-dumb "finger language."

All the friends and relatives endeavoured to express their views by pantomime, and Mr. Denman ascertained that the charge was a trivial one of disorderly conduct.

Then he smiled, shook his head—the shake being the equivalent of the usual magisterial admonition, and understood as such—and waved his hand towards the door.

The faces of the deaf-and-dumb party broke into pleased smiles. As the little woman left the dock and the court she began to dance a sort of fandango, with one hand held up and the other waving like a semaphore. The public laughed silently.

When the party had departed the usher, who has been shouting "Silence in court!" for years, was understood to remark that he never wished to hear a better-conducted case.

1914
TAKING THE OATH.

A Comedy.

PLAYED TO-DAY AT STRATFORD POLICE-COURT.

Characters.
The Clerk ....Mr. F. A. Stern
A Witness ....Mr. Perry

The Clerk (administering the oath): Say "I swear by Almighty God."
Mr. Perry: Yes.
The Clerk: Repeat after me—"I swear by Almighty God——"
Mr Perry: I swear by Almighty God.
The Clerk: That the evidence I give——
Mr. Perry: That's right.
The Clerk: Repeat it.
Mr. Perry: "Repeat it." [The court laughs.]
The Clerk: Yes—"That the evidence I give——"
Mr. Perry: "Yes—that the evidence I give——"
The Clerk: Shall be the truth——
Mr. Perry: It will, and nothing but the truth.
The Clerk: Repeat what I say.
Mr. Perry: I am no scholar, you know. [The court again laughs.]
The Clerk: We can appreciate that. Just say, "shall be the truth and——"
Mr. Perry: Shall be the truth and——
The Clerk: Say "nothing——"
Mr. Perry: All right. [Further laughter.]
The Clerk: Say "nothing but the truth."
Mr. Perry: Yes.
The Clerk: Can't you say "nothing but the truth"?
Mr. Perry: Yes. [Very loud laughter.]
The Clerk: Well, do so.
[Perry repeats the words, and his evidence is taken.]

1916
AN AMERICAN PRISON.

"Man's Inhumanity to Man" in California.

MY LIFE IN PRISON, by Donald Lowrie. London, John Lane, 6s. net.

By Tighe Hopkins.

The first enclosure that a prisoner enters at San Quentin, California, is the graveyard: "Rows of white boards, each with its black number staring out across the road." The second is "a beautiful flower garden, a fountain surmounted by a figure of a white swan in the centre." The graveyard is for the prisoners; the flower garden is not.

Donald Lowrie tells us that he got 15 years for a burglary (his first offence) after three breadless days and nights in the streets. In the cell, eight by ten, that he shared with four other convicts was a consumptive boy who had received five years for stealing three dollars from a drunken man. By-and-by the boy had the luck to be carried to the hospital, where he died. There are fewer than 700 cells in San Quentin for nearly 2,000 prisoners; and "the floors of the cells are never washed the ventilation is fearful."

Experience Teaches.

Little by little Donald Lowrie learned the topography of the "antiquated and inhuman prison": Crazy Alley, where the lunatics were herded; the Dungeons, where men lay in darkness in strait jackets; the Solitaries, where even worse things happened; Death Row, where the condemned awaited the hangman; Execution Chamber, the topmost storey of the gaol, where the gallows stood always ready, the rope dangling from the beam. There was a parrot that took an interest in new-comers, hopping up to them as they sat on the "mourners' bench" in the yard, with the question, "What did you bring?" (i.e., "What sentence have you got?")

Donald describes his first dinner in prison, each prisoner dipping into the common receptacle with the spoon with which he eats:

If a man is compelled to eat like a pig he is bound to acquire pig instincts (twelve minutes only are allowed for dinner), and he is bound to carry these pig instincts out into the world with him. True, there are a few men who become chronic fasters, eating just enough to keep body and soul together, but are they not also irreparably injured? I have seen a new prisoner sit at the table day after day, nibbling at a piece of bread and sipping his "tea" or "coffee," and then, after the lapse of a few months, I have seen this same man sit down at the table and eat like a hog.

A Mill of Tragedies.

Donald, being young and able-bodied, was assigned to the jute mill. The mill, like most other departments of San Quentin, has its tragedies:

I know of several instances of insanity directly due to prolonged work at a refractory loom. I have watched a man do his best day after day, his face drawn to a tensity painful to behold, only to meet with disaster and punishment in the end. When I worked in the mill the rule was that a man should go to the "hole" on bread and water from Saturday night till Monday morning if he failed to have his task (100 yards to be woven in the day) completed at the end of the week. And then, after spending this period in the "hole" he would be brought back to work on Monday morning and expected to get out his task for that day.

Donald tells in detail what this means. A sentence to the "hole" or dungeon usually carried with it a sentence to the "jacket":

The jacket consists of a piece of canvas about four and one-half feet long, cut to fit about the human body. When spread out on the floor it has the same shape as the top of a coffin, broad near one end, for the shoulders, and tapering either way. Big brass eyelets run down the sides. It is manufactured in various sizes, and is designed solely as an instrument of torture.

The jacket is spread out on the floor, and the prisoner ordered to lie face down upon it. The sides are then gathered up over his back and a rope, about the size of a window cord, is laced through the eyelets.

If the word has been passed to "give him a cinching," the operator places his foot upon the victim's back in order to get leverage as he draws the rope taut, and when the lacing is finished the remnant of rope is wound about the trussed body and tied. Then the victim is rolled over on his back and left to think it over. He is left in one of the dungeon cells, where there is no light and where it is cold and damp.

After the Jacket.

Prisoners have been taken from the jacket paralysed, to die in hospital. Others have lost the use of their limbs for life. A man who had been jacketed said to Donald:

"Talk about the Spanish Inquisition and people being monsters in those days! Huh! I guess the world's just about the same, only things were done in the open then, and now they're done under cover. I went through that torture, and I've never been the same man since. I'll never be the same man again, and you can see that for yourself."

The man had been kept in the jacket for 130 hours, fed once in the day with a little water and a crust of bread. This punishment left him a physical wreck, and he never recovered.

A certain R——— was jacketed for making shell ornaments in his cell. It was thought that he had been making them for the guard, and he would not confess. After a long period of trussing, six hours on and six off, his frame had shrunk so greatly that a tighter jacket was requisitioned:

In a few minutes his screams of agony were piercing our brains... Every man who heard them unconsciously kept as quiet as possible... Without reasoning about it, we wanted those screams to have full sway, to reach everywhere.

The screams had to penetrate two steel doors and wind through the cellar-like passage way to the outer air. Their very faintness made them more horrible. It sounded like a man being tortured in the bowels of the earth. After the dungeon-keeper had timidly reported at the office twice—he was always fearful when he came to report screams, because he was sometimes sent back with a reprimand about being chicken-hearted—the captain went down to investigate, but refused to release the victim. He came back, jangling the keys at his side and humming "Annie Rooney." After a time the screams became fainter. Finally they died away.

Bad and Foolish.

This is rather bad and foolish of America in the twentieth century. If we leave out of the reckoning (though we are not called upon to do so) the sheer inhumanity of it, this method of treating criminals in prison is very shortsighted and very costly. When Prince Kropotkin or my friend Mr. G. H. Perris exposes the horrors of the Boutyrki Prison in Moscow or any prison of the exiles in sub-Arctic Russia, our feeling of sickness and loathing is not accompanied by any feeling of surprise. But America has long been a party to the International Penitentiary Congress, and from America have come in recent years some of the wisest books on criminology, the science which seeks to show, among other things, that no country can any longer afford to make fools or victims of the inmates of its prisons.

Perhaps someone asks: Do you believe all these stories of Donald Lowrie's—an ex-convict? Yes, I believe them all. For this hideous record of San Quentin Prison is not the sole revelation of its kind. It is not even the ghastliest. Worse things have been published about this Californian inferno than anything told by Donald Lowrie.

With a few splendid exceptions, on which it would be grateful to enlarge, the innumerable prison systems of America are a chaos, in which the political jobber and the contractor pull together to defraud the State and bring the prisoner to ruin.

In its terrible way, Donald Lowrie's book is fascinating from end to end, and it will be a pity if it does not find its way to a host of sympathetic readers.

Catchpole with which wrongdoers used to be captured in Edinburgh.

1905
"BEAUTY PARLOUR."

Negroes Go Gladly to Gaol, in Hope of Losing Their Colour.

According to a despatch from Macon, Missouri, negroes about there are almost breaking their necks to get into the county gaol.

The explanation offered is that the damp condition of the gaol, which has been condemned, has exercised a remarkable effect upon certain negro prisoners, "bleaching them almost white," and it is undisputed in America that most negroes do not like their natural colour.

When the good news circulated, the negroes, says the "Daily Telegraph," began pleading guilty to all sorts of crimes.

The sheriff allowed fifteen to go to gaol, and, addressing other aspirants, said: "I've tumbled to your game. If any more want bleaching you'll have to use sandpaper or a file. I ain't going to entertain any more of you in what you seem to think is not a gaol, but a beauty parlour."

1931
ESKIMOS WHO TRY TO GO TO GAOL

SEATTLE (WASH.), June 4.
Point Hope, Alaska, has ordered the construction of a large gaol because the old one is so popular with the Eskimos that it cannot hold all those who have committed crimes in hope of being arrested.

Some time ago the local United States Marshal arrested two natives for a minor law violation. They were fed so well and the gaol was kept so warm, the prison official said, that they spread the happy news when they were released. Then Eskimos started breaking all sorts of laws just to be sent to the prison.—Reuter.

1934
Prison Run by Criminals

SURPRISE RAID REVEALS AMAZING SCANDAL

From Our Own Correspondent

NEW YORK, Wednesday.
Astounding conditions at Welfare Island, New York's venerable city prison, were uncovered today when Mr. Austin H. MacCormack, the newly-appointed Commissioner of Correction, paid a surprise visit to the institution.

"**I am ready to believe this is the worst prison in the world,**" said Mr. MacCormack, when he came to the end of his inspection.

"I found it virtually administered by a group of gangsters. I found favoured prisoners living in ease and comfort, ruled by Joie Rao, a racketeer, assisted by a so-called Board of Strategy, consisting of three gangsters."

Large quantities of narcotics and weapons, including blackjacks, long-handled razors, glass cutters and kitchen knives, were found in cells by the raiding party.

LIVING IN LUXURY

When the Commissioner and his party entered the so-called Politicians' Ward of the hospital they were amazed to find 50 prisoners with reputed political connections living almost in luxury, with Rao in charge. Examination by a doctor who accompanied Mr. MacCormack showed that of these 50 only six were ill.

In a second ward of 43 prisoners only 12 were in ill-health. Their overlord was a convict named Eddie Cleary, who was found living in a large comfortable room overlooking the river, guarded by a vicious dog named Screw Hater.

RULED BY MURDERER

This dog, always on guard at Cleary's bed, had the duty of keeping inquisitive visitors away.

The Commissioner was also astonished to find that Boss Cleary owned 100 homing pigeons, which were apparently used as a regular postal service to take messages and small parcels in and out of the gaol.

Mr. MacCormack described Rao as chief of a prison drug ring.

Although this man was involved in a murder in the prison 12 months ago, he had become its virtual ruler, issuing his orders from his office in the Politicians' Ward, and under his direction the prison had become a club for his favourites.

Extraordinary scenes took place during the raid on the cells, as, with prisoners shouting and cursing, piles of forbidden articles were removed, including:

*Private food stores,
Weapons,
Wireless sets,
Sacks of flour,* etc.

Among 150 men removed from the west wing, 100 were said to be drug addicts and were taken to hospital for treatment. All the other prisoners were locked in solitary confinement.

The Warden (Governor) was dismissed on the spot and the Deputy-Warden placed under military arrest.

One amazing feature of the raid was a round-up of a number of young men, rouged and painted, and wearing costly jewellery and rich attire, who had apparently been given the complete freedom of the building.

Commissioner MacCormack is an eminent penologist, who was recently appointed by New York's new Mayor, Major La Guardia.

1913
STRIKING ARTICLE
BY
MR. G. K. CHESTERTON

"ANARCHIC POWERS."

THE NEW WORK OF THE POLICE.

"The New Power of the Police" is the title of a characteristic article by Mr. G. K. Chesterton in "Nash's Magazine."

When we come to our precious modern Social Reform (he writes), we seem to submit instantly, and swallow the thing as reform merely because it calls itself so. And in order to effect such dubious changes we are strengthening and sharpening that very machine of police violence and arbitrary power by which all the tyrannies of the past have been maintained.

Thus, to take the most obvious passing case, the White Slave Bill enormously increases police despotism at the very moment when we are inquiring rather painfully about police integrity.

We have been deafened with tales against despotism since our infancy; but if we catch sight of somebody standing in the street whose face we dislike, we instantly cry out: "Arrest that man! Oh, fetch me a frightful fierce despot with a great big sabre to arrest that man!" And we let the sabre do its work without even stopping to cleanse it from the blood of More and Sydney, Essex and Alice Lisle.

Queer Contrast.

The contrast is the more queer, because America has really been investigating its policemen, while England has been merely magnifying and extending them.

The very same newspaper that announced the conviction of American policemen as thieves and liars announced the enthronement of English policemen as judges. The mental state of the English has led them into many muddles; but the *worst* muddle they have reached yet has been the attempt to trust and distrust the policeman at the same time.

To give a person new powers on Monday, and then to begin to inquire whether he has abused his old powers on Tuesday, does not seem to me a good example of the working English compromise.

It is not in the least necessary that I should say that the policeman is inhuman. It is quite sufficient if I say that he is human. For the optimism about him in the educated classes practically maintains that he is divine.

This is because educated people nowadays prefer to have unknown gods; and they worship the constable because they never come in contact with him—except as an object in the landscape.

On this subject the cultured class happens to be the ignorant class. But for the purposes of this protest, nothing more is needed than the concession that policemen were not created before Eden as a separate order of seraphs; that policemen are descended from Adam and Eve—or from the Missing Link, if that makes their innocence more indisputable.

A Magisterial Defence.

I will not encumber the argument with particular cases that are known to everybody: a shorter way of proving the point is to take the defence actually offered in public by one of the justices of this country.

A magistrate, who had heard some of this common sense in some sort of echo from the common people, went out of his way to rebuke the rising tide of the suspicion against police evidence. He said it was very wrong to suspect police evidence: because magistrates were often reduced to relying entirely on police evidence; and that courts of justice often could not get a conviction, except by police evidence. I think we may leave it there. It is one of the most glorious remarks ever made in this world. Translated into English it runs thus: It does not matter whether this witness has lied; because if he had not lied, I never could have hanged the wrong man.

But it is quite clear that the intermittent occurrence of such perjuries does not arise from any special sin in policemen, but from that variety of original sin which is most natural to all groups that are separated, systematised, and more or less hated.

We are asked to give policemen purely anarchic powers. And all the time everybody knows they could arrest half Piccadilly Circus if they were using, honestly the powers they already possess.

If we say that some grocers cheat and that all grocers ought to be subject to laws against cheating, we are not immediately vilified for questioning the honour and chivalry of grocery. If we say that some butchers are bullies and that no butchers ought to be bullies, we are not hooted at for throwing mud on the sacred uniform of the blue apron.

But when the wealthier classes (in England, and I think in England only) hear any one suggest that the police want watching, like the whole human race, they have a sort of fit.

Facts About Police.

Now the three main facts about the police, besides the evident fact that they are necessary, are substantially these: first, that they are men of the poorer classes in a proletarian country, and if they were not policemen, would probably be porters or bricklayers or plasterers; second, that they are such men organized on a military model, and according to a peculiar and partly inevitable ethic, which gives more importance to obedience and solidarity, less importance to liberty and truth, than the everyday ethic of humanity; and third, that, while their ultimate moral justification is an effort of the community to cope with all its crimes, the overwhelming preponderance of the practical work they have to do consists in the protection of property, and therefore, largely, of propertied people.

All these three things are obvious about them; they cannot help them, they cannot be blamed for them. But anybody who can calmly say that they do not together make up the possibility, or probability of a certain number of hired bullies and perjurers is speaking with a lie in his soul.

A soldier can be flogged or shot if he pillages the people he has conquered. A policeman ought to be punished as fiercely as by flogging or shooting if he is found telling lies against the people over whom he is in a permanent position of occupation and conquest.

Now we all know that this is not the case. We all know that while the police are entrusted with heavy powers, they are seldom or never subjected to heavy punishments for the abuse of those powers. They have all the soft side of militarism; but (so far as legal inquisition is concerned) none of the hard side.

Before and, after Wellington called the English army the scum of the earth, the colonel and the court-martial have tended too much to regard the common soldier as a ruffian.

But it is equally certain that the magistrate and the court of justice have tended too much to regard the common policeman as an oracle. His evidence, in the vast number of cases, is never sifted at all. He is never examined—let alone cross-examined. He is the only man in court who is allowed to contradict himself.

KNUCKLE-DUSTER JUSTICE

AMAZING REPORT ON U.S.A. POLICE METHODS

From Our Own Correspondent

NEW YORK, Monday.

SYSTEMATIC brutality in the use of the "Third Degree" is practised by the police throughout half of the United States, according to a report of the Wickersham Commission, presented to-day to President Hoover.

The report bears the significant title "Lawlessness of the Law." This document, written by three distinguished lawyers, attests at least 100 cases where torture was used to wring statements from reluctant prisoners.

Actual examples are given of men denied sleep until they confessed, of handcuffing men upside down while spraying them with tear gas, of forcing suspects into cells with diseased persons until fear of infection unsealed their lips, of administration of water torture, of severe beatings by rubber hose and sandbags.

These Chinese methods are defended on the ground that only drastic action can check the crime wave, but the Wickersham investigators discovered that professional criminals and gangsters rarely found their way into the torture chambers.

The principal victims were poor persons, friendless immigrants, negroes and those suspected of Communist sympathies. The Commission leaves it to be inferred that gangsters are powerful enough to buy protection from such horrors.

THE STRONGER FEELING

It is unlikely that there will be any public agitation to end the Third Degree as a result of the Commission's report, for fear of crime and of Communism is now stronger than humane feelings. The Commission itself acknowledges that in great cities like Chicago the public is more concerned with the reduction of crime than with official lawlessness. They were told that in Chicago it was the exception when suspects were not subjected to personal violence.

Some examples of ingenious torture given in the report are as follows:

In Miami a man accused of murdering his wife was chained to the floor of a mosquito infested cell and later questioned with the scalp of his dead wife at his feet.

A Finn in Los Angeles, arrested without cause when he argued with policemen, was beaten with brass knuckles till covered with blood.

A negro boy in Arkansas was whipped over a period of six days till he confessed to a murder, but the Appeal Court reversed the conviction as against the evidence.

In El Paso a young Mexican woman, charged with having killed her child, was relay questioned for 35 hours till she confessed.

In Clarksdale, Mississippi, a negro, charged with murdering a white man, was tied to the floor and water poured up his nostrils, half suffocating him, till he confessed.

THE POLICE CASE

Commenting on the police argument that third degree methods get results, the Commission points out that this benefit is overweighted by the fact that many confessions thus obtained are false, and of 106 appeal cases studied nearly half of the convictions were reversed because of third degree methods.

"The effect upon the police is obvious. Third degree must brutalise those who practise it. Their fight against lawlessness, if waged by forbidden means, is degrading itself almost to the level of a struggle between two law-breaking gangs."

New York police are instanced in report as practisers of such methods, and authoritative proof is adduced that mediæval weapons exist in many stations here.

"Recent methods employed included punching in the face, whipping with rubber hose, kicking in the abdomen, tightening the necktie almost to choking point. Arrested persons come to station houses or headquarters in good shape and are seen shortly afterwards in the Tombs Prison with swollen faces, all sorts of bruises and cuts, and often with blood spots scattered over them.

"A distinguished magistrate reported to us that when several Italians were brought before him for alleged violence he looked at their backs, and there was hardly a spot which was not raw from recent beating.

"Michael Fiaschetti, a former head of the police squad, is reported as admitting his resort to brutality in the following words: 'I went to the Tombs and got myself a sawed-off baseball bat and walked in on those dogs. Yes, they came through with everything they knew.'"

"HOODED" PRISONERS IN JAPAN.

After Williams, the Eastbourne murderer, was arrested his features were carefully shrouded from the public gaze, a plan which is adopted in Japan. Above are some of the 113 prisoners charged with burning down police-stations and other public buildings arriving for their trial at Tokio, their heads covered with huge straw helmets.

AMERICA'S SLAVES.

WHITES IN BONDAGE IN TEXAS.

From Our Own Correspondent.

NEW YORK.

Slavery in the form of peonage and involving even whites in its grip is now reported from Texas. A man named Straps and his wife, who were flogged by five masked men, will be used as witnesses against D. Osborne, who is charged only with assault. A man and his wife, relations of Straps, were also flogged.

It is stated that Osborne was employed by their owner, the tenant of the farms these people occupied, and that the floggings were done to drive them away and make the Straps work two farms.

A case recently reported of a negro who escaped from Florida alleging that he had been kidnapped when his car broke down ended in the freeing of a large plantation owner, who admitted thrashing negro men and women with a strap, but brought witnesses to deny peonage.

A characteristic outbreak of whipping seems spreading in the South. A schoolmaster and three other men at Toccoa, Georgia, have been arrested on a charge of almost flaying to death a woman they charged with loose behaviour, and her son, aged 15, who tried to defend his mother. Three other floggings were disclosed, two of them of women. The victims assert that the floggers belong to the Ku Klux Klan.

In the State of Mississippi, on the very day that New York was acclaiming Lindbergh as the type of American chivalry an armed mob seized two negroes accused of shooting a foreman in a quarrel, poured petrol over them, and burned them to death.

1898
TREADWHEEL HORROR

According to the evidence at the inquest, he was admitted to jail on Sept. 30th. On the following day he was certified by the prison doctor as fit for first-class hard labour. He must then have been in good health if a medical certificate is worth anything at all. After this certificate of the doctor he was put on the treadwheel by order of the prison Governor. He worked on this wheel till the 10th October —that is, for ten days. On that day he complained to the doctor that he was not well and could not work the wheel. The doctor gave Cooper some medicine, and told him he must work the wheel. Three days afterwards, on the night of the 13th, Cooper was found by one of the warders in a semi-delirious condition. He was removed to another cell. Next morning, at six o'clock—a few hours before his death— he was ordered to get out of bed. His bed was taken from him, and, as he was unable to put on his clothes, he was left lying naked on the floor. Each time a warder pulled him up he sank down again from sheer weakness and exhaustion. At a quarter-past eleven poor Cooper rallied a little and asked for some water. At twelve o'clock, when the cell-door was opened, he was lying dead upon the floor. The Home Secretary says he has inquired into this horrible case. We trust that Mr. Lough will ask him to lay the particulars of that inquiry on the Table of the House.

1915
JUSTICE AND THE LAW.

Yesterday the Court of Criminal Appeal quashed a sentence of twelve months' imprisonment with hard labour passed on an unfortunate man found guilty of receiving a stolen threepenny piece. The Court held that there was no evidence at all to show that the man knew the money was stolen. Only a day or two ago another case came before this Court in which a man had pleaded guilty to entering a house for shelter. This was taken as equivalent to a plea of housebreaking (there was no evidence that he intended to steal anything), and he was sentenced without trial to nothing less than seven years' penal servitude. This sentence also was quashed, the Court declining to order a new trial. If there had been no Court of Criminal Appeal (as there was not ten years ago) both these iniquitous sentences would undoubtedly have been served. It is an interesting, if painful, reflection on the boasted purity of our law and justice that such sentences can be passed at all; and more interesting and more painful still to reflect that before the bitterly opposed establishment of the Criminal Appeal Court quite a number of people may have suffered yearly under similar gross miscarriages of justice.

1929
WORLD'S MOST ROMANTIC DETECTIVE.
Master of Eight Languages Who Visited Germany During the War.

ONE of the most remarkable detectives ever attached to Scotland Yard, and a man whose career borders on the incredible, has been dismissed the Force in Inspector Hubert Ginhoven, who, with Sergeant Jane, was found "Guilty" of breaches of duty.

Both officers had been entrusted with special political and secret service work, and their dismissals follow recent disclosures regarding the leakage of Scotland Yard secrets to prominent Communists.

Tall and pale-faced, with a perfect knowledge of eight languages, including Turkish, Russian, and German, ex-Inspector Ginhoven was looked upon as one of the most romantic detectives in the world.

He served in many parts of the world, and his mastery of languages gives colour to the stories of how he often disguised himself as a native of various countries in the quest for information regarding the enemy.

On many occasions he penetrated behind enemy lines to gather vital information. It is stated that on one occasion he was dropped from an aeroplane with the aid of a parachute inside the Bulgarian lines on the Salonika front.

Then, disguised in German uniform he entered a Zeppelin shed and destroyed a Zeppelin before escaping back to the lines of the Allies.

After another exploit an enemy Government put a price on his head.

Twice during the war he travelled as a Dutchman through Germany, and even into Krupps's works—disguised as an infirm German labourer.

Ginhoven's father was a Dutchman who became naturalised. He joined the London police over twenty years ago.

His knowledge of languages made him an exceptionally useful officer. On one occasion he created a minor sensation in court by interpreting the case from the English into French, German, and Yiddish.

This brought him to the notice of Sir Patrick Quinn, the then chief of the Special Branch, and Ginhoven joined that service.

Detective-sergeant Jane was formerly in the Bristol City Police Force, and was a police tailor for a time before he joined the Metropolitan Police. He also had a good record in the Special Branch of Scotland Yard. He had specialised in political missions, and was regarded as an authority on the Communist movement in this country.

1918
BOLSHEVISM IN U.S.
Judge's Blunt Denunciation in a New York Trial.

The New York correspondent of the Central News writes:—

We are dealing pretty sternly with the Bolshevik element in this country— Eugene Debs, Mrs. Phelps Stokes, and the rest of them.

Federal Judge Clayton, of Alabama, addressing six men and one woman, all disciples of Lenin and Trotsky, who were before him on a charge of conspiracy to violate the Espionage Law, said that when he was in Congress he voted to restrict immigration, and he was now satisfied that he voted rightly.

The indicted woman complained that the Government was making efforts "to stifle free speech," and Judge Clayton retorted: "Freedom of speech is one thing and disloyalty is another.

"I am sorry for the people of New York who have to deal with individuals who have no more conception of what free government means than a billygoat has of the Gospel.

"This Court is not going to follow the example of the Bolsheviks, who appear to have a half-baked idea of government composed of socialism and nihilism.

"I want to say that when this war is over the United States will be the principal agency in assisting the Russian people to attain an orderly form of government."

1926
ISLAND THAT AMERICA ONCE FORGOT.

Modern Utopia—No Laws, No Gaols, One Tax.

LITTLE WORLD ON ITS OWN.

Special Wire to "The Star."

DAMARISCOTTA (Maine), Friday. Muscongus Island, a scant mile off the southern Maine shore, is America's closest approach to Utopia, for it has no laws, no gaols no candidates, no elections, and almost no taxes.

One hundred and fifty fisher folk live in prosperity and comfort on this three-miles-long and mile-wide island.

Legally Non-existent.

"Uncle Sam's" map-makers, many years ago, forgot about Muscongus Island, and legally it became nonexistent. Muscongus and Maine did not discover this at once. The islanders continued to pay taxes to the township of Bristol, and to abide by the township's statutes, but in 1863 the island's 28 votes swung a close State election.

Court Challenge.

"Uncle Sam's" map-making error was then dug up. The election was challenged in the courts, and denial of the right of the islanders to vote was the outcome.

Muscongus raised the cry of the Boston Tea Party. "No vote, no taxes!" they proclaimed, and they had their own way

The State government stepped in recently, and levied on the island a nominal land tax, but apart from this the island is a little world on its own.

MISCELLANEA

LOUIS XIV.'S HEART.

Amazing Story of its Burial in Westminster Abbey.

A remarkable story regarding the heart of Louis XIV., and how it came to be buried in Westminster Abbey is told in this week's "Truth" by Mr. Labouchere, who says that the story was told to him by the late Colonel Harcourt, and confirmed by his brother, the late Sir William Harcourt.

The Harcourt who lived during the first French Revolution had many connections in France, and invited a good many of the emigrés to visit him. Amongst them was a Canon of St. Denis. On leaving, the Canon expressed the thanks of himself and of other Frenchmen for the kindly hospitality of their host, and produced from his pocket a something that looked like a piece of dried leather, an inch or so long, which he presented to him. "I was," he said, "in the Cathedral when the royal tombs were broken open and the contents scattered to the winds. This is the heart of Louis XIV. It was kept in a separate receptacle, and I managed to get away with it."

The heart, having thus got into the possession of the Harcourt family, was occasionally produced for the inspection of visitors as a curiosity. The late Dr. Buckland, Dean of Westminster, was on a visit, when it was brought out for his inspection. He was then very old. He had some reputation as a man of science, and the scientific spirit moved him to wet his finger, rub it on the heart, and put the finger to his mouth. After that, before he could be stopped, he put the heart in his mouth and swallowed it, whether by accident or design will never be known.

Very shortly afterwards he died; and was buried in Westminster Abbey. It is impossible that he could ever have digested the thing. It must have been a pretty tough organ to start with, and age had almost petrified it. Consequently the heart of Louis XIV. must now be reposing in Westminster Abbey, enclosed in the body of an English Dean.

1905

Old Wives' Cures in Harley-street

A. P. Luscombe Whyte

A recent medical journal describes how a child raving with rheumatic fever, her limbs swollen with pain and her temperature rocketing, was brought for treatment. The fever defied ordinary methods. But five injections of bee venom cured it. Another paper tells how a labourer, crippled with rheumatism, was ordered by a courageous doctor to get stung five times a day. Painful ... but he soon walked.

The wise women didn't know of the valuable counter-irritant properties of the formic acid found in bee venom. But they knew, partly by instinct, partly by simple reason, that it would cure rheumatism. Bee-keepers, who often got stung, never seemed to get rheumatism. They didn't stop to debate each discovery. That's why they were so often right.

There are millions of country—and thousands of city—folk who still rely upon the old folk-cures. The more fantastic have been laughed out. They no longer stuff a cockroach, boiled in oil, into a bad ear, or rub an infusion of mice on a sprained back. But they successfully treat a whole dictionary of ailments with the simple products of the soil and the kitchen.

For centuries the farmer's wife used to reach for the teapot when she burnt her hand. Tea leaves bound on the burn drew out the pain. Harley-street has just perfected the last word in treatment for burns. They are sprayed with tannic acid.

The Druids used mistletoe (meaning, literally, Heal All) as a universal panacea. For ages the country people doctored blood-pressure, thumping headaches, vapours and hysteria with mistletoe "tea."; and still do.

Yesterday a doctor showed me a tube of French tablets. They were the latest cure for blood-pressure, epilepsy, St. Vitus's dance, and a host of nervous troubles. They acted ideally, without any depressing action on the heart. They were made of mistletoe.

Garlic has always figured in the histories of folk-medicine. Eaten whole, or its juice drunk, it was considered an infallible cure for tuberculosis, coughs and (rubbed on) for wounds. Some chest troubles were treated by making the patient inhale the fumes into his lungs (he must have been unbearable for hours). Tuberculosis of the skin yielded, they said, to the juice.

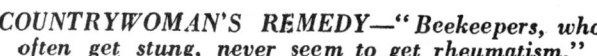

COUNTRYWOMAN'S REMEDY—"Beekeepers, who often get stung, never seem to get rheumatism."

But it was not till quite recently that medicine discovered that the essential essence of garlic, containing allyl sulphide, was an excellent medium for chest and tuberculosis treatment.

The sense of smell and colour did much to influence the instinctive doctors of long ago. Lavender, that calm and fragrant bloom, must, they thought, have soothing effects. They made essence of lavender and used it in a dozen ways as a nerve-soother and soporific. As long ago as 1721 it appeared in the London Pharmacopœia as "Palsy Drops." It is still being used in Wessex.

Recently I read an article in a French paper in which a French scientist described the extraordinary effects of lavender. Its action in slowing down motor (muscle) activity made it of utmost use in the treatment of palsy, St. Vitus's dance and neurasthenia. It had even been used to send patients to sleep.

The old Wiltshire farm-folk never had headaches. They could charm away the most stubborn (they said) with a plaster made of black pepper, bound in a handkerchief and saturated with camphor. Their instinctive choice was almost uncanny. Any modern doctor will tell you of the fever-relieving properties of pepper and how its volatile oils will soothe away pain wherever they are applied. Camphor, of course, is to-day known as the most valuable of pantry-shelf anæsthetics through its power to depress local nerves and damp out pain.

Scores of other such folk-cures have since been endorsed, and often adopted, by medical science. A hot fig to draw out the pain or the abscess of toothache. Mandrake as a pre-operative anæsthetic. Poppyheads, bruised in wine, as a pain-killer and soporific. Boiled raisin juice for quinsy. Marjoram for headache. Wormwood as a tonic. Ivy-salve for rheumatism and neuralgia. Meadow-saffron for gout....

Even in America there are, according

Miscellanea

1923
ONE LEGGED CRICKETER.

Mr. S.-J. H. Corner, the one-legged veteran of the East Ham Corinthians, who still keeps wicket for his club every Saturday.

1920
More Epitaphs.

How would Leighton Buzzard's new censor of epitaphs regard some of those that find favour in Western America? Here is one from a Nevada burial ground: "Sacred to the Memory of Hank Monk, the Whitest, Biggest-hearted, and Best Stage-driver of the West, who was Kind to All, Thought Ill of None. He lived in a Strange Era, and was a Hero, and the Wheels of his Coach are now Ringing on the Golden Streets." Another, also from the Far West, runs: "To Lem S. Frame, who during his life shot 89 Indians, whom the Lord delivered into his hands, and was looking forward to making up his hundred before the end of the year, when he fell asleep in Jesus at his home at Hawk's Ferry."

Guildford Churchyard contains a good specimen of the vigorous epitaph:

Reader, pass on, ne'er waste your time
On bad biography, and silly rhyme,
For what I *am*, this cumbrous clay ensures,
And what I *was*, is no affair of yours.

An epitaph of somewhat similar type used to be shown in the churchyard of St. Mary's, Islington:

Pray for the soul of Gabriel John,
Who died in the year 1601:
Or if you don't, it's all one.

to one authority, thousands of city dwellers who believe in the old remedies.

One doctor tells me he credits the old country-folk for keeping alive many sound old cures, and the quack doctors for developing new ones.

"The quacks helped to develop electro-therapy, hydropathy (bath treatment), the sun-ray, osteopathy and glandular treatment. They realised long ago that certain parts of animals (containing important glands) were valuable for treating specific diseases. We are still only on the fringe of the jungle they gaily entered."

Don't despise mad old Martha of the village. She was wise in her generation.

1947
SAVE THE COUNTRYSIDE

IN your excellent leader on September 7 you say that within twenty years the beauty of our country may be entirely ruined by arterial roads and motor monstrosities.

But you did not mention the worst evil of all —the extension of street lamps over rural roads, parks, commons and peaceful villages.

A public lamp blots out our view of the clouds and stars and stabs the quiet night, which Nature made to rest and restore.

Of all the horrors of modern civilisation, I know of none more destructive to the beauty of life than the abuse of artificial light.

Hampstead, N.W.   TAB CAN.

George Ives

1928
A Literary Ford.

America has now produced a literary Ford; it has been left to Mr. E. Haldeman-Julius, an American publisher, to perfect the art of "merchandising" the world's classics.

During the last ten years he has sold over 100,000,000 copies of his cheap reprints, and in his newly-published book, "The First Hundred Million," he describes with American frankness the methods by which he has achieved his astounding success.

If Mr. Haldeman-Julius is to be believed, what sells a book—that is, a classic—to the masses is its title. As a general rule that title must have some connection with the three great subjects which appeal passionately to the reading masses:—

1—Sex.
2—Self-improvement.
3—Attacks upon respectability and religion.

Starting on the premise that by their titles ye shall sell them, Mr. Haldeman-Julius was able very soon to divide his classics into healthy and sick: the good-sellers with the good titles, and the bad-sellers with the bad.

How It Is Done.

Every one of his reprints which failed to sell his standard of 10,000 copies a year was sent to his book hospital, where its commercial defects were analysed. If they were in the text the book was dropped; if in the title the title was ruthlessly altered.

In many cases a new title saved the book. For instance, in 1926 a translation of Victor Hugo's play only sold 8000 copies under its original title of "Le Roi s'Amuse." Next year, under its revised title of "The Lustful King Enjoys Himself," it sold 38,000. Similarly, Gautier's "Golden Fleece" makes a far wider appeal when it is re-christened "The Search for a Blond Mistress," while Maupassant has also been "doctored" with great success.

Schopenhauer's "Art of Controversy" and De Quincey's Essay on Conversation sell like hot cakes under their self-improvement titles of "How to Argue Logically" and "How to Improve Your Conversation."

It is all very simple and all very successful. I can see authors fulminating, but Mr. Haldeman-Julius *does* sell the classics and he never interferes with the text.

1926
'LOVE COLONY' SCANDAL ENDS IN PRISON AND HUGE FINE.

Former Eton Boy Who Took 'Soul-Mate' to Live with His Wife.

Behind a message from New York, announcing that the "Love Colony" at Allentown, Pennsylvania, has been brought to an end by a sentence on its founder, Charles Garland, an ex-Eton boy, of sixty days' imprisonment and a fine of £100,000, lies an extraordinary story of a young man who spurned wealth, brought home another woman to live with his wife and child, and generally tried to practise a new social doctrine of complete freedom for the sexes.

"REYNOLDS'S" CORRESPONDENT.

NEW YORK, Saturday.—The fines and imprisonment have been inflicted on Charles Garland on charges of adultery.

Garland called his retreat the "April Farm Love Colony," and attracted to it from time to time a considerable number of young and prepossessing women. The "Love Colony" had been in existence for several years.

Nearly six years ago, when he was twenty-one, Garland, heir to a million dollars (£200,000), not long down from Harvard, one of America's most distinguished universities—he was at Eton about 1912—and a nephew of Mr. Charles Tuller Garland, the well-known English racehorse owner and a leading member of the Warwickshire Hunt, startled American society and many friends in England by declaring his adherence to a new social doctrine.

He stated that, in his view, no one had the right to possess so much money as he was heir to, and that he did not intend to accept it.

He was then tilling a small patch of ground on Long Island and living in a shack.

"A Soul-Mate" Passion.

At first his pretty young wife shared his views, but after spending a winter in a cold and sparsely furnished shack she changed her mind. Garland then decided to accept the money, but to settle three-quarters of it on his wife and little daughter Margaret.

He proposed to retain only £100 himself and to hand the residue to ten friends whom he could trust to administer the money for the benefit of the community. This was done and the money used for helping young artists, sculptors, and authors.

Then came domestic difficulties. Young Garland conceived a "soul mate" passion for his mother's secretary, a former Boston art student named Lilian Conrad, whom he brought to share his home with his wife.

His wife refused to accept the triangular arrangement, and they separated.

"I admit," said Garland afterwards, "without shame or fear that my love for my mother's secretary, Lilian, brought about my separation from my wife."

Then he made this remarkable declaration: "The man who can love two women with an equal spiritual depth and true emotion is gifted with just twice the depth of soul possessed by a man who can love only one."

Miss Conrad's contribution to this discussion was: "I accept Garland's proposal to share his home with his wife. I love Garland. My philosophy is the same as his. I also love Mrs. Garland more than any woman I know. I am truly sorry for her."

"Unthinkable Arrangement."

Mrs. Garland's statement was brief and to the point. "I refused my husband's suggestion," she said, "that I should share my home with Miss Conrad. Such philosophy, such an arrangement, is unthinkable. So we parted."

It was not long after this that the soul mate, Miss Conrad, left Garland, and he went back to his shack minus wife, soul mate, and fortune.

Subsequently, he found the Love Colony, where, with a few kindred spirits, he carried out the doctrine for which he has now been sentenced and fined.

Last January there were ten members of the Love Colony—five men and five women. The colony declared that the relations of men and women were a "personal matter," and that it was not for the Government to regulate them "unless the persons concerned disturb the peace and health of the community."

CHARLES GARLAND.

The doings of the colony became more and more notorious, until the authorities were compelled to take action.

How the means were found to run the colony is not clear, but presumably some of the residents of it had resources of their own to conduct their social experiment.

It has now come to an end, with the ruin of the man who started it.

Mr. Charles Tuller Garland, who was reported to have stated in an interview that he would not be surprised at his nephew doing all this, had his polo and cricket grounds and a fine riding school on his famous English estate at Moreton Morrell. They were reputed to have cost £250,000 to lay down.

1903
RED HAIR AND CHARACTER.

"All nations are agreed that there is something wrong with the red-haired man," said Professor Karl Pearson to a Birmingham audience last night.

The professor was talking of the value of any estimate of the mental and moral character by means of the physical character, and supported his contention with regard to the red-haired person by pointing out that in the Passion Play of 1500 one of the necessary properties was a red wig for Judas Iscariot to wear, while in the mediæval paintings Judas was invariably represented with red hair. Professor Pearson gave some credence to what had been said in relation to the colour of the eyes: "Blue eyes go to heaven, grey to paradise, black to purgatory, and green to hell."

1920
CHARACTER IN FACE.

How Parents and Teachers May Decide Vocations.

How to tell a child's character and to discover from its features the career for which its talents are best fitted was described at the College of Preceptors, Bloomsbury-square, yesterday, by Dr. Henry Chellew, of the London School of Economics, in a lecture on Vocational Guidance. Dr. Chellew contended that it was the duty of parents, in conjunction with schoolmasters, to diagnose from the child's character what his vocation should be and put the child to that vocation. It is undoubtedly the case, he said, that "Nature seems to decide in advance by face and gesture what many people were best intended to be."

Dr. Chellew's system of character reading is thus summarised:

Triangular full face.
 Essentially a mental type. Unromantic, strenuous, "eats little; thinks much. Feels little, sleeps little." Usually makes good accountant, chemist, or engineer.

Round full face.
 Essentially a vital type. Sentimental, easy-going; "sleeps and eats all the time, does little work." Makes usually a good mathematician.

Pointed profile ("such as the Chamberlain family").
 Uncompromising, inclined to procrastination.

Convex profile ("such as Mr. Horatio Bottomley").
 Egoistic, self-reliant.

Convex features (type usually called "pugnacious").
 Alert, keen, practical, penetrative, impatient.

Concave features.
 Mild, reflective, patient.

Receding forehead.
 Quick thinking.

Advancing forehead ("such as that of Sir Oliver Lodge").
 Great capacity for deep thought, but "will never live to keep pace with the man or woman whose forehead slopes back."

An ear situated a long way behind the eye, said Dr. Chellew, indicated strong vitality, while the higher the ear in the head the greater the intelligence of the child.

Under the modern system of education "either you 'fit in' or the school gives you up. The many people who do not 'fit in' are often the biggest successes."

PHENOMENA

Obiter Scripta.

A Mystery.

Although it has just been stated on oath at an inquest that upon the body of a man struck by lightning there were the unmistakable photographs of a fern leaf and the leaf of a tree, the scientists will to a man bid us dissociate the impressions from thought of lightning. It is impossible, we are told, for lightning to convert the human body into a sensitised plate, and upon it leave a photograph. Which is disconcerting in view of the abundant stories told every year to the contrary. Rightly or wrongly attributed to lightning, there are many cases on record in which the "facts" have been against the dicta of the critics. Only last year a man lying in a hospital was found to have clearly imprinted upon his flesh the image of a crucifix planted at the head of his cot. This was ascribed to a flash of lightning which had passed over him as he lay there. Similar was the experience of a lady upon whom there remained the indelible picture of that part of a chair against which she had leaned when struck by lightning; and of a farm girl upon whose body there was imprinted the outline of the cow she was driving when struck by lightning. The pictures get there, if not by the aid of the lightning, then by some process as inexplicable as the presence of the fly in the amber.

1905

1934
NATURE'S LANTERNS : By Hellier

READING BY TOADSTOOL LIGHT.

IN BRAZIL, BORNEO AND MANY OTHER PARTS OF THE WORLD GROW LARGE 'FUNGI' (TOADSTOOLS) WHICH GIVE OFF ENOUGH LIGHT TO READ A PAPER BY. THE EFFECT IS VERY GHOSTLY AND YOU EXPECT GNOMES TO APPEAR AT ANY MOMENT.

'ST. ELMO'S FIRE'

A LOVELY SIGHT IS SOMETIMES SEEN AT SEA. POINTS OF BRILLIANT LIGHT APPEAR AT MASTHEADS AND OTHER PARTS OF THE SHIP AND WILL EVEN SURROUND A SAILOR WORKING ALOFT, OUTLINING HIM WITH FLAME, BUT WITHOUT HURTING HIM. THIS LIGHT COMES FROM THE ELECTRICITY IN THE AIR. IT OCCURS ONLY ON DARKEST NIGHTS AND APPEARS EVEN IN GALES AND RAIN.

LIVING JEWELS.

THE FIREFLY IS A BEETLE. ITS LIGHT COMES FROM TWO SPOTS ON ITS HEAD, ALSO FROM ANOTHER SPOT UNDER THE BODY. S.AMERICAN LADIES SOMETIMES FIX FIREFLIES TO THEIR HAIR AND DRESS.

SHINES FROM BIRTH.

THE GLOW-WORM IS ALSO A BEETLE. ITS EGGS ARE LUMINOUS, ALSO THE GRUBS. THE FEMALE GIVES THE MOST LIGHT, WHICH COMES FROM THE END OF THE TAIL.

'WILL O' THE WISP'.

FROM EARLIEST TIMES WE READ OF A MYSTIC LIGHT LEADING TRAVELLERS TO THEIR DOOM IN THE MARSHES. THIS 'WILL O' THE WISP' IS REALLY INFLAMMABLE MARSH-GAS, CAUSED BY DECAYING VEGETABLE MATTER IN MARSHY WATER, THE LIGHT BEING CARRIED ACROSS THE WATER ON THE BREEZE. IN PARTS OF ITALY AND SICILY, WAVERING LIGHTS OF MARSH-GAS ARE SOMETIMES SEEN AT SEA OFF MARSHY COASTS AND LOOKED UPON AS BAD OMENS BY FISHERMEN.

1938
These Trees are Lightning-Proof

"Reynolds" Correspondent

THE Thunderstorm Census Organisation, whose 2,000 members record thunderstorms and information about them, has amassed many interesting facts.

Mr. S. T. E. Dark, a London schoolmaster and a research member of the organisation, revealed some of them to me yesterday.

Of 164 trees struck by lightning in the past four years, he told me, 51 were oak, 32 elm, 27 ash, 13 poplar and nine firs. No beech trees were struck.

"Why the oak and the elm attract lightning more than other trees we can't yet say," said Mr. Dark, "but we do know that the beech tree gives the best shelter in a thunderstorm and is least likely to be struck by lightning."

1939
——Water-Tree——

Constant clear water trickles night and day from the branches of an old birch tree at Stonehouse Farm, West Harling, Norfolk.

Water began dripping from the tree trunk about a month ago. Then the branches began running.

The villagers scratched their heads, for there is no stream, pond or ditch anywhere in the vicinity. They decided to saw away a branch and now fresh spring water runs steadily from the cut.

Experts say that an underground spring has forced its way up through the trunk of the tree.

1938
BALL OF FIRE FALLS ON MEN, INJURES FIVE

FIVE workmen were injured when a "thunderbolt" dropped in Ipswich late at night. The men were working on a new school in Copleston-road, and when the "thunderbolt" dropped near them a number of workmen were knocked to the ground.

A twenty-gallon drum of petrol exploded, badly burning one man. Electric lighting in the district was put out of order.

J. Hurn, who was handling the drum of petrol, said yesterday he saw a ball of fire fall. "A second later the petrol exploded and I was completely knocked out."

1908
PHOSPHORESCENT TREE.

A phosphorescent tree has been discovered in a wood on the Cleland estate in the Wishaw district, near Glasgow.

A number of young men, says the "Scotsman," were startled by what they thought was an apparition in the woods, but on approaching it they found that it was an ash tree, the trunk of which gave off a light brilliant enough to read by.

1931
METEOR CRASH

SHOCK FELT IN 40-MILE RADIUS

From Our Own Correspondent.

NEW YORK, Wednesday.

A huge meteoric stone fell early to-day on a farm near Malinta, 35 miles south-west of Toledo, shaking buildings in many towns in Northern Ohio.

The stone, which was 10ft. wide and 5ft. in depth, is one of the largest recorded in recent times.

The impact was felt within a 40-mile radius, and scores of persons leapt from their beds fearing an earthquake shock.

Damage appears to have been confined to broken windows, but the shock was so violent that it caused widespread alarm.

Following the crash telephone communication with Malinta was cut off, and it is thought the wires may have been blown down by the rush of air caused by meteor's fall.

A woman, who telephoned before wires were broken, described the object as falling with a noise like thunder.

1908
FREAK WEATHER.

Phenomenal Whirlwind and Two Hours' Torrential Rain.

While a number of farm hands were haymaking near Mountcharles, County Donegal, on Friday evening, several haycocks in an adjoining field were suddenly lifted with a whirling motion.

Revolving rapidly in a wide circle, and still ascending, they rose to a height of three-quarters of a mile and then began to disperse. Part of the hay was subsequently found to have descended in a cornfield a mile distant.

The strangest part of the affair was that perfect calm reigned all around the place.

Yesterday a violent thunderstorm of two hours' duration occurred at Yarmouth. Torrents of rain fell, and the streets were flooded. In Northgate-street, the main approach to the town from the north, the water was a foot deep, and invaded the shops and houses.

1907
TATTOOED BY LIGHTNING.

Curious Seaweed-Design on Bodies of Victims.

Interesting medical evidence was given last night at the inquest held at Goring, near Worthing, on the bodies of the two young labourers, Sidney Charles Orchard and Frederick Bennet Wadey, who were struck dead by lightning on Sunday afternoon.

Dr. J. S. Crook stated that there were deep marks of torn flesh on the skin in patches from the head down over the chest to the feet, but whereas in Wadey's case the bulk of the fluid would seem to have gone down his right leg, in Orchard's case it was the left leg only that was injured.

There was a general blueness and congestion of the skin over both bodies. It was like very delicate, finely-divided seaweed, rather than twigs, and it was not unlike a delicate fern. It reminded him more than anything else of the frost that crystallised on window panes. The marks were more pronounced in the case of a third man who was only injured.

The jury returned a verdict of death from misadventure.

1927
NEEDLE IN GIRL'S BODY.

YEAR'S TOUR FROM FOOT TO HEAD.

Miss Dora Watkinson, a maid at Westley Hall, Bury St. Edmunds, a few days ago drew from between two of her lower teeth half an inch of broken needle, stated to be part of a darning needle that entered her foot a year ago and broke off.

Her foot was X-rayed at the time, and she appeared to feel no ill effects. She discovered the fragment in her lower jaw through her tongue being scratched.

WHERE IS YOUR UMBRELLA?
Lionel Hale
1936

I have often tried to pretend to myself that I leave behind me my umbrella, my gloves or my books, not because I am careless, but for the admirable reason that I am lost in beautiful thoughts. But when I discover the loss, my thoughts are anything but beautiful. On balance, my thoughts suffer.

But when I look at the records of lost property, I realise that my bitter thoughts about my commonplace losses must pale before the thoughts of people who are forgetful on the grand scale. I do not envy the feelings of the man who left an alligator on the Southern Railway—unless, of course, he did it on purpose, which is quite possible.

And what about the owners of the elephant found straying in Camberwell, the goldfish left under the seat of the Tube, various horses and carts discovered derelict, canaries in cages, Alsatian wolf-hounds tethered to seats on the tops of omnibuses, white mice, and a wooden horse with glaring eyes from a travelling fair?

In wet weather, Londoners lose 1,158 umbrellas a day; but we may doubt whether the sum total of their vexation adds up to the remorse of a man who has lost an elephant.

Losses of this kind, of course, are worse than careless; they are inconsiderate. An ordinary loss—a guitar, jewellery, even a wringer mangle—embarrasses only the loser; but an elephant embarrasses the finder as well. Findings, by English law, are not keepings; and nobody who finds an elephant, or a snake, or a skunk in his railway carriage, is likely to quarrel with English law on that point.

Again, the discovery in taxis of human thigh-bones and skulls, and even of complete skeletons, is not likely to give much pleasure to the finder, even though these—by no means uncommon trove—turn out to be anatomical specimens belonging to medical students. At first glance, I fancy, skeletons must seem grisly fellow-travellers.

73 GIRLS FAINT WHEN FOUR BOYS COLLAPSE
1938

From Our Own Correspondent

NEW YORK, Sunday.

SEEING four boys collapse while drilling in a school playground, girl spectators began to collapse, too.

In a few minutes 73 girls had fainted, and for some time the playground—at New Hanover High School, Wilmington, North Carolina — resembled a casualty clearing station.

Here is the explanation, offered today by Dr. William Marston, one of the foremost psychologists in the United States.

"It was a case of mass hypnosis. The girls, watching the drill movements, became emotionally identified with the boys.

"Soothed and unified into a single pattern, they were amenable to the suggestion offered by the collapse of the boys."

All the girls have recovered, though they were ill enough to be sent to bed for the day.

1906
A Blessing in Disguise.

Venice has suffered from a remarkable hailstorm, the hailstones being so large that they killed many cats on the roofs of the houses. The Venetians are rejoicing, as the cats in their city are a perfect plague.

1921
SHOWER OF FROGS.
THOUSANDS OF SMALL HOPPERS FALL AT GIBRALTAR.

During a recent thunderstorm at Gibraltar a shower of frogs fell on the North Front.

Thousands of these small hopping creatures, unusual at the Rock, may be seen in the hedges (says Reuter), and have aroused much curiosity.

Some seven years ago a similar phenomenon occurred, and later a shower of sand covered everything with a pink deposit.

1914
BURNING ALIVE.
GIRL'S ABNORMAL TEMPERATURE BREAKS THERMOMETER.

According to the "St. Petersburg Gazette," there is a girl in Kiev University Hospital, lying ill with typhoid, whose temperature is so abnormally high that it has actually broken a thermometer which was capable of registering up to 113deg. Fahr.

The attempt to take her temperature was made, says the "Daily Citizen" correspondent, with an ordinary centigrade clinical thermometer marked to 45deg. (113deg. Fahr.). The mercury column quickly reached its greatest limits and the glass was shattered.

Professors Obraszoff and Janowsky subsequently took the girl's temperature with a special thermometer, which recorded the heat of the girl's body as being 131deg. Fahr. They declare that she still retains consciousness, but is practically burning alive.

1920
WAS IT THE QUAKE?
Experts Baffled by the Mysterious Stampede of Sheep.

Had the Great Earthquake anything to do with the stampede of thousands of sheep reported in Cambridgeshire at about the same time?

At least 30 widely separated flocks broke out of confinement in a panic, and fled in all directions.

Farmers are puzzled to account for it. One theory put forward by Mr. W. Varney Webb, Chief Constable of Cambridgeshire, is that the sheep were panic-stricken by the meteors and the Northern Lights, which were strikingly brilliant on that particular night.

On the previous day the sheep were very restless and many jumped over their hurdles.

When sheep jump their hurdles this is said to be a sure sign of coming bad weather. From time to time the theory that earthquakes affect the weather has also been put forward.

Lord Lambourne, who has a wide experience of farming, told *The Evening News* to-day that he inclined to believe the theory that the meteors and the Northern Lights were responsible.

In his long experience he was unable to remember anything of the same extraordinary nature happening.

1903
WOLF-CHILDREN.

The story of the Sydney woman who, as reported in yesterday's "Express," has just been fined £1 in an Australian police court for leaving her child to be reared in a chicken run, with the consequence that the little one could do nothing but imitate the fowls in every way, even to roosting at night, has caused much comment.

At the offices of the Zoological Society the opinion of an eminent ornithologist was sought. "Apart from its pathos," he said, "it is an extremely interesting case. I am unaware of any previous instance of a child being reared by birds.

"The nearest approach to it happened in Scandinavia, where a peasant, finding a wild swan frozen fast in a lake, took it home, revived it, and made it a domestic pet.

"One very stormy night his wife was brought to bed with a child. Neither doctor nor nurse was obtainable. A baby was born, and the wife died. The husband was in despair for the baby's life, when he remembered his pet swan, that was accustomed to repose in front of the kitchen fire.

"He took the tiny baby down and laid it beside the swan. The bird seemed to understand what was required, and spread its wings over the baby, which it kept alive and warm for many hours until a nurse was obtained.

Many Instances.

"As regards children who have been reared by wolves there are many true instances, although the case of Romulus and Remus, who were nourished by a she-wolf, is, of course, a fable.

"But Mowgli, the little wolf-child hero of Mr. Kipling's 'Jungle Book,' is founded upon fact. Particulars of such cases have been recorded by Colonel Sleeman and Sir R. Murchison. They have occurred for the most part in Northern India, especially in Oudh The children have all been boys, and were all apparently idiots.

"No grown-up people have ever been found among wolves. The ultimate end of these wolf-children has probably been the obvious one consequent upon their getting into a set of less scrupulous wolves.

"Those animals have frequently carried off infants in the districts of Cawnpore and Lucknow. Some undoubtedly have been eaten, but others have been brought up and educated after the wolf fashion.

"Some have been reclaimed several years later, but have never got rid of a strong wolfish smell, and they have been known to receive friendly visits from little companies of their former savage acquaintances."

Zoologists have a record of a typical case where two soldiers of a King of Oudh surprised and captured three animals who came down to drink on the bank of the Goomtee river.

Two of the animals were evidently young wolves; but the nature of the third was a mystery until the men got near it, and saw that it was a small naked boy on all fours.

1940
"LOST" TRIBES
Primitive Savages of the Everglades

Lost for more than 100 years, descendants of a forgotten Indian tribe still live in primitive savagery in the swampy Everglades south of Florida.

Dr. Laemme, who is excavating ancient Timucuan mounds near St Augustine, Florida, has been told by Seminole Indian chiefs of the "lost" tribe.

Only the old men among the Seminoles have ever seen them at close quarters. They wear no clothes and use flint-tipped spears

If they are Timucuans they must be descendants of survivors of the white man's advance, which few Indians escaped.—B.U.P.

1903
A Wolf-Boy.

He bit and scratched furiously in resisting capture, and when taken into human society drank like a dog, tore up his clothes, and would eat nothing but bones and raw meat, after first smelling it well.

After many months he learned to say the name of a lady who adopted him, but could never articulate more than a few words. His intellect was always clouded, but, dog-like, he was exceptionally quick at understanding signs.

"People who live much among animals always gain some animal characteristics, even if such be confined to the ability to imitate a particular animal's call. For myself, I can cause a stir of curiosity among many birds by imitating their cries, and I have known men who can in that way bring back a tom-cat to a certain spot over and over again cause quite a commotion in a rookery at nesting-time, or put a bird in a complete state of mystery as to the whereabouts of its supposed mate."

Gilbert White has recorded a remarkable case of a boy who lived so much among bees that he became a very bee-bird.

In winter he dozed away the days in a state almost of torpor. He spent all his time by the fire. But in summer bees were his sole food and amusement. He rushed after them all day long in the sunshine, buzzing all the while like a bee.

Every kind of bee was his prey. He was never stung, although he must have caught thousands, and sucked them for their honey. Some he kept in bottles; others between his shirt and his skin, until wanted.

He would actually enter private gardens to steal bees, sometimes turning hives upside down. Needless to say, the boy was a hopeless idiot.

1936
Ape-man Found in Forest

UNABLE TO SPEAK

HELSINGFORS.

A strange creature, half man, half ape [reminiscent of the castaway Ayrton in Jules Verne's "Mysterious Island"] has been captured near Riga, Latvia, by a band of foresters.

The band, engaged in inspecting one of the great forests of the region, suddenly came upon the man-ape, crouching at the foot of the tree. As they approached, the creature fled and, swinging itself on to an overhanging branch, climbed with remarkable speed and agility to the top of a tree.

One of the foresters took a shot at it, whereupon the creature, emitting a wild shriek, crashed to the ground.

The foresters seized it, found it to be entirely naked, and its body covered with long, thick hair.

Upon taking the captive to a nearby village it was discovered that he was actually a farm labourer who h appeared many years ago.

The ape-man can neither speak nor understand anything when spoken to, but lets out yells of delight when meat and fruit are placed before him.—Reuter.

1938
Girl Tarzan Captured

A GIRL Tarzan, her naked body burnt brown by sun and exposure, with long finger nails and uttering inarticulate cries, has been captured by hunters in the mountains of Adana, Anatolia.

They had just killed a large brown bear in the mountain forests when out of the trees came the girl menacing them with cries and gestures.

After being overpowered she was taken to a medical institution at Brusa, where she refused all cooked food.

She also refused to sleep in a bed and was given a mattress on which she slept in a dark corner of her room.

ADOPTED BY BEAR

Investigations revealed that a two-years-old child had disappeared from a nearby village 14 years before and it is presumed the child wandered into the forest and was "adopted" by a bear.

Doctors hope to develop the girl's power of speech.

At present she is incapable of concentrating on any subject, although she responds to music, sometimes bursting into wild, unintelligible songs.

She exhibits most interest in a glass mirror in her room and will sit before it for hours gazing at herself.

"I Walked on All-Fours and Ate Ostrich Eggs"

1939

Evening Standard Reporter

PROFESSOR R. RUGGLES GATES, heredity expert at the University of London (King's College), is now satisfied that South Africa's famous "baboon boy" really was brought up by baboons.

To-day he received a letter from Professor Raymond Dart, of Witwatersrand University, telling him that the police have corroborated many of the stories.

The letter encloses a statement taken from the boy himself, now an adult farm worker at Thornkloof, Trappes Valley.

This reads:

"I can recall only a few incidents of my life among the baboons. My food consisted mainly of crickets, ostrich eggs, prickly pears, green mealies and wild honey.

"I was kicked on the head by an ostrich while raiding its nest, and was often stung by bees while robbing their hives, and once fell and broke my leg.

"**While with the baboons I walked on all-fours and slept in the bush entirely naked.**

"I was busy hunting for food one day with my baboon companions when two policemen shot at us with revolvers, but I was captured by one of the policemen."

The "boy," a native who is now named Lucas, was found near Grahamstown in 1921 by a police patrol who had been chasing a troop of baboons. He was then about 12 and he made guttural noises like the baboons.

He now speaks Afrikaans and English.

1905

"TOAD-IN-THE-HOLE."

As some men were felling an oak tree at Pulham St. Mary, Norfolk, a toad that had apparently been embedded in the tree for years fell out. It died in a few minutes.

KILLED BY A THISTLE.

A potter, of Hanley, has died from blood-poisoning caused by a thistle which pricked his hand.

1929

APE WOMAN SHOT

Theory That Negress Was Brought Up as Member of Herd—Shock for Hunter

Reporting to a German firm which has plantations in the Cameroons, an agent describes how an elephant hunter shooting at what he took to be an ape in a tree found to his astonishment that it was a negro woman.

She was without clothes and did not have the customary tattoo marks.

The mystery was investigated by the authorities, who, says Reuter, came to the conclusion that the woman must have been brought up from childhood by the apes and lived with the herd as one of them.

1934

"WILD" MAN CAPTURED

HE ONLY SPEAKS "ANIMAL LANGUAGE"

Belgrade, Saturday.—A party of men, hunting in the woods near Uzitza, saw what they thought to be a strange animal running through the wood. They fired, and the creature dropped.

When they approached they found a youth of about 15 years of age, completely naked, covered with mud and hair. He was unhurt, but terrified at the sight of his captors.

He was taken back, and it was discovered that he did not speak any known language, and appears to have lived most of his life in the woods, feeding on roots and berries.

He can run amazingly fast, moves naturally on all fours, and can communicate with wild animals and birds by imitating their calls perfectly.—Reuter.

1930

MAN SHARES LIONS' FAMILY LIFE

NATIVE OUTCAST BEFRIENDED IN THE WILDS

(FROM OUR OWN CORRESPONDENT)

JOHANNESBURG, Sept. 28.

Following the spoor of a wounded buck, which obviously had been dragged by a lion, a Northern Transvaal farmer expected to meet the lion in its lair, but was astonished to find instead a native tearing and eating the raw flesh.

Investigations showed that the native, years previously, had been accused of murder in a tribe and hid in a cave, which proved to be the home of a lion family.

The man drove the animals off, but the latter eventually became accustomed to him. The man lived on roots and honey, but one day he found a buck which the lions had killed and helped himself. Afterwards he regularly shared the daily kill.

The lions one by one disappeared as the family grew up, until only a lioness was left, but she regularly supplied his larder until shot by the farmer.

The native was greatly distressed by the loss of his wild companion, but is now a happy member of the farmer's labour staff.

1927
4,000,000-YEAR-OLD MAN?

FILM PARTY'S DISCOVERY.

Two members of the British Instructional Films claim to have discovered in the island of Cyprus a fossilised imprint of the foot of a prehistoric man on a mountain which geologically belongs to the Eocene period.

[The Eocene period is the first part of the third (Cainozoic) geological period, put at from 40,000,000 to 4,000,000 years ago. The earliest evidence so far of the existence of man goes back only about 50,000 years, to the end of the early Palæolithic period.]

The fossil was found during the taking of a film for the Cyprus Government, and it is now in Cyprus Museum. Mr. E. W. Edwards, of the British Instructional Films, said to the "Daily News and Westminster" last night: "In a dry water-course on Mount Hilarion we came upon a fragment of rock similar to the rest of the mountain, and in the fragment there was the imprint. It had filled with a liquid, which had fossilised into flint. If this footmark is definitely identified as belonging to the Eocene period, there will have to be modifications of the date of the 'birth of man.'"

1944
Flowers by the Witch's Grave Stop Her Tricks

"Evening News" Reporter

FLOWERS have been found every Sunday beside the two-ton "Witch's Stone" at the crossroads of Scrapfaggot Green, Great Leighs, Essex, since it was replaced a fortnight ago to stop queer psychic happenings in the village.

"All is quiet since the stone was put back," says Mr. W. J. Sykes, of the St Anne's Castle Inn, "but we can't explain the flowers."

The stone was shifted when bulldozers widened the road for American transport. Then queer things started happening—a great boulder was found one morning outside the Dog and Gun, chickens were discovered locked up inside rabbit-hutches, rabbits were loose in the garden, bells in the church clock chimed irregularly, 30 sheep and two horses were found dead in a field, and a village builder found his scaffold-poles tumbled about like match-sticks. A vigilance committee was formed, but discovered nothing.

Tradition had it that the stone marked the place where a witch had been buried at the crossroads, and Mr. Harry Price, the psychical investigator, recommended the parish council to have it restored to the exact original spot. This was done at night with the use of a compass.

1925
DEAD SNAKE IN HIS SUPPER BOTTLE.

Pouring oatmeal stout into a glass while at supper a Folkestone man was startled to see the head of a snake sticking out of the bottle. He took the bottle to the office of the Sanitary Inspector, and the dead snake, 16 inches long, was pulled out.

How it got into the bottle is a mystery.

1926
EGGSTRAORDINARY.

OTTAWA, Saturday. — "Earthquake, beware April 21," was the warning contained in the shell of an egg found by Mrs. Alfred Turner, of North Bay, Ontario on the floor of her hen house. The inscription is raised and the lettering is slightly darker in shade than the remainder of the shell. The egg was full of meat, and it is held impossible that it could have been lettered from the inside.—Exchange. 1926

1904
BUTTERFLY SWARMS IN MID-OCEAN.

WRITING in *La Nature*, the captain of a boat belonging to the American Board of Public Works gives an account of an extraordinary swarm of butterflies which he and his crew witnessed on the high seas:

The white butterflies appeared as numerous as flakes of snow, and a person might have thought that he was in the midst of a storm, since the insects at times formed very compact clouds that produced the appearance of an approaching squall. During two days the voyage was effected entirely under such conditions. Thinly-scattered swarms were also encountered. Many of these insects fell into the water, while the mass was always endeavouring to ascend, and the wind blowing from the east was ever carrying it seaward.

1925
CLUE IN A DEAD MAN'S EYE.

POLICE REPORT TO BE TESTED IN COURT.

EIGHTFOLD CRIME.

MASSACRE TO CONCEAL THEFTS.

"Sunday Express" Correspondent.

BERLIN, Saturday, July 4.

IS it possible for the eye of a murdered man to retain a picture of his assassin that can be photographed by the police and used as evidence?

The question will figure largely at the trial of Fritz Angerstein at Limburg on Monday.

He is charged with the murder of eight people, and the police allege that a photograph of the retina of one of the victim's eyes revealed a picture of Angerstein with his raised arm gripping a hatchet.

1921
LIFE IN OTHER WORLDS.

Startling Claim by Frenchman.

LIVING SPECKS FOUND IN METEORITES.

From a Scientific Correspondent.

The discovery of the existence of micro-organisms—in other words, specks of living matter—in 21 specimens of meteorites and a number of igneous rocks that have been examined, is claimed by MM. Galippe and Souffland in the French scientific journal, "Comptes Rendus."

They claim further, that even after the samples have been subjected to high temperatures the organisms embedded in them have come to life and multiplied when placed on suitable culture mediums in the laboratory.

If these claims are verified it should lead to great advances in our conceptions of the universe and of man's place in it.

For if micro-organisms can come to life from the romantic dust of meteorites then the belief would be strengthened that Life must also exist in other worlds and in other regions of this far-flung universe, and that its germs must be practically indestructible.

About 23 People Will Vanish Today!
Some For Weeks—Some For Ever

1948

1907
FIGHT WITH A "SEA SERPENT."

A Clevedon (Somerset) correspondent forwards the following story of a strange adventure which he says befel Mr. McNaughten, a Scottish visitor to the town. The incident, which occurred on Sunday last, was, he says, witnessed by many spectators:—

"Mr. McNaughten was quietly rowing in a little skiff about a mile off the Clevedon Pier when a large snaky object, which he describes as 'like a huge mummy, with large sunken eyes enveloped in a sort of hairy flap' suddenly appeared at the rear of the boat—about twenty yards away. It approached by a series of leaps and dives, causing the sea to be greatly disturbed. Mr. McNaughten says that by plunging the oars into the surf he endeavoured to keep his antagonist at bay. But his efforts were only momentarily successful. In a few seconds it had reached within a few yards of the boat.

"'I can only dimly recollect what happened,' he continued. 'The flabby monster seemed to leap straight out of the water—straight as an arrow at me. I hardly know what I did. I think I must have ducked and crashed the oar into the creature. At any rate I was flung violently into the water. When I regained the surface I managed to clamber into the boat. My terrible antagonist was nowhere in sight. In a dazed condition, scarcely knowing what I did, I succeeded in reaching Portishead.'"

1938
THEY'VE SEEN SEA MONSTER

TWO Suffolk fishermen long hardened to the terrors of the sea, came back to Southwold yesterday still frightened at what they had seen when trawling in a calm sea Reason?

The Sea Monster
This is what Ernest Watson said: "A great head showed itself above the water, then flashed past like a torpedo. It struck up such a wash that all we could see afterwards was its camel-like back sticking out. It towered over us, and went so fast that after a few minutes it was out of sight.

"I should never have believed it if I hadn't seen it," said William Herrington, the other fisherman.

"I just saw its head once—when Ernie shouted—and all I saw afterwards was its humped back. It must have been 60ft. long. It was grey and seemed to have a round back. It was big enough to sink any boat of our size if it had come nearer."

1945
Chased monster in a motor-launch

There's a monster at large in the North Sea, according to the crew of a salvage ship working a mile off the mouth of the Tyne.

At first they thought it was a floating derrick, but Skipper Lowrie, of Kincardine, Scotland, and two of his crew, set out in a motor-launch to make sure.

It was a monster all right, says the skipper. "We chased the monster for between five and ten minutes," he said. "Its back was eight to ten feet across."

1942
Monster may be 'Nessie'

DWELLERS on Loch Ness side are convinced that the sea monster washed ashore at Deepdale Holm, Orkney, is their own monster, affectionately known as "Nessie."

On May 2, 1933, it was announced a giant creature had been seen in Loch Ness.

"The Orkney monster, 24ft. long, is covered with hair, and has a head like a cow, only flatter.

"In 1934 our monster was seen off Dores Bay," a Loch Ness man said emphatically. "Obviously it was making for the open sea. I should think this animal at Deepdale Holm is undoubtedly our monster—they leave their homes to die, don't they?"

The carcase at Deepdale Holm is to be shipped to London for scientific investigation.

1905
Blue-blooded Fish.

A hundred eyeless fish have been brought to the surface from one of the wells of the Crude Oil Company, Whittier, California. The fish are transparent, and their blood is blue.

1937
"SEA-SERPENT" CAPTURED

FORTUNE HARBOUR (Newfoundland).

Fishermen have caught a sea-serpent off the coast here after a two-day battle with guns, harpoons, and lances.

The monster was 35 feet long with a girth of 25 feet and a tail nine feet across. It had flippers but no fins.

Fortune Harbour is 25 miles northeast of Botwood, base of the Imperial Airways Transatlantic liners now making survey flights.—Reuter.

1938
Vicar Saw 60 ft. Sea Monster

Confirmation of the report that there is a 60ft. monster in the sea off Southwold, Suffolk—two fishermen claim to have seen it—was given yesterday by the Vicar of Southwold, the Rev. R. N. Pyke.

"I was standing with my wife and another clergymen in my house on the sea front," he said. "when I saw a very remarkable creature pass the pier head at a terrific speed.

"I can quite believe the fishermen who said they saw the monster travelling at fifty miles an hour. I saw it travelling faster than the quickest motor-boat I have ever seen."

Witch Doctor Detective
1934

JUNGLE JUSTICE IN NEW GUINEA

Bamboo Pole "Names" Murderer

SYDNEY.

An extraordinary story of how a murderer was detected by sorcery after all other methods had failed, comes from Salamoa, New Guinea. Here is an eye-witness's account of what occurred:

An excited throng of natives gathered round the "Devil House" in Salamoa, surrounding several gaily-bedecked witch doctors.

The witch doctors were trying to discover the murderer of a native named Tousa, who had been found speared a few days earlier. Making horrible noises and chanting loudly, the crowd, composed of natives from all the tribes in the neighbourhood, eagerly followed the movements of the witch doctors, who were dancing round a bamboo pole, ten feet high, stuck in the grave of the murdered man.

After certain rites had been performed the natives in turn asked the pole questions, just as if they had been speaking to a living man.

"You fella," they cried, "you get cross along boy along Sepik (a neighbouring district)."

"You fella, you get cross along boy along Aitapo," they continued, mentioning in turn the names of all the districts.

When the name of the district of Logui was brought into the incantation the bamboo pole swayed violently backwards and forwards although no one had touched it.

SUSPECT'S FATE

Then a native from Logui stepped forward and began cross-examining the pole as to the name of the murderer. All the suspects in the district were mentioned, one by one, with no result.

Then the name "Topindik" was called, and the pole started thrashing about with the utmost violence.

After this the natives returned to the Devil House, and the tribal court sentenced Topindik to death.

For days he was shadowed until at last he spat out a piece of betel nut. This was straightway taken to the Devil House and flung in a fire.

According to the native's superstition the guilty man, as soon as the nut began to burn, should have felt burning pains in his stomach. Whether this happened or not no one can say, but the same day Topindik was found lying dead, his face twisted with agony, and not a mark on his body.—Reuter.

The above bears out a statement in the annual report of the Lieutenant-Governor of Papua (Sir Hubert Murray) that in many parts of the Mandated Territory "sorcery is still in existence."

1938
COLONY OF WIZARDS

A COLONY of African witch doctors and mystics is to be founded in England by a 54-years-old woman who has spent five years living alone among the native tribes of French Equatorial Africa.

She is Mrs. Elsie Osborne, of Kensington, whose husband left her a large fortune when he was killed in an air crash in America nine years ago.

In her beautiful Kensington home Mrs. Osborne told the Sunday Referee of her plans.

"I am seeking a large secluded house where I can start my colony to teach people in England some of the mysteries that are in common practice among the natives of Africa," she said.

"I have witnessed so many things that even the greatest scientists would think were miracles that I was determined to bring some of the witch doctors to England to teach their magic."

Mrs. Osborne went to Africa with a party of French biologists, but when the party returned to France she decided to stay on.

One night she was taken by the village witch doctor to witness a murder by magic.

A native had stolen a sacred spear. The native from whom the spear had been stolen publicly invoked the spirits to take vengeance on the thief, naming the man and a certain night for the deed to be done.

"Came From Nowhere"

The night the doomed man was to die Mrs. Osborne went with the witch doctor to the native's hut to see what would happen.

"The hut had thick mud walls and there were no windows. No murderer could come through the door because I was standing in the way," she went on.

"I had the beam of my electric torch focused on the man the whole time.

"**Suddenly there was a hiss. The large sacred spear that had been stolen appeared from nowhere and plunged through the man's body.**

"When I asked the witch doctor how it had been done he just shrugged his shoulders and said 'magic.'

"After I had been among the tribe for two years I felt that I would like to see what my own country was like.

"I told a witch doctor about this and he promised that I should see my own country without moving from Africa.

"I Saw Everything"

"Before I went to bed he gave me a peculiar white drug to take.

"Before I knew what had happened I was unconscious. My mind seemed to travel through space till it reached London. I saw everything. When I woke I jotted down the names of plays and cinema shows that were on at the theatres, the newspaper placards—everything.

"*I thought that I might have dreamed it all. But I checked up on my dream when I came back to London a few weeks ago. It was all as I had seen it.*

"But the cult of the witch doctor is dying out in Africa, and I am determined to start a colony over here to save some of their 'magic' so that it shall not be lost for ever."

PUNISHMENT

TONGUE-TIED

They were very thorough in the 18th century. This pleasant little invention is a scold's bridle, used for nagging women. It is on view at the Antique Dealers' Fair at Grosvenor House London. 1938

1938
HANGMAN FOUND STARVING

Found starving in the street, Arthur Ellis, aged seventy-three, who hanged 500 murderers, is dying in Montreal Hospital.

He lost his job as London's hangman in 1935, when he bungled the execution of a woman. The rope was too long, and she dropped 18ft., the jerk decapitating her.

1937
GIRLS UNDER 16 UNSEXED BY "TRICK" OPERATIONS

FROM OUR OWN CORRESPONDENT

NEW YORK, Sunday.

MRS. Kathryn McCarthy, a former member of the U.S. Congress, who startled the U.S. by revealing the fact that seventy-three girls in a State reformatory at Beloit, Kansas, had been sterilised, made still graver charges to-day.

"Eight of the girls operated on were completely unsexed," she said. "One of those unsexed was only nine. Most of them were under sixteen.

"There has been no reason for these terrible operations. In most cases, the consent of the parents has not been obtained.

"In fact, protests have often been ignored.

"The girls were robbed of their right of motherhood by cruel trickery. They were told they were to have appendicitis operations, after which they could go home.

"The promise that they could leave the institution was kept in only a few cases.

As a result of Mrs. McCarthy's charges, Kansas authorities have ruled that there must be no more sterilisation of girls at Beloit, except in the "most extraordinary emergency."

1921
"DESPICABLE CRIME"

Prisoner Who "Ought to be Drowned."

"You are convicted of the most despicable, the meanest crime that I know. You ought really to be drowned," said Mr. d'Eyncourt, the Marylebone magistrate, when passing the maximum sentence of six months' hard labour on Joseph Phillips, alias Faulkner, a waiter, twenty years of age, living in the High-road, Kilburn, for living wholly on the immoral earnings of Daisy Lorraine. Previous convictions of four months for importuning men and five months for being found in possession of cocaine were mentioned by Mr. C. V. Hill, the solicitor prosecuting.

1930
A KISS IN THE TRAIN.

SCHOOLBOY BOUND OVER FOR ASSAULTING WOMAN.

On a charge of assaulting a woman, aged twenty-four, in a train by kissing her, a schoolboy, aged fourteen, was sentenced, at the Notting Hill Juvenile Court, to five years at a reformatory.

He appealed against the sentence at the London Sessions, and was bound over under the supervision of a rabbi.

The woman complained to a porter at Finchley-road station, and the boy is alleged to have said it was right, and that he was a cad.

1903
15 Years for Stealing 1d. Stamp.

NEW YORK, Friday.—Ellsworth P. de France has just been released from Sioux Falls Prison, after serving a sentence of fifteen years for theft of a penny postage stamp.

1904

A convict at Princetown has, it is stated, been sentenced to receive eighteen strokes for striking a warder who had told him not to take a pet mouse into the Roman Catholic chapel during service.

1936
BOY OF 12 FLEES FROM THE CHAIN GANG

'May Become Public Enemy'

FROM OUR OWN CORRESPONDENT
NEW YORK, Sunday.

FUGITIVE from the chain gang, a twelve-year-old boy is believed to be tramping the country after a terrifying experience at the hands of the authorities in South Carolina.

His adventure started when he left his home in a northern town to tramp to the south to see relatives.

A few days later he was caught leaving a freight train in South Carolina after taking a free ride. He was arrested, and a police court Judge sentenced him to thirty days with the county chain gang.

One morning, before starting work with the gang, he escaped and has not been seen since.

These facts are revealed by the journal of the American National Probation Association, which publishes a picture of the boy, but withholds his name.

"Because of the stupid cruelty with which his case was handled," says the journal, "this twelve-year-old youngster is now presumably one of our great army of hoboes and criminals.

"Society, which could think of no better way to treat a truant child than to put him in a chain gang, can hardly blame him if he develops into one of our notorious public enemies."

1906
UNWORTHY JUDGE.

Child of Three Sentenced to 3½ Months' Imprisonment.

[From Our Correspondent.]
GENEVA, Sunday.

A Swiss child, aged three years, has been sentenced at the criminal assizes at Weinfelden, in the canton of Thurgovie, to three and a half months' imprisonment by the presiding judge, for theft.

It appears that the little fellow was passing a toy shop, and seeing some toys dangling in the street helped himself to two or three articles of little value and took them home.

The little fellow was carried into court, and in answer to questions frankly said that he took the toys home to play with his little sister, as they had none.

To the great astonishment of the Court the judge sentenced the infant to three and a half months' imprisonment.

The "prisoner's" parents pleaded in vain that their child's life would be ruined, and that he was not responsible for the act.

The little fellow was carried out of the court crying, and handed over to a prison official. The Swiss Press are indignant at the unprecedented action of the judge, and condemn the verdict as illegal.

1926
"BORN A DEVIL!"
OLD CONVICT'S STATEMENT IN DOCK.

SENTENCES TOTALLING 53 YEARS' IMPRISONMENT.

Presenting a remarkable figure with his long white hair and a flowing white beard, George Lawrence, 82, trembled in the dock at London Sessions while listening to an extraordinary story of his criminal career, which extends over nearly 70 years. Prisoner pleaded guilty to stealing a Gladstone bag and contents from a truck at St. Pancras Station.—A detective stated that there was a list of convictions against Lawrence dating back to 1858, when he was sent to a reformatory school for three years for theft. Since then he had been convicted on 36 other occasions, and sentences totalling 53 years' imprisonment—38 years' penal servitude and 15 years' hard labour—had been passed upon him. The great majority of the convictions were for larceny. The officer added that on a recent occasion when Lawrence had been "in trouble" he had been dealt with very leniently on giving his promise to enter the workhouse. Unfortunately he would only stay there a short while. When he was asked what his objection to the workhouse was he replied that the men he met there were worse than cattle. Lawrence, in the course of a long and rambling statement from the dock, declared that his parents told him he was "born a devil! although his father was a Baptist." He was confirmed by a bishop, but that did not save him from a sentence of imprisonment for theft when he was only 10 years of age. Since then he had received very severe punishment for petty offences. He had been sent to prison for five years for stealing a bottle of wine, and on three occasions he had been given sentences of 10 years for stealing property which was not valued in any instance at more than £3. The treatment which he underwent in prison in the old days was very harsh. At one time it was the custom for warders to hand a man a loaf of bread for his breakfast with one hand and to give him a punch on the jaw with the other.—The chairman, Sir Robert Wallace, K.C., observed that it was extremely difficult to know what to do with such men as accused, who had now reached the 83rd year of a most extraordinary life. He would postpone sentence on the distinct understanding that Lawrence at once entered the workhouse and remained there. If prisoner did not remain in the workhouse he would be brought up again at the court and sentenced to another term of imprisonment.—Lawrence, as he left the dock, exclaimed: "Thank you, my lord. I will stick it as long as I can."

1904

The epidemic of smallpox at Dewsbury is a reminder that the old-time cure for this scourge was a sound thrashing. There are people still living who in infancy were treated for measles by frequent whippings by their parents, and in the parish accounts of old towns there are many such entries as this from Huntingdon: "To whipping two women yt had ye smallpox—8d."

1900

CAPITAL PUNISHMENT.—Mr. George Ives writes to us regarding certain remarks of our Brussel's Correspondent as follows:—"The death penalty has been abolished in many countries, not, in my opinion, in mercy to the unhappy prisoners. For instance, in Belgium real life long imprisonment prevails, and as much as nine years may be spent in cellular confinement. In Italy, too, perpetual imprisonment is carried out under terrible conditions. In fact, we often find that a violent death by execution has been altered for one that is dragged out through years of suffering and solitude, a state compared with which our somewhat savage penalty of the rope would be some almost an act of charity!"

1912

HANGING AS A FINE ART.

SCIENTISTS DISCUSS THE BEST METHODS.

MEN WHO RECOVERED.

"Express" Special Correspondent.
DUNDEE, Wednesday Night.

The British Association separated to-day after what every one agreed was a memorable meeting.

One of the last papers read dealt with an extraordinary subject—"Hanging Without Tears." It was Dr. Frederic Wood-Jones who introduced this rather grisly subject, but, as he explained, it had its uses, because "if you are going to hang a man you might as well hang him properly."

With skulls of notorious murderers as illustrations and lantern slides of gibbets, he related the history of hanging for a thousand years.

"The Anglo-Saxons," he said, "have a great love of hanging, and the science has constantly improved. In mediæval times many of the places where they hanged people were provided with a kitchen with big pots of pitch. The bodies were pitched all over and made waterproof and able to resist the atmosphere. Then they were hung out as a warning to other offenders.

"This was the beginning of gibbeting. Thames pirates once formed one of the most popular sights of gay London, and there was great disappointment among innkeepers when the pirates were no longer allowed to be hung in chains."

He described the evolution from the simple gibbet into the cage shaped like the human form, in which bodies were exposed, the last instance being seen in 1834. The widow of this victim, Dr. Wood-Jones remarked, had only died a few years ago.

Hanging was also used as an anæsthetic in connection with the old practice of killing a man for high treason by hanging, drawing, and quartering him. This kind of hanging did not necessarily kill a man, for five men hanged in 1447—gentlemen belonging to the Duke of Gloucester—had been marked out to be quartered and drawn when their pardons arrived. They were cut down, and soon were none the worse.

This year a case came to light which showed that the up-to-date method of hanging is the same as the Romans used to practise on the Nubians. A man was executed in 1865 by Calcraft, one of Scotland's most fashionable practitioners.

"His skull," said Dr. Wood-Jones, "shows lesions exactly similar to those in the skulls of the Nubians hanged in Roman days—caused by the right-handed knot under the jaw. This produces the same effect as the boxer's knock-out blow."

1934

GIGGLING GIRLS AT EXECUTION

SEVEN NEGROES HANGED IN THE U.S.

NEW YORK, Saturday.

Seven negroes were executed in three Southern States yesterday, all convicted of murder or assault charges.

The execution which attracted most attention took place at Hernando, Missouri, where Isaac Howard, Ernest McGhee, and Johnny Jones were hanged after they had confessed to an assault on the seventeen-year-old daughter of Clyde Collins, who stood next to the sheriff as the latter sprang the trap.

Mr. Collins had sought to become the executioner for the day, but the State Legislature had thrown out the Bill to effect this on the ground that such a procedure was "uncivilised."

One hundred and fifty spectators, including a dozen giggling girls, crowded the hallway beneath the trap and jeered and joked as they watched the bodies fall.

When Howard, who was the first of the three to be hanged, was pronounced dead the sheriff turned to Mr. Collins and said: "That —— won't bother you any more," to which Mr. Collins replied, smilingly: "Hell, no."—B.U.P.

1910

HOW CRIMINALS ARE MADE.

AMAZING SENTENCE ON A BOY OF TWELVE.

SEVEN YEARS FOR 5d.

An astonishing illustration of the English method of making criminals is to be seen in the action of the Hayward's Heath magistrates yesterday.

The Bench sent a boy of twelve—a first offender—to a reformatory for seven years for stealing a lump of coal valued at 5d., as well as ordering the lad to receive six strokes with the birch rod.

The lad's explanation of the theft of the piece of coal was that he did not want to have to go next morning to buy some for his mother. So he went to the wharf in the evening and took the lump home.

The little offender's name is Charles Bulbeck. His father burst into tears on hearing the sentence imposed on the child, and told the magistrates that he thought they were "a bit hard."

The magistrates laughed at the father's plea, and Mr. E. J. Waugh said: "You should look after your boy better."

Although the boy has never been charged before the magistrates ordered the father to pay £1 9s. 11d. costs, and to contribute to the lad's maintenance in the reformatory.

1933

DRESS CLOTHES AT EXECUTION

FOUR MEN AND A WOMAN BEHEADED

BERLIN, Saturday.

Five people, including a woman, were beheaded in Germany to-day, and in each case the executioner wore evening dress and a top hat.

One of the men was guillotined, but the heads of the others were cut off with an axe.

The woman was a widow named Emma Thieme, who, with two men, had been condemned to death for the murder of her son.

Executions in Germany during the past six months now total 31. Previously the death sentence has rarely been carried out.—Reuter.

1921
KEEP ON DOING.

"He was doing nothing when I saw him," explained a policeman charging a man at Ealing, "and as I thought that was unsatisfactory I took him into custody."

1921
A CHESS PRODIGY GOES ASTRAY.

Counsel Thinks Brain May Have Been Weakened.

A child chess prodigy, William Winter, known afterwards to the police as "a Simple Simon among the Communists," appealed to-day against a six months' sentence at Bristol for seditious speeches.

He was described as an international chess player and a student of Cambridge University.

Mr. H. S. Diamond, on his behalf, said he could not really appeal against the conviction, as there was evidence that he uttered the speeches.

During the war, he said, Winter was in the Honourable Artillery Company, being discharged with a good character. He seemed to have left his studies at Cambridge to air his extreme Socialistic views and join the Communist ranks.

It was said that he was under the influence of a woman older than himself. While he did not suggest that chess players all become weak in the head, he submitted that in this case the man's brain was weakened. A term of imprisonment might have a severe effect upon him.

Mr. Justice Branson said no fault could be found with the trial. This young man left his studies and employment to stir up strife amongst those less fortunate than himself.

The sentence was not too severe, for those who made such seditious speeches inflamed and perverted many people. The appeal was dismissed.

1919
HEAVY SENTENCES ON POLICEMEN.

"Expert Housebreakers on a Wholesale Scale."

Two police officers, Thomas Maxwell and Alfred Shaw, pleaded guilty at the Old Bailey yesterday to receiving stolen property, and were each sentenced to five years' penal servitude.

Mr. Travers Humphreys, prosecuting, said the defendants were expert housebreakers on a wholesale scale. Maxwell was a sergeant with 13 years' service, and Shaw, a constable, with 10 years' service. They were stationed at Hampstead, where it was the custom for residents who were going away for a holiday to give notice to the police. They used that knowledge to rob the houses themselves. There were five cases in the indictment, and the house of Sir Edward Elgar was amongst those robbed. Maxwell was afterwards found wearing a coat and trousers which had belonged to the composer.

It was stated that the total value of the stolen property was about £1,000, and only about £400 worth had been recovered.

1924
WOMAN IN IRON CAGE.

EXHIBITED IN COURT AFTER SENTENCE.

JERSEY JUSTICE.

FROM OUR OWN CORRESPONDENT.
JERSEY, Saturday.

Following an old-fashioned practice that smacks of the Middle Ages a woman sentenced by the Jersey Royal Court was placed in an iron cage and subjected to the gaze of a large crowd of visitors who out of curiosity had come to watch the proceedings. In her despair the poor woman went into hysterics and had to be removed.

The woman, Daisy Southard, a native of Exeter and the widow of George William Warren, formerly of the Devon Regiment, was accused of having made a false declaration with reference to the birth of a female child. She stated it was her husband's; whereas it was shown the latter had been dead three years. After being sentenced to pay a £2 fine and to go to gaol for one month she was then placed in an iron cage situated in a corner of the court for all to see, until her shrieks compelled her removal.

∴ In England the practice of publicly exhibiting minor offenders in the stocks fell into disuse about a hundred years ago.

1937
EXECUTIONER WANTED

MANY APPLICATIONS FOR NEW POISON-GAS JOB

Kaunas, Lithuania, Saturday.—Many applications for the post of poison-gas executioner have been received by the Lithuanian Government, following their recent order substituting poison gas for hanging or shooting.

In spite of the numerous applications, no official intimation that the post has been filled has yet been issued. Among the foreigners who want the job are eight Dutchmen, two Germans, two Czechs, and one Hungarian.

One of the Germans is stated to be an artist from Frankfurt-am-Main. In his letter of application he stated that he had a special inclination for the profession of executioner.

No sentences of death by poison gas have yet been carried out, although three murderers have been condemned to die in the new way.—Reuter.

78 Punishment

1939
He Wants The "Cat" For The Drunken Driver

Mr. Robert Pauline, a Senator for the American State of Montana, thinks that people who drive motor-cars when drunk should be flogged.

He has introduced a flogging Bill into the Montana State Legislature.

Under this Bill the drunken driver would receive five lashes for the first offence, ten lashes for the second offence and fifteen lashes for the third offence.—Reuter.

1917
The "Cat" for a Street Pest.

When Robert Trevelyan was charged at the London Sessions with loitering, it was stated that he was arrested while masquerading in feminine attire. He wore a fur hat over his long curly hair, a long coat trimmed with fur, and the bottoms of his trousers were concealed by spats. His face was powdered, his eyebrows blackened, and his lips rouged.

He was sentenced to 21 months' hard labour and 15 lashes with the "cat."

1938
80 YEARS AGO
FEBRUARY 28, 1858

THE victim of the flogging which took place at Newcastle Barracks was a private of the Northumberland Fusiliers, who had been sentenced by court-martial to 50 lashes. The "cat" with which the torture was inflicted had a handle eight inches long and nine tails of equal length, each weighted with pentagonal pieces of steel, 81 in number. The regiment having been paraded on the barracks square, the triangle was set up and the victim was forcibly stripped and tied up. His voice trembling with emotion, he requested them to take his life, but spare him this dishonour. The plea was ignored, and forth stepped one of the burliest drummers, armed with the cat. At the first blow, a piercing shriek rung from the victim in his agony. His lacerated flesh gaped under the blow, and lumps of flesh were detached from his bleeding back at each fresh blow. At the 45th stroke of the instrument—that is, after receiving 405 lashes—the unhappy wretch positively burst his bonds in the contortions of agony, and fell a bloody heap to the ground. He was again tied up and another 45 wounds were inflicted. When the poor sufferer was eventually released from his torture, the whole of his spine had been laid bare. He was carried to hospital in a delirious state.

By means of this instrument, deserters from the Army were in bygone days branded with the letter "D."

1923
CONVICT CAMP HORRORS

Florida's Legislative Committee engaged in examining witnesses on the death of Martin Talbert, of North Dakota, a boy who died in a convict lease camp, has been horrified by the stories of terrible floggings and other cruelties inflicted upon men most of whom are guilty only of vagrancy. Talbert, who was arrested for vagrancy and leased to a lumber company, died a few days after receiving a severe lashing, when, according to fellow-prisoners, he was delirious with fever contracted in the swamps and his feet were so swollen he was unable to wear boots. The inquiry was held at the request of the Governor of North Dakota, and as a result of the revelations, the Florida Legislature has already voted to end the system of legalised peonage. Now it is expected the committee will recommend that flogging be abolished. A witness said Talbert received 119 lashes and was frightfully cut that the sheet upon which he died looked "as if bloody beef had been laid upon it." Overseer Higginbotham, who whipped Talbert, has been indicted and charged with his murder.

1904
FLOGGING FOR ADMIRALS.

"The Chinese, inveterately democratic and logical, flog their admirals as well as their humbler heroes," says Mr. G. Bernard Shaw, returning in the "Times" to his attack on flogging in the Navy.

"If flogging is all that our admirals say it is, the quarter-deck should be strenuously kept up to the mark by the cat and the birch, for an admiral can send a battleship to the bottom where a boy can only hurt his own digestion by a clandestine cigarette.

"The case against flogging is exactly parallel with the case against industrial sweating. Some admirals cannot command without flogging, just as some employers cannot command without sweating. Abler men can and will—that is enough for us."

1919
Flogging as a Privilege.

A foreign visitor, according to the "Manchester Guardian," has discovered that to be flogged at school is a privilege of the governing classes. Old Dr. Parr of Eton might have agreed. A distinguished cleric used to tell how, when he first went to Eton, he was classed as "mediocre," and escaped flogging. One day, however, an assistant master told Dr. Parr he thought the boy had some talent. "Say you so?" replied Parr. "Then let the flogging begin to-morrow."

1936
MINISTER LEADS NIGHTRIDERS

From Our Own Correspondent
NEW YORK, Thursday.

A clergyman who enlisted women members of his congregation in a "vigilante" band of nightriders is responsible for 11 floggings in Colombus County, North Carolina, according to evidence now before a Grand Jury.

The nightriders, who are apparently non-political, chose their victims for moral reasons, threatening them with the slogan: "Change or kill."

Mrs. Bertha Fowler, with her mentally incompetent 14-year-old daughter, are the latest victims.

On the night of June 2 they were taken in cars to an isolated field, where two sheeted and hooded women stripped them to the waist and watched as a man flogged them with a harness strap.

The leader of the band is believed to be a pastor of Clarendon (North Carolina).

RED CROSS ON SKULL

The existence of the terror was discovered by accident when a judge, while hearing a case, ordered Mrs. Fowler to remove her hat while she was giving evidence (says the British United Press).

It was then discovered that the woman's hair had been clipped close to the skull and her head painted with a red cross.

1907

Flogging: Two Phases
The "triangle"—painfully suggestive of the guillotine—to which prisoners guilty of crimes of violence are bound while suffering flogging with the cat or the birch (specimens of which are seen above, gracefully nestling)

1900

There was a happy Day at Leeds on Saturday. His lordship had a case of robbery with violence before him, and the law permitted him to order the "cat." He ordered forty lashes; and who will grudge his lordship his little innocent pleasures?

1930

CORPORAL PUNISHMENT

Fortunately for him, the modern Editor who advocates reform does not run the same risks as his predecessor of a century ago, and it is without fear for our personal liberty that we suggest that the time has now come when this stain upon the British record for humanity and enlightenment should be finally removed. It is not very easy to determine the extent to which it survives, as flogging with the cat is mixed up with the birching of boy offenders in the official statistics. Mr. Clynes stated, however, in the House of Commons recently that in 1928, the last complete year for which figures are available, thirteen persons over twenty-one and three persons aged between sixteen and twenty-one were ordered the cat in England and Wales for criminal offences. To these must be added those who were flogged in prison, of whom there were eleven in 1927. Men may be sentenced to be whipped under five statutes, for the following offences:—

(a) Slaughtering horses without a licence (Knackers Act, 1786).
(b) Being incorrigible rogues (Vagrancy Act, 1824).
(c) Treason (Treason Act, 1842).
(d) Aggravated robbery with violence and garrotting (Larceny Acts, 1861 and 1916; Garrotters Act, 1863).
(e) Procuration and living on the earnings of prostitutes (Criminal Law Amendment Act, 1912).

In practice, we believe, men are only flogged with the cat nowadays for offences (d) or (e), or for personal violence to a warder in prison. Incidentally, it is instructive to remember that this punishment was inserted in the Act covering offences (e) through the insistent instigation of advanced feminists, who ought to have known better.

The nature of the instrument now termed "the cat" is not easily ascertained. We have been informed on good authority that it consists of nine pieces of cord attached to a handle, but it has recently been described in the Press as "made of one thong, one inch in diameter." Official reticence is also observed with regard to the use of this instrument, and, in the absence of any more authoritative account, the following circumstantial description from the DAILY EXPRESS of February 4th, 1930, may be quoted:—

> "The 'cat' is the most dreaded of all prison punishments.... The markings on the back of the prisoner who has received the 'cat' remain there throughout life. Before a man receives the 'cat' he is examined by the prison doctor and his pulse is felt. The doctor himself gives the signal for the whipping to begin, and the strokes are counted by the chief warder. One of the strongest warders in the prison is always detailed for the unpleasant duty of giving the 'cat.' A prisoner usually faints from the pain and shock after ten strokes, and if his punishment is a longer dose, the second stage is given at a later date when the man has fully recovered from the first flogging. Always after the 'cat' a prisoner has to go into the hospital. A convict when he gets the 'cat' is strung up, stripped to the waist, with his arms wide apart, bound to the arms of a cross, and his feet just touching the ground."

1938

Sir—On many occasions it has been my unpleasant duty to supervise the public administration of the cat-o'-nine-tails in the Near East. Never, in my experience, have I known a criminal to come back for a second "dose," and I found that, on release, the man invariably showed the marks left on his back and ribs by the "tails" to his associates—usually themselves "undesirables"—and it certainly acted as a strong deterrent.

I am convinced, in spite of the many arguments I have heard and read to the contrary, that to deal efficiently with the type of man who has no regard for human suffering where his own criminal purpose is served, is to inflict bodily pain on him. Appealing to his conscience or "better side" is futile. He has none.—Yours, &c.,

HAROLD WENTWORTH.
Tunbridge Wells, Feb. 28.

RELIGIOUS MANIA

MURDER IN ZION CITY.

TRYING TO EXORCISE A DEMON.

(From Our Own Correspondent.)

NEW YORK, Friday. Sept. 20.

A terrible murder, committed in the name of religion, is reported from Zion City, where Mrs. Letitia Greenhaulgh has been tortured to death by her own son and daughter and three other members of the sect of Parhamites, who declared that it was necessary to exorcise the evil spirit from the body of the feeble, rheumatic old woman.

The five fanatics knelt by the bedside of the aged patient, and after prayer jerked and twisted her limbs. Mrs. Greenhaulgh's cries were greeted with triumphant shouts as being the agonised exclamations of the demon.

Finally, the old woman's neck was broken and the "demon" ceased groaning.

Then the fanatics began the ceremony of resurrecting the patient, but their combined efforts failed to restore the corpse to life. All five have been arrested and will be tried on the capital charge.

1907

Religious Mania

1927
"A WITCH."
ENGLISHWOMAN BEATEN BY VILLAGERS.
From Our Own Correspondent.

BELGRADE (Jugo-Slavia), Thursday.

A remarkable case of the superstition which survives in some parts of Eastern Europe has involved an Englishwoman, Mrs. Annie Chester, who has been spending a holiday at Travnik, Herzegovina, 45 miles from Sarajevo.

At a village near by Mrs. Chester was seen by the villagers taking photographs and making sketches, and they immediately denounced her as a witch, declaring that she wanted to bewitch their children.

She was attacked with sticks and stones, and fled, but was pursued, and unmercifully beaten. Just outside the village she fell, exhausted, and was taken to a hospital by police.

Ten women and 20 men were arrested.

PRAGUE, Thursday.—The people of a village in the Carpathians declare that they saw a woman, aged 70, "taking a walk with the devil." Eight young peasants dragged her into a forest and tried to burn her as a witch. She was liberated just in time by a hunting party.—Exchange.

1924
STIGGINS OF THE ARCTIC.
ESKIMOS DRIVEN TO RELIGIOUS MANIA.

"Daily Express" Correspondent.
OTTAWA.

A reign of melancholy that led to madness and murder in a tiny Eskimo hamlet in the Arctic circle has been brought to an end by the death of a fanatical evangelist, who reduced the entire community to a state of religious mania.

The story has filtered through from a far outpost of the Royal Canadian Mounted Police.

Neakutuk, company factor and native Crœsus of Kivetuk, on the eastern shore of Baffin Island, announced shortly after the coming of winter that the Great Spirit had ordered him to lead his fellow villagers to the land beyond the stars.

IN AWE.

They watched in awe as the self-appointed prophet pored for hours over his Bible. When he ordered strange rites they obeyed. The entire village abstained from food for days; and at other times gave itself up to orgies.

Many villagers killed themselves in order to escape from his influence. Others went mad. Two of them killed another who dared to doubt, and an illiterate Eskimo was doomed to death for the sacrilege of looking at a Bible.

When daylight followed the long Arctic night, the villagers did not notice the return of the sun, so bound were they by the hypnotic spell. They were set free from their bondage only when Kidlappik, the village strong man, killed Neakutuk because he struck a woman who had broken one of his rules.

1925
60,000 FANATICS EAT BROKEN GLASS.

Feast Of Pain That Went On For 10 Days.

BURIED ALIVE.

MEKNES, Morocco.

Sixty thousand snake-charmers, fakirs and wandering mystery-men assembled here to honour the memory of their patron saint, the Marabout Sidi-Ben-Aissa, and gave an exhibition of immunity from pain and the triumph of mind over matter.

They swallowed live coals, and slashed each other with knives, danced on the edges of knives with bare feet, and let themselves be buried alive for days.

Riffs There.

They came from all over Morocco, Algeria and Tunis, even from the Riff, several hundred of Abd-el Krim's henchmen being "Aissaouas," as the devotees of Sidi-Ben-Aissa are called. The French, respectful of Islamic traditions, did not interfere, and for ten days the feast went on. The war in progress 50 miles away bothered none of these fanatics.

Gifts Thrown.

Raw meat was their staple dish. They tore sheep apart with their hands and devoured the pieces, ate serpents and broken glass, and made a pretence of swallowing sabres. All this took place in the narrow streets, while admirers threw down gifts and food from the windows and roofs.

1936
OFF TO "HEAVEN" BY AEROPLANE

NEGRO PASTOR'S PROMISE TO FOLLOWERS

FLYING UNTIL PETROL RUNS OUT

(FROM OUR OWN CORRESPONDENT)

NEW YORK, Saturday. — A grandiose plan "to blast a way to Heaven for all God's people" is causing great excitement this week-end among the half a million coloured inhabitants of Harlem, New York's negro suburb.

This latest attempt on the altitude record has been announced in a proclamation by Father Divine, self-styled "Dean of the Universe," a black evangelist with dynamic energy and a tremendous vocabulary of expletives.

He has a big following of coal-black disciples, who walk in procession with much shouting and dancing, the chief lieutenants, called "archangels," wearing artificial wings and carrying big tin trumpets.

A red-blue fire, burnt at frequent intervals in "sin-infected" streets, provides illumination in the darkest districts.

Father Divine's proclamation calls upon his followers to assemble to-morrow, to organise "the biggest religious jamboree the world has ever seen."

HIS FIERY CHARIOT

"Swing Low" and other negro spirituals will be sung by a white-robed choir wearing tinsel crowns.

"Bring your drums, tambourines, and cymbals," says the proclamation.

Finally, after a three days' demonstration, Father Divine, in his own aeroplane, lighted by torches to resemble a fiery chariot, promises to fly heavenwards until the petrol is exhausted.

As a curtain-raiser to this frenzied week-end, Divine's officers assembled to-day in their principal tabernacle—called "Heaven"—to which no one was admitted without the password, "Peace, peace, it's wonderful."

In this tabernacle earthly names have been abandoned in favour of such spiritual ones as "Heavenly Rest," "Lovely Peace," and "Tree of Life."

The principal archangels prayed, sang, and danced deliriously until lunch-time to-day, when came an enormous supply of ham and eggs.

The stage is now set for a religious circus, dear to Harlem's coloured folk, and attractive also to tens of thousands of visitors from New York.

1905
WITCH FLUNG INTO SEA.

SEVENTEEN PEOPLE ARRESTED FOR MURDER.

"*Express*" Correspondent.

DANTZIC, Oct. 15.

Seventeen people have been arrested at Putzig on the charge of complicity in the murder of a woman named Anna Ceynowa, who was reputed a witch.

The woman was blindfolded and conducted to the summit of the rocky promontory of Hela, in the Baltic, and then flung into the sea. As she succeeded in swimming ashore the villagers strangled her by drawing the long tresses of her hair round her throat.

They afterwards gave themselves up to the police, as a matter of form, they said, declaring that they had performed a meritorious act in ridding the neighbourhood of a sorceress.

1904

Religious Disabilities.

The "revivalist" mania continues to rage furiously in Wales, and both business and pleasure appear to be either at a standstill or turned topsy-turvy under the influence of this new excitement. At one village the local theatre, which before the outbreak had to put up "house full" every night, is now quite deserted in favour of the rival attractions at the chapel. Football is no longer played—one does not quite see why. It seems rather a slur on the game that it should be considered entirely incompatible with "religion." But so it is, and now that the players are "converted," the tries no longer get a chance. The ordinary business of the day has been in some cases practically suspended for prayer meetings. But the greatest revolution of all is a linguistic one, and it has led to a considerable obstruction of industry. The miners are worst off of all, for being unable to swear any more, they have lost all control of the pit-ponies, who cannot understand the instructions given them in the new expurgated language. Traffic too must suffer a good deal if there be many cases like that of a tram-car driver who, finding himself inadvertently using a powerful expression, promptly fell on his knees and prayed fervently for forgiveness. Like every other great movement, the "revival" seems to have certain immediate disadvantages.

1905

Analysing a Vision.

The ironist will not fail to note the humour in the practical steps which are being taken to investigate the lights of Egryn. The Welsh revival has been accompanied by the seeing of visions and the dreaming of dreams. Strange fires have been descried in the heavens, portents on the earth. Our forefathers wou'd have set them down at once as signals from the unknown—benedictions from Heaven on the outpouring of the spirit. Imaginative Welshmen, looking through the eyes of their ancestors, have been content with a similar solution of the mystery. Then the scientific observer sallies forth carrying maps of the district, surveying implements, telegraphs and cameras. He sees curious lights and prepares to observe them with all the power of his apparatus. Then he discovers that they are but indications of the energy of brother scientists labouring to the same end. The miracles of Egryn are not yet explained, but "it is probable they have no very obscure physical or chemical cause." A material generation bent on finding the truth rather than feeding on fancies!

1904
THE HOLINESS SOCIETY.

A New Religion Creates a Wave of Fanaticism in a Maine Village.

The inhabitants of Beal's Island, a small village in Maine, are experiencing a wave of fanaticism, inaugurated by a new religious body known as the Holiness Society.

The members of the society, which is presided over by Mrs. Beal, have destroyed their jewelry and finer belongings, including much of their clothing, believing it to be wicked to keep more than is necessary for immediate use.

Shopkeepers, under the influence of the mania, have thrown their stocks of tobacco and cigars into the streets.

Dogs and cats have been sacrificed with solemn functions, and Mrs. Beal attempted to kill her baby, saying, "God tells me to kill the child."

She was prevented from doing this by the constables of the town, who (says the "Chronicle" Boston correspondent), being reinforced by the more sober citizens, are attempting to put an end to the fanaticism.

1908
A MAD FAMILY.

ATTEMPT TO CRUCIFY RELIGIOUS MANIAC.

A strange case of a family suffering from religious mania is reported from the Swiss village of Oftringen, says a "Morning Leader" Berne telegram.

There are eight grown children in the family, and recently they were converted by an itinerant preacher. Thereupon the whole family began to neglect their farm and domestic duties, and to spend the day and night in prayer. The cattle were neglected, and would have been starved had they not been fed by the neighbors.

"The Bride of Christ."

One girl named Bertha declared that she was the bride of Christ, and always went about clad in a garment of white. Strange rites, too, were practised. Once at midnight the whole family, dressed in white clothes, assembled around a wood-pile altar in a field and burned a white calf, meanwhile dancing around the burning pile. This was called "immolation."

Then Bertha expressed a wish to be immolated, and it appears that an attempt was made to crucify her. The police, however, got to know of this, and arrived in time to prevent further mischief. Bertha was found ill in bed with nail-wounds in her hands.

Taken to an Asylum.

The girl and two sisters and a brother were promptly removed to the lunatic asylum at Koenigsfelden.

It is recalled by the veterans that 50 years ago in the Canton Thurgau a girl was crucified by a religious sect in a burst of madness.

WONDERFUL WELSH SEER.

1905

Mrs. Mary Jones, of Islaw'rffordd Farm, near Dyffryn, in North Wales, and her daughter. She is said to be accompanied by a miraculous star when she goes about her revival work in the neighbourhood. Sometimes this star appears in the heavens to guide her on her way; at other times a soft radiance illuminates her path. These phenomena have been vouched for by many disinterested witnesses.

1904
ASSISTED BY AN ANGEL.

REMARKABLE STORY OF A WELSH CONVERT.

(From Our Special Correspondent.)

PONTYPRIDD, Thursday, Dec. 22.

No sun rose on the valleys to-day. A smother of thick fog blanketed the villages with the murk of the pits, and at Penygraig, where Mr. Evan Roberts is to-day, the revival surged in the dark like a strenuous mole.

The fog was equal to the best that London can produce, but it had no effect on the crowds who gathered in the chapel.

One of those who testified to-day was a maker of artificial limbs, who said he had leanings towards the stage and had just secured a pantomime engagement. This he would now abandon.

At Pontypridd to-day a man paused in the middle of the street and told in a loud voice how an angel had visited him. He had been carrying sacks up to a loft and found the work too heavy for him, so he knelt down and prayed, and while he was yet on his knees a young man, tall and fair, in shirt sleeves and working clothes, entered and offered to help.

The sacks were then carried up, each taking half, and when the convert went up with the last load expecting to find his helper there, for the ladder was the only approach to the loft, he saw no one, and realised that the young man had not been of earth.

The only doubtful feature of this revival apart from the adoration of Evan Roberts is the presence of a great number of professional converts, who testify with unction, tell elaborate tales of intricate and sometimes unprintable pasts, and gain a hectic credit as leaders and teachers.

These men and women are of all nationalities, and some are even negroes, and they invariably address themselves to creating hysteria and pillorying their too emotional hearers as converts to their preaching.

It is now fairly certain that Evan Roberts will go to London after the New Year, and this is a pity, for the results of his work there will undoubtedly discount the value of the revival here.

While inquiring of a squad of Valley police yesterday as to the decrease in crime, I found that every man was himself a convert.

PERCEVAL GIBBON.

1925
AMERICAN FANATICS
AND THE
DAY OF DOOM.

WEIRD MIDNIGHT WATCH

FROM OUR OWN CORRESPONDENT.

NEW YORK, Friday.

Americans generally are going about their business to-day quite unconcerned by the prophecy that the world will end just after midnight. The followers of Mrs. Margaret Rowen, the Californian prophetess of doom, all "brides of the Lamb" will watch on various American hilltops to-night, and if their Lord does not appear they hope at least to see some sign of faith rewarded. "If Christ," wrote Mrs. Rowen after her last celestial vision, "does not appear to meet his hundred and forty-four thousand faithful' shortly after midnight on Feb. 6 or 7 it means my calculations, based on the Bible, must be revised." Twelve believers living on Long Island met at Patchogue, within a few miles of New York, last night to make final preparations with Robert Reidt, their local leader. Reidt and his wife and four scared children were present, and also a local farmer named Downs, who for fifty-seven years has never left his village, Miss Kennedy, a prim, middle-aged spinster, a mentally deficient, and three negroes. Other strange people of a similar type living in various parts of the United States also met and duly harangued. The real Seventh Day Adventists are extremely annoyed by the masquerading of "advanced" Adventists, whose number, all told, they declare does not exceed 200, and this despite Reidt's boast of "unnumbered thousands."

Reidt was found last night outside his farmhouse, shouting up to the skies through a rude megaphone, "Gabriel, we're ready. Oh, Gabriel." He told reporters last night that "every one of his little flock will be transported by supernatural power, possibly on a cloud, to California. Other believers will similarly journey to California, where, on a hill unnamed, the Lord will come to earth, surrounded by his angels. A musical programme will be given by the angels, and then the earthly brides, bridesmaids, and guests will be taken on high." People who remain on the earth will perish, but regarding the precise method of their death there is apparently no agreement.

To-night the police are standing by at Patchogue to prevent a clash between the Ku-Klux-Klan and Reidt's world-enders. The Klan resents the inhumanity of the prophet in putting fear into the hearts of his children and misguided neighbours.

Joseph Gammel, the leader of the world-enders in College View, Nebraska, says the popular view regarding the end of the world is "illusion." Such an end, says Gammel, "won't be sudden, but gradual. You must discriminate," he said, "between what we believe and mere reporter yarns. The Lord cannot come down from heaven within seven days, because he will pause at some planets en route, to make arrangements for the reception of the saints he plans to take back with him." Mrs. Rowen's suggestion about the hilltop, said Gammel, will not be necessary in the United States, but where the population is thick arrangements will be made for the faithful to escape from the mobs of the unsaved, who will run riot on the seventh day.

Meantime Mrs. Rowen still lives placidly at Hollywood, California, and refuses to make any comment as leader of the strangest lot of fanatics living on this side of the Atlantic. It is not believed her followers are dishonest, but simply are stupid. Reidt said to-day his children had given away their dolls and toys, because they would not want them after to-morrow. Others have sold their homes. "I have nothing left except this old zither, and I play that," he said, showing an ancient instrument, "because I expect to play some day in heaven."

It is recalled the world-end movements in the United States was once almost popular. In 1842 the followers of Alexander Miller were very numerous in the Middle and Eastern States. The Millerites held enormous meetings, and people began to close their shops, and the excitement increased to such an extent that in March, 1843, husbands were murdering their wives for refusing to become converts, mothers were poisoning their children, and men and women committing suicide and going insane. The great day came, and passed as usual, and Miller's stock went down, but some of his friends made small fortunes in selling "muslin for ascension robes."

1928
WATCH FOR END OF THE WORLD.

JERUSALEM SITS UP ALL NIGHT

JERUSALEM, Tuesday.

A curious exhibition of popular credulity was witnessed yesterday when crowds of people, impressed by the prophecy that there was to be a violent earthquake, which would be the prelude to the end of the world, spent the night out of doors

They were rewarded shortly after midnight by the spectacle of a sudden storm of thunder and lightning and even rain, which is remarkable here for this time of the year.—Reuter.

1923
"DREAM PREACHER."

Woman Who Foretold the End of the World Arrested.

BERGEN, Saturday.

In a country district of Finland, one Maria Akerblom, "The Dream Preacher," has been arrested.

Going from place to place on horseback and with flowing hair, she foretold the immediate coming of the end of the world.

She declared that in view of this it was useless to own house or land, to save money or to do any work, and it is alleged that as a result of her preaching all of her large following of peasants have been more or less economically ruined.—Reuter.

Religious Mania

1928
MR. POTTER'S TIDAL WAVE.

WEYMOUTH'S GREAT WASH-OUT.

So far there are no signs of panic in Weymouth, although, according to the Rev. J. W. Potter, a London spiritualist, it is to be destroyed by a tidal wave at 3.53 p.m. next Tuesday. Rooms are still being booked in the town for Whitsun, and there is no record of anyone having taken flight.

Mr. Potter's information is derived from "spirit" messages describing a period of "world tribulation," which is due to start on Tuesday and to last for eight years. Weymouth, he says, is to get the first dose, and possibly the whole of Southern England may be submerged.

One elderly resident in Weymouth, who accepts the prophecy, has received news that the tidal wave has just passed Egypt, and is already pushing on towards the "doomed" town, but generally the residents are not alarmed and there has been no great rush for lifebelts, rafts and bathing costumes.

WHITSUN ATTRACTION.

The Mayor, Alderman Bartle Pye, said to a "Daily News" representative yesterday: "I think you will find Weymouth in its usual geographical position on Tuesday. We are not worrying. Some of us are smiling. It may be that the false prophecy will do us a little good by advertising our charming town. A tidal wave is surely an exceptional Whitsuntide attraction."

Among spiritualists who prophesy eight years of tribulation after Tuesday is the Rev. Walter Wynn, of Chesham, who bases his opinion on certain alleged revelations made in the Great Pyramid at Ghizeh, which he has studied for 40 years.

As long ago as 1925 Sir Arthur Conan Doyle announced that spirit messages indicated that "a great catastrophe, shattering in its nature, is approaching."

A PLEASANT PROSPECT.

Two years later—in December, 1927—Professor Pav, a French astrologer, went further. It was clear, he said, from his reading of the stars that in 1928:

The British Empire will largely disappear.
France will lose many of her colonies.
New oceans will appear in Central Europe.
North and South America will almost vanish into the sea.
The Atlantic will become dry land.
Millions will die from famine.

But his prophecy was not complete. He did not mention the end of Weymouth!

1935
Germans Hail Wotan

"CONSECRATED" HILL FOR NAZIS

A Pre-Christian Celebration

From Our Own Correspondent
BERLIN, June 23.

Bonfires are blazing on hills and mountains throughout Germany to-night in observance of the Summer Solstice. As far as possible fires have been kindled wherever German tribes are known to have held their meetings in pre-Christian days.

1932
Blood-Red Omens in The Sky

CHURCHES THRONGED

"Reynolds's" Correspondent
NEW YORK, Saturday.

AN end-of-the-world panic has seized the people of Asuncion, Paraguay. Terrified by the blood-red appearance of the sky and renewed earth tremors, a wild rumour spread that these signs heralded the end of the world

Awe-stricken crowds are thronging the churches and standing in the city's open spaces, awaiting the dread hour. The priests, realising that the strange phenomenon has a natural cause—the vast upheavals that have stricken the backbone of the South American continent—are striving to calm a populace almost out of control.

Thus, once again, credulity and awe of the marvellous has produced an end-of-the-world scare on a big scale.

Such scares are caused by such events or the prophecies of foretellers of final doom. A few years ago a prophet in Latvia announced the end of the world for a certain date.

DUG THEIR OWN GRAVES

Simple-minded Letts listened to him in awe and believed. In bands of hundreds they set out at Libau to dig their own graves, and the panic continued until the dread date passed like any other day, and confidence was restored.

One of the most sensational false alarms of modern times was given by Professor Porta, of Michigan University. He foretold the end of the world for Dec. 17, 1919. Wild rumours spread throughout America, and in many small towns the people came out of their houses and waited for days for the coming event.

In May, 1922, the brother of the late President Harding of the United States, a prominent Seventh Day Adventist, warned his credulous followers that the end of the world would come before the term of his brother's office was up.

President Harding died in May, 1922. But the old world rolled on

Perhaps the most famous of all scares occurred in the eighteenth century, when Cardinal Nicolas de Cusa, backed by the authority of his office, announced the end of the world

THE INGENIOUS CARDINAL

The Cardinal's argument was ingenious. He said that the Deluge occurred at the 34th jubilee of the Creation, and that the world would cease on the 34th jubilee of the Christian era. The Cardinal's arithmetic was defective. Nothing happened.

Swedenborg, the Swedish mystic, announced the year 1757 for the end of all things: Johann Albrech did not agree. He gave the date as 1836.

In 1836 William Miller, an American Adventist, announced the end for the year 1843, and Dr. John Cummings for 1866.

Old Mother Shipton, who had tens of thousands of followers, gave the date as 1881.

All these prophecies led to wild scenes of panic

1925
ICE COLD BATHS.

Cruel Negro Religious Rites In America.

NEW YORK, Saturday.

Immersion in ice-cold baths, unmerciful flogging of children, and the suspension of women by the thumbs were part of the so-called "religious rites" practised on his followers by James Johnson, the self-styled "King of the God Givers" at Philadelphia.

Johnson, who was head of this negro religious cult, has been sentenced from ten to 20 years' imprisonment, charged with extreme cruelty to nine women and 23 children who adhered to the cult he preached.

The police testified that during their religious frenzy the women observing Johnson's "rituals" would hang for hours by their thumbs.

Religious Mania

1949
Blind, Lame, And Insane Wait 6 Days In Mud For 'New-Day Messiah'

BLIND people, wallowing helplessly in the mud, hundreds of paralytic children, and insane people were among 7,000 sick who greeted Bavaria's "New-Day Messiah" on his return to his headquarters at Rosenheim, a hamlet 30 miles south of Munich.

Some of them had been waiting six days to see the "Messiah," 43-year-old carpenter and faith-healer Bruno Groening.

A sigh went up from the crowd when they caught sight of Groening, with his rugged features, black wavy hair falling almost to his shoulders, and piercing blue eyes.

Before Groening left six days ago on a business trip to Bremen he announced that the ground in front of his "temple"—a former gambling casino—possessed curative powers.

Many pilgrims said they had not left the spot for two, three, and even six days. The supposedly hallowed ground had been churned to a sea of mud beneath their feet.

In Insane Wards

In driving rainstorms the pilgrims kept their vigil, believing passionately that Groening would work miracles and cure them of their ills, from infantile paralysis to blindness.

While they waited the Bavarian Red Cross provided emergency first aid for those (about 100 people a day) who collapsed.

Three people were taken to hospitals in Munich—two to wards for the insane. They had suffered violent spells while enmeshed in the throng of invalids scrambling in the mud.

£4 Tinfoil Wads

Groening claims uncounted cures, including those of a lame duck and a spavined pony, merely by exhorting his followers to faith in God.

Groening has no need for fees. Contributions come in from all over the world. To help his followers to concentrate on their faith he gives them what he calls "Groening balls"—little wads of tinfoil.

They sell for 50 marks (about £4) on the Black Market.—*B.U.P.*

1921
THE "NEW MESSIAH."
Remarkable Credulity in South Germany.

From Our Own Correspondent.

BERLIN, Saturday.

A man who claims to be the "new Messiah," and professes to be able to work miracles, is causing intense excitement in the South German State of Wurtemburg.

Scantily clothed, unshaved, and with flowing hair, he is touring the country calling on the inhabitants "to do penance, for the end of the world is at hand." His claim to work miracles is accepted by villagers and townspeople alike, and hundreds of sick consumptives, weak-minded, war cripples, deaf and dumb are flocking to demand his ministrations, not only from various parts of Wurtemburg and from other German States, but, according to the local newspapers, from Austria and Switzerland.

The "prophet's" call to repentance is meeting with a wonderful response, workmen leaving the factories and farm hands leaving the fields in order to spend, in prayer and meditation, the short time remaining before, as the "New Messiah" prophesies "the world disappears amid thunder, earthquakes, and lightning."

An effort on the part of the Wurtemburg authorities to persuade the "prophet" to leave the country has foundered on the reluctance of his followers to let him go.

The Munich "Medizinische Wochenschrift," after mentioning that followers of the prophet claim that they are able to see and converse with angels, devils, and ghosts, urges the Berlin Government to intervene in the interests of public health, which is endangered by the presence of thousands of sick people who, as mentioned, are hurrying to the prophet in the hope of being cured.

1933
Human Sacrifice in Kentucky

From Our Own Correspondent

NEW YORK, Feb. 9.

A revelation of the ignorance and superstition prevalent in the wilder parts of the Appalachian Mountains comes from Inez, Kentucky, where eight members of one mountain family have been charged with the murder of Mrs. Lucinda Mills, aged 72, as a human sacrifice.

The officers who made the arrests stated that the woman had been strangled with a chain and was about to be sacrificed on a crude altar when they broke into the barred cabin.

The sacrificial ritual lasted for hours, and came to a climax with a period of fasting, in which members of the family chanted and prayed in an "unknown tongue."

The prisoners declare that they were acting "by Divine commands" for human sacrifice. The woman's son, John, is actually accused of strangling her.

A son-in-law told the police that he wanted to prevent the sacrifice, but was afraid to interfere. Another son, a grandson, two sons-in-law, two daughters, and a daughter-in-law, have been taken to gaol and to-day continued shouting, praying, chanting and dancing in their cells.

1937
FAMILY VOW TO CRAWL 300 MILES
ONE DIES: TWO OTHERS CONTINUE

(FROM OUR OWN CORRESPONDENT)

CALCUTTA, Sept. 16.

A family, consisting of a father and his two sons, who started recently to crawl from Sirmoor State on a pilgrimage to Hardwar, in fulfilment of a vow, came to grief on the seventh stage of their journey, when one of the two sons died of nervous exhaustion.

Undaunted, the father, with the surviving son, hopes to complete the remainder of the crawling journey, with a two-day break to enable him to perform his deceased son's obsequies.

When entreated by some of the spectators on the way to abandon the performance the father is reported to have said that he could not flinch from the sacred vow lest he should incur the displeasure of God, and ascribed his son's death while on such a sacred errand to God's will.

The vow was taken when the two sons were critically ill of typhoid some time ago. The family intended covering the distance of 300 miles in 60 stages of five miles daily.

Religious Mania

1928
ORDEAL BY FIRE "FOR PURITY."

GIRL TORTURED IN A FURNACE

"Daily Express" Correspondent.
NEW YORK,
Wednesday, Oct. 31.

The medieval ordeal by fire, self-inflicted as a purification rite, is declared by Miss Elfrieda Knaak, a thirty-year-old Sunday school teacher at Lake Bluff, Illinois, to have been the reason why she was discovered nude and nearly dead from burns beside an open furnace in the basement of Lake Bluff Police Station.

She was found on Monday night by a night watchman with her face and body blackened by fire, her feet badly burned, her forearms burned nearly to the bone, her hair burned off to the skull, her forehead seared, and all her clothing missing.

KEY MYSTERY.

The police station is unoccupied at night. Miss Knaak had let herself in with a key obtained by some means unknown. She was taken to hospital, and it was believed that she was dying, but the doctors now say that she may recover.

She murmured, in delirium, "Hitch, oh, Hitch, why don't you come to me?"

She was later gently interrogated. The police say she meant Mr. C. W. Hitchcock, aged forty-five, who is married, has four children, was formerly a music-hall actor, and is now a teacher of salesmanship and elocution at Lake Bluff. He also acts as a police officer.

Miss Knaak had studied to become a book agent under him for the past four years. She said to the police:—

"A few months ago I got to know him spiritually. This was not a material love affair. Advanced psychology made me understand him. I have been hearing his voice for weeks saying, 'Have faith, have faith.'

"I had an appointment with him for Monday night which he did not keep. I again heard his voice urging me to have faith. To prove my faith I thought of fire. I removed my clothes, and burned them; then I burned myself. I survived. I proved my faith, and I shall live. I knew I would survive. I did it for the sake of purity."

Dr. A. J. Risinger, who is attending her, says he is unconvinced.

TERRIFIC PAIN.

"To believe her story you must believe she first placed one foot, then the other in the furnace, and held them there," he says. "Then she must have thrust her head and arms in also, and held them there in what must have been terrific pain.

"It does not seem possible that a person, even in a trance, could do that. Muscular reaction alone would cause her to jump back from the flames."

Mr. Hitchcock, who is confined to his home with a broken leg, says: "Poor girl, if she had a 'crush' on me, I certainly did not know it."

Miss Knaak's home is at Deerfield, Illinois. She studied at the University of Chicago and the University of Illinois State, and is highly educated.

1945
DEFENCE BY RATTLESNAKE

NEW YORK, Monday.
Police fought rattlesnakes and religious fanatics in a little Virginian town where 5,000 people had gathered at a meeting of a faith healing sect who maintain that God will protect them from anything, even rattlesnake bites.

They try to prove it by letting the snakes bite them. But this time the police broke up the meeting, killed four rattlesnakes and arrested the leaders of the cult.

When the police charged, the faith-healers swung the rattlesnakes over their heads, shouting: "Come and get me. Praise the Lord."

Lips to fangs

One touched his lips to the snake's fangs as he was being put into a police car. Another screamed and pulled a snake from beneath his shirt. It was clubbed to death.

Raymond Hayes, leader of the sect, was arrested shouting: "We fought in the last war and had a mighty hard time. We fought for freedom, and what do we get?—you fellows and the Governor of Virginia trying to run a dictatorship."

1940
LIVE FOR EVER —BY POST

From JOHN WALTERS
NEW YORK, Thursday.

ONE million Americans who believed they would never die were disillusioned today.

The reason—Los Angeles detectives arrested twenty-four luxury-living leaders of the religious cult known as "Eye Am" and accused them of a £750,000 fraud.

The cult's high priestess, Mrs. Edna Ballard, known to her followers as Sweet Saint Joan, and twenty-three apostles were removed from their homes and accused of fraudulently claiming they were able to provide everlasting life through the post.

A million simple men and women in all parts of America sent the cult postal orders.

Said Sex Was Evil

They received in return a guarantee that they would not die.

The cultists taught their subscribers that sex was wicked and prevented immortality. This caused the break-up of many marriages.

Mrs. Ballard and her apostles drove about Los Angeles in a fleet of yellow phaetons bought by followers' postal orders.

1927
£3,000 SEATS FOR THE MILLENNIUM.

GRAND STAND AT THE SECOND ADVENT.

"BISHOP'S" SCHEME.

"I WAS advised that, for three thousand pounds, I could have reserved a seat in the temple from which I should be able to see the second coming of Christ across the waters of Sydney Harbour."

The woman who made this extraordinary statement to a "Daily Express" representative arrived in London yesterday from Sydney, New South Wales, and her remark referred to the "temple" which has been built on the shores of Sydney Harbour by a religious sect known as the Order of the Star in the East.

"Bishop" Leadbeater.

This sect, which is said to have a world-wide membership of one hundred thousand, is controlled in Australia by a man calling himself "Bishop" Leadbeater. It appeals with the promise of the approaching second advent of Christ, and, under the auspices of Leadbeater, it has set to work in Sydney on practical business lines.

Money, subscribed mainly by hysterical women, has so swollen the order's local fund that an old house on the north shore of the harbour has been bought, considerably enlarged, and converted into a "temple."

It is apparently proclaimed by Leadbeater that Christ will reappear walking over the water through the Heads—as the passage into the Pacific Ocean is called—of Sydney Harbour. The house which he has acquired faces the Heads, and below it he has had constructed a vast amphitheatre in the classical style.

Each seat in this amphitheatre—to put the idea in the simplest language—will command an excellent view of the second advent, and each seat may be reserved by members of the order for sums proportionate to their means.

RICHES OR FAME

THE WORLD'S MILLIONAIRES.

No two compilers have made similar lists of the millionaires of the world. China, England, France, Russia, and the United States each claim to be the home of the richest man. The list, exclusive of millionaire sovereigns, given in *T.A.T.*, is as follows:—

Albert Beit, diamonds, London, £100,000,000.
J. B. Robinson, gold and diamonds, London, £80,000,000.
J. D. Rockefeller, oil, New York, £50,000,000.
W. W. Astor, land, London, £40,000,000.
Prince Demidoff, land, St. Petersburg, £40,000,000.
Andrew Carnegie, steel, New York, £25,000,000.
W. K. Vanderbilt, railways, New York, £20,000,000.
William Rockefeller, oil, New York, £20,000,000.
J. J. Astor, land, New York, £15,000,000.
Lord Rothschild, banking, London, £15,000,000.
J. Pierpont Morgan, banking, New York, £15,000,000.
Lord Iveagh, beer, Dublin, £14,000,000.
Senora Isidore Cousino, mines and railways, Chile, £14,000,000.
M. Heine, silk, Paris, £14,000,000.
Baron Alphonse Rothschild, banking, Paris, £14,000,000.
Baron Nathaniel Rothschild, money lending, Vienna, £14,000,000.
Archduke Frederick of Austria, land, Vienna, £14,000,000.
George J. Gould, railways, New York, £14,000,000.
Mrs. Hetty Green, banking, New York, £11,000,000.
James H. Smith, banking, New York, £10,000,000.
Duke of Devonshire, land, London, £10,000,000.
Duke of Bedford, land, London, £10,000,000.
Henry O. Havemeyer, sugar, New York, £10,000,000.
John Smith, mines, Mexico, £9,000,000.
Claus Sprecles, sugar, San Francisco, £8,000,000.
Archbishop Conn, land, Vienna, £8,000,000.
Russell Sage, stockbroking, New York, £5,000,000.
Sir Thomas Lipton, groceries, London, £5,000,000.

1905

1936
Literary Fortunes

RUDYARD KIPLING leaves £155,000.

Other literary wills:

Hall Caine	£250,000
Stanley Weyman	£100,000
Charles Dickens	£93,000
Thomas Hardy	£91,000
John Galsworthy	£88,000
George Moore	£75,000
Anthony Trollope	£70,000
Rider Haggard	£61,000
D. H. Lawrence	£2,500

1921
ENDOWMENT OF BRIDES FOR EUROPE.

No one is really a millionaire who has not an income of 100,000 dollars, and if he is to be a sterling millionaire, his income should be 500,000 dollars. The number of such Americans is, roughly, 250.

One reason why millionaires escape detection is the prevalence over here of tax-free securities. Into these securities flows super-wealth, with disastrous results to the revenue. While the earned income pays, the tax-free dividend escapes.

Still, the big men have been hit really hard, and their power to accumulate wealth will never be what it was. Take Charles Schwab, who returned to the State 80 per cent. of his income. Or take John D. Rockefeller. If his income is 50 million dollars, and he hands back 35 millions, it makes a considerable difference.

DOWRIES FOR BRIDES.

On benefactions you do not pay tax, and there are also brides' dowries which sometimes escape, so far as the United States are concerned. The following is a list of matrimonial endowments of European civilisation.

	Million dollars.
Princess Anastasia (Mrs. Leeds)	40
Mrs. Spender-Clay (Pauline Astor)	10
Lady Craven (Miss Bradley Martin)	15
Baroness Selliere (Emma Riley)	8
Lady Beatty (Ethel Field)	8
Mrs. Colin Campbell (Nancy Leiter)	6
Mrs. Frederick Guest (Amy Phipps)	5
Lady Donoughmore (Elena Grace)	5
Lady Decies (Vivien Gould)	5
Lady Herbert (Belle Wilson)	3
Lady Cheylesmore (Elizabeth French)	3
Lady Arthur Herbert (Helen Gammell)	3
Viscountess Deerhurst (Virginia Bonynge)	3
Duchess of Manchester (Helena Zimmerman)	2
Lady Howe (Flora Davis)	2
Countess Gianotte (Miss Kinney)	2
Lady Johnstone (Antoinette Pinchot)	2
Marchioness d'Andigne (Madeleine Goddard)	2
	124

To these figures the Vanderbilt family have added 20 million dollars, and in the year 1909 it was estimated that up to date the export of dowries had amounted to 250 million dollars.

When it is further remembered that in voluntary gifts to Europe since August, 1914, Americans have contributed more than 2,000 million dollars in addition to home bequests and donations, it will be seen that there are many reasons why fabulous fortunes are now more evenly distributed.

1903
MILLIONAIRE HERMIT.

Mr. John Vanderbilt in His Lonely Mountain Home.

Mr. John Vanderbilt, a member of the wealthy New York Vanderbilt family, is called among his own people the "Hermit of Hexenkopf," by reason of his strange mode of life.

He is seldom seen anywhere; he never travels, nor works, nor writes, nor does anything in fact. Being a misogamist, he has never married, and, though reputed to be enormously rich, he lives in a tiny creeper-covered hut on the summit of a Pennsylvanian mountain, in the midst of the most beautiful scenery.

He is quite alone from year's end to year's end. He does his own cooking and housework, washes his own linen in a neighbouring mountain stream, catches his own trout, shoots his own game, cultivates his own strawberries and vegetables, milks his own goat, and makes his own bread.

The only person with whom he ever holds intercourse is a young farmer, who lives a few miles away, and who is kind enough to bring him flour, eggs, meat, etc., and who does any odd commissions he may wish executed in the outside world.

Mr. John Vanderbilt never receives or sends letters, he objects to newspapers and periodicals, and reads only a few favourite books that he took with him into his solitude; but some people think that he is engaged in writing a great work on an abstruse subject.

It is said that he has no opinion of humanity, male or female, and that he thoroughly despises money and money-makers.

1903
CZAR'S MILLIONS.

COMPARED WITH OTHER PLUTOCRATS'.

Despatches from St. Petersburg state that the "Almanach Hachette," the French equivalent to our "Whitaker," has been confiscated by the Press censor because it contains a comparative table of the incomes of the leading European monarchs.

The list in question is an illustrated page, giving the photographs of the leading European rulers, with their incomes per minute. The Czar of Russia is first on the list, and his income is given at £16 4s. a minute.

If the almanack's data be true, the Czar draws from his countless millions of subjects

£16 4s. a minute.
£972 an hour.
£23,328 a day.
£8,514,720 a year.

Fabulous as this sum appears, and far as it is ahead of any other European ruler, it does not give him an income nearly equal to that of Mr. John D. Rockefeller, the American multi-millionaire, or the South African magnate Mr. Alfred Beit. Both are stated to be equally rich.

Their incomes are approximately:—

£20 a minute.
£1,200 an hour.
£28,800 a day.
£10,512,000 a year.

There are dozens of American millionaires who could produce millions in hard cash far more easily than the Czar of Russia. Thus Mr. Rockefeller's fortune is estimated at £60,000,000, his holding in the Standard Oil Trust alone, which many would be glad to buy, amounting to £10,000,000.

Mr. Russell-Sage, the millionaire-broker, is worth £20,000,000, and Mr. George Jay Gould £16,000,000.

On the whole the American kings of finance receive far larger incomes than royal rulers on this side the Atlantic, as the following list shows:—

	£
John D. Rockefeller	10,512,000
Andrew Carnegie	5,000,000
Russell Sage	1,800,000
W. A. Clark (the Copper King)	1,600,000
George J. Gould	1,200,000
J. Pierpont Morgan	1,000,000

The six European monarchs receiving the largest incomes are:—

The Czar	8,514,720
Sultan of Turkey	3,000,000
Emperor of Germany	628,000
King of Italy	571,600
King Edward	470,000
King of Spain	236,000

No reason is given by the censor for confiscating the almanack. A cynic might say the Czar did not want his subjects to know the amount he extracted from them, or he might be equally near the truth if he thought him jealous of the comparison of his wealth with Rockefeller's.

BLACK MAGIC DENIALS OF AN ENGLISHMAN.

Mystic Talks of His Expulsion From Paris—Exploits of a Former Spy

"Reynolds's" Correspondent.
PARIS, Saturday.

AN Englishman, against whom there are accusations of having practised black magic and of offences against decency, and who has been ordered to quit Paris, has filled the news bill this week. He is Edward Alexander Crowley, and caused some stir in London years ago.

On the day preceding his departure for Brussels I had a long talk with this amazing man in his sumptuously-furnished flat in the Avenue de Suffren. He was in bed recovering from an attack of influenza, and a nurse was in attendance upon him. As he lay there, his striking face lit up by piercing eyes, he related his extraordinary career.

Born in Leamington fifty-three years ago and educated at Malvern and Trinity College, Cambridge, he told me that his profession was that of a poet and a writer on Buddhism. He had, he said, published books for over thirty years, and lived by authorship and on invested money.

A strange, wandering life he led. He travelled through China on foot, and almost succeeded in ascending the Himalayas, and was received at Thibet by the sacred lamas.

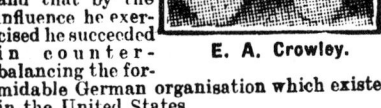

E. A. Crowley.

During the war he went to America and participated in German counter-espionage, but he declares that he lent himself to this rôle in agreement with the British Naval Intelligence Service, and that by the influence he exercised he succeeded in counter-balancing the formidable German organisation which existed in the United States.

"I had no difficulty in ingratiating myself with the New York Irishmen," he said, "for my name, which was that of many of them, served as a passport. I discussed with Bernsdorff, the German Ambassador, the possibility of an Irish revolution, and to further this idea I wrote violent articles in the German paper in New York, 'Das Vaterland,' and suggested that England should become a German colony.

"But I did these things in order to win the confidence of the Germans. The object I had in view was to make the German submarines sink American ships, and so compel America to enter the war. I was well in with the chief of the American Naval Intelligence Service, and I have sent him a telegram begging him to send me a letter, which I shall forward to the French Government"

When he was pressed to give me the reasons why the police had ordered him to leave France, Crowley said that he knew of none. There have been allegations that he had organised parties in his flat, that black magic was practised there, and that he was guilty of offences against morality.

He admits that he has written a great deal about magic, and I saw on the table in his bedroom a book on the subject which he said had taken him twenty years to write. This volume, he said, was only the first part of the work on which he was engaged.

"There is no accusation against me," he declared. "My sweetheart was expelled. She was told that a service was being rendered to her by separating her from me. When she demanded what it was the French authorities had against me they suggested that I was a trafficker in cocaine. This is ridiculous. Afterwards they said: 'It is not that. Perhaps that is not true. It is something else. The real reason is too terrible.'

SURPRISED BY DECISION.

"I have lived in Paris for seven years. I have led a peaceable life, writing during the day, and playing chess at my club in the evenings. I was notified on March 9 that I would have to leave. When the police came here they were much attracted by a coffee mill, and wondered whether it was a machine for distilling cocaine.

"The order against me is not one of expulsion. It is simply a refusal for me to continue to live in France. In other words, my right to an identity card has been withdrawn from me. The decision came upon me like a bolt from a clear sky.

"My case can be likened to that of Dreyfus. The French authorities are not obliged to give reasons for the action they have taken against me, and I repeat that they have given none. The British Embassy has left my case severely alone. It has absolutely refused to help me.

"There was a suggestion that anybody who helped me might be expelled also. What I am insisting on is an open inquiry before which witnesses can be produced who will be prepared to make accusations against me. My case is in the hands of M. Paul Boncour, the Socialist deputy and barrister. I believe that an attempt will be made to hush up the business."

MASTER OF THE OCCULT.

Crowley's literary works include a translation of Baudelaire and a volume of sonnets on Rodin, illustrated by reproductions of the sculptor's principal works.

At one time he was a well-known figure in Montparnasse, where he had a reputation as a master of the occult sciences. Numerous articles about him have appeared in the French Press this week. A woman writer who knew him well at one time has said that he claimed to see through the thickest walls and that he could "dislodge himself from his body"

There were allegations against him in connection with the scandal which led to the expulsion from France of Don Luis de Bourbon, the young Infant of Spain, but Crawley told me in the course of our interview that he had never seen this personality.

It is, he says, his intention to marry his sweetheart, who is in Brussels. His secretary, an American, is also there. He hopes to return to France if and when he is rehabilitated.

Mr. Crowley came into prominence in London in 1911, when his picture was painted by Augustus John. He was hotly attacked as the head of an "abbey" in Sicily, where degenerate rites were alleged to be carried on. He is the author of "The Diary of a Drug Fiend" and works on the occult. It is doubtful if the authorities will welcome him into this country again.

PREVIOUS BOOKS.

"BLASPHEMY, FILTH, AND NONSENSE."

What is the literary record of this Mr. Crowley?

Mr. Aleister Crowley is the author of a number of books, many of them printed privately. His work, considered as a whole, is a blend of blasphemy, filth, and nonsense. The nonsense is flavoured with mysticism. A very small knowledge of pathology enables one to label him as a well-known type.

As an example of his ideas, one may take the dedication to "Why Jesus Wept": "To any unborn child, who may learn by the study of this drama to avoid the good and choose the evil, i.e., as judged by Western or Christian standards."

REVOLTING POEMS.

The numerous allusions to a kind of vague Buddhistic mysticism are clothed in sensuality. Most of the poems are pornographic, many of them revolting, and all of them the product of a diseased mind and a debased character.

In the middle of a long poem called "Alice: an Adultery," there appears this notice: "The editor regrets that he is unable to publish this verse." The titles of his books are, for the most part, either biblical or sexual: "Jephthah," "Jezebel," "Aceldama," "The Honourable Adulteress."

Through all his work runs a loathing of Christianity, and he pays Mr. G. K. Chesterton the compliment of a personal attack on him, as one of the last champions of that outworn creed.

He has written on ceremonial magic, and on the state known as "Ecstasy," which relieves one from the dulness and monotony of a normal life. "My mind is pregnant with mad moons and suns," he writes in one place.

All the time he is obsessed with sex and sexual images.

A large number of his books are printed privately—some of them in Paris. They are either incomprehensible or disgusting—generally both. His language is the language of a pervert, and his ideas are negligible.

1922
BESTIAL ORGIES IN SICILY.

CAKES OF GOATS' BLOOD AND HONEY.

The story of the bestial orgies conducted by Aleister Crowley in Sicily sounds like the ravings of a criminal lunatic, made mad by his own depravity, and was related yesterday to a "Sunday Express" representative by a woman who has just returned from this place to London.

The orgies are carried on as mystic religious rites in an old farmhouse near the village of Cefalu, in Sicily. The main room of the house is windowless, with a flagged stone floor. On the floor is painted a great orange circle, lined with pale yellow. Inside the circle are interlaced black triangles. The room is lighted by candles.

BURNT INCENSE.

A tripod, upheld by three little fauns, burns incense made of burnt goats' blood and honey. In a cupboard are heaps of little cakes, all made of goats' blood, honey, and grain, some raw, and some baked. The raw ones, gone bad, fill the room with their stench.

In this room are carried on unspeakable orgies, impossible of description. Suffice it to say that they are horrible beyond the misgivings of decent people.

Many women come to Cefalu, all with money, for whatever else Crowley may demand of them, money is his primary need. It takes money to supply him with the drugs he uses incessantly, the hasheesh, cocaine, heroin, opium, morphine, every drug known from the Orient to the Occident.

WOMEN VICTIMS.

Three women he keeps there permanently for his orgies. All of them he brought from America two or three years ago. One is a French-American governess, one an ex-schoolmistress, and one a cinema actress from Los Angeles.

Whenever he needs money, and cannot get it from fresh victims, he sends them on the streets of Palermo or Naples to earn it for him. He served once a prison sentence in America for procuring young girls for a similar purpose.

The French-American governess has two children (of which he is the father), who live in the midst of this debauchery. The children of the schoolmistress by him are dead.

Crowley himself, a clever talker, with no little personal magnetism, spends his time smoking opium in a room which is really a gallery of obscene pictures gathered from all over the world.

He bases his "religion" on a few texts gleaned from Pythagoras, which he quotes persuasively when trying to attack a new victim.

But the real facts of his system are much simpler than that. They go down to the lowest depths that human depravity can reach.

PROFESSOR LOMBROSO.

1938
By Apollo!

When Count Potocki, described as a journalist, of Lamb's Conduit Street, Bloomsbury, was asked to take the oath at Clerkenwell County Court yesterday, he inquired whether he might be allowed to swear by Almighty God, but not on the Bible.

Judge Earengey: You may take the oath in any manner that is binding on your conscience

Count Potocki: Then I shall swear by Apollo, to whom I pray every day.

He then took the oath in this way.

Judge Earengey subsequently granted an application by Count Potocki to change his description in the proceedings from journalist to poet.

1909
DEATH OF PROFESSOR LOMBROSO.

Famous Italian Criminologist and Student of Insanity.

GREAT MAN'S WHIMS.

TURIN, Tuesday.—Professor Cesare Lombroso died suddenly this morning.—Reuter.

Professor Cesare Lombroso, the world-renowned Italian criminologist and psychologist, was born in Verona in 1836, of Jewish parents.

At one time he was a determined enemy to spiritualism and its adherents. In January, 1907, however, he wrote: "Until the year 1890 spiritualism had no fiercer nor more obstinate opponent than I."

About this time, in 1892, he encountered, in the course of his medical practice, what he described as one of the most extraordinary cases he had ever seen—that of a girl attacked by a violent hysteria presenting symptoms explicable neither by physiology nor pathology.

This girl at times became blind as regards her eyes, but was able to see, though her eyes were bandaged. When sunlight was centred on her ear she protested she was being blinded.

Next her sense of taste went to her knee, and her sense of smell to her toes. She was also telepathic, and could see her brother when he was absent.

CONVERT TO SPIRITUALISM.

Professor Lombroso was driven to the conclusion that spiritualism would explain the matter, and so, after making experiments with Euspasia Palladino, the medium—all in daylight—the curious psychic phenomena that occurred confirming his growing belief, he became a spiritualist and took up the cudgels in its defence.

It was his work in connection with criminology, however, that won him most reputation, for he was regarded as the great expert on the mentality of law-breakers of all sorts.

It was not his first work. When only fourteen years of age he came under the notice of Mazolo, the great philologist, who taught him Chaldaic, Hebrew, and Chinese. He then turned to the study of diseases at the universities of Padua, Vienna, and Pavia, from which to the study of the degenerate states of the brain that cause a man to become a criminal was only a step.

He took it in Paris, nearly fifty years ago. A notorious French criminal died in prison, and Lombroso performed an autopsy on him in the prison yard.

"I instantly perceived," he narrated, "that the criminal must be a survival of the primitive man and the carnivorous animals . . . . and the whole idea of my future work rose before me like a picture."

From then on he examined every criminal he could, made measurements of their skulls, their facial angles, studied them in every possible way.

He came to the conclusion that their actions were caused by degeneracy, not by volition.

COINCIDENCE OF LAST BOOK.

Personally, though his work lay along such lines, Professor Lombroso was a very mild man and childish in his way, and as absent-minded as the typical scientist of fiction.

When he went a journey he used to stuff his pockets with bank-notes, and whenever he took a handkerchief out, or anything else, a few bank-notes would fall to the ground.

He was as contrary as the most contrary of old people. Were he asked to do anything he more likely than not immediately decided to do the opposite to what was wanted.

Professor Lombroso was an opponent of our punitive penal system.

By a strange coincidence the last book of Professor Lombroso appeared in an English translation on Monday, under the title: "After Death—What?"

OSCAR WILDE AND ZOLA.
A REPLY TO SOME CRITICISMS AND FURTHER REVELATIONS.

BY CHRIS HEALY.

IT was only to be expected that my recent article in To-Day,* on an unknown side of the Dreyfus case, should cause considerable surprise, and that my statement that Oscar Wilde was one of the direct instruments in freeing Alfred Dreyfus should be freely criticised. To the commonplace mind only commonplace things are possible. One critic, in particular, "jibbed" at my statement that Wilde objected to meeting Zola on the ground that the latter was the author of immoral books, and concludes with the remark that "Wilde is understood to have become a reformed character, but he cannot be believed to have suddenly developed into a Mawworm."

What the latter may be I do not know, but, perhaps, even at the risk of disturbing some of my critic's family traditions, I am impelled to add some further facts about poor Wilde. "English law is cruel and senseless," once remarked a well-known barrister to me at the conclusion of a certain *cause célèbre*. "Few of our judges admit a fact accepted by most medical men—that certain forms of crime should be treated by a lunacy specialist rather than by a judge and jury." Those who were best in a position to judge recognised that, despite the splendour of his intellect, Oscar Wilde on one point was as mad as the proverbial hatter. There are innumerable cases of men whose sanity, in business and the ordinary walks of life, is beyond suspicion, and who on one question are completely insane. I have in mind a dear friend of my own, a brilliant chess-player, a consummate man of affairs, and who, despite his income of but a few hundreds a year, believes that he could buy up Rothschild, Pierpont Morgan, Mackay, and Rockefeller, and then have enough money left to repeat the process.

To the many Wilde was an unspeakable person, but to the few he was an accomplished scholar and gentleman, suffering from one of the most terrible and loathsome forms of insanity which two years of prison life increased rather than diminished. I met him in Paris a few weeks after he finally left England, and his appearance was burnt in on my memory. A tall, stalwart figure, with a face scored with suffering and a mistaken life. The grey, wearied eyes, the mocking curves of the mobile mouth, reminded me of Charles Reade's description of Thomas of Sarranza at the time that he sat in the Fisherman's Seat—"a *gentilhomme blasé*, a high-bred and highly-cultivated gentleman who had done, and said, and seen, and known everything, and whose body was nearly worn out."

Wilde was then living in the Rue des Beaux Arts, under the name of Sebastian Melmoth. He invited me to lunch, and we had *déjeuner* at a little restaurant on the Boulevard St. Michel, where for over two hours he talked with the same delightful *insouciance* which had characterised him in his best days. Wilde detested coarse language or coarse conduct, and I remember him moving his chair away from the vicinity of some students who, with their Mimis and Marcelles, were talking in a strain that would have made Rabelais blush. He talked lightly about his trial, but his face lighted up with savage indignation when he spoke of his prison treatment. Of one prison official, he said: "He had the eyes of a ferret, the body of an ape, and the soul of a rat." The chaplains he characterised as "the silliest of God's silly sheep," and gave an instance of the kind of reading they select for the prisoners under their charge. A man had been sentenced to seven years' imprisonment, six months of which was to be endured in solitary confinement. The book served out to him by the chaplain at ——— Prison was "Sermons Delivered at ——— Prison to Prisoners Under Sentence of Death." I had had the advantage of reading "The Ballad of Reading Gaol" in MSS. some days before I met the author, and I asked him whether he intended to write further in the same vein.

"Do not ask me about it!" Wilde said with a sigh. "It is the cry of Marsyas, not the song of Apollo. I have probed the depths of most of the experience in life, and I have come to the conclusion that we are meant to suffer. There are moments when life takes you, like a tiger, by the throat, and it was when I was in the depths of suffering that I wrote my poem. The man's face will haunt me till I die."

The conversation drifted on to Aubrey Beardsley, who was then on the point of becoming a Catholic.

"I never guessed," said Wilde, "when I invented Aubrey Beardsley, that there was an item of aught but pagan feeling in him."

I happened to mention something that Herr Max Nordau had told me the day before on the subject of "The Degenerates," and on Nordau's firm belief that all men of genius were mad.

"I quite agree with Dr. Nordau's assertion that all men of genius are insane," said Wilde, "but Dr. Nordau forgets that all sane people are idiots."

He leaned back in his chair, lit a cigarette, and gazed reflectively at the beautiful scarab ring on his finger. "I shall start working again and trust to the generosity of the English people to judge it on its merits, and apart from their Philistine prejudices against myself. I do not acknowledge that I have ever been wrong. . . . only Society is stronger than me. Should the English people refuse my work, then I shall cross to America, a great country which has always treated me kindly. I have always been drawn towards America, not only because it has produced a very great poet—its only one—in Walt Whitman, but because the American people are capable of the highest things in art, literature, and life."

"Do you not care for Longfellow, then?"

"Longfellow is a great poet only for those who never read poetry. But America is great because it is the only country in the world where slang is borrowed from the highest literature. I remember some years ago, when I was travelling out West, I was passing by a store when a cowboy galloped past. The man with me said, 'Last night that fellow painted the town red.' It was a fine phrase, and familiar. Where had I heard it? I could not remember, but, the same afternoon, when I was taken to see the public buildings—the only ones in this place were the gaols and cemeteries—I was shown a condemned cell where a prisoner, who had been sentenced to death, was calmly smoking a cigarette and reading 'The Divine Comedy' of Dante in the original. Then I saw that Dante had invented the phrase 'painting the town red.' Do you remember the scene where Dante, led by Virgil, comes to the cavernous depths of the place swept by a mighty wind, where are confined those who have been the prey of their passions? Two pale faces arise from the mist, the faces of Francesca da Rimini and her lover. 'Who art thou?' cries Dante in alarm, and Francesca replies sadly, '*We are those who painted the world red with our sin.*' It is only a great country which can turn the greatest literature into colloquial phrases."

He bowed his head for a moment, then he murmured, "When the greatest literary men of the world petitioned the English Government to treat me with less severity, the prison authorities allowed me, whilst I was lying in an hospital bed, to have one book to read. I chose the 'Divine Comedy,' and it saved my reason."

Then he laughed, and began to criticise, good-humouredly, some of his contemporaries. "I look

---
*To-Day, October 8, 1902.

upon Zola," he said, "as a third-rate Flaubert. Zola is never artistic, and often disgusting. As to Flaubert, all I can say is, that whenever I enter a strange town I always order the 'Confessions de St. Antoine' and a packet of cigarettes, and I am happy. I have never read any of Huysman's works, but he must be a great artist, because he has selected a monastery as his retreat. It is delightful to see God through stained glass windows."

Then he referred to English writers, and his opinions on these I forbear from quoting, except in one case. "Poor Richard," he said. "He is an absurdity, but then he is a graceful absurdity." I leave my readers to guess the Richard in question. After a long talk, Wilde concluded, "It would be useless on my part to tell you what I am going to do with my life. Popular authors—and by popular authors I mean authors who are talked about but never read—are in the habit, at certain times, of confiding about two columns of their future intentions to the newspapers. I cannot say what I am going to do with my life; I am wondering what my life is going to do with me. I would like to retire to some monastery—to some grey-stoned cell where I could have my books, write verses, and reverently smoke my cigarettes."

I saw him frequently after this until he left for Naples. It was during this time that he suggested the clue which enabled Zola to successfully defend Dreyfus, and Maître Labori and Mathieu Dreyfus can attest the authenticity of this statement. The last time I saw Wilde he was kneeling in the church of Nôtre Dame. The sun streamed through the windows, the organ was pealing a majestic chant, and his head was bowed, almost hidden. Perhaps some vision of what his life might have been came to him and scourged his soul anew. I only know that when I left him he was still kneeling before the altar, his face hidden by his hands. I heard of his new play being effusively accepted by Sarah Bernhardt, who later on backed out of her offer, and this plunged Wilde into the depths of poverty. I also heard about another play—since produced in London with a well-known person's name attached to it as the author—being offered to an authoress famous for her epigrammatic powers. She was to pay Wilde a certain sum down, and a part of the royalty, but the lady in question indignantly refused, saying that to rob a writer of such a fine piece of work would be monstrous. Others were not so sympathetic—and Wilde never received his share. A few, a very few, of his old-time friends stood loyally by him, but he was a proud man, and suffered his privations in silence, with the same courage he had evinced in Court by refusing to betray the high-placed associates of whom he was made the scapegoat.

The end of his meteoric career is too sad to be dealt with here. Suffice it to say that, if his terrible mania made him sin in the eyes of the world, he suffered no less terribly. Apart from this side of his character, he had a rare delicacy in the things of this world, and his remark that Zola was a writer of immoral books, to which my "Mawworm" critic objected, was said in all sincerity. Those who really knew him made due allowance on his behalf, ignoring the maniac who had fallen under the ban of English displeasure, and recking only of the rare artist, the accomplished scholar, the greatest sonneteer in the world of poetry since the days of Rossetti and John Keats, and the kindly gentleman whose heart was a mine of generosity and good nature. Now that poor Wilde is dead, one may easily forget the little side of his character, and rejoice that such a brilliant star, even after its fall, lighted the way towards a great act of justice.

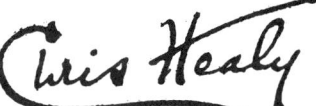

MUSTAPHA KEMAL.

1934

The Man With The Worst Job On Earth

WORKS 30 MINUTES A DAY FOR £3,000 A YEAR

THE latest victim of the 'flu which is sweeping the Near East is a man who earns £3,000 a year for working thirty minutes a day! He is the man whose duty it is to taste the food before it is served to Mustapha Kemal Pasha, the dictator.

Twice a day—until 'flu laid him low—this man with the most uncomfortable job on earth has stood in the kitchen of the President's villa near Ankara, or in the kitchen of the residential-presidential train, tasting every single dish prepared for his master.

After the food is tasted it goes to a hot-plate, where it remains for one hour before it is placed on the dictator's table.

It takes only fifteen minutes to taste the dishes, but the hour must elapse before the dictator tastes the food in case the taster should die in the interval. It is reckoned that after an hour the danger has passed.

Mustapha Kemal has many lurking foes. That is why his taster is so well paid for the nerve-racking job. He belongs to the Turkish Secret Service, and his salary is larger than that paid to many of Mustapha Kemal's diplomatic envoys to foreign Courts.

He is known in Turkey as "the man who never eats."

The pickings from the President's dishes, he says, satisfy him. Some people declare that the thought of powdered glass, powdered diamonds, and snake poison inserted into rissoles, called kebabs, and beloved of Mustapha Kemal, or sprinkled over his vegetables, destroys the taster's interest in food.

The man who waits to drop dead has no appetite!

1927
LAWRENCE OF ARABIA.

By A. J. CUMMINGS.

The only time I ever met Colonel T. E. Lawrence, "the uncrowned king of Arabia," whose singular book, "Seven Pillars of Wisdom," is now being offered in America at the singular price of £4,000 a copy, was in 1920, shortly after the suppression of the revolt in Mesopotamia.

Colonel Lawrence.

I was anxious to obtain his views on British policy there; and when I sought him out in the seclusion of his gracious room in All Souls College I was surprised at the friendliness of his greeting, for I knew tha he hated publicity and had been told that he would run a thousand miles from any journalist. But as I entered the room, Lawrence, by an odd coincidence, was reading a book written by my brother, and thus the way of the interviewer was made easy.

It was difficult at first to picture in this frail, shy, pale-faced, soft-voiced Oxford don a veritable Prince of Mecca, the man whose leadership of the Arabs during the war has become a romance of history, and whose prestige among them was so immense that they invested him with supernatural powers.

Yet when he had forgotten his shyness, and began to talk with profound learning and an indescribable fascination of his beloved Arabs and of his romantic dream of a mighty Arab Federation, speaking Arabic, in Asia, under a great Arab ruler, his eyes shone and his face flushed; and I realised that here was the withdrawn vision of a poet and the leaping fire of a true man of action.

And, then I discovered his secret ambition. The new king of Mesopotamia, I asked, would it be Feisal? His unguarded answer was an astonishing one. "Yes, it may be," he said, looking me straight in the eyes, "but it may be an Englishman."

I have often wondered since whether an imaginative Mr. Churchill, or some other member of the Government of the day, oppressed with a dangerous problem, had actually dangled before him the tempting bait of a real Arab kingship in Mesopotamia.

1929
FOUGHT KING EDWARD.
Boyhood Struggle Over a Sand Castle.

Probably the only man who fought the late King Edward, Dr. R. W. Henderson, is seriously ill at his residence at Rickmansworth, Herts.

Dr. Henderson, who is 85, tells how, when he was a boy of ten, he built a sand castle on the sands at Broadstairs.

King Edward came along with an attendant and kicked the castle over. The result was a "set-to" between them, the attendant allowing the affair to take its natural course.

1905
LIFE AFTER DEATH.
By BULWER-LYTTON.

A WELSH lady, writing in *Blackwood's Magazine* on her visit to Knebworth in 1857, says that Sir Edward Bulwer-Lytton spoke on the subject of spirits:—

He said he did not believe we should reach the highest Heaven when we died. "No," he continued, "it is not likely that we, imperfect as we are, should be suddenly ushered into the Divine Presence on leaving this world; our minds would not be prepared for so much glory: we are far too sinful for that. We shall pass through successive stages of existence, rising higher and higher until we reach the fulness of knowledge and of happiness. We cannot expect instant transition from great darkness to light, which to us would be insufferably bright. Does not everything progress? Is not progression the order of all God's works here? Why not hereafter? It is strange," he went on, "that all spirits, when questioned about heaven, agree in stating that into our next stage of being we shall carry the pursuits and characteristics of mind which were ours on earth, but all refined and ennobled. None of them, however, profess to have reached to the great knowledge of our final heaven, nor to know by what means we shall pass from one stage to another."

HIS SYMPATHETIC SNAILS.

Another subject of which Bulwer-Lytton was speaking was that of sympathetic snails. Snails are so apt to become attached to each other that if you take two snails that have contracted this friendship, put them in different bottles, take them into different rooms, by shaking the snail in one bottle you can always make the snail in the other bottle shake at the same time, no matter how distant they may be. A snail telegraph is said to have been used during the siege of Paris. Discussing this matter, Sir Edward was led to think that possibly two sympathetic compasses might be constructed, the alphabet arranged round them, with the addition of two magnetic needles in such perfect sympathy that whatever letter one of the needles pointed to would be instantly indicated by the corresponding needle. Distance was to make no difference in this mutual influence, which would be just as strong if one compass were in the South Sea Islands and the other in Siberia, as though they were lying together on the same table. Sir Edward employed a clever optician in Holborn: the compasses were made, but some mistake befell about the required conjunction of the stars, and the experiment failed!

1913
THE LATE OSCAR WILDE.

Monument in Paris Cemetery Unveiled Secretly at Night.

In defiance of the authority of the Prefect of the Seine, Jacob Epstein's monument to Oscar Wilde in Père Lachaise Cemetery has been unveiled at night by Mr. Alesteir (?Aleister) Crowley, says *The Times* Paris correspondent.

This monument has remained hidden from public gaze since its erection on account of certain features which were considered to be objectionable.

Mr. Crowley was supported in his action, taken, as he explained, in the interests of the "freedom of art," by some twenty enthusiasts from the Latin Quarter.

The authorities were taken unawares, and knew nothing of the invitations distributed on Wednesday night in the Latin Quarter to assemble at Père Lachaise.

The monument was to be covered up again last night, and a special watch kept by the authorities until their demands had been carried out.

[Mr. Aleister Crowley caused some little stir in London three years ago by the founding of a new religious cult, which met at Caxton Hall weekly.]

SPECTRES

THE GHOST OF OSCAR WILDE

OXFORD MAN TELLS OF MIDNIGHT VISITOR

The ghost of Oscar Wilde—a pale-faced dandy of a ghost in a loose-flowing tie—is reported to be walking again in the rooms he occupied 60 years ago in Magdalen College, Oxford.

The present occupant, Mr. Tony Kelly, claims to have been visited at midnight this week by his predecessor. Mr. Kelly is an Australian, and plays ice-hockey for the University—not a man given to æsthetic fancies.

"I had gone to bed about half-past eleven," he said yesterday, "but for some reason I could not get to sleep. Suddenly I had a most extraordinary feeling, a sort of goose-flesh, as if someone was in the room.

"And so there was. He was standing by the window—a tall man, with a long jacket, very old-fashioned, with rows of buttons and very short lapels. His tie was loose, and tied in a big knot.

"He began to walk up and down. I spoke to him and he didn't answer. I put out my hand as he came near me, and it went straight through where he seemed to be.

"Finally he walked away into a corner of the room, and just faded out of sight. There isn't a door in that corner, either."

It was in these rooms that Wilde wrote the poem "Ravenna" that won the Newdigate Prize when he was an undergraduate.

1934

1935
'Vampire' that Bullets Cannot Harm

SERB PEASANTS IN STATE OF TERROR

(FROM OUR OWN CORRESPONDENT)
BELGRADE.

Several families living in a village near Gnyilane, in southern Serbia, are living in terror of their lives through the manifestations of a supernatural being believed locally to be a vampire. Invisible and impervious to rifle bullets, the vampire enters peasants' houses at the dead of night, opens locked chests, levitates logs of wood from the fire, drenches peasants, their wives and children, with jugs of water, and drives the cattle in the byres to frenzy.

The phantom does not seem to be afraid of the light, for two of the braver peasants ambushed in one of the haunted houses witnessed this efficient imitation of a spiritualist seance and fired on him, upon which he departed giving three final thundering knocks on the door.

1923
GHOST MOVES A PIANO.

THE PHANTOM SAMSON OF BORESFIELD.

FLYING WASHSTAND.

FAMILY BEATEN AT A GAME OF DRAUGHTS.

A correspondent wires:—
The Cambridgeshire village of Gorefield, a few miles from Wisbech, is disturbed by the activities of a ghostly agency in the house of a well-known resident.

Accounts circulated of the happenings in the house have brought people from far and near, anxious to get further particulars and test the truth of the reports.

Persistence!

It is stated that furniture is moved and ornaments dashed to the ground, and if the articles are restored to their right places they are quickly upset again.

Since Monday last the House has been in complete disorder, the repetition of the mischievous doings having induced the occupants to take the attitude that it is useless to restore articles to their proper places, as the "ghost" is thereby only incited to greater assiduity in upsetting them.

Moving Scenes.

Heavy articles of furniture, including a piano, have been moved several feet; a gramophone, standing on a small table at one end of a room, was mysteriously moved to a large table in the centre of the apartment; crockery in the pantry has been thrown down and smashed; while a small table in the kitchen has been seen turning round on the floor, and part of a washstand in a bedroom has been seen flying over the bed.

The disturbances occur at all hours of the day and night.

1923
SURPRISE AT A SEANCE

MATERIALISATION OF A LIVING MAN.

WHAT BELIEF DID.

To the EDITOR of the PALL MALL GAZETTE.

SIR,—Not a few of your readers will attach some importance to the letter on "Magic, Mystic 'Fluence" from your "Special correspondent."

Without wishing to make this subject a matter of correspondence in your columns, I should like to be allowed to meet your correspondent's suspicions with facts above suspicion.

A business colleague of mine became ill. He left town, and, as I was later given to understand, died.

The following year I was present at a test séance with the object, among other things, of seeing a "sister" from the other side. This expectation having been realised, I was next confronted, unexpectedly, with the ectoplastic materialisation of my old business colleague! The likeness was beyond dispute, and, by itself, convincingly evidential that our departed friends return after death.

Sixteen months later, whom should I meet one day at noon in the City but this very business colleague! He had not died, as I had believed; but my believing him to be deceased had simply made of me an excellent subject for the deception practised by some disembodied intelligence at the séance.

A. C. NORRIS.

1928
LIVING WOMAN'S GHOST.

HUNT FOR A VILLAGE APPARITION.

THE FARMER'S WIFE.

"Daily Express" Correspondent.
WHITCHURCH (Salop),
Thursday.

The Shropshire village of Northwood, midway between Wem and Ellesmere, is in a state of excitement over a series of mysterious nightly visitations.

Stories are told of a woman's figure, which has been seen by several people, all of whom agree that she is

Dressed in sombre clothing, as distinguished from orthodox ghostly habiliments.

The image of a local woman—a farmer's wife, who lives in the neighbourhood.

A farmer named Morris and a workman named Peate were returning homeward one night with a horse and trap when they saw the woman, and stopped the horse with the view of giving her a "lift," as they knew her well. She disappeared suddenly, and although the men actually got out of the trap and searched for her she was not to be found. Two nights later Mr. Morris saw her again.

HUNT FOR A BODY.

Subsequently a man named Egerton, in the same district, was walking along the road late at night and distinctly saw the woman in the glaring light of a passing motor-car. As the car passed onwards, over the spot where the woman was standing, the man rushed forward expecting to find the body in the road, but nothing was visible.

Mr. Arthur R. Ellis, a wireless factor, of Wem, was driving his car in the same district, and distinctly saw the woman, whom he knows well. She was standing in the road, and he jammed on the brakes and swerved to avoid her, pulled up, and found—nothing. This story is corroborated in every detail by a boy named George Bache, who was in the car at the time.

Many of the more adventurous spirits are prowling the roads at night, and it seems that those who have deliberately gone out to watch have drawn blank every time.

1904
FIGHTING GHOST.

MIDNIGHT STRUGGLE WITH A SPECTRE.

The ghost of Tondu, Glamorganshire, has reasserted itself in the most aggressive fashion.

According to a correspondent of the "South Wales Echo," a respectable resident of the district which the uncanny apparition haunts and terrorises was proceeding at midnight along a lonely, narrow roadway adjoining the deserted buildings and coke ovens of the abandoned Ynishawdre Colliery—an ideal spot for ghosts—when he was actually attacked by the unnatural monster.

The gentleman is muscular, but the sight which suddenly met his gaze at the far end of a tunnel-like bridge made him turn hot and cold. An exceptionally tall, cadaverous figure was standing there. A silent, motionless sentinel, it was shrouded in white, the orthodox garb of the genuine ghost.

The head, as the frightened observer now describes it, was like a death's-head covered with wrinkled parchment: the eyes were hollow sockets, in which was a cavernous glow. Suddenly the eerie thing advanced towards the trembling man under the bridge. It approached within twenty yards, and then swiftly glided towards him with its long arms outstretched.

It clasped him as though in a vice, and then began an uncanny tussle in the darkness. The man could not grip. There seemed nothing more tangible than air, but he felt himself held as though in the folds of a python, and the glowing sockets were bent full upon him. He turned to flee, but could not escape from the power that held him. With a frantic effort he clutched again at this supernatural assailant, and it was gone.

Women and children creep indoors when nightfall comes, and bands of stalwart men sally forth to lay the terror of Tondu.

1904
ABBEY GHOST HUNT.

Mysterious Spectral Visitor at Kirkstall.

Kirkstall Abbey, near Leeds, the famous ruins of which are beloved by antiquaries and pleasure-seekers, is reported to be haunted.

A station porter was pacing the platform at midnight recently when he noticed a spectral figure, clad, apparently, in a long grey sheet, down which streamed a long streak of red.

Shortly after the appearance of the mysterious figure the signalman saw the porter dashing frantically about; but the signalman himself saw nothing of the ghost, and the porter that night found no trace of it.

A passenger alighting at the station early in the morning a day or two later called the attention of the same porter to a weird figure gesticulating from the roof of one of the wooden sheds which lie behind the station buildings.

Closely followed by the booking clerk, the two ran towards the ghost, which was immediately seen moving towards the exact spot where the porter had previously lost sight of it, and here, for the second time, the apparition disappeared.

On another night strange lights were seen flickering around the station and the neighbourhood of the goods shed, and again the ghost appeared. This time a party was formed with the object of solving the mystery, but although each one took a different direction, the search was again fruitless.

1903

MAN'S STRANGE FREAK.

PENRITH.—A mysterious personage, known as "The Hairy Man," who, it seems, is endeavoring to take the character of "the wild man from Borneo," is having a nice little game on the mountains just now. He occasionally makes a mysterious appearance in one of the small mountain towns, demands food, and then disappears into the bush again. He visited Springwood about a week ago, and gave the residents a great scare.

1921
GHOSTLY EVIDENCE.

A man has been arrested in America and charged with murder in consequence of a vision.

Some time ago a Mr. Freeman, a Philadelphia engineer, found one morning the dead body of his daughter lying on a couch in the drawing-room. She was shot through the head. There was no clue to the crime. But, last Monday, Mr. Freeman was visiting his daughter's grave. The dead girl, he declares, appeared to him in a vision and uttered the words: "Father, go and see Edwin King. He can tell you everything." King was arrested on Tuesday and charged with the murder. He protests his innocence.

This is merely the first chapter—rather, the first paragraph—of what may prove to be a remarkable story. At this stage, we can only note the possibility of the vision being the result of the father's subconscious suspicions. But the case offers curious analogies with the affair of Maria Marten; the Murder of the Red Barn. Maria was missing from home. Her mother dreamed that she had been killed and that her body was buried in the Red Barn at Polsted in Suffolk. The dream proved to be veridical; and William Corder was executed for the murder ninety-three years ago.

1904
FACETIOUS GHOST

Hits a Policeman in the Eye with Half-a-Pound of Butter.

The ghost, whose antics have disturbed the village of Coedkernew, in Monmouthshire, for the past week, has crowned its misdeeds by striking the sedate village policeman right in the eye with a half-pound of butter.

The ghost has previously turned the pictures on the walls in a farmhouse, compressed a piece of beef into a jug while the farmer's back was turned, threw a bundle of hay into the yard, dropped 200 pieces of crockery in the kitchen without breaking them, and carried beds round the room and partly down the stairs.

Ten persons sat up all night in the farmhouse waiting for the ghost to appear. The trustworthiness of the company of watchers was guaranteed by the presence of the local constable, but for some time it seemed as if the policeman's attendance had frightened the ghost away.

The ten men of Coedkernew were losing faith, when suddenly an eerie sound made the hair of the more sensitive begin to rise. The sound was followed by the rapid flight of an object which, thrown with unerring aim by an unseen hand, hit the policeman in the eye. It was butter.

Then there was a ghost-drive, but no ghost was found. Other pranks which the ghost has recently played have taken the form of putting soda into a tub of newly-clarified lard, and the emptying of a jar of pickled cabbage into a large quantity of cream. Another bed is said to have been found halfway downstairs, and the name of Mrs. Parsons's first husband traced on the glass of a lamp.

THE ANGELS OF MONS.

1930

"EXPLANATION" OF THE "VISIONS."

PICTURES ON CLOUDS FROM AEROPLANES.

The British troops really saw in 1914 what they called the Angels of Mons, if a story by a former member of the Imperial German Intelligence Service is to be believed.

This ex-officer, Colonel Friedrich Herzenwirth, whose narrative is pub-

lished in a newspaper in New York, says:

> The Angels of Mons were motion pictures thrown upon "screens" of foggy white cloudbanks in Flanders by cinematographic projecting machines mounted on German aeroplanes which hovered above the British lines.

The reports of British troops during the retreat from Mons on Aug. 24, 1914—that they had seen "angels the size of men," which appeared to be in the reurguard of the retreating army—were attributed by psychologists to mass-hypnotism and hallucination.

A MISCALCULATION.

Colonel Herzenwirth says the object of the Germans responsible for these scientific "visions" was to create superstitious terror in the Allied ranks, calculated to produce panic and a refusal to fight an enemy which appeared to enjoy special supernatural protection. But the Germans miscalculated.

"What we had not figured on," adds the Colonel, "was that the English should turn the vision to their own benefit. This was a magnificent bit of counter-propaganda, for some of the English must have been fully aware of the mechanism of our trick.

"Their method of interpreting our angels as protectors of their own troops turned the scales completely upon us. Had the British command contented itself with simply issuing an Army order unmasking our trickery it would not have been half as effective."

SUCCESS ON RUSSIAN FRONT.

Col. Herzenwirth, however, explains that the Germans were more successful with their cloud motion pictures on the Russian front in 1915.

The Virgin was shown with uplifted hand, as if motioning to stop the murderous Russian night attacks. As had been the case in Flanders, the German planes carrying the magic lanterns with enormously powerful Zeiss lenses flew above the enemy lines.

A dense snowbank in the sky above the German Army was used as a screen. Entire regiments who had beheld the vision fell upon their knees and flung away their rifles, Col. Herzenwirth says.

The trick was repeated several times on the Russian front and was invariably successful. "We knew from prisoners we took," says the Colonel, "that in some cases companies actually killed their officers and flung their rifles away, shouting that they would not be guilty of firing upon an army over which the Mother of God hovered in protection."

ST. JOAN AND ST. GEORGE.

With the French in Picardy and the Champagne region the Germans made another miscalculation, however. "Instead of taking the figure of a woman that we threw upon the clouds one night as that of the Virgin or a saint protecting our army, the French promptly recognised Joan of Arc," he says.

"The tables were turned upon us once more when we changed from a woman to a man in Flanders. The British said it was St. George."

1930

HOAX: SAYS GERMAN WAR OFFICE.

MYTH: SAYS AN AUTHOR.

COL. HERZENWIRTH ? — !

Were the Angels of Mons myth or reality?

The quotations in yesterday's "Daily News" from a narrative published in a New York newspaper, which purported to give an explanation of the phenomena, have again raised the dust of controversy.

This "explanation," by "a former member of the Imperial German Intelligence Service, Colonel Friedrich Herzenwirth," was that:

> The Angels of Mons were motion pictures thrown upon 'screens' of foggy white cloudbanks in Flanders by cinematograph projecting machines mounted on German aeroplanes, which hovered above the British lines.

According to "Colonel Herzenwirth," what was intended as German "frightfulness" was interpreted by the British as a portent of ultimate victory.

"NO SUCH PERSON."

Following is a message received yesterday from our Berlin Correspondent: "A prominent member of the War Intelligence Department in the present German Ministry declares that the story is a hoax; Herzenwirth himself a myth, or, if existing, a liar. It is officially stated that there is no such person."

Mr. Arthur Machen

Mr. Arthur Machen, the author, told the "Daily News" yesterday that the whole story of the apparitions was a legend invented by himself.

It arose, Mr. Machen said, from a story—"The Bowmen"—which he wrote and which was published on Sept. 29, 1914.

"The story told how, during the retreat from Mons, some English soldiers in the trenches saw the advancing Germans dropping down by whole regiments. That, they supposed, was due to the fact that one of them said, half in a joke: 'May St. George be a present help to the English!'

"The tale is that St. George came along bringing with him the ghosts of the bowmen of the old days and the Germans were supposed to be pierced by ghostly arrows.

"Nothing particular happened for the next few months, but some time in 1915 it was pointed out that people were taking the story as true. Then they began to turn the bowmen into angels. They elaborated the story and changed it about in all sorts of ways."

A SOLDIER'S VISION.

Against this it is interesting to recall that there is in existence an affidavit, sworn by Private Robert Cleaver, of the 1st Cheshire Regiment, which reads:

> I, Robert Cleaver (No. 10515), a private in the 1st Cheshire Regiment of His Majesty's Army, make oath and say as follows:
> That I personally was at Mons and saw the Vision of Angels with my own eyes.
> Sworn at Kinmel Park, in the County of Flint, this 29th day of August, 1915.
> Robert Cleaver.
> Before me, George S. Hazlehurst, one of His Majesty's Justices of the Peace acting in and for the County of Flint.

Mr. Hazlehurst gave the following report of Cleaver's account:

The men were in retreat and lying down behind small tufts of grass for cover. Suddenly the vision came between them and the German cavalry. He described it as a "flash." I asked him if the angels were mounted or winged. He could say no more than that it appeared as a "flash." The cavalry horses rushed in all directions and were disorganised; the charge frittered away

* * *

A "Daily News" reporter was informed yesterday by an official of the War Office that the official archives dealing with that part of the war contained no record to support any statement that an apparition was seen at Mons by the British troops.

1933
CHURCH VISIONS

PARISHIONERS PROTEST AGAINST CLOSING

Parishioners of Middleton, near Sudbury, Suffolk, demonstrated yesterday because the church and grounds had been closed to the public.

When the police moved them on they held a protest meeting in a barn and decided to meet again next Sunday.

The rector, the Rev. Clive Luget, and Dr. Thornber claim to have seen visions of the Virgin Mary and Dr. Thornber yesterday repeated that he had seen a vision of the Virgin Mary on the lawn.

1940
Acid Drops

The heavenly vision of angels has turned up again, this time in Greece. The *Daily Mirror* of November 22 reports the following: A few days ago news spread through the South of Greece that Greek soldiers on a lonely parade on the Athenian front encountered a veiled figure in the darkness who, when challenged, threw aside her veil revealing the face of the Blessed Virgin. To the awe-struck soldiers the virgin declared "It is I, I will not forget to revenge myself through my Greek soldiers on my own day." Angels and virgins! They are getting quite plentiful. At least we have here an explanation of the Greek advance. And we believe this vision to be as true as any other vision of angels that has ever been seen. Good Christians should remember that the chief authority they have for the divinity of Jesus is the message of an angel. The Italians are "up agin it."

1915
"A RING OF ANGELS."

'Scientific" Theory Advanced for Reported Psychic Phenomenon.

"There is a scientific reason for the appearance of a ring of angels round a contingent of Germans, which was reported in the Press on the information of two officers."

This statement was made to *The Evening News* by Mr. F. L. Rawson, a well-known authority on occult phenomena.

"This case of the apparition which caused the Germans' horses to become unmanageable may easily have been caused through one of the English being a very religious man and believing that this would take place.

"If it was his particular form of belief that angels would surround a man, then his thought could sufficiently intensify the matter to enable another man who was psychic to see the apparition. That person might not know that he was psychic, but, seeing the ring, he would state the fact aloud. The thoughts of those around would intensify the form, and all present would see them.

"The horses would see it easily, because animals are more psychic than human beings; that is to say, they can see finer forms of matter than the ordinary human being can possibly see."

1948
'HEADLESS GHOST IN PRE-FAB'

By Sunday Dispatch Reporter

THE ghost of a headless man is causing considerable alarm to people living in prefabricated bungalows in Page-road, Bedfont, Middlesex—so much so that the police have been called in.

The bungalows, which are detached, were built by Feltham Council on land which once formed part of the notorious Hounslow Heath, one-time haunt of highwaymen.

For weeks past strange "things" have been happening in house No. 42, occupied by Mr. Joseph Wilkinson, a coach driver; Mary, his 27-year-old wife, and Patricia, their four-year-old daughter. They have been haunted by a headless figure.

One night the little girl screamed to her parents: "There's a man sitting on my bed."

Then, when the Wilkinson's dog Dusty went hysterical with fear overnight, the family sought refuge with a neighbour, Mr. Walter Luke, ex-naval petty officer, who lives at No. 44 with his wife and four-year-old daughter.

Book Mystery

It was Mr. Luke who sent for the police, because strange things began to happen in his bungalow.

One night last week the stillness was shattered by the crash of a heavy book on the floor. That, said Mr. Wilkinson, was not so alarming as being unable to find any book on the floor afterwards.

Mr. Luke is now thinking of asking psychic research investigators to visit his bungalow and the Wilkinsons' home next door.

1934
Girl Typist Who Saw a Ghost Fall in City Street

MENTAL VISION OF TRAGEDY OF WHICH SHE HAD NEVER HEARD

A London typist on her way home fainted on passing an office building. She was carried into a chemist's shop in Aldwych.

On recovering, she declared that she had had the impression, as she walked, that a girl had fallen from the window of a high building and crashed at her feet. The shock was so great that she collapsed.

Exactly eighteen months ago, the tragedy she described actually happened—a girl fell from an upper story and was killed at the very spot where the typist, who had never heard of the accident, fainted.

What is the explanation of this remarkable occurrence?

A famous psychologist told the *Sunday Pictorial* that there are people with such sensitive minds that they can conjure up sub-consciously pictures of past events.

These people, placed in environments where tragedies have happened, can describe in minutest detail the particulars of the tragedy.

And the experience of the typist is by no means uncommon.

The psychologist said: "Recently I had a patient who told me she could not pass a certain street corner near her house as she always seemed to see a motor-bus pinned against the wall there.

"I made inquiries and found that seventeen years previously—during the war, and long before she came to the neighbourhood—a bus ran on to the pavement at this spot and seven people were killed.

1934
BLACK MAGIC IN THE CONGO

AN EXPLANATION WANTED
FROM A CORRESPONDENT

Indian magic, such as the "Rope Trick," "The Growing Mango Tree," and others, has been explained in detail, but I have not yet read how the African works his. The reason, I suppose, is that he is so seldom seen in action.

Once when hunting on the Upper Congo I came upon some native women making a clearing in the bush. Immediately it flashed across my mind that "Ju ju," or some other devilish rites, were to be observed, so I asked the women what was toward.

"We are preparing the arena for Maluka, the great magician, who is to give an exhibition of his powers to-morrow," was the reply.

I asked whether a white man would be permitted to see the performance. The women replied that if I asked Noguru, the petty chief, they thought there would not be any difficulty. Next morning I presented myself at the chief's village and asked to see Noguru. I was ushered to the largest hut, where, seated in front of the doorway, was a pleasant-looking, well-built native of about 40.

After making him a generous gift of calico I broached the subject of my visit, and asked him if I might be allowed to see the show.

"Certainly," he replied, "it is public and open to anybody." He then asked if I had a strong stomach, as, he said, if I was at all squeamish, what I should see would turn me up. I said I would risk that. "All right, then. Come along as soon as it begins to get cool."

Four o'clock that afternoon saw me at the clearing. Half an hour later two very powerful savages entered, each carrying a little girl of about nine years old on the palm of his right hand. The children looked dazed, as if they had been drugged.

The two child-carriers now faced each other, about five yards apart, and began tossing the children to each other, the little girls landing in a sitting position on the palms of the throwers' hands, which were used as platforms. The more the audience applauded this game of shuttledore with human battlecocks the faster was it played, until at last the thrown children passed each other in mid-air with the swiftness of volleyed tennis balls.

Next, at a signal from Noguru, Maluka strode into the clearing. He wore a grass mask and his body was striped with whitewash, which gave him a zebra-like appearance. He was followed by two boys, one bearing a crate containing half a dozen live fowls, the other a large bundle of dry bamboos, the most inflammable material in that part of the country.

Maluka nodded to the fuel-carrier, who immediately made a bonfire, upon which —when it was in full blast—he placed the crateful of fowls. It may have been my fancy or hallucination, but I could have sworn I smelled the pungent aroma of burning feathers. I was about to rush in to rescue the chickens, when Noguru stayed my hand.

"The chickens will not come to any harm," he said quickly.

Within a few minutes the crate was reduced to ashes.

"Now go and examine the crate," said Noguru.

I did so, and found it intact with the fowls inside, very much alive. There were no traces whatsoever of a fire.

The fowl-burners then made way for the *pièce de résistance*. A tall native, with his hands manacled and with a rope, fastened by a slip-knot, around his neck, was dragged into the centre of the arena.

Noguru then told the assembly that the man who had been marched in was under sentence of death, and was about to be executed by Maluka. Not only would he be killed, but after being dead long enough to see the error of his ways, he would be brought to life again by the agency of Maluka.

This awe-inspiring speech made a profound impression. In deathly silence, Maluka, still masked and whitewashed, walked into the circle bearing a 4ft. sword, whose edge he tested with the thumb of his disengaged hand, at the same time uttering a gibberish that none could understand. Then he went up to within a few feet of the condemned man, and proved his distance, as a cavalryman would, with the sword. He then brought the weapon well over his left shoulder, after the manner of a golfer terminating his stroke, and, with a mighty back-hand stroke to the right, severed the head from the body as easily as if it had been stuck on with putty! The head immediately fell to the ground and rolled away a few feet. The trunk remained upright for some seconds, and then slumped to the ground, blood spurting from the neck like a fountain.

I was horrified and tongue-tied. I wanted to protest aloud at a cold-blooded murder, for there, not 20 yards away, lay the head, and, a few feet from it, the decapitated body.

While I was staring fascinated or mesmerized, the whole scene changed. Maluka vanished. So did the head and the body. I pressed my hands over my eyes to assure myself that I was not dreaming. No, it was real enough; for when I looked again there was the same crowd, including Noguru. But Maluka and his victim had dissolved into thin air.

Suddenly a deep-throated murmur went round, and, at the same time, Maluka— minus his mask and paint—walked into the arena, leading by the hand the man he had beheaded—the latter grinning all over his face as if he had much enjoyed the performance.

1941
Ghost Caused Court Martial

ONLY one ghost has ever been the cause of a court-martial—that of Anne Boleyn, Henry VIII's ill-fated consort.

In the year 1864, a rifleman of the 60th Rifles was at his post in that part of the Tower of London known as the Lieutenant's Lodgings, where is the small oak-panelled room in which the Queen was confined until she was led out to execution.

Later on, when the officer of the guard was going his rounds the sentry was discovered prostrate on the ground, in a complete state of insensibility.

Under the impression that the man was drunk or had been sleeping at his post, the officer had him put under arrest, and later there was a court-martial to inquire into his neglect of duty.

To the surprise and doubtless to the amusement of the court, the sentry stammered out a fantastic tale as to how he had seen a dim white figure emerging from the room known as "Anne Boleyn's Chamber."

* * *

"I challenged it," the sentry asserted, "then, as it took no notice, I challenged it again. Then as it still did not stop, I charged at it with my bayonet. But I went slap through the figure, striking my head so badly against the wall that I fell down unconscious, and remembered nothing till I found myself under arrest in the guard-room."

The officers forming the court disbelieved the sentry's story until two Beefeaters corroborated it by stating that from their room above the post they had seen the mysterious figure—and this, they asserted, was nothing less than the ghost of Anne Boleyn, such a familiar object to the Beefeaters that they were in the habit of referring to it as "the Queen."

Several other persons said that they also had seen the spectre frequently, and the court finally decided that there was nothing else to do but to acquit the sentry.

Later on the post had to be abandoned, as sentries were shy of doing duty there.

So in the prosaic records of the War Office there is preserved the finding of this court-martial establishing the authenticity of the ghost of Anne Boleyn.

A.C.B.

1908
AMBUSHING A "GHOST"

Man with Pistol Faints at Sight of Nine-Foot "Spectre."

A queer story of a nine-feet-high "spook" that terrorises Galway is told by the Dublin correspondent of the Central News.

"It is said," reports the correspondent, "that two young men coming into Galway from Newcastle made a short cut by the railway line, and when opposite a place called Glanville they observed coming towards them on the line a dark object which they both agree in relating was of human form and about nine feet in height. When the object came within a few yards of them they state that it vanished, but they again saw it about forty yards along the line, and this time it passed on towards Lough Corrib and again disappeared.

"On coming into Galway the young men told of the weird occurrence to their friends, and accordingly a party was organised to visit the place the following evening and lay the ghost. At 8 o'clock the party started, armed with sticks, shotguns, and revolvers.

"Arriving at the spot, they lay in ambush for the spectre. They had not long to wait, for straight in front of them it suddenly appeared, whereupon one of the party raised his revolver. But he never fired the shot. The weapon dropped from his hand, which became powerless, and he fell in a swoon into the arms of one of his companions, while the 'ghost' vanished from view.

"General terror prevailed among the ghost hunters lest the case of their companion might become serious, and the hunt of the spectre was forgotten. The young man was conveyed into Galway, where he had to be medically attended, but it was some hours before he was brought back to consciousness.

"The affair only incited others to take up the hunt, and on Tuesday night a large party started for the purpose of encountering the apparition. But although they remained hidden for some hours no ghost made its appearance. A year ago several persons stated they had seen a spectre near the scene of the present apparition, and there is great terror in the district over its reappearance."

1933
A "GHOST TRAIN" IN SWEDEN

NOISELESS EXPRESS SEEN BY FIVE PEOPLE

(FROM A CORRESPONDENT)

A "ghost train" appearing between the Orresta and Tortuna Stations, on the Vaesteraas Railway, in Central Sweden, has frightened and mystified the country people of that district. Recently a party of five persons, while walking on the road near the railway, suddenly saw a lighted train at high speed glide noiselessly along the railway line. It looked exactly like the ordinary train, which was due half an hour later, except for the head and tail lanterns, which were unusually bright and powerful. It was clearly seen by the entire company, but no one heard the slightest sound from it.

On several previous occasions the same sight has been seen by single persons in exactly the same spot, but no one has been able to account for it or to offer a satisfactory explanation. Some years ago the railway bank caved in at this section of the line, and the old people of the district now prophesy some serious accident. Scientists have somewhat vaguely explained the phenomenon as a kind of mirage.

A similar sight one or two years ago frightened the Lapps (and the reindeer) in a desolate part of Lapland, where a phantom train was seen rushing through the forest in a district where there was no railway at all. This sight also remains entirely unexplained.

1929
SECRET OF PEEL CASTLE.

BLACK DOG THAT ONCE HAUNTED THE PLACE.

"Will anything be brought to light about the 'Moodey dhoe'?" Peel folk are asking uneasily, in connection with the excavations now being made at Peel Castle.

"Moodey dhoe" is Manx for black dog, and Peel Castle, for centuries, has been famed—if for nothing else—for its tradition concerning the apparition of a black dog which is said to haunt the place.

When the castle was used as a soldiers' garrison, the black dog was often seen, it is said, and although the soldiers became used to its appearance, they never relished the idea of it being there, and always refrained from using strong language in its presence.

DOWN THE DARK PASSAGE.

On one night, however, a soldier, while drunk, made up his mind to follow the mysterious animal and find out what it really was. He set off after it down a dark passage, much to the alarm of his fellow-soldiers.

When he returned he was sober enough and speechless with terror. He died shortly after, without disclosing what had happened.

After that no person was brave enough to go into the passage; it was built up and another way was made. The tradition was related to Sir Walter Scott by his brother, who resided in the Isle of Man, and he immortalised it in "The Lay of the Last Minstrel."

Superstitious folk about Peel believe that it is as well to let sleeping dogs lie, and they hope that no effort will be made to pry into the secret of the closed passage.

1934
Ghost Bus of Kensington

STATEMENT AT AN INQUEST

"Cause of Many Accidents"

During an inquest at Paddington yesterday, the junction of St. Mark's-road and Cambridge-gardens, North Kensington, was stated to be the place where local people had reported that a ghost 'bus was seen.

The inquest was on Ian James Steven Beaton, aged 25, metallurgical engineer, of Hamilton-road, Dollis Hill, who died following a collision between the car he was driving and another driven by Mr. George Pink, the chauffeur of the Hon. Samuel Vestey, of Manchester-square.

The jury returned a verdict of accidental death and exonerated Mr. Pink.

Frederick Robinson, of Chesterton-road, Kensington, a witness, asked whether the junction was noted for accidents, stated that he was told that it was the second within a week.

In reply to a further question as to whether this was a place where a ghost 'bus was stated to have been seen, Robinson replied, "So some of them say."

The legend of the phantom 'bus is well established in the neighbourhood.

THE LEGEND

A woman resident in Cambridge-gardens said: "The legend of the phantom 'bus has been going strong for years. I have never met anybody who has seen the 'bus, but the version I heard was that on certain nights, long after the regular 'bus service has stopped, people have been awakened by the roar of a 'bus coming down the street.

"When they have gone to their windows they have seen a brilliantly-lighted double-decker 'bus approaching with neither driver nor passengers.

"According to this story, the 'bus goes careering to the corner of Cambridge-gardens and St. Mark's-road, and then vanishes. A number of accidents have happened at this corner, and it has been suggested that the phantom 'bus has been the cause."

Another version is that a 'bus, which a woman had been told by a conductor to board, "vanished into thin air" when she approached it.

STRANGE DEATH

END OF A PERSECUTION.

JEANNE WEBER ACQUITTED AT BOURGES.

A FEROCIOUS MAGISTRATE.

The court at Bourges yesterday afternoon acquitted Jeanne Weber, who had become known throughout France as "the Ogress," and ordered her to be set free immediately.

This is the last act of one of the most extraordinary judicial tragedies in the history of the country.

Nearly two years ago, says the "Express," Jeanne Weber was accused of having strangled two of her own children and two of her little nephews. In each case the child had died after it had been alone with Jeanne Weber.

After a long trial, Jeanne Weber was acquitted and set free.

She was obliged to change her name, as no landlord would take her in, for nobody with children would live in the same house with her. For a few months she lived unmolested in a wretched lodging in Paris. But one day a former neighbour recognised her in the street, followed her home, denounced her, and she had to go again.

She decided on suicide, and threw herself into the Seine, but she was rescued, and the magistrate before whom she was taken gave her money to go out into the country, where she could live unmolested.

But a strange fatality dogged her footsteps, and two months ago, in the house of a woodcutter where she had taken refuge, a small child died of convulsions.

It was discovered that the woman on whose knees the child had died was Jeanne Weber, and her persecution began again.

The unfortunate woman was imprisoned again, and subjected to ferocious cross-examination by the examining magistrate, who declared himself convinced of her guilt.

It was proved that the child had died from natural causes, yet there was another trial.

1908

1923
"WE ARE TOO HAPPY."

Strange Tragedy of a Bride and Bridegroom.

From Our Special Correspondent.
PARIS, Tuesday.

"We are killing ourselves because we are too happy."

That is the strange reason given in a letter addressed to the police for a double tragedy which took place at Suresnes (near Paris) this morning, when M. Paul Albert Liebaut and his wife Germaine were found shot dead in a bedroom of their home.

The police believe that the woman, who was wearing her wedding dress, first shot her husband and then committed suicide. They had only been married six days. Liebaut was 30 years of age and his wife 22.

The letter to the police contained also the following phrases:

"We do not need money, for we are worth over 30,000 francs."

"We have good health and a wonderful future before us, but we prefer to die now because we are the happiest people in the world."

"We adore each other, but we would rather descend into the grave together while we are still so happy."

1908
154 NEEDLES SWALLOWED.

Remarkable Death of an American Woman.

[From Our Correspondent.]
[BY MARCONI WIRELESS.]
NEW YORK, Thursday.

Mrs. Mollie Dessler has died in the hospital from having a needle, which she had swallowed, pierce her heart. Her case is one of the most curious on record. Thirteen months ago, being deserted by her husband, Mrs. Dessler attempted to commit suicide by swallowing needles. By degrees she swallowed 154, and within a short time was tormented with pain.

She was taken to the hospital, and after twenty-six operations, extending over a long period, the doctors were able to extract 134 of the needles, partly by means of strong magnets. The needles were taken from her abdomen, back, nose and hands. It is believed that she supplemented the original dose in her anxiety to kill herself, and yesterday one of the needles that was left in her body entered her heart, killing her instantly.

"It was the final desperation of a plucky girl, who would rather die than go on without her husband," a friend said to me this evening.

1933
'I'm Going Into Space'

FLEW ON—TILL END OF 4 HOURS' FUEL

"I'm just going out into space to find out what it's all about; if there isn't anything, that will be O.K., too."

AFTER Mrs. Louise Turck Stanton, a wealthy and youthful member of an aristocratic family of Jacksonville, Florida, had written this in a letter she borrowed an aeroplane.

She had enough petrol for a four hours' flight put into the tank.

Then, climbing into the cockpit, she took off and, heading east over the Atlantic, flew high and straight . . . on . . . and on . . . and on . . .

Four hours later the letter was found, and airmen dashed in pursuit. They found nothing . . . . and there is no hope.

A fortnight ago Mrs. Stanton's husband was killed in a motor accident. They were devoted to one another.

104 Strange Death

1933
WICKET-KEEPER KILLED BY STUMP
A Fast Ball Mishap

MYSORE, Tuesday.

A wicket-keeper has been killed in a cricket match here. The wicket was shattered by a fast ball and the metal shoe of a stump pierced the player's heart, a bail also striking him in the eye.

The wicket-keeper was a 17-year-old student named Nurayana.—Exchange.

1938
1,000 PICTURES OF PIGS DROVE MAN TO DEATH

DETECTIVE-OFFICER WEBB scratched his head when he came to the end of his search in the office where Dugan, big business man, had been found shot.

Obviously it was suicide. But why was the office full of pictures of pigs? There were a thousand of them. A large canvas in oils was, from the paunch and the clothing, a portrait of the dead magnate—except that the head of a hog appeared in place of the man's face.

Yes, there was a resemblance. Dugan had looked like a pig, and people who did business with him had afterwards used that term to describe him.

The bewildered detective asked the dead man's secretary how all the pigs had come to be there. "They came every day, by post, express messenger, in parcels, every possible way," she said. "We don't understand it. Mr. Dugan couldn't go to a banquet without finding drawings of pigs on the place cards, or dangling from chandeliers."

The mystery was cleared up when Webb interviewed a young man and his fiancée.

"Maybe we didn't do right," said the young man. "Anyhow, you know what a wrecker of other men's businesses Dugan has been, and what a rotter he was."

Ruined Her Father

He told how Dugan had determined to marry the girl, and, because she would have nothing to do with him, had ruined her father. Then he smashed her sweetheart's business, driving the young man's father to suicide.

Dugan went on pressing the girl and nearly drove her mad with his unwanted attentions.

Then the young man had an inspiration. It occurred to him that Dugan might have a little conscience left, so he organised all Dugan's enemies to send anonymous pictures of pigs to him.

"I thought," he explained, "that Dugan might not be able to face himself as we all saw him, seeing those leering pigs at every turn."

Dugan could *not* face life when he saw himself as others saw him.

David Seabury, famous American psychologist, tells the story in his book, "The Art of Selfishness," recently published in America.

Mr. Seabury holds that the young avenger and his friends had no more committed murder morally than they had legally. They were acting in self-defence.

1921
KILLED BY A MONKEY.

At an inquest on a Lewisham man who died in an epileptic fit, a sister said he had had fits ever since an organ-grinder's monkey jumped on him 19 years ago.

1924
"DEATH WAITS FOR ME."
Coroner Reads Poem Found in a Dead Woman's Hand.

A poem, said to have been written by a woman who had suffered for years from neurasthenia shortly before she took her life by coal-gas poisoning, was read at an inquest held by Mr. H. R. Oswald, the West London Coroner, on Saturday:

Headed "Death Waits for Me To-night," the poem was as follows:

"Even now my summons echoes from afar
And grave mists gather round my star;
I am weary and am travel worn,
My faltering feet are pierced by many a thorn.
This cruel world has made my faint heart bleed.
When dreamless rest is mine, I shall not need
The tenderness for which I long to-night."

The stanzas were found in the hand of Florence Martha Miller, 40, a dressmaker, of Richmond-crescent, Shepherd's Bush found dead from gas poisoning. After reading them the coroner said: "If original it is an excellent example of versifying."

The coroner recorded a verdict of "Suicide while of unsound mind."

1935
Suicide by Spider Bite

YOUNG MAN'S STRANGE ATTEMPT

Victim in Hospital

From Our Own Correspondent

NEW YORK, June 2.

A fantastic method of self-destruction that rivals in fiction the inventive genius of Rohmer is reported. A man of 26, despondent over his failure to obtain employment, lies unconscious in the Worcester (Massachusetts) Hospital with the deadly venom of the black widow spider in his veins.

The man, Stephen Liarsky, obtained the insect by post from California.

In a glass container in the hospital laboratory is the insect—a large-bodied creature with eight legs. There are small pincers at the head. The spider is entirely black except for a red dot under the body.

The man is slowly suffocating as the poison is causing liquid to form in his lungs. Practitioners, who admitted they knew no way to combat the poison, administered a mixture of oxygen and carbon dioxide and injected adrenalin glucose.

The black widow spider was found in a perforated cardboard box beside the man's bed. In the box were postal cards bearing printed information that the insect's bite was deadly and there was no known cure.

The card stated that for five dollars a larger black widow with infant might be purchased.

1934
BURIED ALIVE BY HIS OWN ORDER

Abbot's "Life Work Done"

SIMLA, Tuesday.

Pilgrims from Bhaironji, near Bareilly, United Provinces, declare that Shambunath, the 125-year-old abbot of the temple, has been buried alive at his own request, as he considered that his life's work was over.

He had been at the temple for over 50 years.

For centuries it has been the custom of the abbots to practise self-immolation once they considered their usefulness at an end.—Exchange.

1936
MAN BITES MAN
INNKEEPER'S DEATH AFTER QUARREL WITH CUSTOMER

Munich, Saturday.—An innkeeper has been bitten to death by an angry customer at Elsbach, Western Bavaria.

When he presented his bill for six quarts of beer, the customer, 24-year-old Oskar Zaettel, protested that he had been overcharged.

In the quarrel that followed, Zaettel bit the innkeeper severely in the neck. Infection set in, and five days later the innkeeper, whose name was Derer, died.

For his savage bite, Zaettel has been sentenced to three years' imprisonment.—Reuter.

1924
WOMAN BANDIT'S FATE IN CHINA

Executed By "Slicing Process."

WIPED OUT A VILLAGE.

"Old Mother" Djao, said to be the most notorious bloodthirsty bandit the Province of Shantung ever produced, has been executed at Ichowfu, in Shantung, according to reports received in Shanghai by mission organisations, says Reuter.

The unfortunate woman underwent that most fearsome of Chinese death penalties, the ling-che, or, in English, the slicing process.

Forty-seven years old, and an expert horsewoman, "Old Mother" Djao led a band of several hundred outlaws who terrorised a wide area.

Attack on Village.

It is related of her that last summer she planned an attack against Ichowfu, after calling to her aid two other groups of bandits.

They had assembled at a place near the village of Balihsiang, when a homeguard of villagers, known as the "Big Knife Society," apprised of their purpose, attacked them and suffered utter defeat.

The villagers were driven back into Balihsiang, and the bandits followed them. Then the gates of the village were closed and every man was shot down.

Even Cattle Killed.

Sixty women and children were lined up, and "Old Mother" Djao was asked what to do with them. Her orders to kill them all were carried out, with the result that every man, woman, and child who was within the walls after the gates had been closed was slain. Even the cattle and dogs of the village suffered the same fate.

Ling-che is vivisection, done by experts in such a manner that the victim survives in a conscious state through hours of a terrible ordeal.

1916
DRIVEN BY DEAD MAN.
Horses' Strange Journey In London Streets.
UNCANNY INQUEST STORY.

The imagination of novelists has often weaved a story round the grim idea of the dead steersman, whose rigid, lifeless hands still held the wheel.

As grim a story, but far more extraordinary, for it actually happened in the heart of London, was told yesterday at the Poplar Coroner's Court.

It was the story of two horses, with a load of timber, travelling from Blackfriars Wharf to Mile End with the dead driver sitting in his seat, holding the reins.

Through the roar of crowded traffic—in and out of the maze of slow and swift vehicles—passed Death, seated above the swarming life of the pavements.

The dead driver was a man named Charles Thornton, aged sixty, and at the inquest yesterday another driver explained how the horses kept their right position in the traffic.

Richard Dean, who went with Thornton on another van, stated that the man was all right when he left Blackfriars. Thornton was behind him on the way home, and his horses must have followed those driven by witness through crowded streets, in spite of the fact that the driver was dead.

Medical evidence showed that the man's heart weighed 36oz., as against the normal weight of 16oz., and that death was due to a large rupture.

Death from Natural Causes was the verdict returned.

1905
KILLED BY CHURCH BELL.

The bellringer of Stoke-on-Trent Parish Church has met with a terrible death in his belfry.

The ringer, Thomas Rose, went up the tower on Saturday evening to get the bells oiled for Sunday, leaving two of his little children below. After a long time they called to him, and getting no reply went to fetch their mother.

She came with the sexton, and together they ascended to the belfry, and the sexton was horrified to find Rose pinned between a huge bell and the beam. He had been crushed to death, and when the wife realised the tragedy the sexton had great difficulty in getting her down the spiral staircase.

Assistance was procured, and by the light of a hurricane lantern men worked to relieve the body with crowbars. It was a dangerous task, the bells being liable to swing on them.

Rose, who had been bellringer for twenty years, leaves a widow and eight children. At the inquest yesterday the jury returned a verdict of accidental death.

1903
A HUSBAND'S TERRIBLE EXPERIENCE.

The Liverpool City Coroner on Friday held an inquiry into the deaths, under extraordinary circumstances, of William Shortis, a rent collector, and his wife, Emily Ann Shortis. According to the evidence, the couple, who were bordering on seventy, were last seen in their house in Oakes-street on Monday, August 10. Three days later, as neither had been seen going about, the house was entered, when the old man was found lying at the bottom of the stairs in a dazed and dying condition, with the dead body of his wife on the top of him.

A police-constable stated that the husband was completely pinned down under the body of his wife, who weighed about sixteen stone. Witness was of opinion that the couple had been going upstairs, and that the woman had fallen backwards, carrying her husband with her to the bottom.

According to the medical evidence, the woman had died immediately from concussion of the brain, and the husband had thus remained in his terrible position for over three days, having apparently been so seriously injured as to be unable to extricate himself.

The jury returned a verdict of "Accidental death" in both cases.

1924
SUICIDE IN SLEEP?

Evidence that he may have cut his throat while asleep was given at the inquest at Bangor on Saturday on Mr Thornton Jones, a solicitor. He lived 80 minutes after the infliction of the wound, during which time he cried out to his wife and son, "Forgive me, forgive me." Then motioning for a paper and pencil he wrote "I dreamt that I had done it. I awoke to find it true."

1942
Jap 'willed' his own death

From William Courtenay, "Sunday Chronicle Special Correspondent."

NEW GUINEA, Saturday.

A JAPANESE captured by the Australian Forces in New Guinea willed himself to die—and died.

The Jap was being brought to Milne Bay in a launch. He had slight leg wounds.

On the way he called on his god to slit his throat.

Then he attempted to jump overboard and later seized a guard's bayonet and tried to stab himself.

All his suicidal efforts having been frustrated, he lay down on the deck and died. His guards were convinced he died by sheer effort of will.

1906
TERRIBLE STORY.

A terrible story of the degenerating effect of certain classes of literature was told yesterday, when Karl Brunke, a bank clerk, nineteen years of age, was sentenced in the Brunswick Criminal Court to eight years' penal servitude for murdering two sisters, Martha and Alma Haars, at their own request.

The German criminal code differentiates, says the Express Berlin correspondent, between ordinary murder and murder committed at a victim's request. Paragraph 216 of the code provides for punishment of at least three years' imprisonment for murder committed at the serious and plainly expressed desire of the victim.

Brunke, in replying to questions addressed to him by the judge, said he was keenly interested in literature, and had read Kant, Schopenhauer, and other philosophers. He had written many plays, all of which had been rejected by theatrical managers.

A few months before the tragedy he began to teach music to both girls, who were respectively twenty-two and twenty-one years of age. He declared that Martha Haars, like himself, became a victim to melancholia because her literary aspirations remained unfulfilled. Alma desired to die because she was deeply attached to her elder sister. Whatever the reason may have been, Brunke and the girls agreed to die together.

1928

'LAST THOUGHTS' BY A SUICIDE.

PENCILLED STORY IN NOTEBOOK.

"IT IS GOOD TO HAVE LIVED."

Wistful, wanton, wayward, wild
Sceptic head yet heart of child.
God, who shaped the land and sea,
Why has Thou so mismade me?
God, who doeth all things best,
Tell me, dost Thou sometimes jest?
Ideals, lofty practice,
Low mouthing, yes.
But acting no.
Why, O Architect Divine,
Didst thou warp this mind of mine?

These lines were contained in a remarkable document, entitled "My Last Thoughts," written by Horace Pitt, aged 52, the proprietor of Oakfield School, Newport, Mon., before he shot himself on the cliffs at Penarth.

When he was found a revolver was clutched in one hand and a pencil in the other.

The document, contained in a notebook, was read at the inquest at Penarth yesterday. It stated:

"When this morning I decided to cut short this weary life of artificial make-believe, I felt temporarily elated, like one who, gasping and groping along a stifling subterranean passage, wins suddenly into the lucid and champagne air of a breezy English upland.

"About 11 p.m. The night has fallen. ... I have lived about 40 years in three hours.

"Thank God for life. It is good to have lived, and as for death, I cannot dogmatise but shall know in 60 seconds. Bang."

A verdict was returned of "Suicide while temporarily insane."

1934

NINE GIRLS DIE FOR LOVE

Bound in a River

SHANGHAI, Monday.

An amazing story of the mass suicide pact of nine Chinese girls, aged from 13 to 19, comes from Hewian, Fukien.

They are reported to have roped themselves together and jumped into a river.

According to vernacular newspapers, the group suicide was due in each case to unrequited love.—British United Press.

1905

"THE CURSE OF LIFE."

CURIOUS LETTER OF A PRISON SUICIDE.

Sentenced on November 22 to eighteen months' imprisonment for housebreaking, James Montrose, aged twenty-three, committed suicide by hanging himself in his cell at Swansea Gaol with a piece of cord and a hook which he used in mat-making. An extraordinary letter, which he wrote on a slate, was read at the inquest yesterday. In it he said:

"I had a hard task to keep from hanging myself while I was awaiting trial for two months, and it was then I made up my determination that the first warder that reported me for any paltry offence I would murder for the purpose of getting hung out of this miserable curse of life.

"But as I hate the law, and therefore do not wish to die by it, I have changed my mind, and take the curse of life away myself. Rather than have a life in the cursed gaols of England, which are ruled by gangs of brutal tyrants, I would sooner die; and I say again that it were far better to be down in the grave. I am happy in the thought that I will soon be no more."

A verdict of Temporary insanity was returned, and no blame was attached to the officials.

1919

PREYED ON HIS MIND.

Committed Suicide After Conviction.

A curious story of how being fined for the possession of an anti-Zeppelin bullet so preyed on a man's mind that he committed suicide was told at an Edmonton inquest on John Garratt, aged 47, a labourer, who was found dead in his room with his head buried under an overcoat and with a gas ring turned on lying near.

His son stated that some time ago his father was charged with having in his possession a Pomeroy bullet which was used in bringing down Zeppelins, and which, it was alleged, he had obtained unlawfully. He was detained in custody for some time and then fined £1.

This, said witness, had broken his heart, as the bullet had been given to him and he had kept it as a curiosity. He was ashamed to go back to his work, although his employer treated him with every kindness.

A note found in the deceased's handwriting asked the wife to forgive him and the son to look after her.

The coroner found that death was due to coal-gas poisoning and recorded a verdict of "Suicide whilst temporarily insane."

1929

PIN PRICK DEATH.

At a Lambeth inquest yesterday, on Winifred Brosnohan (51), of Ingravestreet, Battersea, it was stated that she died from toxemia after running a pin into her thumb.

At a second inquest, on Lancelot Hugh Beaver (17), a Bedford Modern School boarder, a doctor said he died of an infection which probably arose from an abrasion on a small corn on his foot.

1926

LOVERS' SUICIDE.

GRAND GUIGNOL SEQUEL TO BELGRADE TRAGEDY.

From Our Own Correspondent.

PARIS, Friday.

A tale of horror which might figure on the repertoire of Grand Guignol is reported here from Belgrade.

Two young people, aged 18, Imra Blaj, son of a wealthy tradesman, and Mizzi Stachitch, a butcher's daughter, whose union was opposed by their parents, decided to commit suicide.

On Tuesday they went together into the country, descended a railway embankment and threw themselves before an engine.

The young man was dragged several hundred yards by the cowcatcher of the engine and torn to pieces. His sweetheart was decapitated and her head thrown through the window of a cabin in which the wife of the level crossing keeper was playing with her children. The woman, seized with horror, snatched her two infants to her bosom and fell dead of shock.

1901

EXTRAORDINARY SUICIDE.

At a Leyton inquest yesterday it was shown that Malcolm Jamieson, 63, a plasterer, committed suicide by cutting the back of his neck. The muscles were cut through and several arteries severed.

Dr. Clarence Wright said that he did not believe there was another case of suicide like it on record.

It was shown that deceased had been very strange in his manner. He used to rave and mutter to himself, and would frequently exclaim, "Oh, my poor head!" and "I'll do it before I leave this earth."

A verdict of "Suicide whilst temporarily insane." was returned.

1938

"TOO MUCH IN LOVE"

COUPLE WHO DREADED PARTING, FOUND GASSED

"They were too much in love," declared the mother of 29-year-old Alfred Carter at a Chertsey inquest on her son and his wife of five months, Edith, 23, who were found gassed at their home in Derwent-close, Addlestone, Surrey.

Police found the couple lying in a last embrace in their locked kitchen. On the table was a slice of their wedding cake.

Mrs. Carter told the coroner that during the recent international crisis, the couple stayed with her at East Barnet. They were always together, and were afraid the husband would be called up as a reservist. They dreaded to be parted.

Mr. Carter, the dead man's father, declared, "My son had a very hasty, jealous temper. His wife was the same. I think they just said, 'Let's make an end of it,' and this is what they did."

An uncle expressed the view that the cause was jealousy.

"Both seemed to be madly jealous," he added.

The verdict in each case was "Suicide while the balance of mind was disturbed."

1926
KILLED BY JAZZ?

Noted Musician Drops Dead on Hearing U.S. Band—Last Protest

News of the tragic death in remarkable circumstances at Coney Island, U.S.A., of Mr. Nicola Coviello, a noted London professor of music, was received yesterday by his son.

Mr. Coviello, who was seventy-nine, was taken to Coney Island by a nephew whom he was visiting, says *The Daily Mirror* New York correspondent.

He listened for a few minutes to a jazz band playing at furious pace and turned to his nephew, declaring, "That isn't music. Stop it." Then he swayed and fell dead.

Mr. Coviello had for thirty years conducted a school of music at Balham, residing in Boundaries-road Balham.

1934
Poisonous Snakes Put in a Bed

OGPU CHIEF KILLED

HELSINGFORS, July 12.

The death of General Sirov, the chief of the Transcaucasian Ogpu (secret police) is reported here.

On retiring to bed the General was bitten by two poisonous snakes, which are alleged to have been deliberately inserted between the sheets.

In spite of all efforts to save his life, the General died in great pain.

The snakes are stated to have been stolen from the local zoological gardens.—Reuter.

1934
KILLED BY MOCK EXECUTION

How a University sacristan was killed as a result of the flick of a wet towel which he really believed to be an executioner's axe was described by Dr. J. Burnett Rae, a physician in charge of the Department of Psychological Medicine of Croydon General Hospital, in an address to the National Council for Mental Hygiene last night.

"He was a sacristan at my old University of Aberdeen years ago," said Dr. Rae, "and was unpopular with the medical students."

After a mock trial the man was taken to another room. His head was placed on a block, his neck was flicked with a wet towel—and he died.

1904
TRAVELLER'S TERRIBLE DEATH.

Accidental death was the verdict returned at an Islington inquest in as strange a case as ever came before a coroner's court. Mr. Welch, thirty-three, a wine trade traveller, was expected home at seven p.m., and three hours later his wife found him with his limbs paralysed, lying near the front door steps. He told her he had been lying there for two hours, and that he had fallen over the steps coping, a foot high. He died in hospital, as the result of dislocation and fracture of the spinal column.

1941
SIX KILLED WHEN WALKERS BUMPED INTO WALKERS

SIX cases of pedestrians being killed by bumping into each other are reported by the Royal Society for the Prevention of Accidents.

Five of them occurred in the black-out.

Twenty-two others were killed by walking into lamp-posts or other obstructions or slipping on pavements.

1934
Death from "Housemaid's Knee"

IT was disclosed at an inquest at Stepney to-day that the death of Mrs. Elizabeth Alice Gregory, aged 47, who had been employed for ten years as a cleaner at London Hospital was due to "housemaid's knee."

The Coroner (Dr. Guthrie) asked: It is very rare to get a death from it, is it not?

"Yes, very rare," replied Dr. A. S. Wesson, medical officer of Mile End Hospital.

It was stated that one of Mrs. Gregory's daughters died on the same day.

Dr. Guthrie recorded a verdict of death by misadventure, adding that death was "consequent upon her kneeling on the floor to do her work as a scrubber."

1906
MURDERER BURIED ALIVE.

Expiation of Monstrous Crimes.

Reports received at Tangier from Marrakesh state that the cobbler Mesfiwi, who murdered and buried about thirty women, has duly expiated his monstrous crimes.

It had at first been determined that the murderer should be publicly crucified, but at the last moment orders were issued that he should be walled up alive. Previously, however, Mesfiwi was subjected to daily floggings.

The final act of the tragedy also took place in public. When the masons were at work a mob jeered at the trembling wretch.

When the walling in had been completed the mob still remained hurling insults at the doomed man.

For the two first days Mesfiwi screamed continuously, while the mob exulted in his agony.

On the third day (says the Central News) the living tomb gave forth no sound, and it is presumed that by that time the murderer had died from exhaustion.

108 Strange Death

1924
OCTOPUS EGG MYTH.

Yarn with Several Places of Origin.

The story that appeared in the "Daily News" the other day of a girl who swallowed an octopus egg, which hatched inside her, has aroused a remarkable amount of interest But the most remarkable thing is that the incident seems to have happened in various parts of the country. A "Reader" writes:

"Having read a certain paragraph in your paper which dealt with a girl swallowing an octopus egg, I would inform you that what you think is a fable is quite true.

"The girl, who has now succumbed, was an employee in a Nottingham factory. I must conclude by saying that your paragraph seemed to me very callous."

"A Constant Reader" says:

"With reference to your article concerning the factory girl on holiday, I should like to inform you that the incident occurred at Whitley Bay, in Northumberland. The girl was caused an immense amount of pain. . . . the octopus died shortly after the girl, which happened about 14 weeks ago."

Another reader writes to say that it was a Bradford mill-girl who swallowed the egg.

1904
LOVE STRICKEN AT 75.

Old Lady Puts on Bridal Dress and Lays Down to Die for Her Lover.

Lovestricken for a boy of twenty, who told her he was engaged to another girl, a soft-hearted spinster of seventy-five determined to die.

She lit a charcoal fire, clad herself in a white gown, which she had bought for her bridal dress, and scattered orange-blossoms on her couch, then lay down.

She was quite dead when found the next morning, having been stifled by the fumes of the charcoal.

As forgiving as she was fond, says the "Telegraph," she has left her small fortune, bringing in an income of £120 a year, to the young man.

1903
KILLED BY LOT.

"Express" Correspondent.
BERLIN, Tuesday, Nov. 3.
According to a despatch published by the "Tageblatt," a Russian soldier, while drilling with his regiment at Wilna, stepped out of the ranks and killed his colonel with a bayonet thrust. The act was greeted with cheers by the regiment.

Investigations revealed that a conspiracy was formed among the men, who decided to kill the colonel, and selected the murderer by lot. The colonel was hated owing to his severity.

The Russian Minister of War has despatched a commission from St. Petersburg to make further inquiry into the circumstances of this extraordinary affair.

1923
MANIAC WHO KILLS LOVERS.

SERIES OF MURDERS BY "SPOONER-KILLER."

"Sunday Express" Correspondent.
NEW YORK, Saturday, June 30.
A maniac who kills affectionate couples as they pass him in the park or street is terrorising the city of Memphis, Tennessee. Already he has six murders on his blood-list, and he is still at large.

Mrs. Tucker.

The sight of a man kissing a girl seems to enrage him, and although he has been known to rob his victims of small sums, this seems to be his chief reason for killing. His haunts vary, but he usually chooses motor parkways or shaded drives in the suburbs.

He often fires at a motor-car containing a man and woman.

1923
KILLED BY A BALL OF FIRE.

MOST DANGEROUS FORM OF LIGHTNING

ONE IN A MILLION CHANCE

"Reynolds's" Correspondent.
GRIMSBY, Saturday.—"The chances of death in this way are one in a million," said the Grimsby coroner, to-day, after William Hicks, coal merchant, had described the circumstances in which George Beeson, a Cleethorpes boilermaker, was killed during a thunderstorm.

"I saw a ball of fire, probably three feet in diameter, come rolling slowly through the sky," said Hicks.

"It seemed to touch a chimney stack; and instantly there was an explosion. The chimney stack was shattered, the roof split, and windows were broken. Among the debris on the ground I saw Beeson, lying unconscious."

Beeson had been standing beneath when the stack was struck, and a falling tile fractured his skull.

"Ball lightning," commented the coroner, "is the most dangerous form of lightning there is The fireball travels slowly through space harmlessly until it encounters some physical object, then it explodes, exactly like a shell."

The verdict was "Death from misadventure."

1921
SUICIDE IN A GRAVE.

Grim Discovery Follows Paris Murder.

From Our Own Correspondent.
PARIS, Tuesday.
Three nights ago an Italian woman named Cressini was found dead in a flat in the Rue Philippe de Girard. There was a bloodstained knife near the body, alleged to belong to a man named Bullano, with whom she had lived. Bullano had disappeared.

Preparations were made for the funeral, and a grave was dug in the Pantin Cemetery. In it has now been found the body of the missing man, face downwards. He had shot himself through the heart, upon which he had kept to the last a photograph of his victim.

1927
CHILD DIES OF FRIGHT.

SHOCK AT SIGHT OF A POLICEMAN.

"Sunday Express" Correspondent.
ELGIN, Saturday
Nannie McKerron, a seven-year-old Elgin girl, dropped dead to-day when she saw a policeman approaching.

The girl was of a highly nervous disposition.

1928
PROFESSOR'S SUICIDE.

From Our Own Correspondent.
VIENNA, Friday.— Professor Leo Bruck, who was connected with a grammar school in Budapest, committed suicide in an extraordinary manner in a classroom in the presence of his pupils.

He had lectured on Socrates and, as if to describe in a telling way the equanimity with which the philosopher drank a cup of hemlock, he seized a glass of water on the desk in which, as was afterwards ascertained, he had put poison and drank it.

He continued to lecture but soon dropped unconscious to the floor. The pupils raised an alarm but medical help proved futile.

1934
HIS BLOOD WAS BLACK

"Extremely Rare"

A pathologist said at an inquest at Coventry on John Charles Clarke, aged 39, of Longford, Warwickshire, that a post-mortem examination showed all his blood to be coal-black, of the consistency of tar.

The pathologist was Dr. Wright, who added that the heart was studded with black spots. He attributed death to melanotic sarcoma, an extremely rare form of malignant growth.

A verdict of Death from Natural Causes was returned.

SUPERSTITION

SACRIFICES TO THE "RAIN GOD."

BARBARIC SURVIVAL IN RHODESIA.

From a Correspondent.

JOHANNESBURG, January.

A story almost incredible to European ears of the savage man's faith in human sacrifice to propitiate the weather god has just reached here from Rhodesia.

Following continued drought, an unfortunate native was seized, bound and publicly burned to death as an offering to the Rain God. A tragic coincidence was the almost simultaneous breaking of the drought, and this, of course, despite the fact that 63 men have been arrested on a charge of murder in connection with the affair, is the surest guarantee that a custom which has already sent some 70 unfortunate men to a horrid death will be continued.

1923

1919

Soldiers' Superstitions.

I have heard of some strange superstitions, but this, related to me by a demobilised gunner, took me by surprise. He said, quite seriously, that his battery discovered that whenever any of Sir Rider Haggard's books were sent to them an S.O.S. signal was immediately received. He assured me that this always happened, and that one evening, while he was reading "Allan Quatermain," three such urgent signals were received. The battery decided to bar the books in future, and as soon as any arrived they were burnt. A marked decline in the number of S.O.S. calls was then noticed. The story might not be so surprising if the books had not been Sir Rider Haggard's and the battery itself had appealed for help. One could understand the arrival, say, of a consignment of the works of Walter Pater causing some consternation in the average battery. As the story stands, it is more fantastic than most soldiers' superstitions.

1912

AIRMEN'S NEW PERIL.

Aeroplane Shot At as Bird of Ill Omen.

[From Our Correspondent.]
PARIS, April 9.

Corporal Gilbert, the well-known aviator, has just experienced a new danger with which airmen may henceforth have to reckon. He was flying over the country around Brioude last week, where the superstitious people of that district are on the look-out for a gigantic bird of ill-omen, which is supposed to render sterile all the fields over which it flies during Holy Week.

Seeing Gilbert's aeroplane hovering over his farm, an old farmer of 83 fetched his gun, loaded it, and fired upon the aviator, whom, however, he fortunately missed. Gilbert, unaware that the farmer had fired at him, and believing that the gun had been discharged as a sign of enthusiasm, responded by throwing out a handful of aviation pamphlets, entitled "Our Future is in the Air" and then disappeared in the distance.

The octogenarian farmer, seeing the papers fluttering to the ground, supposed they were feathers from the "bird," and joyfully declared to his wife and grandson, "Though my sight is not so good as when I was 20, I have winged him all the same."

1925

MAN-WOLF STORY LEADS TO MURDER.

CONSTABLE KILLS A "SORCERER."

VILLAGE OF TERROR.

PEOPLE WHO FEARED WITCHCRAFT.

"Sunday Express" Correspondent.
STRASBOURG, Saturday, Nov. 28.

"I SAW a wolf with a human face—the evil face of a sorcerer. He had haunted my house for days. One night I flung open the door and shot the man-wolf through the heart."

This was the defence of a constable on trial for murder at Uttenheim, an old-world village in Alsace where the legend of the werewolf still persists. Tales of sorcery during past weeks had worked on the inhabitants to such an extent that they became panic stricken. Vague terror filled their minds, and they walked in daily fear of being bewitched.

Joseph Sur, the constable, believed that his cottage was haunted. "Animals with human faces" appeared at night when the lights were out and people were in bed. Misshapen, evil dogs and cats appeared, he declared, to harm the village.

BOYS' "HAUNTINGS."

He communicated his fears to his family of three sons and two daughters, and then to his neighbours. The whole village, with the exception of two mischievous boys, soon became a prey to nerves. The two boys encouraged the villagers in their beliefs, and then began to play on their fears by "haunting" hedges and cottage gardens at night.

The remarkable part of these strange events is that the villagers knew what the boys were doing, but their credulity was so extraordinary that they came to believe that the boys themselves were the sorcerers with power to change their bodies at night and until dawn into the forms of maleficent animals.

Thus one evening when the constable saw outside his house a dim figure with the face of one of the boys he shot him dead. The arrest of the constable and the trial followed. The man's sons and daughters swore in court that they had seen the evil animals at the same time as their father.

VILLAGERS' NERVES.

Others testified that the boys had "the power of turning themselves into animals and passing through small apertures in the walls of houses to disturb people in their sleep."

The villagers during the trial were in a state of nerves, and once the judge had to clear the court. A number of women had worked themselves up to such a pitch that they had to be taken home.

Sur, who pleaded that he had acted in self-defence against the sorcerer's influence, was sentenced to two years' imprisonment, but the man-wolf legend is still alive in the village, and the belief in sorcery persists.

1928

SAILORS' DREAD.

FIRM BELIEF IN "JONAH" SUPERSTITION.

Twenty-nine survivors of the ill-fated Vestris were aboard the Celtic. Did that number include the bugbear of sailormen, a "Jonah"?

Science may not be able to explain whether there is any psychic influence which operates in a passenger in such a way as to cause disaster to the ship in which he or she is travelling. Men who earn their living by the sea, however, are positive that "Jonahs" exist. They will quote classic instances.

"WOMAN'S INFLUENCE."

"Thousands of both our rank and file believe in the theory," said an official of the National Union of Seamen to a "Daily Express" representative yesterday. "They still talk, for instance, of the possible occult influences exerted by a woman whose last sea accident happened in the same vessel, the Celtic.

"A Mrs. Murray, the wife of an American naval lieutenant, experienced three disasters. She was saved when the Titanic crashed into the iceberg and foundered in 1912. It was pure luck that she was found. She was aboard the Lusitania when the ship was torpedoed during the war, and she was rescued with difficulty. Mrs. Murray was a passenger in the Celtic in 1927 when that ship and the steamer Anaconda came in collision.

"No one can say if ill-luck follows a person; seamen swear it does, and I have known voyages where the men have sailed with fear in their hearts, believing that a comrade was a 'Jonah.' Often their premonition has proved accurate."

1905

Daniel Flickinger Wilberforce, a negro who has been working in the mission field of Africa for twenty-five years, has relapsed to savagery, having become chief of his old tribe of devil-worshippers.

1906

CHURCH OF MURDERERS.

Cult of the Executed Criminal in Sicily.

A description of one of the most remarkable churches in Europe was given by Mr. E. S. Hartland (Glos.) at the international congress for the History of Religions at Oxford yesterday, in the course of a paper on the cult of the executed criminal.

In the city of Palermo, he said, there was a building only frequented by the poorer class of the inhabitants. Originally it was a church and was now known as the Chiésa dei Decollati (Church of the Executed). Decollati were executed criminals, and herein lay the interest of the church. Formerly criminals of rank, whose friends did not succeed in securing their bodies, were buried there. The church was in consequence the shrine of a remarkable cult—the cult of the Anime dei Decollati. It was filled with votive offerings of wax legs, heads, feet, babies, and so forth—testifying to the various benefits for which the intercession of the Decollati was besought.

In a side case was a representation in relief of Purgatory, with three or four persons in the flames. Their necks were hung with hearts and other amulets. Above, in the case, was a crucifix, to which they were apparently praying, and in the case also were several pairs of votive eyes in wax.

Most curious of all, however, was a case of water-colour drawings outside and adjoining the church on either wall of the burial-ground. These drawings represented persons suffering from internal hemorrhage, or various wounds. They represented accidents, shipwrecks, and attempted murders. Some unfortunates were tumbling from scaffolds, some were being crushed by tramcars, some by falling trees, and so forth. Bystanders and relatives were represented in attendance.

They, or the persons immediately concerned, appeared to be praying to the Decollati, who were shown in one of the upper corners, to the number of three or four, up to their waists in purgatory. They were generally manacled; some of them had ropes round their necks. The Decollati, on the other hand, were praying from Purgatory to the Virgin and Child frequently shown just above them.

The veneration of the souls of the departed was by no means confined to Palermo and its neighbourhood. It was known from Acireale, on the east coast, to Trapani, on the extreme west. The cult of the executed criminal in Sicily was not an isolated example of the vagaries of human emotion.

1898

AN "ANGEL-MARRIAGE."

Gross Superstition and Fraud in Darkest Bavaria.

A truly extraordinary story is sent by the Vienna correspondent of the *Daily News*.

The invalid daughter of a poor couple named Wohlfahrt, living at Kempten, Bavaria, persuaded a neighbouring farmer named Kottrich that she was in correspondence with the Virgin Mary, and also with Kottrich's deceased daughter Crescence. On this pretence the invalid's parents obtained numerous large sums from Kottrich. By-and-bye the invalid (Agnes) reported that Crescence had

MARRIED AN ANGEL.

She wished to have her dowry sent, and 1,000 marks for furnishing her new home. Then after a time came the news that Crescence, who was very happy, had given birth to a child. Would they send money for the wants of the baby?

Agnes or her mother for her made more preposterous demands every day — the Kottrichs had to borrow loans and pay high interest for them. One day the Virgin Mary herself asked for the loan of 2,500 marks, promising to pay good interest, to decorate the heavenly rooms, erect new altars, &c.

Eventually Kottrich saw that he was being defrauded, but this was not until he was practically ruined. So he consulted the police, and the Wohlfahrts were arrested. Agnes, in the meantime, had died. At the trial the Kottrichs produced fifty-two letters which Agnes had transmitted from heaven, and these were not all, some being lost. The letters which came from the Virgin Mary direct were written in Latin letters, those from Sister Crescence in German letters; every sheet of letter paper had the picture of a saint upon it. Those from the Virgin Mary had a gilt edge. Imagine the

SENSATION IN COURT

when the Public Prosecutor read a receipt "from the Mother of Christ" for 150 marks; a request for a higher amount signed : "In Heavenly glory, Joseph and Mary." A letter expressing thanks for money received and for excellent potatoes; another announcing the receipt of 2,500 marks, signed "Daughter, son-in-law, and little baby," with the remark added, that when the money arrived "all the angels in Heaven blew their trumpets."

Perhaps the most remarkable fact of all is that "Our Lady" and "Sister Crescence" sent their dear ones some things from Heaven, from "the heavenly hall"—a sofa, a large milk loaf, pieces of clothing, a silver watch, and a gold ring, but this last had to be returned after a short time. Frau Kottrich herself baked a fine tart for the Virgin Mary.

The woman prisoner was found guilty and sentenced to two years' imprisonment. Her husband, who is too stupid to have helped in the deceit, was sentenced to two months' imprisonment for receiving stolen goods.

1904

A TATTOOED CRUCIFIXION.

A man who recently came into the hands of the Church Army at their new labor home at Bow was found to have a representation of the Crucifixion tattooed on his back.

He explained that he had had it done many years ago as a protection against flogging!

He had been in the Army, and there was a notion prevalent amongst soldiers that no officer would dare to order a man to be whipped whose flesh bore this symbol, nor any comrade be found to carry out such command if given.

1936

Peasants Riot for Old Calendar

FIVE KILLED IN RUMANIA

From Our Own Correspondent

BUCHAREST, Sept. 14.

At least five people were killed and 18 seriously wounded in a "calendar war" which broke out to-day in the Province of Moldavia, in Northern Rumania.

The affair is reminiscent of the mediæval outbursts of religious fanaticism. It arose out of the arrest of a notorious peasant "saint" named Glikerie, leader of the movement for the reintroduction in Rumania of the old Julian Calendar instead of the Gregorian Calendar.

Several thousand peasants armed with scythes and pitchforks, preceded by a column of children, women, old men and cripples chanting hymns, marched to the town of Piatra-Neamtz and threatened to storm the local prison if their " saint "was not released at once.

The mob became violent and attacked the gendarmes, six of whom were seriously wounded. Troops were called out and order was restored only with the aid of machine-guns and rifle fire.

Glikerie claims that the Balkans are being destroyed as a consequence of the introduction of the "modern" Gregorian calendar. He remains under arrest, together with some 200 additional calendar crusaders who were arrested during to-day's revolt.

The Gregorian Calendar ordained by Pope Gregory in 1582, was adopted by Rumania in 1919.

1910
RUSSIAN CHOLERA.

STRICKEN VILLAGERS "HAND IT ON" TO NEIGHBOURS.

(From Our Own Correspondent.)

Berlin, October 12.—The Russian newspapers are daily publishing the most astonishing revelations as to the attitude both of the people and of the officials to the cholera scourge, which is still carrying off thousands of persons every week. The revelations would be incredible were they not attested by trustworthy persons.

Dr. S. V. Balkovetz, sanitary inspector of the Minsk Zemstvo, publishes, in the organ of the local medical association, a description of the attitude of the peasants towards the epidemic. The peasants, says Dr. Balkovetz, refuse to be treated for cholera, on the ground that it is "God's scourge," and as the divine reason for thus afflicting the nation they quote a rhyming proverb, which reads, "If the people did not die the heavens would fall."

This passive attitude, however, is not universal. Some villages have no objection to getting rid of the cholera by non-medical means. A favourite practice is "handing it on." The villagers take useful articles out of cholera-afflicted cabins, and strew them on the paths connecting with other villages where there is no cholera. The calculation is that persons belonging to the cholera-free villages will find and take home the infected articles, and with them the disease. The peasants, however, are now becoming too wise, and refuse to fall into the trap; so that the roads are in vain baited with death in the shape of household goods.

Disinfection as "Tyranny."

The enmity to the "dokhturs" is intense. The "dokhturs" poison the people—such is the universal belief. The only way to avoid death is to do what they forbid. Thus the muzhiks persistently drink bad water, and when the inevitable attack begins they refuse all treatment, and do their best to "hand on" the disease to others. "Endless efforts, incredible labour, is spent by the doctors in order to disinfect houses, clothing, and coffins of the dead. The disinfection is regarded as tyranny and mockery of the dead. The sprinkling of disinfectants calls forth screams and sobs. Enmity and hatred meet us at every village. To drive off the doctors is the battle-cry everywhere."

The peasants naturally have their own way of fighting the plague:

"Perfuming the villages, surrounding them with a thread spun in a single night, wearing a wooden cross, burying alive cats and pikes—these are the methods employed in Minsk province, especially in the Poliessk districts. Sometimes, in order to prevent the spread of the disease, the muzhiks force the priest to bury the victims face downwards." Water, "whispered to by wise women," is another means much used.

The "poisoned" medicines constitute a burning question. Sometimes the peasants force the doctors to drink their own medicines. "Often the question of poison or no poison is only decided after tests on flies, cats, and dogs. This causes the spreading of the wildest legends; the dosed flies are represented as carried away by magic; cats, having taken the medicine, cry out with human voices, and dogs vanish altogether."

In the Eastern provinces the same conditions prevail. The Moscow newspapers of October 7 contain the following telegram from the province of Ufa. "The communal council of the Tcheremess village of Bedeeve passed a decree declaring that the first woman who had died of cholera was a witch, and was now flying by night in the shape of a pillar of fire. The village police were therefore ordered to disinter her body, turn it face downward, and drive iron spikes into its back."

Dr. Kuznetsoff, a Volga-side sanitary officer, gives some further details as to the popular attitude in this district.

"In some villages the peasants obediently take the medicines prescribed; but when the doctor's back is turned they mix it with mud taken from a pond rich in frogs. This, it is believed, 'kills the poison,' but allows the curative elements to work. A doctor at Michailovo returned and made a scene when he found a patient thus swallowing mud, whereupon the sick man's relatives seized him and bound him to an oak-tree. There he remained all night.

"Often doctors arrive and find perfectly healthy men and women hung up by the heels to the ceiling. Thus they are 'cured.' The doctor pronounces them healthy, and this increases the popular belief in the efficacy of the cure, so that many really afflicted persons are so hung up, and thus left to die.

Belief in Witchcraft.

"Witchcraft is here universally believed in. When one man who suffered from a trivial complaint was 'treated' by the villagers for cholera by the hanging method, he ran away and hid in a forest. The peasants declared that he had turned into a hen. They seized the first hen they saw, killed it, and buried it. In this village no man died of cholera, and the fame of the hen-treatment so spread that every village within reach began sacrificing its fowls. The fact that the 'cholera-patient' came back from the forest did not make the least difference in the popular superstition."

According to the newspapers the attitude of the officials is little more enlightened, and with less excuse. The sanitary inspector, Dr. Malinowsky, sent to Odessa to take measures, is thwarted and fought by the notorious Prefect Tolmatcheff, who holds that sanitary inspectors are of no use, and that cholera can be prevented by methods resembling martial law. M. Tolmatcheff, who is a known Jew-baiter, drives through the city on tours of inspection, and levies administrative fines on all Jews who break the sanitary regulations, while Christian offenders nearly always get off. When bubonic plague lately broke out, the Prefect offered ten roubles for every case reported. The result was that hooligans raided the city, seized perfectly healthy persons by the score, and dragged them to the sanitation barracks. In other cities the anti-cholera regulations are being exploited in order to punish Liberals.

The sanitary authorities in vain telegraph to the Premier asking for protection in their work against the all-powerful local officials.

1935
Witchcraft Act Case Fails

ONLY TWO PROSECUTIONS IN 100 YEARS

A Workington (Cumberland) hawker's wife, Mrs. McGee, was acquitted at Carlisle Assizes yesterday of a charge brought under the Witchcraft Act of 1735 of undertaking to tell the fortune of Mrs. Rothery, of Beckermet.

She was also charged with her husband, Thomas McGee, and her brother, James McCourt, with conspiring to obtain goods by means of a worthless cheque. All were acquitted.

In the fortune telling charge, it was stated that only two prosecutions had been brought under the Act in the last hundred years, the other being in 1904, and Mr. Justice Singleton told the jury that they were making history.

1905
FAMILY BEWITCHED.

REMARKABLE STORY FROM MONMOUTHSHIRE VILLAGE.

Our Newport correspondent telegraphs: The quiet parish of May Hill, near Chepstow, is excited. Some time ago a small farmer reported that he had lost £50 from his house. Someone, he said, had taken from its secret hiding place the key of the box in which his wealth was stored, had taken the money, and then replaced the key. Suspicion fell on a resident, whose house was searched, but without any trace of the money being discovered.

Then it was suggested that a "witch" should be imported from Wales, and the suggestion was acted upon. The result has been strange and unforeseen. Immediately the "witch" arrived on the scene the farmer's daughter and granddaughter showed unmistakable evidence of madness, and one of them, a married woman, has been removed to the asylum at Gloucester. Then the farmer's wife became affected in the same way, and went out into the woods, where she remained in hiding.

It was reported yesterday that one of the farmer's sons had developed similar symptoms, and had become such a terror to his wife and the neighbours that it had been necessary to place him under restraint. He produced a quantity of what he described as "witch wood," which he urged his wife to grasp tightly and to pray, so as to circumvent the "witches," which he seems to imagine have influenced the family.

1930
"TWILIGHT BELIEFS"
Fairies, Pixies, and Wish-Hounds

TO THE EDITOR OF THE MORNING POST

Sir,—Why does Mr. James P. Park so confidently assert that "we live in an age when these old twilight beliefs are disappearing"?

I have lived for ten years on the borders of Dartmoor. I could an I would introduce Mr. James P. Park to a bridge that cannot be crossed at midnight.

To a dell where fairies are still seen to dance.

To a dangerous locality where an earthbound spirit dwells causing terrible accidents.

To a well-known and universally respected lady who has seen a pixy and heard the wish-hounds.

I could take him to visit a witch in her cottage, at the risk of being overlooked.

Cornwall.   PADDY SYLVANUS.

1909
DEATH-WARNING "HEN."
Curious Story of Irish Superstition Told by Relatives to Registrar.

A strange story of Irish superstition was reported yesterday from Drumavale, near Clones, Co. Monaghan.

A "hen" is declared to have entered a farmhouse and begun to crow. Mindful of the old Irish superstition that such an incident is a warning of death, a Miss Clarke, aged eighty, seized the bird and cut its head off.

Up to that time, the relatives have informed the registrar of deaths, the woman had enjoyed excellent health, but a few days later she was seized with illness and died within an hour.

1902
LINGERING SUPERSTITIONS.

The survival of a curious superstition was brought to light at Essex Assizes yesterday during the hearing of a charge of stabbing. In order that the wounds might the more speedily heal, the knife with which they were inflicted was greased and laid on the bed on which the prosecutor slept. It certainly happened that no serious results followed the injuries.

1936
Peasants Kill Farmer and His Family

BUDAPEST, Monday.

Superstition led to the deaths of four persons in the district of Temesvar, Hungary.

When the sow of a wealthy farmer had a litter of 12, one of the pigs had four eyes and eight legs and this led the villagers to believe that the farmer was possessed of the devil.

A child of a neighbour died, and the peasants attacked the home of the pig owner and set it on fire. The farmer, his wife and two sons were burnt to death as no one would raise a hand to rescue them.—Exchange.

1931
YARD HUNT FOR A SATANIST.

BUT LONDON IS NOT THE H.Q NECROMANCERS.

PARIS BLACK MASS.

"DEVILISH" TRICKS OF AN INFAMOUS CULT.

SCOTLAND YARD is now hunting a necromancer. Police at Hensingfors, Finland, found that more than 50 bodies had been exhumed and used for the rites of a small crowd of occultists, and because one of them had a book printed in English, they asked Scotland Yard to take a hand in rounding up the leader.

Scotland Yard's first discovery is that the headquarters of the unsavoury movement are in Paris—not in London.

The head of the gang has been turned out of several countries, but he goes on his way, preaching and practising his infamous cult and winning other crazy people to his creed.

He has been visiting and lecturing in and near London recently, but his fellow Satanists are keeping his secret. The police do not know where he is, and they find it harder to break through the taboo of a lunatic sect than to induce an ordinary criminal to squeal.

DEGRADED TYPES.

It is thought that there are two people at the head of the organisation, but there are many acolytes. One of them now abroad has been closely questioned by detectives, but they have not gone much further with their knowledge.

Black magic has strange haunts, outside the pages of thrillers. It has been practised in universities and in mansions, as well as in cellars.

Mr. Harry Price, of the National Laboratory of Psychical Research, told "The Star" to-day that there are many Satanists in England.

"The devotees are a degraded type, and they find secrecy one of the allurements of the cult. That hampers the police.

"I am of the opinion, however, that the headquarters are not here. I know there is one in Lyons, and also there are many followers in Paris.

AN ADVENTURE IN PARIS.

"All this is the more surprising, when one realises that Scandinavia, Norway, and Finland are the least psychic of all countries.

"Had this broken out in Paris, it would not have been so unusual. I have attended a Black Mass in Paris. It was both spectacular and startling, but most of the performances are reserved for the initiates. They are to be guessed rather than described."

1933
HAPPY RATS
BELGRADE.

Thousands of rats and field mice have invaded the countryside and houses around Jajtze, Bosnia. Peasants cannot sleep for the mice running over their bodies during the night, and the crops are threatened with destruction by the plague.

No one dares attempt to drive the vermin away, since Marko Kajtaz, a rat-catcher, was struck dead by lightning while at his work in the fields. The peasants see in this the hand of God.—Reuter.

1903
THE DEVILPHONE.

It has been found impossible to establish the telephone at Saint-Etienne des Gres, in the Tarascon district, says the Paris correspondent of the "Telegraph."

Under the odd impression that the invention was the work of the Evil One, the inhabitants determined to oppose its entry and resolved to arm themselves with their agricultural implements and to make a fight for it.

The carter conveying the apparatus thereupon said he would not risk his life in the adventure and the cart has been left at Tarascon.

1937
VOODOO VICTIMS SAVED

Trembling with fear negro wife Mrs. Verlen McQueen and her daughter, aged eleven, sought sanctuary in Detroit, U.S.A., police headquarters yesterday, stating that they were condemned to be boiled alive as Voodoo Cult sacrifices.

Police raided the McQueen home and arrested the husband as he tended the steaming vessel of sacrifice, says British United Press.

1906
"MULTIPLYING DIAMONDS."

The theory advanced by Mme. Cavalier in a lecture on Thursday that diamonds have sex, and if placed together in a box will multiply, is described by Professor Pringle, of the Museum of Practical Geology, South Kensington, as absolutely untenable. All jewels are the result of chemical formation, he says, and unless fused to liquid form it is impossible to add anything to them.

Superstition

1935

Having done their best to empty Germany of some of its best brains, the Fascists have created a fearful and wonderful biology of their own. The latest edict is to prohibit the use of lemons, because " only the products of the German soil can create German blood. Only from them derives that pulsation of the blood which with its effect upon body and soul determines our German character." This seems to go with the " Proletarian biology " and " proletarian psychology " of which we used to read. The next step in Germany should be the repudiation of Newtonian gravitation, as coming from an Englishman, and the rejection of the earth's motion round the sun because Copernicus was a Pole.

1928

BLACK MAGIC MURDER.

BOYS SET FIRE TO A FARMER.

VOODOOISM.

"SUNDAY DISPATCH" CABLE.
NEW YORK, Saturday.

A tale of witchcraft, as strange as anything out of the Middle Ages, is revealed by the murder of Nelson Rehmeyer, a farmer of York County, Pennsylvania.

An extraordinary confession by two youths and a self-styled "powwow" will be made the opportunity for a complete investigation into the prevalence of Voodooism and other forms of black art which are still practised by hundreds of people in the south of the State.

A witch doctor and two youths are now under arrest, charged with the murder of the farmer, who himself practised the art of Voodooism.

Their story is that Rehmeyer had bewitched the family of one of the boys and caused a road they wished to open to be closed.

One of the boys, William Hess, aged 18, summoned to the family's aid a witch doctor, reputed to have power to remove evil enchantments.

THE LOCK OF HAIR.

After a consultation with "the word from beyond," the "doctor" declared that the evil spell could be removed by burying a lock of Rehmeyer's hair eight feet beneath the ground. The fee for the revelation would be £8.

According to a confession made to the police, a visit was paid to Rehmeyer, who, however, proved singularly unwilling to lose his lock of hair.

Thereupon the "doctor" and the two boys struck the farmer on the head with a piece of wood, poured kerosene over the unconscious man, and set fire to his clothes.

The braying of Rehmeyer's neglected donkey first drew attention to the murder, which is the second in the last six years to occur in York County through belief in witchcraft.

1928

150,000 PEOPLE WHO BELIEVE IN MAGIC.

MURDER FOR HAIR.

"Daily Express" Correspondent.
NEW YORK, Sunday, Dec. 9.

ASTOUNDING revelations of the prevalence of so-called witchcraft and "pow-wow" necromancy rites among the 150,000 residents of York County, Pennsylvania, and the neighbourhood have been made in consequence of the investigation of the recent murder of Nelson Rehmeyer, aged fifty-nine, famous locally as a practitioner of black magic.

John H. Blymyer, aged thirty-two, a rival worker in witchcraft, and his two assistants have been arrested and accused of the murder. One of the prisoners, it is alleged, confessed that they killed Rehmeyer in an effort to obtain hair from his head for burial behind a chickenhouse in order to "cure an evil spell" which Rehmeyer was accused of casting over Blymyer and the family of M. J. Hess, thus causing household discord.

LONELY FARMHOUSE.

The murder occurred on the night of November 27, at Rehmeyer's lonely farmhouse in a suburb of the city of York, following a terrible struggle in which Rehmeyer resisted efforts to cut his hair.

Blymyer, who is awaiting trial, is quoted as saying, " I did not expect to kill Rehmeyer, but now I no longer feel bewitched. I can now eat and sleep "

Mr. Lu Zech, the coroner who investigated the murder, declares that three-fourths of the population of York County believe in witchcraft and practise "pow-wow" rites. He asserts that five infant deaths during the past two years are traceable to black magic.

York County's early settlers were Germans, and their present-day descendants still remain under the spell of medieval German necromancy. One of their sacred words is "hex,' said to be corrupt German for witch.

"Pow-wow" doctors abound in the neighbourhood, having thousands of patients, who have unbounded trust in their charms. "Pow-wow" is the North American Indian word, apparently adapted because of its mysterious sound.

Investigators who have been making inquiries during the past week found a general belief that a flitch of bacon drives away warts, that a key hung down the back stops bleeding at the nose, that linen taken from a body reduces swellings, and that pulling a child backwards through a bramble bush cures whooping cough.

There are scores of other such "cures," which must be accompanied by the pronunciation of mystic words or the display of secret signs for efficacy.

The "witch doctors" use as witchcraft guides "The Sixth and Seventh Books of the Magical Spirit Art of Moses" (sometimes called "The Black Art Bible"), and the "Himmelsbrief," or "Heaven's Letter."

SPECIAL RANK.

Few of these volumes are in circulation, and possession of them therefore gives special rank in Pennsylvania witchcraft circles.

Blymyer denies the accusation that black magic secrets have been passed to him through generations of ancestors. He declares that he was taught "pow-wowing" by Mrs. Emma Knopp, of Marietta, near York, aged seventy, a wrinkled, witch-like dame who looks a hundred, and has but one remaining tooth—a long, sharp-pointed fang.

America is greatly stirred by the revelations. Efforts are being made by Pennsylvania civic bodies to devise means of stamping out the sorcerers, but prosecutions are seldom successful. Almost any jury summoned to hear cases in York County contains believers in witchcraft who make "guilty" verdicts more difficult.

The city of York, the capital of York County, is a modern municipality with handsome buildings, and is a wealthy centre of a fertile agricultural region, yet witch "pow-wow" doctors ply their trade in the city equally with the country districts, where almost every farmhouse is said to be tainted with belief in witchcraft.

TABOO

PURITANICAL LAWS IN THE STATES.
COMICAL RESULTS—LYNCHING THREATENED.

An amazing state of things is reported by Dalziel from the village of Winstead, in Connecticut, where certain of the old "blue" laws of the State, regulating the private conduct of citizens in various extraordinary and puritanical ways, have just been revived with highly amusing results. The position of affairs, indeed, as reported, is more suggestive of comic opera than actual fact. And the joke of the matter appears to be that political spite rather than excessive virtue has been at the bottom of the business—one party having caused the enforcement of part of the laws in question and the other retaliating by calling into effect the balance. As a consequence yesterday every place of business was rigorously closed, trains forbidden, and cycling disallowed. Indeed, a number of men and women who went for rides on their machines were arrested. The "blue" laws regulate Sunday labour, so twenty prominent citizens have been arrested on the charge of having their Sunday dinner cooked. Correct deportment was a strong point of the old laws, and thirteen men were consequently arrested for kissing their own wives, this being an offence which the law expressly forbids. Owing to these and other repressive measures Winstead is almost in a state of rebellion, and the victims threaten to form a committee to lynch the responsible politicians.

1898

1929

"LA PUDEUR BRITANNIQUE"

The traditional English respect for appearances is upheld by this Serpentine study. In a moment the boy bather in the portable tent will join his naked friends without embarrassment, but the conventions will have been honoured

1899

THE DEMOCRATIC SHOW.

> To fan
> And winnow from the coming step of time
> All chaff of custom, wipe away all slime
> Left by men-slugs and human serpentry.

Felixstowe is an alleged watering place into which civilization is slowly penetrating. They take objection in that town to the cut of your bathing drawers and have just fined County Court Judge French, of all men, 40s. for preferring his own pattern to that of the municipal donkeys of obscure Felixstowe. I wonder what these noodles would have done with Adam and Eve had they wandered in this quarter, even after they pretended to find out that God had made them indecent. Why is a "great mass meeting" not held at Felixstowe to denounce God for having made us as we are? Felixstowe is a place for bathers to avoid in future.

1899

GOD'S HANDIWORK DESPISED.

Sir,—Your delightful paragraph about Felixstowe in last week's issue prompts me to offer a few considerations on the subject of bathing costume. During the last fifteen years or so there has arisen a diseased and artificial dread of viewing the human body. We see the tendency widespread. Those detestable vices known as bathing drawers have crept in, even upon our quiet rivers, to hide our self-made shame from the unspotted swans, and are enforced at closed and high-walled swimming baths. I begin to feel more and more Walt Whitman's respect for the animals who never reach our depth of degradation.

Is it really true that the modern Puritan regards the supple forms of youth—"the fair young larch-poles of our Empire," as "Branca" calls them—as being unclean and impure? Pink coral statues, with the breath of hay—are even they corrupt to the alleged moralists' view? Perhaps; for the Puritan's mind is coarse and it is the revolt against himself that makes him a Puritan. What is called morality is convention. It cannot be in sanity that men can say that the human shape looks better and more seemly with a piece of red rag round it.

I will only briefly assert, as a diver of some skill and a devoted bather, that water garments are insanitary, preventing much that is most beneficial and threatening much that all would wish to escape. A good half of the benefit of swimming consists of drying in the sun and open air. Through drawers the wind strikes chilly and the pores of the skin are kept covered. I will only say on the "morality" side, that if these very "modest" people would study the origin and purpose of clothing in the history of savage races, they would discover that garments were mostly worn to allure others and that no attraction is considered to be so strong as that which is unseen.

I am glad to see that on the Thames they have apparently gone a little too far even for the heavy British public and that there seem a chance of a good row. May the day come when only in absolutely public places will anything so ugly and inconvenient be tolerated as clothing for a swim.

B.A. Cantab.

George Ives

The censored drawing.

1940
VICE DANGER IN SHELTERS

BAPTIST pastor thinks "it has now become dangerous to a young man's moral reputation for him to be seen coming out of an air-raid shelter at night."

He is the Rev. W. G. Cripps, and he was talking about Weston-super-Mare.

Speaking to a mixed congregation in his church there, he accused girls aged about seventeen of soliciting in the streets and taking men into air raid shelters which have no lighting system.

"My wife was asked to give temporary lodging to some young girls who were described by the authorities as unbilletable," he said.

"They won't stay in at night, and prefer to go out on the streets. Then they are found in air raid shelters not alone Can we afford to overlook things like this?"

Moral welfare workers in the district are urging the authorities to install lighting in sea-front surface shelters

Dr Remmett Weaver, Medical Officer of Weston-super-Mare, told the *Daily Mirror*: "I hope certain steps will be taken before long"

1921
POSTER BANNED BY UNDERGROUND.

PEOPLE WITH A PAST.

NOT VERY NICE TO KNOW.

The Underground Railway, it seems, have a nice taste in advertisement posters. At any rate, they are very scrupulous and selective, and very anxious that nothing should offend in the slightest degree the susceptibilities of the millions who use their lines.

It is for this reason that a new poster, which has been submitted to them by Messrs. Pope and Bradley, the West-End tailors, has been politely, but firmly, refused.

It appears that the picture contains the portraits of a number of famous historic personages of whom we should say in these days that they were "not very nice to know, you know," and lest the more sensitive of the public should be shocked, the Underground authorities refuse to paste the picture on the walls of their stations.

The foreground of the picture is occupied by a modern couple in the act of dancing a very modern dance. But no adverse comment is made about these. The trouble has arisen over the little group of figures clustered in the background.

Here one is able to recognise, among others, such famous personages as Antony and Cleopatra, Queen Elizabeth, Sir Walter Raleigh, Charles II., Nell Gwynne and Byron. These personages, it is pointed out, are unfortunately "people with a past."

The picture is by the well-known artist "Jacques d'Or," and is entitled "Masters and Mistresses." The Underground authorities in returning the posters say:

In our opinion they are lacking in taste, and may be the cause of adverse criticism from our passengers. With regard to "Masters and Mistresses," this is open to objection in that the figures shown in the background are historical personages whose moral characters were not above reproach.

Whilst not setting up to be the defenders of public morals, we think it is only right to see that all passengers can travel on our railways without fear of offence.

So you may beguile the short waits on the tube stations gazing at the art collections without fear, and safely take your wife and daughter. The gentleman who has been going strong for a hundred years has an impeccable past; the lamplighter who breaks the lamp (but not the mantle) is a respectable married man, and the dazzling tooth-paste girl is beyond reproach.

Mr. Dennis Bradley told a "Daily News" representative yesterday that the refusal of the poster was vastly amusing to him and to his friends. It was incredible.

1922
ULYSSES
James Douglas

A famous dramatist told me that an eminent novelist had lent "Ulysses" to him. His remarks about the book are unprintable. Then a friend in Paris brought a copy to London and lent it to me. I have read it, and I say deliberately that it is the most infamously obscene book in ancient or modern literature. The obscenity of Rabelais is innocent compared with its leprous and scabrous horrors. All the secret sewers of vice are canalised in its flood of unimaginable thoughts, images, and pornographic words. And its unclean lunacies are larded with appalling and revolting blasphemies directed against the Christian religion and against the holy name of Christ—blasphemies hitherto associated with the most degraded orgies of Satanism and the Black Mass.

THE BIBLE OF THE OUTCASTS.

And here let me say frankly that I have evidence which establishes the fact that the book is already the Bible of beings who are exiles and outcasts in this and in every civilised country. It is also adopted by the Freudians as the supreme glory of their dirty and degraded cult, which masquerades in pseudo-scientific raiment under the name of "Psycho-Analysis."

1913
WOMAN TRAMPLED ON.

Sequel to the Wearing of a Daring Slit Bathing Suit.

American people are deeply exercised by the case of Mrs. Charles Lanning, the wife of a wealthy New Jersey hotel proprietor, who was assaulted at Atlantic City when she appeared on the beach clad in a daring swimming costume.

The beach was crowded with many thousands of men and women in elaborate bathing suits. Into their midst strolled a handsome woman attired in a brilliant purple bathing suit, the skirt of which, according to the *New York Herald*, was "slit clean to the waist."

She led a toy poodle, white except for a ribbon bow collar which was the exact shade of purple worn by the dog's mistress.

As the bather approached the water's edge a strong gust of wind caught the ends of her skirt, and they flew back, revealing a pair of vividly purple tights. The revelation caused a mighty shout to go up from the other bathers.

A man hurled a handful of sand at Mrs. Lanning, and a moment later everyone was pelting her. She was buffeted backwards and forwards amid the indignant mob until one man, catching her by the leg, threw her to the ground, where the mob trampled on her.

Only after a severe fight, says *The Daily Mail* New York correspondent, could the police rescue the woman from her tormentors. She was carried by motor-car in an unconscious condition to the nearest hospital, where she is now recovering from her injuries. Her expensive purple bathing suit was torn to shreds.

1930
PARIS CINEMA WRECKED

EGGS FILLED WITH INK

"MODERNIST" FILM RESENTED

From Our Own Correspondent
PARIS, Dec. 8.

A cinema hall was wrecked and its screen damaged here, when a part of the audience manifested its objection to the film shown. The demonstration was pre-arranged, the demonstrators, who occupied two rows of the stalls, having armed themselves with ink grenades, stink bombs and other explosive material.

The ink grenades were ingeniously constructed of hollowed-out eggs which burst on being hurled against the screen, covering the pictures with large black splashes. At a given signal a regular barrage of these missiles was launched, while an appalling clamour of cat-calls, whistles and syrens drowned the sounds of the film.

At the same time a gang of men invaded the foyer and bar and proceeded to tear down pictures and smash furniture. Meanwhile a free fight had started in the hall between the demonstrators and their partisans and the section of the audience who objected to the film being interrupted.

"THE GOLDEN AGE"

Order was only restored on the arrival of the police, who arrested the organiser of the attack and his assistants. The former is a well-known unofficial protector of public morals, who made himself notorious a short time ago by wrecking a bull ring at Melun. The cinema in question belongs to the modernist or "advance guard" movement initiated after the war by a literary and artistic clique calling themselves the "Sur - Realistes." It specialises in the more original kind of film, and has come in for severe criticism before.

The film which provoked Friday's outrage is entitled "The Golden Age." It is an extraordinary mixture of satire, buffoonery, parody, and obscenity, and makes a good many obvious digs at such recognised institutions as the Roman Catholic Church.

The film was described by the critic of the "Figaro" as an obscene attack on the foundations of civilised society. Surprise is expressed that the film was authorised by the censor, as the extreme crudity of many of the scenes would preclude exhibition by any ordinary Paris cinema, even although the film is said to have been cut before being passed.

1927
PARK SUN BATHER.

QUESTION ABOUT BOXERS UNANSWERED.

Mr. Mead: I am going to hold, rightly or wrongly, that to expose the upper part of your body is indecent.

Defendant: What about the Milligan-Walker fight? They were stripped to the waist, dressed as I was, and they were not arrested, and there were 30,000 present.

This was a striking passage from a sharp dialogue between the Marlborough-street Magistrate and Harold Hubert Vincent, the sun-bathing advocate, who was charged with an offence under the Hyde Park regulations.

Police evidence was that defendant was lying on an overcoat on the grass by the western end of the Serpentine road, wearing a pair of shorts only.

Vincent (to a constable): Have you ever heard of sun-bathing?

Magistrate: I am not going to have nonsense of that sort. Sun-bathing, as you call it, may be a proper thing practised in privacy, but it is not to be indulged in if it is indecent and offensive to other people.

Vincent (to the constable): Do you know the effect of the sun on the human body?

Mr. Mead: Don't answer him.

Addressing the magistrate, Vincent said: "I am fighting a greater cause than that of personal freedom, nothing less than that of the regeneration of an ignorant and degenerate people.

"I am going on with this fight even if it means my going to the gallows," and he thumped the front of the dock with his fist.

He was remanded for a medical report.

1929
SEIZED PICTURES.

POLICE RETURN WORKS OF BLAKE.

The "Daily News" was informed yesterday that the police after their raid on the pictures by Mr. D. H. Lawrence at the Warren Galleries on Friday night returned and confiscated a set of William Blake's pictures and books. Later they returned the set.

Blake died in 1827.

They apparently thought Blake was living. He died in 1827, and when they found that proceedings should have been taken over 100 years ago, they returned the set.

On the application of the police summonses were granted on Saturday in connection with the 13 seized pictures. It is understood that the summonses have not yet been served.

There was a steady stream of visitors to the Gallery on Saturday to see the remaining pictures, nearly all of which bore the red "sold" label.

1931
CURIOUSER AND CURIOUSER.

WHERE CHILDREN MUST NOT READ "ALICE."

All the world is now joining in the merry sport of banning books. During the past few months all sorts of famous books have been banned in various countries and for various reasons.

Now comes news of the queerest ban of all.

In the Chinese province of Honan an official order has just been issued, says Reuter, which prohibits schoolchildren from reading

ALICE IN WONDERLAND.

The Governor of Honan, General Ho Chien, explains that he has banned Alice" because:

"Bears, lions and other beasts cannot use a human language, and to attribute to them such power is an insult to the human race. Any children reading such books must inevitably regard animals and human beings on the same level, and this would be disastrous."

This is a serious matter for the children of Honan.

Not merely will it prevent them from reading "Alice." It will prevent them from reading Kipling's "Jungle Books" and the Brer Rabbit stories. It will prevent them from reading "Puss in Boots" even.

1930
CLEANING-UP U.S. FILMS.

NEW CODE OF ETHICS FOR TALKIES

SCREEN TSAR'S EDICT

From Our Own Correspondent.

NEW YORK, Monday.

A SWEEPING new ethical code for films was adopted by the board of directors of Motion Picture Producers and Distributors of America at a meeting here to-day.

Mr. Will H. Hays, known as "the film Tsar," announced that these new standards, made necessary by the coming of talking pictures, would govern the character of practically all films shown to a world audience of 250,000,000 people weekly.

Mr. Will Hays.

Among the interesting regulations in this attempt of Hollywood to put its house in order are the following:

Sanctity of marriage and the home shall be upheld.

Adultery shall not be explicitly treated or justified.

Scenes of passion shall not be introduced when not essential to the plot.

Sex perversion or any inference of it is forbidden.

The subject of White Slavery shall not be treated.

No religious faith may be ridiculed.

Ministers of religion should not be used as comic characters or villains.

The use of the flag shall be consistently respectful.

The history of institutions, prominent persons and citizenry of other nations shall be represented fairly.

Pointed profanity is forbidden.

Such subjects as hanging, electrocution, third degree methods, brutality, apparent cruelty to children or animals must be treated within careful limits of good taste.

It is provided that every effort shall be made to reflect in drama and entertainment better standards of life. Law, natural or human, shall not be ridiculed, and sympathy shall not be created for the violation of laws.

CRIME ON THE SCREEN.

The code says: "Crime, brutality and vice are among the facts of life, but it is recognised that there is a right and a wrong way to present such facts on the screen. Crimes against law shall never be presented in such a way as to show sympathy with crime as against law and justice.

"Acts of murder or brutality shall be presented only in such a way as will not inspire imitation. Methods of crime shall not be presented in explicit detail. Revenge in modern times shall not be justified as a motive.

"WET" SCENES.

"The use of liquor in American life shall be restricted to the actual requirements of the characterisation or plot."

To-day's ratification of this code, drawn up by Mr. Hays, follows a series of meetings with the production chiefs of leading Hollywood studios, at which Mr. Hays secured their signatures to it.

The code is described as a voluntary act of self-discipline and self-government by the motion picture industry.

1930
AN EXPURGATED BIBLE

CHICAGO.

Mr. Frank R. Chandler recently celebrated his 90th birthday, and took the opportunity to comment upon the "20th Century Bible" which he has just published.

"In it," he said, "I have expurgated all immoralities, indelicacies, and irrelevancies. I have left stars to denote the deletions. For instance, in the Bible it says that Noah got drunk. Why do we need to say that? As the Bible stands now I would not want a daughter of mine to read it, but expurgated, as I have made it, it is fine literature."—Reuter.

1934
A Nudist Wedding

MINISTER THE ONLY ONE CLOTHED—IN A GOATSKIN

CHICAGO, June 29.

Wearing nothing, a girl from Amarillo, Texas, was married here to-day to a man from Milwaukee, similarly naked, in the midst of a strictly nudist gathering. The minister was the only person present who departed from the rules. He was arrayed in a goatskin.

Nine unclothed friends of the bride and bridegroom attended the wedding. Round about the party stood models of Dinosaurs triceratops, and brontosauri, and other monsters of bygone ages, for the ceremony took place in a section of the Century of Progress Exhibition, named "The World Millions of Years Ago."

The bride is a member of the nudist colony of Rose Lawn, Indiana, and her bridegroom comes from the Mirror Lake, Wisconsin Colony. After the wedding they put on clothes to make the journey to the nudist colony where they are setting up home.—Reuter.

1919
SHOCKING BARRY'S MODESTY

Snapshots to Shame Women Bathers.

The modesty of members of the Barry Council was shocked when they received a report from their surveyor of a troubled interview he had with two women bathers recently.

He reported that he saw the women, without covering, bathing in the children's pool near the rocks. He rebuked them, but the women only laughed, and one of them told him that if he did not go away she would smack him. When she came out of the water and dressed she actually smacked his face.

The Committee empowered the beach inspector to take legal proceedings, and it was decided that snapshots of bathers be taken in future further to shame the women should any impropriety be noticed.

1921
LOW NECK ARREST
In Prison for Breach of Modesty Law.

Arrested by the Chief of Police in person as she stepped from a train, a young American woman, Mrs. Sarah Johnson, has been removed to gaol pending trial on the following counts:

Wearing short sleeves which exposed the arm above the middle of the forearm.

Wearing a blouse of transparent material.

Wearing a blouse with neck cut below the junction of the base of the neck and collarbone.

Lest the news should cause a panic among fair readers of the "Daily News," it should be explained that the arrest did not take place in London under D.O.R.A., but in Zion, under the "Modest Dress Ordinance." Not the Zion of song and scripture, but Zion, Illinois, which is a very different place indeed.

Mrs. Johnson, according to Reuter's correspondent, is 21. When the Chief of Police called her attention to the matters set forth in the count, she observed, in the saucy spirit of her years:

"When you pay for my clothes, you can tell me what to wear."

But what the Chief of Police said to this is not evidence.

DRESS CENSORS ON CHICAGO'S BATHING BEACH

1913
VENUS IN TROUSERS.
STATUES CLOTHED TO PLEASE MRS. GRUNDY.

St. Louis (U.S.A.) is suffering from a bad attack of Mrs. Grundy, to win whose favour the cafes and restaurants presented an extraordinary spectacle, most of the pictures and statues there being partially covered with some article of clothing. Under a city ordinance cafe and restaurant proprietors are forbidden to display pictures, paintings, or statues in the nude, a form of decoration which has been almost universally approved. The other day regular patrons of one big town cafe found Venus wearing a pair of diaphanous trouserettes, while "The Lady with the Goose," which is a well-known group at the same establishment, covered herself with a slit skirt. In another cafe, where the proprietor boasted a group depicting Pan piping to a bevy of wood nymphs, Pan has been forced to wear overalls, while the nymphs are dressed in pyjamas and nightgowns. The cafe proprietors have let their fancy run riot in the matter of clothing their treasures, and the "sleeping beauty" who has for years slumbered peacefully and unclothed on a slab in another establishment, now wears a policeman's uniform — the proprietor declaring that he could think of no more fitting garb for a sleeping figure. Still another cafe manager, in whose place is a bronze figure, has dressed the figure in a short white linen garment, while a statue of a Bacchante, a copy of a work which was refused by Boston, now wears a complete motoring outfit, including goggles and veil.

1904
BRIGHTON SHOCKED.
Young French Ladies Undress and Bathe From the Beach.

Frequenters of the front at Brighton were greatly shocked the other morning when a party of young French ladies undressed on the beach and plunged into the surf, wearing somewhat scanty costumes. The police interfered after they had dressed, and told them that in England ladies were only allowed to bathe from machines.

The protest of the police was quite in order, but the beach regulations might be more strictly applied all round. There are certain periods of the day when hundreds of men and boys, clad in the very scantiest of costumes, disport themselves on Brighton Beach at points where they can easily be seen from the piers and the front. Indeed, the space between the groins and the piers is the favourite bathing ground of hundreds of gamins, who much prefer to take a bath "mid noddings on."

As the season has so far been such a grand one for bathers the question of suitability of costume has been raised at many watering places on the east and south coasts. Bexhill, where mixed bathing is permitted, is deeply concerned about the matter, and so also is Ramsgate.

The difficulty could easily be solved by the local authorities taking over the bathing machines and cabins, and running them on up-to-date, popular lines. The average bathing machine is a draughty, ill-constructed structure, with broken floors and scanty appointments. Cleanliness, too, is very often conspicuous by its absence. Cheaper and better accommodation is the true remedy for scanty costumes, and al-fresco bathing from the beach.

1928
THE FREEDOM OF THE PRESS

ONE hopes that Mr. Stanley Unwin will follow Mr. Cape's example and send the Home Secretary a complimentary copy of a book just published by him: "The Struggle for the Freedom of the Press, 1819-1832," by William H. Wickwar (Allen & Unwin, 16s.), and it seems only right that if Sir William Joynson-Hicks spent one week-end reading "The Well of Loneliness," he should spend another reading of how his predecessors, one hundred years ago, tried unsuccessfully to prevent people expressing opinions, discussing subjects, or writing books of which Home Secretaries disapprove. Tom Paine's "Age of Reason," Palmer's "Principles of Nature," Southey's "Wat Tyler," Shelley's "Queen Mab," Byron's "Cain," "Don Juan," and "The Vision of Judgment," were among the books which the "Jixes" of 1828 thought should be suppressed as seditious, blasphemous, or obscene. The judges of those days agreed with the "Jixes"; the aggregate number of years which people spent in prison for publishing Paine and Palmer must have been enormous; the Courts held that "Wat Tyler," "Queen Mab," "Cain," and "Don Juan," were all seditious, blasphemous, or obscene, and Leigh Hunt's brother, John, who in 1812 had been sent to jail for two years because he wrote that the Prince Regent was "a corpulent man of fifty, a violator of his word, a libertine over head and ears in disgrace, a despiser of domestic ties, the companion of gamblers and demireps," was in 1824 found guilty and sentenced for publishing the poem which most people now consider to be Byron's masterpiece. It is significant that these very poems, which the authorities tried to suppress as blasphemous or indecent in the twenties, are included in the Collected Works of Southey, Shelley, and Byron which were presented to me at the age of twelve at my private school in 1891 and 1892 as "Good Conduct" or Scripture Prizes. One trembles to think of the books which may be presented in 1990 as "Good Conduct" Prizes in Girls' Schools.

* * *

Mr. Wickwar has written an admirable book because he gives one the facts and his authorities for them. It is not altogether an easy book to read for that very reason; the volume is literally packed tight with facts, and Mr. Wickwar rarely, if ever, interrupts his narrative by the obtrusion of his own opinion or prejudices. It is a work of real historical value which ought to be—though one cannot hope that it will be—read by all judges, magistrates, Home Office officials, Public Prosecutors, Home Secretaries, and politicians. It is because every generation so effectually buries its own dead, its own political stupidities and cruelties, that political progress is so slow and the law always lags from fifty to one hundred years behind contemporary civilization. It is almost inconceivable that, if the full history of the persecutions and prosecutions of 1819 to 1832 were widely known, rational people would allow the law with regard to expression of opinion and the publication of books and newspapers to remain as it is to-day.

* * *

The history of those persecutions and prosecutions is the main theme of Mr. Wickwar's book, for it forms the struggle for what is called "the freedom of the Press." Until I read his book, I had no idea that books and pamphlets played an even greater part in that struggle than newspapers. After the Napoleonic Wars the governing classes were faced by what, looking back, we now see to have been the rising tide of democracy. They tried to stem the tide by forcibly suppressing all opinions with which they did not agree. Their weapon was the law, which still exists, governing seditious, blasphemous, and obscene libels. A publication was—and is—a seditious libel if it tended to bring into hatred or contempt or excite disaffection against the King, the Government, the Constitution, Parliament, or the administration of justice. The governing classes—and, therefore, of course the judges—in the twenties interpreted this law to mean that, in effect, it was a criminal offence punishable with fine or imprisonment to criticize King or Government or to advocate any change in the Constitution. One judge held that "to make the people discontented with the Constitution under which they live" was a "gross and seditious libel"; another that to "make the people dissatisfied with the Government under which it lives" is "unconstitutional and seditious." Under this law, Burdett was sentenced to three months' imprisonment and a fine of £2,000 for sending an Open Letter to the Electors of Westminster protesting against the Peterloo Massacre; and hundreds of poorer and obscurer men suffered fine or imprisonment for writing or selling publications which criticized the Government. John Hunt was sentenced to one year's imprisonment for saying what, eleven years before the Reform Act, everyone knew to be true, namely, that the House of Commons was "for the main part composed of venal boroughmongers, grasping placemen, greedy adventurers, and aspiring title-hunters, or representatives of such worthies."

* * *

The people who fought the battle of the freedom of the Press were the Radicals, and for the most part they had both Whig and Tory against them. Politically the battle was part of the great struggle for Reform of the House of Commons. But because the Radicals were in the forefront of the battle, the law of blasphemous libel became as important as that of seditious libel. Richard Carlile, who, according to Professor Trevelyan, "suffered and achieved more for the Liberty of the Press than any other Englishman of the nineteenth century," and many others who followed in his footsteps were deists, rationalists, or atheists, and they claimed the right to express their opinion about religious questions. Here the battle was fought over the right to publish books criticizing the Christian religion. The governing classes maintained that any book criticizing the Christian religion, provided that it was sold to the "lower orders," was a blasphemous libel, and the judges supported them. Carlile forced the issue by republishing Paine's "Age of Reason" in 1819 and selling it in the famous shop at No. 55, Fleet Street. He was sentenced to two years' imprisonment and a fine of £1,000. It was the beginning of a truly heroic struggle. Carlile's wife reopened the shop, was prosecuted, and sent to join her husband in Dorchester Gaol. Her place was taken by Carlile's sister, who was immediately sent to prison for twelve months for selling "Appendix to Paine's Theological Works." There followed a long line of volunteer shop assistants who were prepared to suffer and suffered in the cause of freedom. The story of how the cause triumphed in the twenties and how the Government failed should be read in Mr. Wickwar's pages.

LEONARD WOOLF.

TRANSVESTISM

1921
VERA, THE BOY IN SKIRTS.

21 YEARS AS A GIRL.

FROM OUR OWN CORRESPONDENT.
NEW YORK, Wednesday.

A quaint story of a boy having been raised to manhood as a girl comes from the little island of Ocracoke, off North Carolina, whither, after a brief struggle for a living in Baltimore, Charles C. Williams, 21, has just returned, declaring that he much prefers wearing skirts, sewing, household work, and the companionship of girls.

When Williams was born his mother was bitterly disappointed that he was not a girl. She called him Vera and dressed him as a girl. Ocracoke supports some 600 persons, mostly fisherfolk, and with the exception of the mother none knew that Vera was a boy.

He grew up to be a quite good-looking girl with blonde hair and fair complexion, and he did not leave the island until his 21st birthday, when his mother took him, dressed in women's clothes, to the mainland, where he made the discovery that Ocracoke was only a small place in the world.

On his return to the island Vera wrote to a mail-order house and obtained by parcels post an outfit of men's clothes. He cut off his long hair, took the money he had earned by sewing, and rowed to the mainland. Then he wrote to his mother that he was tired of being a girl.

She replied telling him that his real name was Charles. For two months Charles worked as a waiter in Baltimore. Then he became disgusted with the world. He has now returned to Ocracoke and the society of his girl friends.

1929
MOLLY, A JOLLY JACK TAR.

Masquerade as Sailor —and Fight with a Bully.

"Sunday Chronicle" Correspondent.
Brighton, Saturday.

A Brighton girl of 21 who

Served as a sailor before the mast,
Rescued three men from drowning,
Knocked out the ship's bully,

has just returned to her home tired of adventure.

She is Miss Molly Flynn, the daughter of a retired sea captain. Twelve months ago she went to America as a typist and shorthand writer to a commercial firm in New York. Tiring of the monotony, she worked her way to San Francisco and, dressed as a boy, got a job as a sailor on a schooner bound for the South Seas.

A pretty girl with bobbed hair and a muscular figure, Miss Flynn told me to-day the story of her remarkable experiences.

ACHING IN EVERY BONE.

"I little dreamed what I was letting myself in for," she said. "I had my hair cut short like a boy's, and bought a suit of old clothes. I had no difficulty in passing myself off as a man, as I have naturally a deep voice.

"Added to the ordinary hardships of life in the fo'castle was the fact that the crew was made up of the scourings of the seven seas. They were the most hard-bitten crowd imaginable; and their language!

FIGHT WITH A BULLY.

Miss Flynn's fight with the ship's bully took place one night on deck. He was a herculean Swede, who was the terror of the fo'castle.

"As I was the youngest of the crew," she said, "he made me his butt, and was continually cuffing me about. One night, in desperation, I lost my temper and caught him a stinging smack on the side of the face.

"When we got on deck he made a rush at me. I dodged, and as he swung past me I aimed a kick at his legs. I caught him on the ankle and brought him down with a crash that smashed his wrist. He left me alone after that."

To the end of the voyage Miss Flynn kept up her masquerade without anybody having a suspicion of her sex.

1918
SAVED BY DISGUISE.

Escaped Prisoner Impersonates Dead Girl for Six Months.

A soldier of the Middlesex Regiment, one of 400 prisoners returned from Germany, who arrived at Cannon-street Station yesterday morning, had a unique experience.

He was taken prisoner in 1916, but made his escape. After wandering about for six days he asked for food at a small farmhouse. He entered, half expecting to find soldiers billeted in the house. The only occupant was an old woman, who was wailing over the body of her daughter, who had died that morning.

Being able to speak a little French, he suggested to the old woman to let him impersonate the daughter. At first she objected on religious grounds to his burying the body, but he overcame her scruples.

He buried the girl that night in the garden, and for six months wore her clothes and worked in the fields. A few of the neighbours were told, but they kept the secret.

Among some 300 British prisoners who arrived in Denmark from Germany yesterday were Lieut.-Col. Lord Farnham, Lieut.-Col. Sloggett, Lieut.-Col. Wickermann, Major Walker, and Capt. Milburne. General Ravenshaw and his staff also arrived.

1910
WOMAN'S LIFE AS A MAN.

5 YEARS' MASQUERADE

(From Our Own Correspondent.)
NEW YORK, Monday.

After successfully masquerading as a man for more than five years, Mrs. Lena B. Smith, an attractive widow of thirty, with closely cropped brown hair, to-day cast off her disguise and resumed the garb of her own sex. She announces her intention of retiring from the profitable business she established in the assumed character of a Spanish commission agent.

Mrs. Smith, who lived for several years in South America, disguised herself as a man five years ago in order to win a wager that any woman possessed of histrionic talent could pass unsuspected as a member of the opposite sex. The wager was made at Boston, where a physician offered her £500 a year as long as she could maintain the deception. Mrs. Smith came to New York and secured an engagement as a clerk at a wholesale tobacconist's.

In the course of her male career she occupied positions of confidence in half a dozen well-known business houses, and finally went into business on her own account, renting a flat together with a Boston girl. They were supposed by their friends to be a married couple and entertained frequently and made numbers of friends.

Mrs. Smith declares that one girl clerk fell so deeply in love with her as to propose an elopement.

The interviewers to-day visited each of the business houses where Mrs. Smith occupied positions. The majority of the employés expressed profound surprise, not unmixed with chagrin, at learning that the "jolly young Spaniard," known to them as Mr. Martinez, was in reality a woman.

Mrs. Smith states that on the whole her experiences have not tended to raise the male sex in her estimation.

JOHNSON HOOD, a Peterborough plateworker, who had a weakness for masquerading as a woman.

1920
U.S. SENSATION.

Police Raid Ex-Mayor of Los Angeles House.

MEN GOWNED AS WOMEN.

A tremendous sensation has been caused in Los Angeles over a raid made by the police at the home of a former Mayor, Mr. Arthur C. Harper. In all, twenty-one men, seven dressed in elaborate women's evening gowns, were arrested.

Among these was the former Mayor's youngest son, Joseph H. Harper, 24 years old. He was one of those dressed in women's costume.

The charge made against the party was "vagrancy and lewdness."

According to young Harper, they were "giving a party just to have a little fun."

At the party was a huge punch bowl, from which the men graciously took cups of the punch and offered them to the "ladies." The "women" were painted and powdered, and wore elaborate wigs, and their corseting was perfection itself.

As the men and their "ladies" drove up to the door of the house they were met by a lackey in livery and introduced to those already present by the various women's names.

The police had been informed of the party by a former soldier now in the police department who had been accidentally invited to attend.

Many of the members of the party drove up to the house in their own limousines, the licence numbers of all of which were covered up. The men wore diamonds, and their dress gave every indication of wealth. There was a strong suspicion among the police that some of them at least were prominent locally, and were giving false names.

According to the police and the other witnesses, dancing on the floor was conducted just as if the camouflaged men were really women, and that the actions on the ballroom floor and elsewhere were such as to warrant, without any doubt, the arrest of the members of the party.

After the raid the party was taken en masse in their costumes to the police station. The gowns worn by the "women" constituted one of the most extraordinary sights ever on display at the police station. They were not only elaborate, but expensive, one "woman" wearing an ostrich plume worth at least £10 alone.

The strange part about the scandal is that the former Mayor, his wife, and daughter, were upstairs, and knew nothing of what was going on, only that a party was taking place.

1939
Bride was 'man' for 50 years

Sunday Chronicle Correspondent
PARIS, Saturday.

AFTER living as a man for more than fifty years Jeanette Bosquanne, now aged fifty-six, of Moulins, France, has just been married to the only man who knew her secret.

Just before Jeanette was born her two-years-old brother was killed in an accident.

The tragedy so preyed on the mind of Jeanette's father that he swore that if the new baby was not a boy he would kill it.

Jeanette's mother, fearing that the threat would be carried out, told her husband when Jeanette was born that the baby was a boy. So the girl was brought up as a son.

Jeanette promised that as long as her father lived she would keep the secret.

Six months ago, with the death of her father, Jeanette for the first time took her place in the life of the village as a woman.

1913
POSED AS A WOMAN.

Extraordinary Mania of a Peterborough Man.

A "SECRET INFLUENCE."

The story of a man's extraordinary mania for feminine impersonation was told at Peterborough Police Court before Alderman W. Cliffe, when Johnson Hood, a plate worker, was charged with being a wandering lunatic. Inspector Kyle said that he met the defendant, who was dressed as a woman, about noon on Thursday. He had on a green straw hat, trimmed with blue ribbon, and a veil to match; a white blouse; a blue skirt; a white apron; a brown wig, and patent shoes. Hood, said the inspector, was holding up his skirt as he came along the road, and witness called out to him. Defendant did not stop, but witness caught him up and said, "I believe you are a man masquerading as a woman."

Hood replied, "I know I am; I am the son of King Edward VII., and King George is my brother." He was taken to the police station, and on being searched was found to have on a complete outfit of women's clothes—even to a pair of open-work stockings.

Alderman Cliffe: You admit being dressed as a woman? Defendant: Yes, I do.

The Chief Constable was told by Hood that he thought he had been hypnotised, and he imagined that some secret influence had been at work. It was further stated that on inquiries being made at the Labour Exchange the deception had been so complete that Hood had been enabled to register himself as a cook out of employment, and gave his name as Mary Johnson.

The Chief Constable stated that a remarkable feature in the case was that Hood on one occasion went down to the works where he was employed dressed as a woman and inquired for himself. He was ushered into a waiting-room whilst a messenger was despatched into the works to inquire for Mr. Hood. After some time the messenger returned and said he regretted to inform the visitor that Mr. Hood was not at work that day. The "lady," apparently rather upset by the information, thanked the man for his trouble, and departed without "her" identity being discovered.

Defendant's wife, giving evidence, said that masquerading as a woman was her husband's failing. He had been doing it for many years—ever since he was eleven years of age. He had always said the police could never touch him, and she wished they had caught him earlier, then he would never have carried it on.

After consultation the defendant was released, his wife and son agreeing to take him to Birmingham and to look after him. Hood himself undertook not to masquerade as a woman again.

1920
GIRL "HUSBAND"
FOUR YEARS OF MARRIED LIFE WITH ANOTHER WOMAN.

"Daily Express" Correspondent.

NEW YORK, Friday, Oct. 1.

The Philadelphia police have discovered that a girl named Jacqueline Gay, aged twenty, has been living with another woman, Winifred McVaugh, also aged twenty, as Winifred's husband for the past four years, after a formal wedding ceremony.

Jacqueline Gay is an Oklahoma Indian, and formerly worked in a religious mission. She says she took to man's attire to protect herself. The facts came out when she was arrested and charged with trafficking in narcotics. She explained that girls whom she had nursed through illnesses while she was at the mission taught her the drug habit.

She has implicated Felix Cardullo, a wealthy resident of the Italian quarter in Philadelphia, as one of the leaders in the illicit traffic in narcotics.

1937
"DARBY AND JOAN" WHO WERE NOT
TWO WOMEN "WEDDED" FOR FORTY YEARS
DEATH REVEALS THEIR SECRET

(FROM OUR OWN CORRESPONDENT)

PARIS, Saturday.—Even more remarkable than the "Col. Barker" story in England is one revealed by a dossier submitted to the Ministry of Justice here.

This brings to light the extraordinary life of two women, who for 40 years had lived together as husband and wife near Juan-les-Pins, on the Riviera.

They were regarded by neighbours as the local "Darby and Joan."

"Darby" was for all the world **Monsieur Camille Bertin,** a Frenchman of independent means.

He came to the Riviera in 1897, accompanied by a young woman, Miss Hilda Mary Joan Scott, a native of Cambuslang, Glasgow.

Miss Scott was presented as "M. Bertin's" fiancée, and, after the usual notice at the local Mairie, they were married.

Within a period of six years after the marriage there arrived at the house of the young couple, at intervals, three baby daughters, who were recognised as children of the union.

In the 40 years of their married life the couple entertained lavishly, but it was noted as something peculiar that their guests were always women. Never was a man received at their table. Furthermore, the three daughters were brought up to avoid the opposite sex.

Less than a year ago the "wife" died, and Camille Bertin survived by only a little over 11 months.

JUDICIAL INQUIRY

Because of the suddenness of the death there was a judicial inquiry, conducted with unusual secrecy, and as the result the amazing discovery was made that Camille Bertin, the model husband, was a woman.

It was not difficult to carry out the deception at the Mairie, where the marriage took place, because Camille is a name common to both sexes in France, and a simple alteration of the entry under "sex" in the birth certificate presented by the smartly-groomed "bridegroom" disarmed suspicion on the part of the official whose duty it was to make the necessary arrangements for the wedding.

It is now revealed, on the strength of a sealed letter the dead "husband" deposited with the family lawyer, that the pair had met in London. Both had had an unfortunate love affair in their teens, and had decided to console each other.

In all the 40 years of their married life no one suspected the truth, and even their three "daughters," were in ignorance, and are still mystified about their own origin.

Neither the lawyer nor the police can throw any light on this mystery, for, if there was adoption, the records have not been kept.

CONDITION IN WILL

The French law recognises the marriage and the birth registration as perfectly legal, because, for purposes of legalisation, the only things that carry weight in France are the papers presented by the persons wishing to marry or to register births.

Therefore, in law here there is nothing to show that Camille Bertin was not a man, and that the three children were not born of his union with Miss Scott.

The will of Camille Bertin leaves all the estate to the three "daughters," subject to the condition that they do not marry. They have assented to the condition, but it is not binding on them, because there are well-known decisions of the French law courts laying down that clauses of a will restricting marriage and the possibility of bringing children into the world are against public policy and therefore illegal.

An amazing thing is that, though Camille Bertin was frequently ill in the years immediately preceding his death, the doctors called in had no suspicion of his true sex.

He had made careful arrangements to avoid the possibility of the secret coming out after death, but his plans were defeated by the suddenness of his death and the inquiries ordered by the police.

The original birth certificate of Camille Bertin has been found in the archives of a Mairie of the Allier Department, and thus it will be possible for the local authorities to issue a burial certificate for Camille Bertin under her real sex.

But that will not prevent the tombstone recording that the body buried is that of "Monsieur Camille Bertin, beloved husband" of the woman who lies beside him in the name of Mme. Camille Bertin.

1912
THE CASE OF "CHARLEY WILSON."

Cases of women who posed as men in order to join the Army or go to sea were by no means uncommon in the seventeenth and eighteenth centuries. One of the most famous of these women was Hannah Snell, who assumed male attire with a view to searching for her faithless but still loved husband, a Dutch sailor named Summ, who had deserted her. Both as soldier and as marine she went to the wars, being 12 times wounded at the Siege of Pondicherry, in 1749. Her identity was eventually discovered, but she ended her days as a Chelsea Pensioner.

A well-known figure in the City at the close of the 18th century was the "Baron de Verdion," an eccentric book dealer, whose sex was not known until her death in 1802. She was the daughter of a German architect named Grahn.

Of the several instances in recent years the most notable is that of "Charley Wilson," whose identity with the "manwoman" mentioned in a manuscript by Charles Reade, the novelist, then published for the first time, was announced in "The Daily Chronicle" of September 6, 1911.

"Charley Wilson" was then 78 years of age, and was living in a Somersetshire village under her own name as Catherine Coome. Married at the age of 16, she was separated from her husband three years later, and resolved to earn her living as a man. This she did for over 40 years, 17 of which she spent at sea. As Charley Wilson she courted and married three women, living with the first for five years, and with the second for 22 years, while the third departed after about 12 months. The secret of her sex was known only to one or two persons until hard times drove her to seek relief at the West Ham Workhouse.

Marie le Roy passed for 25 years as "Harry Lloyd" at Enfield, and her sex was only discovered at her death two years ago. For five years Mrs. Elena Smith carried on business in New York as "Mr. A. L. Martinez" for a wager.

A case in which a woman actually achieved distinction and honours in the guise of a man was that of Dr. James Barry, M.D., who entered the Army medical service as hospital assistant in 1813. She was promoted through the various ranks until at her death in 1865, at the age of 71, she was Inspector-General of Army Hospitals. During her last illness at her house in Down-street, Piccadilly, she refused to be medically attended, and an inquest held after her death revealed for the first time that the Inspector-General was a woman.

"COLONEL" BARKER.

1929
LONDON FASCISTI LEADER.

HUNTED AND BOXED AND SEEMED A "JOLLY GOOD FELLOW."

A WOMAN'S astounding life as a man—posing as Captain Leslie Ivor Victor Gauntlett Bligh Barker she was a leader of the National Fascisti in London, she ran a restaurant in the West-End, she obtained a post as restaurant reception clerk at the Regent Palace Hotel—came to an abrupt end when she was arrested a day or two ago for contempt of court.

The arrest was made at the Regent Palace Hotel by the tipstaff of the Bankruptcy Court. The offence was "contempt of court in failing to appear for public examination in bankruptcy." And when the tipstaff made the arrest he did not dream that "Captain Barker" was anything but a man.

But at Brixton Prison—a man's prison—the secret was revealed. "Captain Barker" was immediately transferred to Holloway Gaol—a woman's prison.

And there "Captain Barker" is now—this woman who for years had posed as an Army ex-officer with a distinguished war career, and had boxed and hunted in so manly a fashion that no one dreamed of the secret.

The sole reason for this astonishing masquerade seems to have been an idea that the world offers more opportunities for advancement to a man than it does to a woman.

1937

POSED TEN YEARS AS WOMAN, DANCED IN CHORUS, "MARRIED"

FROM OUR OWN CORRESPONDENT
NEW YORK, Monday.

AFTER masquerading as a woman for ten years, during which he obtained a job as a "chorus-girl" in a New York theatre, twenty-six-year-old William M. Richeson was to-day unmasked by the police.

Richeson, alias Mary Baker, started wearing women's clothes at the age of sixteen.

In 1931 as Mary Baker he "married" a man who, according to the police, was unaware until yesterday that his wife was a man.

"Loved Hoaxing"

It was before this marriage that Richeson danced and sang as a chorus girl.

Among other jobs he has held are those of hospital nurse, waitress and chambermaid.

Richeson said he first began posing as a woman because he loved hoaxing people.

1906

"I AM A MAN."

Badge Worn to Satisfy Local Authorities in America.

Randolph Milburn, a music teacher of Washington, Ohio, was recently arrested for appearing in the streets dressed in woman's clothes.

He declared that as a certain Dr. Mary Walker is allowed to wear man's apparel he was entitled to wear skirts. After consulting legal authority, it was ascertained that the laws of Ohio permit a man to wear what he likes, providing "he makes no attempt at deception regarding his sex."

To obviate further trouble, says the "Telegraph" correspondent, Milburn, while promenading in woman's raiment, now bears a large silver badge, inscribed "Randolph Milburn. I am a man." This description apparently satisfies the local authorities and amuses the public.

1907

Sixty Years' Masquerade.

A woman, eighty-three years old, who successfully masqueraded as a man for more than sixty years, has died in the municipal hospital at Trinidad, Colorado. Her real name was Katherine Vosbaugh, she was born in France, and emigrated to America at the age of eighteen. She found it difficult to get employment, and adopted male attire, and became a clerk at Joplin, Missouri. She proposed marriage to a girl. Vosbaugh revealed her sex at the time of the proposal, and exacted an oath from the girl that she would never betray her. The "marriage" actually took place, but Vosbaugh's "wife" deserted her soon after. Vosbaugh went to Colorado, and worked for many years as a shepherd and cowboy. For the past twenty years she had been employed as a messenger in Trinidad.

1915

THE MASQUERADER.

Familiar Figure in Skirts Proves to be a Man.

(FROM OUR OWN CORRESPONDENT.)
NOTTINGHAM, Saturday.

The sensation created in Nottingham by the arrest of a weirdly-dressed woman who for ten years has been a conspicuous figure in the city has been increased by the announcement that the prison authorities have discovered the supposed woman to be a man.

Prisoner was arrested on Wednesday by pure chance, when she happened to call at the house of a police-sergeant collecting for a charitable and religious organisation. Papers in her possession described her as "Helen Phillips, Minister of the Christian Police Mission."

For years the prisoner has been an extraordinary figure, parading the streets covered with beads, rosaries, crucifixes and other bizarre ornaments. The deep copper hue of her face and hands, the police now state, is dye. She wore on her deformed left arm a man's boot laced up.

When remanded on Thursday prisoner said "she" was a Servian. When the police visited "her" home in Woolpack-lane they found on the door sign the words "Miss Dr. Vien, F.R.H.S., Astronomy Recorder; Astrology; Clairvoyance."

In a tiny living room an attempt had been made to erect a sort of altar after the fashion of the Greek Church and a coloured picture of the Cross was surmounted by a holy ikon, the whole surrounded by numerous candles and oil lamps, one of which was apparently kept constantly burning.

It is stated Phillips professed to carry on some kind of healing, and about the place were books, papers, and bottles, presumably used for this purpose. Prisoner will be brought up again charged with masquerading.

1906

MADMAN'S CAREER AS "COUNTESS."

REMARKABLE MASQUERADE.

SUICIDE ON THE POINT OF DISCOVERY.

(From Our Own Correspondent.)
BERLIN, Sunday, Dec. 9.

One of the most amazing psychological hoaxes on record, a sort of matrimonial Koepenick case, was revealed at Breslau yesterday by the suicide of a man who had been living as a woman, and, under the name of the Countess Dina Alma de Paradea, of Paris, "she" was about to become the wife of a local school teacher, but has been identified after death as the middle-aged stepson of a prominent Berlin physician and a victim of hereditary insanity.

The "countess" was taken suddenly ill a few days ago, and a doctor who was summoned wished to make an examination. The "countess" entered an adjoining room, drank a bottle of poison secreted in the pocket of her dress, and, returning to the room where the physician was waiting, sank dead at his feet.

The police were sent for, and discovered the corpse to be that of a man about thirty-five years of age, who had masqueraded as a woman with the aid of false hair and other devices. Communication with the Berlin police soon established the "countess's" identity, but it has not been revealed, beyond the fact that "her" stepfather is a physician whose name begins with "H" and that the mother died a year ago in the same lunatic asylum where a brother is still confined.

The Breslau school teacher, who had fallen in love with the bogus countess, met her a few weeks ago in Paris, where he had gone to spend his vacation and to learn French. "She" represented herself to be the daughter of the French Consul at Rio Janeiro, and their acquaintance was speedily followed by an official engagement. At the end of the teacher's leave of absence the couple journeyed together. The "countess" dressed elegantly and wore beautiful jewels, and presented other evidences of belonging to a wealthy and distinguished French noble family. She went to live with her "fiancé's" relatives, who gradually began to be sceptical regarding their lodger's sex. Their doubts were confirmed by yesterday's tragedy.

In the "countess's" rooms the police found an extensive wardrobe of exquisite and costly French costumes and lingerie, in addition to a large collection of false jewels. "She" had lived in various European capitals upon an allowance of twelve guineas a month from "her" stepfather since "her" departure from Berlin several years ago on account of heavy debts.

WOMAN'S MASQUERADE AS A MAN.

The death of Nicolai de Raylan, clerk in the office of the Russian Consul in Chicago, revealed the fact that de Raylan was a woman. On the left, one of the two wives whom the impostor married. On the right, the masquerader.

1907

THE MAN-WOMAN.

RUSSIAN HEIRESS'S INTRIGUE.

LEAVES A WIDOW AND TWO DIVORCED WIVES.

(From Our Own Correspondent.)
NEW YORK, Wednesday, June 26.

An extraordinary career of intrigue and deception is revealed in the diary and correspondence published to-day of Nicolai de Raylan, secretary to the Russian Consul in Chicago, who, after masquerading as a man for eighteen years, was discovered on her death at Arizona last December to be a woman. Nicolai was thrice married and twice divorced, and it is only within the last week that the widow could be persuaded to abandon her claim to inherit her "husband's" property, and admit that "he" was a woman.

Nicolai's real name was Taletsky. She adopted a man's guise when quite young in order to levy blackmail on her mother, a wealthy lady of Kieff, to induce her to reveal the true secret of her parentage. With astounding cunning she had her mother prosecuted for contravening two Russian statutes which provide a long term of imprisonment for anyone who gains entrance for a boy into a girls' school or seeks to evade the law of compulsory military service by hiding the sex of a male child. At the age of seventeen Taletsky, as a man, appealed to M. Pobiedonosteff, the Procurator of the Holy Synod, for assistance. He took up the case and testified before the courts at Odessa that she was a man. As a result the mother was cast into prison.

At this juncture the young woman fled to Finland to evade medical examination, first writing to M. Pobiedonosteff that filial devotion forbade her to testify against her mother. Nevertheless, according to her diary, the procurator proceeded with the case, appearing as the chief witness of the Government in support of the contention that his young protégée was a man. It was only when the attorney for the mother produced convincing evidence to the contrary that M. Pobiedonosteff would admit that he had been deceived.

The next few years Nicolai spent in evading the secret service men whom the humiliated statesman set on her trail. She lived an extraordinary life, successfully making love to young ladies of good family in Finland, Belgium, and finally America. Though addicted to habits of gross dissipation, her posthumous papers show that she was a poet of no mean order. After a third marriage, she lived for thirteen years as secretary to the Russian Consul, supporting with extraordinary histrionic ability the character of a man devoted to sport and fast living.

TWISTS OF FATE

The Sorrows of Genius.

Apropos of the vagaries of fortune, Sydney Smith discovered an interesting letter relating to the discoverer of the uses of steam. This was a certain Salomon de Caus, who wearied Cardinal Richelieu with the story of what steam would do. "To listen to him you would fancy that with steam you could navigate ships, move carriages; in fact, there is no end to the miracles which, he insists upon it, could be performed." Richelieu, angered by the man's insistence, confined him in a lunatic asylum. Lord Worcester went to see him after he had been years a prisoner, vowing that he was not mad. "He is indeed mad now," said the Englishman, sorrowfully; "misfortune and captivity have turned his brain. But it is you who have to answer for his madness. When you cast him into that cell you confined the greatest genius of the age."

1905

Twists of Fate

1928
A LIVE SLEEPER.

This story from Mount Vernon, Washington, was sent by the British United Press correspondent.

Because he is a sound sleeper, John Finch, a youth of Mount Vernon, is alive to-day. He was asleep on the track with his head against a rail when a passenger train passed. A portion of his straw hat was clipped off by the wheels of the train.

The train staff, expecting to find him dead, had to awaken him from his still sound sleep.

They said that had he been a light sleeper, awakened and raised his head as the train was passing he would have been killed.

1906

It is very rarely that such an absolutely symmetrical coincidence can be recorded as that of the six births which took place on board the North German Lloyd liner the *Grosser Kurfürst* on the voyage from Bremen to New York. Three mothers gave birth to six children, and the happy events are classified as follows:

First Class	One Child.
Second Class	Twins.
Third Class (steerage)	Triplets.

Besides the singular coincidence of each class registering its own number in this manner, it is interesting to see how nearly the proportions are to the statistics given in the recent London University report on the birth-rate question. According to that report, the higher the social status the lower the birth-rate, and vice versa, so that 25 per cent. of the population produce 50 per cent. of the children. In the case of the *Grosser Kurfürst* 50 per cent. of the babies were born of 33 1-3 per cent. of the mothers.

1906
STRUCK BY LIGHTNING IN PULPIT.

[From Our Correspondent.]
ROME, Monday.

While a large congregation was assembled in the parish church of Cologno a, near Bergamo, to hear Abbate Maffi preach, a terrific storm swept over the country. A thunderbolt crashed through the campanile, scattering a shower of débris on the congregation. The Abbate Maffi was exhorting the people to calm when a lightning flash seared his left cheek and eye, and tore his vestments to ribbons, burning his clothing to the skin. The venerable preacher thus struck down in the pulpit was borne away in a dying condition.

1912
LIGHTNING AT FUNERAL.

Fifteen Mourners Struck Down at the Graveside.

SERIOUS INJURIES.

There was a remarkable and tragic scene in the New Primrose Cemetery, Germiston, South Africa, during the funeral of a man named McCann, who was killed by an explosion. The committal service was being read at the graveside when there was a rending crash of thunder and a blinding flash of lightning, which dazed the throng. The officiating priest and others who were not badly injured have given the following account of the scene:—

From where the priest stood it seemed as if for a fraction of time a mosaic of umbrellas and livid faces was wreathed in pale blue flame. For another moment there was a terrible silence and then a great cry. A second or so more and then one or two saw that on one side of the grave the ground was strewn with prostrate men, women, and children, and on the other side were shrinking groups of people, still more or less erect, but cowering together instinctively as if for refuge from the overwhelming horror. Some there were who ran blindly for varying distances, they knew not wherefore nor whither. The reverend father felt the shock comparatively little. To quote his own words, "It was as if red-hot pins and needles had been thrust into his left leg just above the ankle."

He was one of the first to grasp the situation, and though the sequence of events is naturally tangled and confused, the tragically interrupted rites of the Church seem to have been speedily completed. Several men rallied round, and while some attended to the injured others helped to lower the coffin, which had meanwhile rested on the bars laid across the grave. The service completed and the coffin lowered, all joined in succouring the injured. Of those struck down the larger number had risen unaided, others rose with slight assistance, but it was soon found that about a dozen were in a much more serious condition, and one person, Michael Connell, a well-known engineer, was dead. Of the injured, who numbered fifteen, Mrs. Blane was seriously burned, one shoe being torn off, her hat burnt, and serious wounds inflicted on her body. Mrs. Taylor was badly burned from the neck downwards. One very serious case, that of a man named Huggin, was taken to the New Primrose Hospital. Serious though Huggin's injuries are, his recovery is expected.

Mr. McCann, brother of the man who was being buried, says that the priest was thrown a distance of 6ft. McCann's nephew was lifted right across the coffin, and all the buttons were torn from his clothes. The stone on an adjoining grave was split in two, and all the glass wreath covers on surrounding graves were shattered.

1925
TALE OF A LOST LEG.
MOTOR-CYCLIST'S FIND IN ROAD AT NIGHT.

A woman's leg, complete with laced boot and stocking, is being cared for by the Ongar (Essex) police until it is claimed by the owner.

It was "found" by Mr. W. Lane, an Ongar motor-mechanic, in unusual circumstances. Motoring at night through Stanford Rivers he ran over something, and when he dismounted discovered the limb.

He searched for a body without success, and, considerably mystified, took the leg to the police station. There it remains, and so far no one has come forward to claim it.

1907
THE DROWNED DOUBLE.

Two Months After Burial Albert Steer Returns.

In the matter of the mystery of Albert Steer, the police confess themselves helpless and at fault.

Two months ago Steer left his family in Bickley with a vague word of a journey into Surrey, and the next day a drowned man's body was taken up from the Thames near Chelsea Bridge.

By the description of it the body seemed to be that of Albert Steer. When his son and daughter viewd it at the Horseferry mortuary all their doubts were removed.

It was certainly their father. Not only were the features and build familiar to them, but all accidental marks were there.

Albert Steer had lost an eye, this drowned man was one-eyed. One of his toes had ben crushed, and the body had a crushed toe. Albert Steer's face was marked with a dent over the eye-brow where a piece of bone had been taken away, and here was the same dent in the same place.

So Somerset House registered the death of Albert Steer, a coroner's inquest declared that he had been found drowned, and a memorial stone has been put up in the cemetery on Bromley Common.

And now Albert Steer, with an uneventful story of two months' work for a gardener at Little Malden, reappears to his sons in the bar of a London public-house.

The Registrar-General must therefore cancel an entry in his books, and the Steer family, in the interest of accurate genealogy, must erase the inscription on a tombstone in Bromley Cemetery.

All that remains for the police to do, as an "Evening News" representative learned to-day, is to recover from the Commissioner of Police the only photograph of one who is once more an unknown man found drowned near Chelsea, and to advertise again for the friends of a one-eyed man with a broken toe and a dent above the eyebrow.

1941
FORGETFUL TRAVELLERS

No fewer than 244,000 articles were left in London transport vehicles and on the Board's premises in 1941. These included 47,000 umbrellas, 26,000 pairs of gloves, 30,500 handbags, purses and similar articles and 48,000 tin hats, gas masks and rifles.

1940
PASTOR CHASED "DEVIL"

FROM OUR SPECIAL CORRESPONDENT
NEW YORK, Tuesday.

WHEN several unfortunate occurrences happened all within a week to the Rev. James Boysell, pastor of a Jersey City (New Jersey) church, he announced to the congregation that the devil was giving him special attention.

Here were the pastor's grievances:

Church chimes got out of order; Church heating furnace exploded; Pastor's car run out of petrol in heavy traffic; and When he entered the church a board fell on his head.

Mr. Boysell told his parishioners that he would personally drive the devil from the church. A young man dressed in satanic costume stood before the congregation as the pastor berated him with logic and bade him begone.

To cap the performance the "devil" ran down the aisle with the pastor in pursuit. They disappeared out of the church door.

The pastor fell and broke his arm.

1949
Cripple Is Cured By Turning Mangle

CRIPPLED since birth, 39-year-old Mabel Slocombe, of Fern-street, Ogmore Vale, Glamorgan, wrenched her back while turning a mangle.

A few hours later she had stopped limping and was walking normally.

Her legs had always been of different length, and one arm was two inches longer than the other.

1927
"DROWNED" MAN RETURNS.

14 MILES SWIM.

TRAMPED OVER THE PYRENEES.

From Our Own Correspondent.
NOTTINGHAM, Tuesday.

Harry Glee, the stoker who was reported by the steamer Trelevan as having been drowned at sea after diving to save the mate, who was washed overboard in a rough sea in the Bay of Biscay on Jan. 27, has turned up in Nottingham.

Having received a letter from the captain of the ship describing how he saw the mate and his would-be rescuer sink together, Mr. and Mrs. Taylor, of Sherwood-place, Nuncar Gate, Nottingham, were surprised yesterday to receive a letter from Glee from 30, Peel-street, Nottingham, describing how he swam 14 miles to land on the coast of Portugal, where he lay unconscious until peasants took him to a cottage.

"I was there three weeks," he writes, "and then came the day when I was well enough to start back home. With a suit of overalls on, no boots or socks, walking between 20 and 30 miles a day, begging food as I went along, I tramped through Portugal and Spain, over the Pyrenees and into France, where I met English-speaking people for the first time since leaving the Trelevan. They applied to the British Consul to help me."

"In the meantime," he continued, "I worked in Toulon Harbour. News came a week ago for me to come to England. I called at Elder Dempster's office in London, got my kit and money, saw the mate's wife on Saturday, and came on to Nottingham, where I have been taken in by my new captain."

Glee describes how he swam with the mate for some miles until the mate died. The stoker lived with Taylor at Nuncar Gate before going to sea.

SILENT SHIP MYSTERY.—This schooner, the Marion G. Douglas, was found derelict in perfect condition off the Island of Bryher, Scilly, on November 27. Her boats were intact, together with a smart motor-launch, while on board was a cargo of timber. This mystery of the whereabouts of the crew is still unsolved, and the circumstances recall the case of the Marie Celeste, which was found deserted in 1872.

1933
IT HAD ITS VICTIM
The "Vampire Lake" Wins Again

The "Vampire Lake" near Varna, Bulgaria, has lived up to its sinister reputation, says Reuter.

According to legend, the lake must have a human sacrifice once a year on a certain day. On this day no one goes near the lake for fear of its power, but this year Anna Costantinova forgot the tradition, and went to the lake to bathe.

She had hardly entered the water before she was sucked under and drowned.

1931
LEGEND OF THE POND
DISTRESSING ECHO OF GIRL'S RIDICULE.
SUICIDE AFTER LAUGHING AT TALE OF TRAGEDY.

Closely connected with the tragic fate of a girl, which a coroner and jury investigated at Chalfont, Bucks, yesterday, was a gruesome legend concerning a pool above which a dead hand was reputed to appear.

The story was treated with ridicule by the subject of the inquest:—

Florence Barley, 23, of New Bradwell, Bucks,

whose body was recovered from the pool, which is known as the Half Hour Pond.

Evidence showed that the girl obtained a situation locally in order to be near her sweetheart, George Roberts. The latter one day told her of the legend connected with the pond. This was to the effect that a girl once drowned herself there after vainly waiting for her lover for half an hour. According to the legend, if anyone ran

ROUND THE POND THREE TIMES

they would see the girl's hand above the water.

Miss Barley laughed over the story and said, "What a silly girl." On Sept. 12 she was visited by her father, and upon leaving him gave him 5s., saying, "Give this to mum." The next morning she was reported missing.

After a search lasting five days two local workmen saw a girl's hand above the water in the middle of the pond. They cleared the weeds and then recovered the body.

Miss Barley, it was declared, was happy and cheerful, and had no worries.—The coroner remarked that in some mysterious way her mind must have become unhinged.

A verdict of "Suicide while of unsound mind" was returned.

Chalfont people, it is stated, are now afraid to go near the pond, and take circuitous routes home to avoid it after dark.

1948
The Samkey Just Vanished from Sight—Owners

AT noon on January 31 the 7,200-ton Samkey, bound for Cuba without cargo, and with a crew of 43—including 25 Londoners—radioed a weather report to the Azores. Then she disappeared.

"She was overwhelmed by some catastrophe, so sudden in its onslaught or dire in its effect that no signal of any sign was heard from her," said Mr. Hewson, for the Transport Ministry at the inquiry to-day.

"The view of experienced seamen was that the Samkey was overwhelmed by some phenomenal sea," he said. But there was no question of negligence in the sailing, storage or ballasting.

1941
CREWLESS SHIP REACHES PORT
BERTHED HERSELF
Daily Telegraph Reporter

It was revealed last night that a ship without a crew and with her engines running all the time berthed herself in a deep water inlet on the coast with only an inch to spare from dangerous rocks. She had travelled about 60 miles.

The ship, which provides one of the most amazing stories of the sea, had been on fire, and her crew must have escaped in a hurry, for they had left behind all their belongings, even their pocket wallets containing money.

The vessel continued with her engines running slowly, and in time the fire burned itself out while the ship still travelled on. When villagers saw her berthed in the inlet they told the lifeboat authorities, and the vessel was taken in tow to a British port

One of the salvage party told me that with comparatively little expenditure she would be as good as ever.

1919
THREE DESERTED SHIPS.
UNEXPLAINED SEA MYSTERIES.
VANISHED CREWS.

For the second time within a fortnight derelict schooners have been discovered in the Channel, with everything on board in order, but no crews.

To-day comes the news of a derelict French ketch, "Lucienne" of St. Malo, found by Walmer boatmen stranded on the Goodwin Sands. All her sails were set and a half-consumed meal was laid on the table, but there was no one on board.

The reason for the crew abandoning the vessel is a mystery. The "Lucienne" had apparently been sailing aimlessly about the Channel until she struck the sands. Her boat was missing. She was refloated and taken to Ramsgate. She was loaded with cement.

A fortnight ago another three-masted schooner was seen to the north of the Scilly Islands, off Shipman Head, and from her behaviour it was apparent she was a derelict. On boarding her the Brighter men were astonished that though every member of the crew had left, everything was in perfect order and in no way damaged. All her sails were furled, and all the boats were on board, including a smart motor-launch.

1926
"MIRACLE" FOR LOTTERY.

A PROPHET WHO FAILED.

FRENZIED CROWDS & WILD SCENES.

From Our Own Correspondent.
MILAN, Sunday.

Unprecedented scenes were witnessed throughout Italy on Saturday at the State lottery shops.

During the past few days the country has talked of little else but the alleged miraculous powers of a crippled peasant named Torraca. News that he had given a doctor who attended him some years ago four numbers which had won a large sum thrilled the faithful devotees of the lottery, and excitement became intense, and spread to nearly all sections of the people, when it was announced that four more "infallible" numbers were to be given for Saturday's draw.

Pressmen went to interview Torraca, who claimed that his family, "assisted by the hand of God," had found "the key to the lottery." The secret, he said, had been divulged by his father on his death-bed, accompanied by the injunction that Torraca should benefit the people, but never go in for the lottery himself.

ARMED PROTECTORS.

Interest grew to fever pitch as Saturday approached. Shoals of telegrams, some from emigrants in New York, Paris and Brussels, and thousands of express letters poured in imploring Torraca to communicate the "miraculous numbers." Visitors from all parts of Italy thronged to San Ferdinando, the village where he lives, and armed men took on themselves the protection of the precious cripple from the clamouring crowds surrounding his house.

Many poor people sold their beds, furniture, clothes and household utensils to provide the stake money. At Milan frenzied crowds had to be regulated by police at the lottery shops, where long queues formed, and windows were broken. A well-dressed man was nearly lynched by an angry queue for having kept them waiting. Similar scenes took place at most other centres.

DISILLUSION.

That disillusion came when the draw ceremony took place. Not one of the promised numbers emerged. Soon it was realised that nowhere had Torraca's prophecy come true.

The crippled tipster-prophet has thought it discreet to disappear. But perhaps he deserves the gratitude of the Government for the many millions of lire in excess of the usual lottery receipts which have passed to the State coffers.

1930
A HE-MAN'S HUG.
It Broke Two of Her Ribs.

MINNEAPOLIS (U.S.), Saturday.
Miss Anna Mitlow, a local beauty, sued her young man for £15 damages because he hugged her with such enthusiasm that he cracked two of her ribs.

It cost her 12s., she told the judge, to have a doctor repair the damage.

"I'll give you judgment for the 12s. doctor's bill," said the judge, "but as regards the other £15—well, a good squeeze like that is worth £15."—Reuter.

1923
REAL RELIC OF THE "STONE" AGE.

Truth About The "Million Year Old" Skull.

SAD DAY FOR 'OLOGISTS.

There has been, we imagine, the biggest shindy in American scientific circles which has occurred since the breaking up of the Society on the Stanislow.

It began in Buenos Aires where, according to Reuter, a committee of scientists has been examining the "million-year-old skull" which was found in Patagonia a few months ago by Dr. J. G. Wolf.

'Ologists Get Busy.

The doctor stated that it was a skull of the tertiary period, and thus caused prodigious excitement all over the world, since, up to the present, no traces have been found of man in that period.

All the anthropologists and the conchologists and the entomologists got busy at once, and it was announced that this Patagonian pericranium belonged to the oldest man in the world—500,000 years older than the Java ape-man, "pithecanthropus," and 900,000 years older than the Piltdown skull found in Sussex.

Now the Committee at Buenos Aires has decided that the skull is only a curiously shaped stone, and has no scientific value. The parallel with the scientific society on the Stanislow is almost exact.

1926
PRISON DREAM
FOILS ASSASSIN.

From Our Own Correspondent.
Rome, Saturday.

FOR forty-six years Alessandro Saraceni has languished in prison—a murderer according to the law, sentenced to perpetual imprisonment.

But now Saraceni is a free man, and one to whom the law owes a debt it can never pay. For Saraceni's 46 years in prison have been the martyrdom of an innocent man.

In vain he had pleaded his innocence of the murder of the man who was found dead on the road near Naples in 1880, soon after he had passed by on his mule.

A Cry in the Night.

The victim bore only one death mark, and that corresponded with the hoof-prints of the mule. But a jury of his fellow-citizens held that Saraceni had murdered the man, and he was sentenced to life imprisonment with a proviso that there should be no abatement of the "life" term.

Saraceni remained in gaol, however, passed from the prime of young manhood to middle-age, knowing all the time that he was innocent, but impotent to upset the law's decree. Forty-six years of deadly, dreary prison routine, and in that long period there was only one incident of note.

But it is to that one incident—a dream—that Saraceni owes his freedom.

Some 14 years ago, in his cell, Saraceni had a dream of extraordinary vividness. He saw King Victor of Italy on the point of being assassinated.

Cries he uttered in his sleep brought a warder rushing to the cell. The prisoner, awakened, excitedly explained his dream or vision, with minute details.

Struck by the clarity of the story the warder reported the matter to the governor of the prison, who, probably as much as a joke as anything else, sent information to the Italian Chief of Police.

Three Shots at King.

To the police chief the thing did not seem a joke at all, for the story fitted in with the fact that on the morrow King Victor was to ride through the city of Rome with the Queen Elena.

As the King and Queen rode, an anarchist, D'Alba by name, fired three shots at them. Thanks to the astonishing story of the man in prison, such precautions had been taken by the police chief that the Sovereign and his consort escaped injury.

Only recently did the story of his dream come to the ears of the King whose life it had saved. King Victor ordered a rehearing of his case. This time Saraceni was cleared, and the mule (long deceased) was found guilty of the murder.

1913
THE EXCITEMENT OF WALKING.

Accident Follows Paralytic's "Miracle Cure."

(FROM OUR OWN CORRESPONDENT.)
NOTTINGHAM, Saturday.

The "miracle cure" of a Nottingham paralytic, which was reported in *The Evening News* yesterday, has been followed by an unfortunate accident.

For four and a half years Samuel Flecknoe was paralysed and helpless, but, to quote his own words, "something" told him to get up last Sunday.

He amazed the members of his family by walking downstairs to breakfast.

Last night he insisted on walking unaided, but while on the stairs he stumbled and fell back.

Doctors were called, but Flecknoe had not recovered consciousness to-day.

FELL WHILE EXCITED.

Dr. Watkins, who gave the case up as beyond treatment two years ago, stated today that should Flecknoe recover from the effects of the fall, there are indications that he will still have the use of his limbs.

Flecknoe, who is thirty-two years of age, apparently fell owing to his excitement in being able to walk about. His mother said she frequently begged him to sit down, but he refused.

"I have been sitting down long enough," he said. He could hardly be induced to take a seat for meals.

On Friday afternoon he walked to a theatre matinée—his first entertainment for four and a half years—and for to-day he had mapped out an extensive programme.

His brother, who has carried him to bed nightly, proffered to assist him last night. "Go away," Samuel replied. "I will carry you if you like." A minute later he fell downstairs.

1929
AIR BLACKMAIL

PLANE FOLLOWS A PIGEON.

From Our Own Correspondent.
BERLIN, Tuesday.

An extraordinary case of attempted blackmail has been counteracted by the police.

General Pattberg, of Homburg, on the Rhine, received a mysterious parcel at his house a few days ago, and when he opened it was amazed to find inside a carrier pigeon, with a letter demanding £250, to be attached to the bird and set free.

In the event of non-compliance he was threatened with death.

The General immediately got in touch with the police, and arranged for an aeroplane to go up and follow the pigeon.

When released, the bird was followed to a pigeon loft and aerial photographs were taken of the house where it settled.

With the help of this evidence the police were enabled to arrest the criminal.

1938
LIFE SAVED BY VIPER'S VENOM

HÆMOPHILIA PATIENT

From Our Own Correspondent
SHEFFIELD, Monday.

By the application to his tongue of a preparation made from the venom of deadly vipers, the life of a Sheffield man who was choking to death has been saved in the City General Hospital.

He is Walter Woodbine, 41, of Walkley-street, Sheffield, who is said to be a descendant of Fletcher Christian, the leader of the Bounty mutineers.

Mr. Woodbine suffers from hæmophilia, a condition of the blood which prevents it from clotting and which renders its victims liable to bleed to death should they cut themselves.

When Mr. Woodbine bit his tongue in falling from a ladder, bleeding inside the tongue caused it to swell to many times its normal size and block the air passage.

He was taken to the hospital, where the "viper venom" was applied by means of a swab to the tip of his tongue. The bleeding stopped and the swelling diminished.

Although Mr. Woodbine has recovered sufficiently to talk with difficulty, he is still unable to eat and can take only iced water.

The venom may mean death to ordinary persons because it causes their blood to clot, but on account of this property it is beneficial to sufferers from hæmophilia.

There have been several previous cases of its successful application to such patients.

1921
ROMANCE OF A BROKEN SCENT-BOTTLE.

"How Delicious!" Founds a £2,000,000 Fortune.

PARIS, Saturday.

How a fortune of £2,000,000 had its origin in a broken bottle is related by M. Coty, a wealthy French perfumier.

As a young man he began in a most modest way to compound new scents, and one day he took a bottle of new perfume to the manager of the Louvre, the big Paris store, in the hope of obtaining orders. The manager declined, however, to buy.

Manager's Resource.

As M. Coty was leaving the shop he accidentally dropped the bottle, which broke.

Several women customers who passed exclaimed: "What a delicious scent. Where can we get a bottle?"

The manager, with commercial presence of mind, replied: "It's our new Louvre mixture, madame. We are expecting a large supply by the end of the week."

He immediately gave M. Coty an order for £3,000 worth.

1925
HER OWN MURDER FORESEEN.

WOMAN WHO LOOKED INTO HER NEPHEW'S MIND.

PROPHETIC LETTER.

"I SEE MYSELF STRANGLED."

"Sunday Express" Correspondent.
VIENNA, Saturday, March 7.

THE remarkable case of a famous woman psycho-analyst who probed her nephew's mind, discovered that she would meet her death at his hands, and then died as she had predicted, is exciting all Austria.

The facts have been revealed at the trial of Rudolph Hug, aged nineteen, who has just been sentenced to twelve years imprisonment for strangling during her sleep Dr. Hug-Helmuth, his aunt, the distinguished teacher and disciple of Professor Freud.

Legal, medical, and scientific circles throughout Austria have shown the greatest interest in the case, especially as it was known that Dr. Helmuth had prophesied her murder by her nephew after psycho-analysing him.

HER LETTER.

Shortly before her death Dr. Helmuth wrote to a friend:—

"My whole life now is an expectation of a blow I am terribly uneasy. I see myself with him standing before me and then squeezing me around the throat."

Dr Helmuth lived in terror for some weeks, and one night the boy Rudolph entered her room and strangled her.

His motive for the crime, as stated at the trial, was that he resented his aunt's experiments on him and the ruthless exposure of his childhood in a book she had written on the value of psycho-analysis.

Rudolph was placed in the care of his aunt when his parents died, and despite his careful upbringing, on Freudian lines, grew to be a ne'er-do-well and wastrel.

1930
SIGHT AFTER 30 YEARS OF DARKNESS.
BLIND MAN ENTERS WONDERFUL NEW WORLD.

From Our Own Correspondent.
NEW YORK, Friday.

A man whose sight has been almost miraculously restored to him after 31 years is looking upon a new world that is stranger and more wonderful than he had ever imagined.

He is Mr. J. F. Fish, a well-to-do business man who, while on honeymoon in 1899, was struck by a falling tree, an injury blinding him by paralysing the optic nerves. For three decades specialists were engaged in vain attempts to restore his sight, Mr. Fish spending £10,000 in the quest.

WIFE FAINTS WITH JOY.

This week, while sitting at home listening to his wife reading, vision suddenly returned to the left eye. It was veiled, but sufficiently strong to enable him to recognise objects.

"A wonderful thing has happened, my dear!" he exclaimed. "I can see you again."

Mrs. Fish was incredulous, but when her husband was able to identify objects in the room, she fainted with joy.

"How different my wife seemed from what I had expected," said Mr. Fish, describing the new world he had discovered. "All these years I had retained the image of her as she was when a girl, but she's more beautiful to me now.

"Friends of a lifetime almost bewilder me, now I can see their faces. I feel like a visitor from another planet —all at sea. The only things in the world that remain the same are the flowers, the trees and the sky. Everything else startles me.

UNREALISED PERILS.

"I was astonished not to find women wearing bustles, or men with side-whiskers, as they were when I lost my sight. I wondered what had happened to the little horse-cars that used to run on the streets. I'm appalled, when I see the height of the skyscrapers and watch the traffic tearing about, to realise that this is the perilous city I've been living in all these years.

"I knew about all these changes, of course, and discussed them, but never actually realised them till now."

Despite the handicap of lost sight, Mr. Fish has made a success as a teacher and business man. It is hoped that the restoration of his sight will be lasting.

1942
HIS EYE FELL OUT
YOUNG MINER'S SINGULAR MISHAP
From Our Own Correspondent

Blackwood, Mon. Saturday. — When, after completing a shift at Oakdale Colliery, near here, Ronald Cutler, a young Blackwood miner went to the pithead baths, he blew his nose to eradicate coaldust.

To his astonishment his eye fell out.

Ambulance men replaced the eye and Cutler was able to go home. He appears little the worse for the occurrence, for the eye is functioning, although it will need further treatment.

1947
He Left His Glass Eye on the Train

Although umbrellas are in short supply, 5,630 were left behind in L.M.S. trains last year.

Travellers on the L.M.S. have forgotten other things, too, such as a glass eye, a barrel organ, a case of butterflies, a cage containing a calf with two heads, a three-legged cock, artificial teeth, and artificial limbs.

1945
27 BLINDED BY EATING FRUIT
FAR EAST 'CHERRIES'

Through eating what looked like ordinary English cherries, 27 soldiers, who have returned to Britain from New Guinea, are totally blind. This was stated by Mr. Charles D. Torvell, scientific adviser to the Forces in the Far East, at Liverpool yesterday.

The fruit, which was discovered at the end of 1942, was still "hush hush," he said. Even now he could not give its scientific name or the areas in which it grew. The lay name for the fruit was "finger cherry."

"You can eat one or two and nothing happens, but if you eat nine or 10 within a few hours you are totally blind," Mr. Torvell added. "Science has found no means of restoring sight in these cases."

1936
BABY LEFT IN CINEMA
FORGOTTEN BY PARENTS

This story was vouched for by Lady (Beddoe) Rees at a meeting at Romsey, Hampshire, yesterday:

A young married couple roused a Hampshire cinema proprietor in the middle of the night and said they had left a valuable article in his cinema. Impressed by their anxiety, he opened his cinema and the couple began a frantic search of the empty building.

Eventually they found their treasure. It was their baby. The child, which was fast asleep, had been forgotten by the couple when they hurried from the cinema.

1911
A MAN OF MYSTERY.

The death has taken place in Dunfermline of a man whose identity has been a mystery for ten years.

Ten years ago he was seized in the streets of the town with a stroke of apoplexy. He was picked up by a policeman; but it was found that he had been struck deaf and dumb. A stranger to the locality, he could neither read nor write, and his identity has never been established.

1923
FEVER CAUGHT FROM A BOOK.

The Medical Officer of Belchamp (Essex) Rural Council reported yesterday that he had traced an outbreak of scarlet fever to a book.

Twenty years ago the book was used by a fever patient. It escaped disinfection, and was never again used by the family. The book was read by the present patient, who thus contracted the disease. The book has now been destroyed.

1923
LAWYER STRUCK BLIND.
TRAGIC INTERRUPTION OF HIS SPEECH IN COURT.

"Daily Express" Correspondent.
VIENNA, Oct. 1.

During a criminal trial in Vienna the Public Prosecutor, Dr. Wunderer, was addressing the court when he suddenly stopped, and after shaking his head several times, exclaimed to the judge: "I cannot see; I have gone blind!"

He was rushed to the Vienna University Hospital, where famous professors who examined him declared that there was little hope of restoring his sight.

Dr. Wunderer, who is fifty, and one of the cleverest lawyers in Austria, is known as the "terror of criminals."

"THE MAN FROM NOWHERE"

This man, who states that he remembers nothing before he was found wandering in Belfast two years ago, has started work as an analytical chemist at Lancaster. He describes himself as the man from nowhere.

1930

1907

TRANCE POST-MORTEM.

VICTIM TRIES TO ATTACK THE DISSECTING SURGEON.

"Express" Correspondent.

VIENNA, Tuesday, July 23.

Johann Kovacs, a railway station porter at Bihar, in Hungary, had yesterday a narrow escape of being dissected alive.

Two days ago he fell down unconscious while at work, and was taken to the hospital. The doctors pronounced him dead, and a post-mortem was decided on, for which all preparations were made, the body being put on the dissecting table, where a lecture was delivered over it to the students before the body was opened.

At the first prick of the knife Kovacs awoke with a start, and as soon as he realised the position, endeavoured to assault the surgeon who held the dissecting knife. He had to be forcibly restrained by the other doctors.

1930

DEATH CHEATED BY POISON.

From Our San Francisco Correspondent.

For twenty years Mrs. Ashbaugh, who is 71, had carried poison in her purse.

"Some day I may want to use it," she thought.

Then came the day. She was lonely and destitute. She swallowed the drug. She was found on the steps of the University and in her hand was a note: "I leave my body to the University for scientific purposes."

But she will not die.

The poison she had carried for twenty years had lost its potency.—International News Service.

1923

TRIAL BY MUSIC.

Regina Kohn, newly arrived from Hungary, faced deportation yesterday unless she could prove herself entitled to classification as an artist, and unlikely to become a public charge. Kohn, who is aged 38, offered to play the "Träumerei" on the violin before a special board of inquiry at Ellis Island. She played so artistically, breaking down almost with emotion, that the board, whose musical appreciation had not been rated hitherto very highly in New York, decided the player might disembark, provided that a brother living here would be responsible for her maintenance till she can open a music studio.

1902

Very Absent-Minded.

Among the forgotten articles left behind on one of the railways, and to be sold, are twenty-five volumes of the "Encyclopædia Britannica." Other trifles that slipped from some absent passenger's waistcoat pocket are a machine for generating laughing-gas and an artificial leg. One wonders if that last owner is still hopping absently on one leg.—"Globe."

1937

TENSE MOMENT AT A CORONATION

WHEN THE CROWN WAS NEARLY DROPPED

A tense moment at the Coronation of Edward VII., when it was feared that the Imperial Crown might fall from the shaking hand of the then Archbishop of Canterbury, was recalled by Mr. Lawrence Tanner, Keeper of the Muniments and Sub-Librarian at Westminster Abbey, in a lecture to the Mothers' Union at Westminster yesterday.

"The Archbishop," he said, "was aged and infirm and was given the Crown with some difficulty by the then Dean of Westminster, who was equally aged and infirm.

"For one terrible moment it was thought he was going to drop it. The Crown shook over the King's head, but he got it on. As a matter of fact, it was back to front, but that did not matter, because everyone was so thankful that the Crown was actually on."

1936

STABBED BY MAN HE PUT INTO A TRANCE

BUDAPEST, Wednesday.

A HYPNOTIST giving a demonstration was stabbed by a man he had "put to sleep" at Izsak (Hungary).

In his performance the hypnotist appealed to the audience for a volunteer whom he might hypnotise.

A young farmer, Karoly Szani, accepted the invitation and was soon in a trance.

"Here is a knife. Take it," commanded the hypnotist. "Stand up, here comes one of your enemies. You hate him because he has stolen away your sweetheart."

The farmer responded perfectly to the orders of the hypnotist.

"Look out, your foe is going to attack you," shouted the hypnotist.

The farmer sprang—at the hypnotist.

The audience, in two minds as to whether it was part of the show, hesitated before going to his help.

At that moment the knife struck the hypnotist close to his heart.

The hypnotist is now in hospital in a grave condition.

The farmer's trance was so deep that the local doctor had difficulty in rousing him.—Reuter.

WAR AND PEACE

A FRIEND of mine has sent me the enclosed postcard (above), which is, I understand, being sold in the streets of Milan. We have heard a great deal of the anti-religious propaganda carried on in Russia, but I doubt whether anything so damaging as this to Christianity has been published in that country. CECIL. 1936

1917

A correspondent writes:—

I have again to thank you for my weekly "cold bath." By which I mean the strong and bracing tonic of the *Freethinker*. What you say about war is too true; but there are other forces arising which will make it unpopular. The nations cannot afford it as carried on under modern conditions. The glorious "free" press loses money by it; and the Philistine gets hit in his "little Mary," and never in the heel, as depicted in erroneous mythology.

Meanwhile Europe has, as it were, placed a sieve in the hands of Death, through which pass the young and the sound. Fancy, if any breeder of animals raised stock in that manner! And the "Imperialists," or pirates, of the world scream out for more babies, much as a miller would ask for flour, that he might grind it. Truly, all wise men contend against the same enemies. And they have no worse foe than Christianity, which corrupts the minds of the living through the fears of the dead.

George Ives

1930

MISS 1930 HITS BACK AT HER CRITICS

Worse Things Than Nose Powdering in Public!

WHAT IS "BAD FORM"?

"Average Girl" Replies to Countess and Professor

Is nose powdering in public bad form?

To those who think it is Miss 1930 has a decisive answer.

Dr. Winifred C. Cullis, Professor of Physiology at the London School of Medicine, has told the Bournemouth School for Girls that she objected to nose-powdering in public.

The Countess of Denbigh told the *Sunday Pictorial* yesterday that she thoroughly agreed with this view.

"I think," said Lady Denbigh, "that we older women have some rights, and one of them is that when we dine in public we should be protected from the demoralising exhibition of girls making-up at the very table where we eat.

"Last night we were dining out and when I saw young girls almost ostentatiously using their make-up outfits I longed to box their ears.

"It is idle to say that customs change. The fundamental laws of good form, which come from good breeding, never alter."

The man's point of view was given by the Earl of Denbigh, who was present.

"ATROCIOUS"

"There is no question at all about it," he said. "The practice of girls powdering their noses or daubing their mouths with lipstick in public is not merely bad form. It is atrocious."

The average girl, however, is angry with Dr. Cullis.

"Why should I secrete myself to apply a little powder to my nose?" said one girl to the *Sunday Pictorial*.

"The truth is that what is bad form in one generation is good form in another.

"The other day I saw a dainty ivory wand armed with claws in a shop in St. James's-street.

"I was told by a friend that it was known as a back scratcher and was as familiar an object as a fan in the most fashionable ballrooms as recently as 150 years ago.

"And they object to us powdering our noses!

"What is more, it is only thirty or forty years ago since it was quite good form for a man to drink himself under the table.

"And they object to us powdering our noses in public."

1920
Milestone and Corpse.

At one point, where both French and German trenches cut across the Paris road, there stood a milestone on a rise between them. The French, photographed it, had an exact copy made in steel with an observation eye-slit covered with gauze, removed the real stone by night and set up the camouflaged one, dug a tunnel to it from their trench, and used it for months unsuspected as an observation post.

In another case "a huge, dead, yellow-bearded Prussian lay, on a point of vantage, staring at the sky. He, too, was photographed and copied, and from the hollow shell, clothed in his uniform, another observer fulfilled his duty."

1915
PULPIT BLASPHEMY.
MISSION TO "CRUCIFY HUMANITY."

ASTOUNDING GOSPEL PREACHED BY GERMAN PASTORS

"Whom God wishes to destroy, He first makes mad." That would seem to be the only explanation of the appalling blasphemy preached from German pulpits at the present time in justification of the campaign of bloodshed and outrage waged by the Prussian War Lord. The Rev. Fritz Philippi, a prominent Lutheran pastor, dealt with this subject in a sermon delivered in Berlin, from which the following characteristic passages are extracted:—

"My text to-day is Luke xii., 49 ('I come to send fire on the earth; and what will I if it be already kindled?'). The words of the Gospel are to-day the language of Germany. How righteously may we, indeed, the most peaceful people under the sun, repeat those other words of the Prince of Peace: 'Do not believe that I have come to bring peace to the world, I have come to bring not peace but the sword.' Just as the Almighty caused His Son to be crucified for redemption, so Germany is destined to crucify humanity for the renewed salvation of mankind. Humanity must be redeemed by blood, by fire, and by the sword. German warriors do not willingly shed the blood of other nations, but they

DO IT AS A SACRED DUTY,

which they dare not neglect without committing a sin. Above all, our adored Emperor abhors the horrors of war. For many long years he laboured incessantly to maintain the peace of the world. Germany has never used her strength to menace the independence of any other nation. Just for this reason, on account of our clean record, we have been chosen as the Almighty's instrument to punish the envious, to chastise the evil-doers, to bring the sword to the sinful peoples of the world. Germany's divine mission is to crucify humanity. It is therefore the duty of German soldiers to strike blows of merciless violence; they must kill, they must burn, they must work wholesale destruction. Half-measures would be impious; there must be thorough war without compassion. The wicked, the friends and allies of Satan, must be wiped out of existence. Satan himself, who has come to the world in the shape of a great Power (England), must be crushed, and to Germany has been entrusted the intensely holy duty of accomplishing the destruction of the embodiment of Evil. When that work is done, fire and the sword will not have come in vain; humanity will be redeemed; the reign of righteousness will be established on the earth, with Germany as its creator and its armed protector."

1941
Rouged German Airmen

BY A SPECIAL CORRESPONDENT

OFFICERS of the German air force in a prisoners-of-war camp in England spend part of their pay on face creams.

Two shot down had waved hair, rouged cheeks, painted lips and enamelled fingernails and toenails.

The medical profession has a word for men of this type. It classifies them as moral deviates, a class with curious tendencies, including outbursts of emotional violence admirably suited to the ruthless tactics of the Luftwaffe.

Sir James Purves-Stewart, K.C.M.G., C.B., celebrated neurologist, who has had active service in previous wars, discovered this abnormal German desire for face cream when he was inspecting what at that time was the only prison camp for German officers in this country.

"These young men, everyone of whom was wearing at least one iron cross, were ill-mannered, aggressive and supercilious," he told me yesterday.

"They were of good physique. Their physical courage could not be denied. But though they were officers, they were certainly not 'officers and gentlemen' in the accepted sense of the word.

Painted Lips

"Had they worn mufti and mixed with a group of our own officers similarly dressed you would have picked out our own men immediately.

"This particular form of perversion happens to flourish most vigorously in Germany, and particularly in Berlin, where it receives open encouragement. It was particularly blatant a generation ago, at the time of the Eulenburg scandals at the Imperial German Court.

"Some time after visiting this camp I was on an official mission in Spain and was given corroboration of this state of affairs by a reliable medical colleague. During the Spanish war he had personally seen a German officer shot down. This airman had waved hair, rouged cheeks, painted lips and enamelled finger and toe nails.

Violent Outbursts

"A Scots acquaintance told me that a German officer with precisely similar make-up had recently been shot down in Scotland.

1918

One kind of faux pas that it is well for propaganda orators to avoid is that represented by the recent declaration of a British War Aims speaker in America that, among other achievements, we had " rescued 300,000 acres of good corn land " in Mesopotamia. The audience of citizens of a country that had entered the war pledged to get nothing out of it received the assertion in stony silence.

1915
CAT-O'-NINE-TAILS IN THE TRENCH.

TEUTON OFFICERS' BRUTALITY.

PRISONER SHOWS WEALS RAISED BY LEADEN POINTS.

From Our Special Correspondent
NORTH OF FRANCE, Sept. 1.

Monsieur Pierre Dumont certifies the authenticity of the following facts, which demonstrate the lack of enthusiasm displayed by the German troops in the firing line, and the means their officers employ to oblige them to perform their military duties.

A few days ago a French regiment captured a German trench by a surprise attack. The Germans had not the time to put up any resistance. The French counted 30 prisoners, amongst whom was a conceited young lieutenant, also three machine-guns, one bomb-thrower, and a quantity of hand-grenades.

According to the German fashion the machine gun servers were attached to their guns, which, however, did not surprise the French, who were familiar with this spectacle, but what did surprise them, however, was to find in the lieutenant's dug-out a rather unexpected object—a cat-o'-nine-tails with lead points at the end of the thongs, a real instrument of torture.

The Prussian officer when questioned maintained a sullen reserve, but one of the Saxon prisoners, whose gold-rimmed spectacles indicated a certain status, kindly answered in his stead. He proved to be a university professor, and in extremely correct French he explained that during the last few weeks the use of this little instrument had become very frequent in the German army in order to oblige the men to leave the trenches.

To prove the veracity of his story he unbuttoned his tunic and showed the marks of a beating received the evening before; the welts raised on the skin by the leaded tips were plainly visible, and the shirt was bloodstained.

The French soldiers were unable to restrain a movement of indignation at the sight. During this scene the officer with difficulty restrained his rage, but a little later when the troupe of prisoners departed, he sprang upon the professor with clenched fists. The French soldiers separated them, and obliged the lieutenant to fall back.

1938
SWING MUSIC SWEEPS CINEMA CROWD INTO MAD HYSTERIA

New York, Thursday.

MOB hysteria caused by the music of a famous swing orchestra brought psychologists and other mental specialists to New York's huge Paramount Cinema to-day to observe and make notes.

For the second day this cinema, seating 3,000, was packed with screaming audiences writhing, grunting and dancing in front of their seats and in the aisles.

There was such confusion in the cinema yesterday that a riot call brought ten mounted police and scores of foot police, who tried vainly to quieten the music-crazed mob.

"Get Hot! Swing It"

Psychologists, observing similar scenes to-day, described them as "perfect examples of mob behaviour," and compared them with those at religious revival meetings.

Bedlam broke loose in the cinema as soon as the swing orchestra conducted by Benny Goodman started playing.

Swept by the music into hysteria, people danced in the cinema's aisles, and some even leapt on the stage, dancing the Big Apple, and screaming loudly.

"Get hot!" yelled a young girl, leaping from her seat and flinging herself into a wild execution of the Big Apple. "Swing it!" "Feed it out!" screamed others.

Standing in the aisle with a notebook the noted psychologist, Dr. George Vetter, of New York University, commented:—

"I've seen food riots and strikes, but I've never seen the mob mind working so beautifully. Note how they're all writhing in unison. Their screams are like the noise of excited goats.

"Most of the audiences are young, and are maturing sexually with no outlet for their emotional urges.

"Music and the darkened theatre have broken down their inhibitory checks. Played in this atmosphere music is just as powerful in its effect on the nervous system as whisky."

A cinema official said: "I think they're just plain nuts!"

1931
Through Their Hats.

Fearing the growth in the numbers of men who go hatless to business, the Federation of the British Felt Hat Manufacturers requests all the bank and insurance company directors in Britain to order their employees to wear hats. It is only another instance of the growing belief in some quarters that men and women exist merely for the convenience of the makers of manufactured articles. Luckily, the modern employer has ideas of his own. Unlike the Victorians, he does not insist on his clerks coming in silk hats, tail coats, and cuffs. What he does want from them is efficiency, not servitude.

1926
Where America Leads.

I am not as a rule impressed by the mere marshalling of statistics, but the published returns for the number of motorcars in the world certainly provide food for sorrowful reflection on the economic regression of Europe and the astounding prosperity of America since the war.

At the end of 1925 there were 24,564,574 motorcars in the world. Of this total no less than 21,094,980 were in America. Europe's share was only 2,675,891, while Australia, with a population of less than six millions, had 416,586! As far as the general standard of living is concerned, these figures seem to prove conclusively the ascendancy of the new world.

1922
MODERN GIRLS AND MORAL VALUES.

AMATEURS WHO SIN FOR PLEASURE.

WHAT KNOWLEDGE HAS DONE.

1904
CAPTAIN AND CANNIBAL.

Captain Foote, of the British barquantine Mary Hendry, now at Barbados, states that during a recent cruise on the African coast he entertained King Ogby, the ruler of the Jakrimen, who inhabit Southern Nigeria.

The dusky monarch was much impressed with the vessel. While feasting on roast pork he inquired if it was the flesh of a white man. The king has over a thousand slaves, numerous wives, and quite a crowd of children. Captain Foote asked him for a piece of tanned skin, with which to make a pair of slippers, and the next day a slave came to the vessel with a parcel from the monarch. It contained the hide, from the neck to the waist, of a negro who had been killed by order of King Ogby for the sake of his skin.

1928
SHADY JAZZ PERILS.

BIG INCREASE IN SEX OFFENCES.

GOOD-BAD GIRLS.

From OUR SPECIAL CORRESPONDENT.
LEEDS, Saturday.

WANT of self-discipline, self-control, and self-respect; lack of home life and of supervision; shady dances and pictures and trashy reading are among the causes given me to-day by social welfare workers here for the increase of sex offences in parts of Yorkshire.

1907
WHISKER LICENSES.

Mr. Frank Richardson Supports Tax on Beards.

GRADUATED SCALE.

Whisker-adorned men in London are eager to learn further tidings respecting the New Jersey legislator who has introduced a Bill for the taxation of beards.

This daring reformer proposes that the tax should range from £1 for ordinary whiskers to £10 for a "goatee"; red whiskers 20 per cent. extra. He declares unfeelingly that the beard habit is increasing, and that men cultivate whiskers in order to save barbers' bills and the expense of neckties.

1929
WOMEN'S NEXT CRAZE.

Paris Fears Of Violet Hair And Green Teeth.

Fears that a craze for violet hair or green teeth might follow have led the newspaper "Paris-Midi" to launch a campaign against the present Paris fashion of women of painting their finger-nails a bright vermilion.

1939
GOD ON OUR SIDE?

THE movement for sanctifying this war rapidly increases.

God has been handed a gas mask and told to fight for Britain.

Easily the best recruiting sergeant so far in this unpleasant line of talk is Judge Richardson.

This legal (and presumably religious) gentleman has been acting as chairman at a tribunal for conscientious objectors.

His observation, made two days ago, will go down in history Said he:

"I AM CERTAIN, AS SURE AS I SIT HERE, THAT IF CHRIST APPEARED TO-DAY HE WOULD APPROVE OF THIS WAR."

So the Almighty approves of the slaughter of countless German men women and children, does He?

Let's hang up the machine gun, the poison gas cylinder and the bomb alongside the Cross as Holy symbols.

Listen, Judge Richardson!
God isn't on our side.
God isn't on Hitler's side.
Let's keep Him out of this dirty, hideous, mechanised campaign of bloodshed.

The whole thing adds up to the simple fact that we are out to save our necks by getting the other fellow first—and that's all! Also, it's less blasphemous.

War and Peace

1942
"MOSLEM" HITLER

Japanese short wave radio is trying to propagate "the absurd allegation that Hitler is a Moslem, a direct descendant of Mohammed," said Ankara radio.—A.P.

1921
MAN IN SEARCH OF A SMALL WAR.

Body and Soul for Sale—but Bars Morocco.

After his taste of aerial fighting as a member of the 135th Aero Squadron of the American Expeditionary Forces, C. C. Seale has no use for peace, and (according to the Paris correspondent of the Central News) is willing to take part in any war.

"Where shall I find a small war where a trained army airman is needed?" asked Seale, of the Advertising Department of the *New York Herald* of Paris, as he left an advertisement offering his body and soul to Mustapha Kemal Pasha, the Bolshevist, the Riffian tribesmen fighting the Spanish, or anybody wanting him.

Seale returned to his home in Texas after the signing of the Armistice, but he found life there dull. He returned to Paris recently and offered his services to Spain as lieutenant in the Foreign Legion in Morocco.

A few days in this service, however, convinced him that the motley groups of Bulgarians, Czechs out of work, Londoners, and unnaturalised "Americans" in the Spanish Foreign Legion would never meet his ideas of discipline, and he promptly resigned his commission.

1918
"SEND HOME OUR SONS!"

U.S. PARENTS AND SIBERIA
From Our Own Correspondent

WASHINGTON, Tuesday.—Declaring that "in absolute usurpation of his power the President of the United States is waging war against a friendly people," Congressman Mason of Illinois aroused great enthusiasm in the House with the demand that Congress compel the immediate return of American troops from Siberia.

"Half of the troops in Siberia," he said, "were conscripted in Illinois, and soldiers' parents make ceaseless demands for the return of their sons." He showed that only one per cent. of recruits are willing to go to Siberia.

Referring to the official explanation that troops are defending railroads in Siberia, Mason asked, "Whose railroads, in the name of God?" Have you stock there? Are you willing to fight there? Then go and fight for it, but don't take my boys to fight for your dirty stock, your dirty bonds, and your dirty railroads."

Mason referred to Koltchak as scum of the Tsar, who lived in a box car and cabled to America for money.

1936
FREE LOVE AMID GUN-FIRE ON BATTLE FRONT IN SPANISH WAR

FREE love, with a "wedding" feast served to the accompaniment of machine-gun fire, was sanctioned on Spain's battle front in Aragon yesterday.

The ceremony was "presided over" by Senor Buenventura Durruti, the powerful Anarchist leader from Barcelona.

The bride was beautiful Carmen Martinez, a Red Cross nurse, the bridegroom Manuel Garcia, an artilleryman.

Durruti said:—

"I could bless you or make you sign a document, but I shall do neither; first, because neither you nor I believe in blessings, and, secondly, because a document would show a lack of confidence incompatible with true love."

Perfect Freedom

"You are joining hands in perfect freedom because you love each other. Likewise you can separate with perfect freedom if some day you cease loving each other.

"If love dies, no document, no matter how many signatures it bears, can revive it. It would become a chain which would make you hate each other.

"Have confidence in yourselves. Remember that nothing unites you except your own wills. Love each other as lovers and as companions. If she loves you and you love her, nobody can undo the knot of your affection."

The couple kissed, and the ceremony was over.

Durruti lent the couple his car, gave them a hundred pesetas and sent them to Lerida for a five-day honeymoon, with orders to return to the front on the sixth day.

1929
SERMON ON MOUNT BAN UNDER D.O.R.A.

QUOTATIONS A WAR-TIME OFFENCE.

A strange bit of war-time history was revealed yesterday at the Norwich Assembly of the Congregational Union.

During a debate on pacifism, the Rev. Leyton Richards, of Carrs-lane, Birmingham, said:—

Publication of the Sermon on the Mount, printed separately during the Great War, was an offence under the Defence of the Realm Act.

Interviewed afterwards, Mr. Richards said he had irrefutable authority for the statement. In Hansard of June 29, 1916, Mr. J. M. Robertson was quoted as saying, for the Government:

"If the Sermon on the Mount or any other portion of any other sacred book were used for the deliberate purpose of preventing men from enlisting or accepting enlistment, that would be a military offence."

He added that a weekly journal submitted for publication without comment a number of quotations from the Bible which were struck out by the Censor.

1921
English Adventurers in Spain.

The formation of a British Legion of ex-soldiers by Spain to deal with the rebellion in Morocco has its precedent in the Legion formed by Lord John Hay to assist Queen Isabella against the Carlists in 1835. It attracted the Byronic, chivalrous youth of England, as Disraeli's novels testify, and under the command of Sir de Lacy Evans these gentlemen adventurers fought gallantly at Hernani and St. Sebastian.

It is noteworthy, in passing, that until the Boer War the British Army always included hired foreign troops. In the Crimea, for instance, we had a Foreign Legion of 3,500 Germans, Swiss, Portuguese, Americans, &c. Indeed, the Boer War was the first war England ever fought without enlisting alien professional soldiers.

1917
ATTEMPT TO FIRE A CHURCH.

Pastor Pushed from His Pulpit in Uproar.

PACIFIST MEETING.

Riotous scenes took place in North London yesterday, when pacifists endeavoured to hold a meeting in the Brotherhood Church, Southgate-road, Kingsland.

Not only was the meeting broken up, but an attempt was made to fire the church, and the pastor (the Rev. F. R. Swan) was thrown from the pulpit.

The meeting was to have been addressed by the Hon. Bertrand Russell on the subject of "International Relations."

That the police anticipated disturbances would follow any attempt to hold it was evident from the fact that there was a force of at least 200 men on duty, with about twenty mounted men in readiness in case of emergency.

SOLDIERS IN THE CROWD.

As half past three approached two cordons of police were drawn across the road facing the church, and the crowd was gradually worked back in both directions from it for a distance of about fifty yards.

After a few minutes some soldiers and civilians passed the police lines and got into the church, in which when the service began there were only about fifty persons in all.

When the service began the pulpit was occupied by the pastor, and seated close to him was the Hon. Bertrand Russell. The opening hymn was sung without any interruption, after which Mr. Swan rose to speak.

He was at once met with a howl of derision and cries of "You ought to be ashamed of yourself" from some women.

Hon. Bertrand Russell.

The organ at once began, but immediately its sounds were drowned by the strains of "Keep the home fires burning."

At this point a man, who is very prominent in his efforts to break up pacifist meetings, mounted one of the pews and was about to denounce the meeting.

Unfortunately for himself, he was mistaken by a soldier for one of its sympathisers and knocked down with a blow.

The din continued for a little, when the pulpit was rushed, by which time Mr. Russell had disappeared.

A soldier made for Mr. Swan and, catching him up in his arms, threw him into the body of the hall towards a door close to the pulpit, through which he disappeared.

One of the men who had taken possession of the pulpit called out: "The National Anthem," which was immediately begun.

FIRE BRIGADE ARRIVES.

Before the first verse was ended a flame of fire shot up from beside the pulpit to a height of about 6ft., and it was at once seen that an attempt was being made to burn down the church.

The flames caught the carpets at the bottom of the pulpit and increased in volume, and inside a minute some of the rails at the back of the pulpit caught fire.

Someone raised the cry of "The church is on fire!" and several policemen dashed into the building.

They had their capes with them, and with these they proceeded to beat out the flames.

The church was then cleared. Meanwhile the alarm had been given, and within a couple of minutes a fire engine and escape dashed up to the church door.

It was on Saturday, July 30, that this same church was the scene of a pacifist riot, which resulted in the hall being wrecked, after being besieged by an infuriated mob.

The police made one arrest following the disturbance.

1918
GAOL FOR MINISTER

Pulpit Jeers at Men Who Die for Britain.

EX-M.P. AND LEAFLETS.

Mr. George Tinsley Peet, superintendent minister of Peel Wesleyan Circuit, was charged at Castleton yesterday with making statements calculated to prejudice recruiting.

It was stated in evidence that in the course of an address in Castleton Church, defendant said he would rather go to hell with a conscientious objector than go to Heaven with drunken, swearing scoundrels who happened to die for their country in Flanders, and that he prayed "God would go on sending our lads to hang in bits on the barbed wire and go on sinking our ships until He had knocked some sense into our sinful hearts."

When defendant was sentenced to three months' imprisonment there was applause in court. Notice of appeal was given.

1918
INTERNMENT OF ALIENS.
To the Editor of *The Daily News*.

Sir,—We are obliged by the rule of our profession to remain anonymous, but we cannot refrain from expressing our astonishment that, on arriving from a country where resident enemy subjects are not necessarily regarded as enemies, we find that the subjects of one of the countries fighting for justice and humanity are agitating for the internment of persons who have satisfied the police of their respectability and good behaviour, and whose only offence is that they were born in enemy territory.

Many of these persons have British-born sons fighting for our cause. Will these sons fight better for knowing that their parents are imprisoned and their homes broken up?

SIX U.S. ARMY OFFICERS.
London, July 9.

1918
The "Repatriation" Scandal

Even the "Intern-them-all" party is shocked, or alarmed, by the spectacle of several hundred British-born wives of Germans being "repatriated" to Germany, a country they have never seen, whose language they cannot speak. The tragedy is that these women are going to Germany and facing all its horrors because they have been so persecuted by other women that they found life here intolerable. Their crime was that of doing in time of peace what Queen Victoria did—marrying a German. The bitterness against them has been mainly due to the Northcliffe-Bottomley-Billing campaign in the newspapers, and it is a disgrace to the country. Now, as a final climax, those who have done this mischief are professing to be appalled at its result, and are shedding profuse tears about its "infamy" and "cruelty."

INVENTED WAR HORROR

1937

Gandor Szakats, inventor of the flame-thrower used during the Great War, was buried at Budapest yesterday in a pauper's grave. He was forty-four, says Reuter.

1917
EARTH AS A FOOD.

Germans Urged to Adopt the Diet of the Bongos.

The "potato bread spirit" in Germany is to be followed by the "dirt-eating" habit.

The "Eilenburger Tageblatt" has announced a new food-stuff, "fossil flour," by the use of which Germany will be able to hold out till her enemies give up the struggle.

This so-called "food" is found in layers in Sweden, Lapland, and Finland, and also in Bohemia and certain parts of Germany.

Geophagy, or "dirt-eating," is in vogue with some of the lowest and most miserable races on earth. The chief of these are the Bongos, a tribe of Equatorial negroes, who will eat anything from reptiles to putrid flesh.

Other Geophagi.

The same resource is adopted in seasons of hunger by the Ottomac Indians in South America, by the Hudson Bay Indians, the Lapps, and by certain of the "mean whites" in the mountainous districts of Tennessee and Kentucky.

They usually eat clay or chalk, which, of course, can supply no nourishment to the frame, but by occupying the attention of the membrane lining the stomach may quiet for a time the sensations which we call "hunger."

The particular "food" which the cheery German is recommending to his countrymen is called "Bergmahl," or "mountain meal," in Sweden, and "fossil flour." It is an infusorial earth, which is taken off the lower surface of the limestone beds.

Flinty Particles.

It is a very fine white powder, composed of the microscopic fragments of the shells of the diatoms. In seasons of great scarcity it has been eaten by the Lapps, not alone, but mixed with ground corn and bark.

It must be injurious to the internal organs since it is silicious, or "flinty," in composition, and in the United States it is used as polishing powder to take stains off metal.

1918

What a thing it is to possess a "conscience" in a Christian country! 625 conscientious objectors to militarism have been court-martialled twice; 510 three times; 210 four times; and 18 have received five successive sentences. In addition, large numbers have been deprived of their votes in Parliamentary elections.

1904
A TRULY IRON NERVE.

It is related of the Russian Field-Marshal Paskievitch that in the course of the siege of Varsovie, being somewhat discommoded by a hot fire from a certain battery, he ordered it to be shelled, but to no purpose. His troops did not seem able to locate the enemy, and their shot had no effect. Finally the Field-Marshal himself galloped forward and sternly demanded:—

"What imbecile is in command here?"

"I am," answered an officer who approached.

"Well, captain, I shall degrade you, since you do not know your business. Your shells have no effect."

"True, sir, but it is not my fault. The shells do not ignite."

"Tell that to others. Don't come trying to fool me with such chaff. You will receive your punishment this evening."

The captain coolly took a shell from a pile near by, lit the fuse, and holding it in the palms of his hands, presented it to the marshal, saying, "See for yourself, sir."

The marshal, folding his arms across his breast, stood looking at the smoking shell. It was a solemn moment. Both men stood motionless, awaiting the result. Finally the fuse burned out, and the captain threw the shell to the ground.

"It's true," remarked the marshal, turning away to consider other measures to silence the enemy's fire.

In the evening, instead of punishment, the captain received the cross of the Order of Saint Wladimir.

1918

The following story has been sent to me by Miss Colenso:—

A minister friend of mine told me the story of a young Scottish boy of his acquaintance, now a military prisoner in Germany. I forget for the moment in which camp. This boy received a letter from home one day telling of his mother's serious illness and the doctor's verdict that she could only live a few weeks. The German commandant, finding the boy in great distress, asked him what was the matter, and on learning the cause of his grief said: "Would you like to go home to your mother?" The boy sprang up exclaiming indignantly, "How can you mock me, when you know it is impossible." "But you shall go, my boy," said the commandant. "I will pay your return fare on condition that you give me your word of honour to come back here." The boy went home to Scotland and remained by his mother's side for about three weeks till her death, when, true to his word, he returned to Germany.

I agree with Miss Colenso that well-attested stories of this kind ought to be given publicity as well as the infamies of the enemy.

1916
Field Crucifixion.

And now let us ponder the following letter:—

Sir,—Did you know one of the punishments in the Army is crucifixion? It is imposed when the men lose their gas helmets. Mrs. —— has learned that her son, with five others, lost their gas helmets in a marsh. They were tied by the neck, waist, hands and feet to cart wheels for one hour; when released her son was dead. Mrs. —— says: "They murdered my son; the indignity would kill him." He was on the eve of coming home, having joined the second day of the "Pals" (Corn Exchange Section), and served his country for nearly two years.

I have known that gentleman by repute since he was a boy, and a better all-round man never lived; a joy and a pride to his home.

The soldier to whom that letter refers was a volunteer, a man forty years of age, who left a good position to serve his country. No doubt he, like thousands of men in the ranks, might have had a commission had he wished. And he was treated in that savage and degrading manner.

There is not one word to be said for such a punishment. The officer or statesman who invented such a barbarous and Boche-like penalty ought to be retired into private life. Such a punishment could only have been invented by a brutal boor, and any officer who would inflict it, or tolerate its infliction, ought to be relieved of his sword.

1928
NUDE CULT DEFIANCE.

VILLAGE PROTESTS TO THE GOVERNMENT.

DOUKHOBORS AGAIN.

"Daily Express" Correspondent.

MONTREAL.

DOUKHOBORS of both sexes are disturbing the residents of Nelson, British Columbia, by appearing nude in the streets.

There are some two hundred men, women, and children who have left the main colony, twenty miles east of Nelson, and appear entirely naked in the highways and in the villages, defying the officers of the law.

Protests have been made to the Government at Ottawa.

It is nearly ten years since Western Canada has been disturbed by these parades of nude Doukhobors.

The Canadian Mounted Police on the last occasion arrested a large number and confined them in prison.

The leaders preach in Russian, their native tongue, and their followers keep alive on little food and shelter themselves in the bushes at night. The local authorities declare it is impossible to control these wandering nude Doukhobors, except by placing all of them in prison.

"SPIRIT WRESTLERS."

The Doukhobors, or "spirit-wrestlers," as the word means, are variously described as a religious community conducted on super-Tolstoyan lines.

They were first heard of in the eighteenth century in Russia, were later subjected to persecution for their refusal to bear arms, and about thirty years ago more than 7,000 of them emigrated to Canada.

The Doukhobors object to all forms of government, and to food or clothing procured by the death of animals, and decline to pay rent or taxes, basing their refusal on a literal interpretation of the text, "The earth is the Lord's and the fulness thereof."

WEDLOCK

EIGHTEEN YEARS FOR MARRYING.

White Husband and Black Wife Punished for Wedding Against Virginian Law.

NEW YORK, Friday.—A striking instance of the severity with which the American laws prohibiting the intermarriage of whites and negroes are enforced in some States was afforded at Richmond, Virginia, yesterday, when a white man and a negress were sentenced to no less than eighteen years' imprisonment for miscegenation—contracting a marriage contrary to the Virginian colour laws, which forbid unions between white and black people.—Central News.

1909

1926

NO MORE HAREM LIFE FOR TURKISH GIRLS.

Wealthy Husbands Angry at New One-Man-One-Wife Laws.

Polygamy and harems have been the accepted privilege of the Turk for nearly a thousand years; now bigamy is a crime in the Land of the Crescent. A Turk, no matter how wealthy, may have only one wife, and he cannot divorce her by simply telling her to go back to her mother.

THE most startling and sweeping change ever made in the established laws of a country has just been made in Turkey.

The Turkish National Assembly has adopted the Swiss civil code, supplanting the old Mohammedan religious laws which have governed family life and personal status since the chronicling of Turkish history.

MARCH OF FEMINITY.

Not only has Turkey cast aside her ancient customs and "Westernised" herself, practically at one fell swoop, but the country has resounded to the modern march of feminity. A few years ago Turkey was, as she had been throughout the centuries, a land where a man was a woman's lord and master in the true meanings of the words. A wife could be repudiated at will, and exchanged or bartered.

To-day the Turkish girl enjoys equal rights with a man in the obligations of matrimony. She must be wooed and won in the accepted sense.

The new laws came into force at midnight on October 4, and until the stroke of twelve a Turk could divorce his old wives and marry four new ones—four was the legal number.

The result was that the change caused a tremendous rush on the part of those who wished to enjoy to the full the last day of multiple marriages and easy divorces.

LAST HOUR WEDDING RUSH.

In Constantinople there were 300 demands for marriages under the old system. Scores of wealthy husbands divorced their wives in the old time-honoured way and then rushed to the "registrars" with two, three and four new ones.

In a large number of instances, however, the Turks who tried to drag young girls to the altar under the old polygamous laws, were faced with a new and hitherto unprecedented difficulty. The girls simply would not obey.

By hook or by crook many of them managed to preserve their independence until midnight, when they were able to "snap their fingers" at their would-be husbands and rejoice in a legalised freedom.

One effect of the present law is to raise the marriage age of girls from fourteen years to eighteen years.

A journalist writing from Constantinople says that one, Ali Hassan, told him all about the mighty change that had fallen over the land as he sorrowfully sipped black coffee and mused on women and life.

"Evil days have fallen upon us," said Ali. "I can't see any good in this new notion. It is against the Law of the Prophet. Mohammed said if a man couldn't get along with one wife he could marry three more.

THE BRAVEST IN BATTLE.

"I believe it was a good system, although many people think it had something to do with all the wars Turkey has been in for the last 600 years.

"The Turkish Army always reported that the men living with four wives were always the first to enlist for service at the front, and seemed more at home in battle than their unmarried brothers.

"The Koranic Law gave him the means of ridding himself of undesirable wives whenever, and as often, as he pleased.

"All he had to do was to drop three stones in front of his wife, and repeat three times, 'You are no wife of mine,' and that finishes it."

Ali added that the men would take to the new law about as readily as they would take to a bubonic plague.

1927
Doctor's Story of a Terrible Suspicion.

HOPELESS FUTURE OF LITTLE COLOURED CHILDREN.

FROM Liverpool to Cardiff—from Cardiff to Newport and Bristol. That is my trail in search of the remedy for this appalling problem of the growing thousands of little coloured children who are being born—born only to increase the alarming number of "unemployables" in Great Britain.

"We see so much of it," said a high Newport official. "We have hundreds of coloured seamen passing through the port every year, and it is only natural that they leave a burden behind them. It's been a devil of a job to keep the place clean.

Tragic Young Mother.

"I know of a case where a handsome young girl showed such ability that she obtained a good position here. She had always been told her father was drowned at sea. Her mother, who was regarded as a widow, slaved for years to give her offspring a good education. Later this talented young woman moved in good social circles and she eventually married a man far above her station in life. The man worshipped her; they lived in a large house where a staff of servants waited on her.

"Her first and her second child were handsome white boys. They went to the best school, and it was while the boys were away at college her third baby was born.

"To the horror of the parents, the third child, a girl, was perfectly black. Husband and wife were frantic. The husband accused his wife of all sorts of things.

"She, poor thing, could only plead innocence. Then the man took to drink and left her to nurse her negro baby.

"Knowing the woman, and recollecting something of her past, I called on the girl's mother and cross-examined her. Then she confessed that as a young girl she had made the mistake of associating with a native sailor at a place where she was in service.

"She told me," continued the official, "that the man wanted to marry her, but he looked so repulsive in daylight that she left her situation and fled while the native was out. Later she came to Newport, where she found good work, and had managed to send her girl to a boarding-school.

"That woman simply lived for the happiness of her daughter. She was so terribly affected by the things I told her that she only lived a little while afterwards. That was one of the greatest of life's tragedies that could ever have happened.

Always Some Weakness.

"It's the old-old story, the spread of the Semitic and Hamitic races who tried years ago to overrun Egypt," said a medical man who resides within a stone's throw of the native locality. "I find the children susceptible to mental influences common among the negroid races. The father is only once removed from the grandparents of the child. In his younger days the father witnessed his parents practising cannabalism and human sacrifice, black magic and other horrors conducted by the witch doctors of the bush. Less than thirty years ago these men were savages.

"It has always been inexplicable to me, as it must be to every thinking person, how a white woman can hitch her wagon to a black star. There must be some mental deficiency on the part of the woman? Or is it kind of sex-intoxication?

Terrible Cases.

"In his own country the man is all right; he may be a bushman, or he may be of a race which looks upon people from the bush as you or I would upon beasts of prey. I often wonder what the girl or her parents would think if they could see their relatives in their native surroundings.

"Now, I am not talking from book-learning. I have been in Africa, as well as most countries. I have seen women and men dress in Bond-street fashion to associate among Europeans at church; they have carried their silk stockings over their shoulders and their boots in their hands until they reached the porch. Nature did not intend them to suffer agonies by wearing boots or clothing.

"In less than an hour after church I have seen these people emerge from their mud huts in loin-cloths, perfectly happy in their primitive nudity, washing clothes on the banks of a stream like the harmless, happy children they were intended to be.

"I don't know of a single case where a native would dare to be seen talking to a white woman in his own country, unless he was a house boy or a cook. A white woman who has travelled in native countries would be horrified at the idea of cohabiting with a negro or a man from India. I find it difficult to make people in Britain realise this.

"We have to tolerate it here because the law allows it. Take the case of the children. I have had whole families of half-castes under me at one and the same time. None of them had the stamina one expected to find in such strong-looking bodies; there is always a defect of some sort or another. I have even found it amongst children of exceptional intellect. The kink is there.

"You know when a negro says: 'I go live for die,' and he just coils himself up and dies. Those ideas are sometimes impregnated in the children, and if they get really sick they drop off like moths round a candle.

"I have seven cases urder me now that I do not care to speak about; they are terrible. These men are in hospital on board ship, and there they will remain until they die or recover. We cannot let them loose on the community."

The remedy for the alarming state of affairs in our seaport towns is being sought in an official way. Already, as exclusively announced in "The Sunday News," an influential committee has been formed in Liverpool. It is hoped that other large centres will fall into line.

1945
NAZI "STUD FARMS" OVERRUN

With the U.S. First Army, Saturday.—A number of Nazi "stud farms" still occupied by unmarried mothers and babies have been overrun by the U.S. First Army near Winterberg.—Exchange.

1936
Bushmen's White Chief Gaoled

BRUNO LEMKE, White Chief of the Bushmen of the Kalahari Desert, and the only European ever to learn the secret of the native arrow poison used by the fierce tribesmen, has been sentenced to two years' imprisonment at Windhoek, Cape Colony, for living with a black woman.

Lemke became chief by his prowess with a rifle with which he hunted food for an entire tribe. He took part in strange rites never seen by any other white man.

He was formerly an officer attached to a force sent to stamp out cattle smuggling along the Bechuanaland border. Later he roamed the desert for years, ruling over the nomadic tribes (says the British United Press).

1940
Free Love for Nazis

"I AM a soldier, 22 years old, tall, blond, blue-eyed.

"Before I go away to give up my life for my Fuehrer and my country, I want to meet a German woman by whom I could leave a child and heir for the glory of the German Reich."

This "agony column" advertisement is typical of hundreds which appear daily in the Nazi Press.

Soldiers invite girls to become mothers of children by them before they leave for the Front. Women, in turn, advertise for a soldier to give them a child.

"A German girl wants to become the mother of a child whose father is a German soldier fighting for National Socialism," runs one such advertisement in the "Schwarze Corps," the organ of the Gestapo.

The paper has made a speciality of this kind of advertisement

Marriage is seldom mentioned by the advertisers, who are frankly advertising for promiscuous sexual relationship.

The Nazis encourage the practice. Any woman who has a child by a soldier is given preference for Government positions and the child is brought up at the expense of the State.

1939
Could Marry at Seven

From Our Own Correspnodent

NEW YORK, Friday.

Seven-year-old children can legally marry in Maryland, U.S.A., it was ruled today by Attorney - General Walsh, when granting a marriage licence to a girl of thirteen.

"There is no statute in Maryland fixing the age of persons contracting marriage," he said, "but in common law a marriage of any person under seven years old would probably be void."

1917
POLYGAMY ENCOURAGED
GERMANY SEEKS TO INCREASE POPULATION.

It is reliably reported that brochures are being circulated in the German trenches, under official authority (says a Central News Zurich telegram), arguing that for the purpose of increasing the German population it is the duty of every able-bodied man to have several mistresses as well as a wife, and that the wives of soldiers should be permitted to provide herself with a substitute for her husband during his absence at the front!

Mr. Bonn, a member of the Swiss National Council, in a letter to a Zurich paper, writes in justification of the idea promulgated in the German brochure, and declares that in the Middle Ages the Popes sanctioned a "second household."—Central News.

1937

HIS WEDDING GIFT TO HER WAS A DOLL

Nine - year - old Mrs. Johns (Eunice Winstead, of Tennessee), with her twenty-two-year-old farmer husband. Eunice, described as about four feet one and a half inches tall, light build, bobbed fair hair, blue-eyed, pretty smile, winning childish ways. Husband, six feet, muscular, serious-looking, could be mistaken for father.

MARRIAGE AT NINE SHOCKS U.S. WOMEN

FROM OUR OWN CORRESPONDENT

NEW YORK, Sunday.

WOMEN of America are raising the greatest outcry U.S. has known since Lincoln's anti-slavery campaign, to end the marriage of nine-year-old Eunice Winstead and 6ft. twenty-two-year-old Charles Johns, of Sneedville, Tennessee.

Plans are being drawn up to change the U.S. Constitution so that such a marriage can be forbidden by law. At present in Tennessee a child can marry at any age with the parents' consent. Over the age of thirteen parental consent is not required.

Eunice's is the second child marriage in the district within two weeks. Ella Green, thirteen-year-old schoolgirl, eloped with Charles Newbery, seventeen.

Just before Christmas, Irvene Rhoades, aged twelve, married Clarence D. Leach, a young factory worker at Wabash, Indiana.

Mrs. Ellen Walker, of Panacea, Florida, married in 1935 at twelve, has borne a son to her husband of twenty-two, Cullen Walker.

1920
WOMAN MARRIED TO HER FATHER.

ALWAYS THOUGHT SHE WAS HIS STEP-DAUGHTER.

TWO CHILDREN.

DREAM REVELATIONS AFTER MANY YEARS.

An amazing story is told in a Bill of Complaint which has just been filed in the Baltimore Circuit Court by Anna Belle Jones, for the annulment of her marriage with William M. Jones.

The plaintiff says she has now learned that her husband—the father of her two children—whom she had supposed to be her step-father, is in fact her real father.

SUPPOSED STEP-FATHER.

Mrs. Jones declares in the Bill, says the Central News, that prior to her marriage she had lived with her parents without the slightest inkling of her supposed stepfather's actual identity; and the story is rendered the more remarkable by the assertion of the plaintiff that the true facts were revealed to her in a dream.

Two children were born of the marriage, both boys, aged three and eight years respectively, and both are said to be perfectly healthy and normal.

1931
"WORST CASE," SAYS CORONER

Father and Daughter With Eight Children

"This is the worst case of its kind I have ever known, or, I should think, that anybody else has ever known. It is horrible."

This was the comment made by the Deptford Coroner, Dr. W. H. Whitehouse, at the inquest on Henry John Virgo (63), who was stated to have had eight children by his own daughter.

Lavinia Virgo, the daughter, said he had given her to understand he was not her father. She had seven children by him, besides one that died.

Police evidence was that inquiries were made after an anonymous letter had been received.

Virgo, when questioned, said he had been living with his daughter, and promised to bring marriage and birth certificates to the police station next morning.

He was found in Greenwich Park with his throat cut.

A verdict of "Suicide while of unsound mind" was recorded.

1946
PUT 'CRUSADER' BELT ON WIFE

AN American carpenter who made a Crusader-type "chastity belt" from inch-thick chain-mail, then locked it on his 33-year-old wife was charged at Atlantic City yesterday with "atrocious assault and battery," cables the *Sunday Dispatch* New York Correspondent.

The police said the carpenter, named Truax, aged 39 told them he did it to stop his wife running around.

After he had gone to work she telephoned the police.

A locksmith failed to open the unusual padlock, which had to be filed off before the belt could be removed.

When she was released the wife exclaimed: "I hate men—all men."

Truax was remanded on £250 bail.

1944
BROTHER AND SISTER

GAOL FOR "VICTIMS OF CIRCUMSTANCE"

For years a brother and sister lived together without knowing their real relationship. They believed they were cousins. When a child was born of the association, however, they were informed of the truth of their own births and legal position.

In spite of this, their devotion to one another was such that they continued to live together, and three more children were born.

This unusual story with many pathetic features was told at the Old Bailey when Frederick Joseph Ross, 42, Royal Corps of Signals, and his sister, Mrs. Elizabeth Martha Hart, 45, both of Findongardens, Rainham, were each sentenced to six months' imprisonment for offences arising out of their association.

When sentence was passed, Mrs. Hart broke down and sobbed bitterly, whereupon Ross turned to Mr. Justice Asquith and begged to be allowed to take a double punishment in order to save his sister from gaol.

Telling the story, Mr. Sebag Shaw, prosecuting, stated that when Mrs. Hart, the elder of the two, was born, she was a burden on her parents. When still a baby, therefore, she was adopted by her uncle, and grew up believing him to be her father.

She married, but her husband died, leaving her with two children. She and Ross then set up home and had lived together for five years before they were informed they were brother and sister.

Nevertheless, they continued to live together as before. Then, in 1940, when it seemed likely Ross would be called up, they discussed the question of the Army allowance, and decided it would be best to "marry."

The ceremony took place at Romford on May 17 last. Subsequently Army allowances amounting to £178 were obtained.

1939
MARRIED NEGRO CHAUFFEUR

U.S. WOMAN'S SUICIDE

From Our Own Correspondent
NEW YORK, Tuesday.

A funeral held at Queen's Borough, New York, to-day, revealed the suicide of Mrs. Laura Stedman Gould Dees, a distant relative of President Cleveland and a member of a socially prominent family, who 11 months ago married her coloured chauffeur, Milton Dees.

It is learned that Mrs. Dees, who was 55, hanged herself in a house in the negro quarter, where she had been living since she returned from an extended tour of the United States. The ostracism to which she had been subjected by her family since here marriage is believed to have caused her great unhappiness.

Dees is a well-educated man and is both a poet and a composer. Mrs. Dees was formerly the wife of Dr. George Gould, a gifted author and oculist. She collaborated with him 30 years ago in writing a biography of Lafcadio Hearn.

1920
SECRET TRIALS.

Strongly Condemned by Mr. Justice Darling.

"PUBLIC SHOULD KNOW."

Another strong protest against secret trials of certain cases was made by Mr. Justice Darling at the Old Bailey yesterday. He urged that the holding of incest trials in camera was wrong, and that the matter should be taken up in Parliament, and the provisions of the Act ordering trials in secret reconsidered.

At the end of a case of this nature, he said a brother and sister had pleaded guilty. They were the parents of nine children, six of whom were dead, and one was mentally deficient and tuberculous. "When these people began cohabitation," he went on, "their crime was not punishable. It had been punished in the Ecclesiastical Court long ago, but this had ceased, and, in 1908, Parliament made it a criminal offence, punishable with seven years' penal servitude. These two particular people received no information that what they were doing was a crime. Many people—their relations—knew they were living in this way, but nothing occurred.

1924
BROTHER AND SISTER.
REVELATION YEARS AFTER MARRIAGE.
FROM OUR OWN CORRESPONDENT.
ADELAIDE, Monday.

Horace Stephen Maplesden, 23, and Ethel Susannah Maplesden, 21, brother and sister, were committed for trial here on the charge of having married.

The evidence showed that the family home was broken up when the accused were small children. Both were placed under the care of the State children's department.

Fifteen years later they met as strangers with different names and became fond of each other. They married and had a child.

Subsequently their mother reappeared and identified both. The son informed the authorities and pathetically told the court that he was anxious and willing to keep his sister and child.

1913
ABOLISH THE HOME!
LECTURER DECLARES IT "A WIGWAM SURVIVAL"

The abolition of the home was advocated by the Rev. W. Mortiz Weston, D.D., Ph.D., at a meeting of the Women's Freedom League at Caxton Hall on "The Independence of Married Women." Mr. Weston, who is reported in the "Daily Herald," said he had formerly been an antagonist, but was now one of the most convinced supporters of the cause.

With regard to the economic independence of married women, he said he was anxious to arrive at a practical solution of the difficulty, and went on to illustrate how he thought this could be brought about. The first thing was the abolition of the home. The home was archaic, a survival of the wigwam, one of those conventions by which women had been enslaved for generations.

With the abolition of the home would come co-operative housekeeping. With a properly-trained staff, including one for the care of children, the economic independence of married women could be brought about without separating them from their children, which is often the case to-day where the mother is obliged to be the wage-earner. Conventions, too, must go, along with Mrs. Grundy. Women were the descendants of serfs, and at present afraid of liberty.

The economic independence of men, he said, was largely artificial, owing to the unequal laws of inheritance. Daughters should have legacies and bequests rather than the sons, as women were not physically as fitted for work as men.

On eugenic grounds this was most important, as then a woman would be able to choose her mate, instead of, as now, marrying a man because he has money, however undesirable he may be in other respects.

1940
THIS TIME—SCANDALOUS
From JOHN WALTERS
NEW YORK, Friday.

BECAUSE she omitted a third marriage ceremony when she began living with an ex-husband from whom she had been twice divorced, Mrs. Eva Small, who has been wed seven times, has gone to gaol for an indefinite term.

It was alleged at her puritanical home town of Newton, Massachusetts, that she had caused an "aggravated public scandal."

The man—William Tennihan—appears on Mrs. Small's list of marriages as husband No. 3 and No. 5. The fact that he was No. 8 only unofficially shocked the neighbours.

They agreed that if the couple had gone through the marriage formalities a third time, no one in Newton would have objected.

Mrs. Small admitted that the oversight was an error.

"Ain't marriage wonderful," she added.

Tennihan was gaoled for a year.

FOOTNOTE.—This is the list of Mrs. Small's husbands: 1, Clifford Mendall; 2, Wendell Small; 3, William Tennihan; 4, Julius Burns; 5, William Tennihan by remarriage; 6, John McGhee; 7, Wendell Small by remarriage.

1949
JUDGE SAYS: "MY MOST SHOCKING CASE"
SEVEN YEARS SENTENCE

"This, without exception, is the most shocking case of this kind with which it has been my misfortune to be concerned," commented Mr. Justice Streatfeild, passing a sentence of seven years' imprisonment at Exeter Assizes.

The sentence was on Cyril Daniel Sandford, aged 49, a quarryman, formerly of Farley Mill, Trusham, Devon. Sandford pleaded guilty to offences against two of his daughters, aged 20 and 15, who, between them, bore him five children in addition to 15 born to his wife.

Mr. T. Field-Fisher, defending, pleaded that Sandford should not be too hardly punished because he was the breadwinner of a large family, was a first-class workman, and had not been in trouble before.

Addressing Sandford, the judge remarked: "One of these five children—four by the elder girl and one by the younger girl —is dead, but there are four, at any rate, who, in due course, if not now, will be able to call you both father and grandfather at the same moment."

He said he would have taken into account a plea regarding the overcrowded condition of the house, but for the fact that incidents had been in the day-time, and they did not take place, except in one case, in a bedroom.

1928
BROTHER AND SISTER.
JUDGE SHOCKED BY BAD HOUSING CONDITIONS.

"I don't know how you can expect people to go straight under such circumstances, all hoarded together in a small house," observed Mr. Justice Sankey, at Bedford Assizes, when Henry James Loveridge Cullip, 18, leather currier, pleaded guilty to incest with his 14-year-old sister. —Supt. Tingey stated that prisoner was one of a family of 16, of whom 10 were illegitimate. The mother was deserted after she had given birth to four children, and afterwards lived with a man, by whom she had a family of 10. She was now living with a third man in a small cottage, rented at 4s. 6d. a week. Four children slept in one bedroom, and the girl of 14 in another on the same landing, the woman and the man being downstairs. Prisoner had an excellent character as a workman. —The mother was called into the witness box, and, after she had been asked a few questions, accused swayed backwards and forwards in the dock, and then collapsed in the arms of warders. His mother also fainted, moaning, "God help me!" Both were revived with water, and the judge ended the distressing scene by ordering the lad to be put in the care of the probation officer for two years, his mother becoming surety for his good behaviour during that period.

1916
HER HUSBAND'S SISTER
Relationship Revealed by a Locket.

WIFE'S STRANGE DISCOVERY

CHICAGO, Saturday.

Mrs. Rodger W. Newton fell fainting when she saw evidence that seemed to prove that the man she had married nine years ago is her brother, older by two years than herself. The discovery came through the husband's finding, in an old trunk, a locket containing an old tintype of his parents, recognised by the wife as a photograph of her own father and mother, the tintype the same as one she once had possessed.

This locket was the only connection with the past left with Newton in 1880, when, a child of three years, he was placed in an orphanage in Spokane, Washington. He was soon adopted by a couple, who gave him their own name and who moved to Wisconsin with him.

Knew He Was Adopted.

He was reared in comfort and was schooled till graduation from the University of Wisconsin. He knew he was an adopted child, but assumed he had been taken from some institution in the State of his rearing.

After leaving college Newton's business, that of insurance, took him to Portland, where he met Miss Elizabeth Porter, then attending a seminary. They were married and left on a honeymoon trip, intending to return to visit the bride's parents. But Newton secured a position for a hardware firm and the visit was never made.

Failed to Find Foundling.

History supplied by the sister wife is that her father, destitute and injured by an accident, left her little brother in a Spokane asylum. Later, when in better circumstances, he tried to find the child but failed. The couple have gone to meet what they believe to be their mutual parents.

WOMEN

THE MUSCOVITE MILITANT : A Russian Joan of Arc
Madame Kokovtseva, recently awarded the Cross of St. George for bravery, is the Colonel commanding the 6th Ural Cossack Regiment. She has been twice wounded while fighting. Portrait by C. Bulla, of Petrograd. **1915**

1929
WOMAN SUPERSEDED

Replaced by Man as Sequel to Raid on Birth Control Clinic

NEW YORK, Sunday.

Mrs. Mary Sullivan, director of the Women's Bureau of the New York Police Department, has been superseded by Mr. Whalen, Chief of Police for New York City, and a male police officer has been placed in charge of it.

This drastic action by the Commissioner is the result of the nation-wide protests against the recent raid by the New York women police upon a birth control clinic (one of the many established by Margaret Sanger, the Marie Stopes of America, here and in various parts of the country).

Both the conduct of the police on that occasion and also the fact that private medical history sheets of women patients were removed as evidence caused a storm of indignation in medical circles.—Reuter.

1905
THE ULTIMATE DESTINY OF MAN
IS TO BECOME A WOMAN!

IN the *Westminster Review* for April the indomitable Mrs. Swiney pursues her triumphant way, demonstrating (1) that man is but undeveloped woman, (2) that he is the product of starvation, and (3) that when the millennium arrives he will disappear by absorption into the victorious female, who will alone survive. Is it not written in "The Sayings of Jesus," "When that which is perfect is come, then that which is imperfect shall be done away; and 'the two shall be one, the male as the female.'"?

MAN BUT AN IMPERFECT WOMAN.

Mrs. Swiney exults in believing that the old superstition is dying which ascribed to the male the gift of life. Science now recognises the male factor as of secondary biological importance:—

The male was primarily short-lived, puny, feeble, undeveloped, dependent and parasitic. What is more, its appearance, even among the higher species and where it has developed to great complexity of organic function, is directly attributable to a defective state of malnutrition in the maternal organism.

The latest word of modern research is that "adverse circumstances, especially of nutrition, but also including age and the like, tend to the production of males, the reverse conditions favouring females."

HIS ASCENT TO WOMANHOOD.

Man, being thus the product of starvation, is temporary and will pass. The process of evolution will gradually evolve him into a woman:—

As man approaches the industrial age, of which the highly evolved instincts of the bee and the ant are the precursors, we cannot but recognise that the characteristics of humanity are becoming the same in the men and women of the higher civilisation. Height, bearing, vigour of muscle, equality of brain power, decrease of hairiness, assimilate the boy and the girl.

The male begins to develop certain rudimentary organs hitherto entirely feminine, thus proving the oneness of the constructive creative elements in the male and female organisms, and the ultimate goal intended by natural evolution. In extreme cases in the lower species, the male develops in a certain period, generally of two or three years, entirely into the female; such is the case among those curious animals, the *Ostracoda* and *Cirripedia*. There is no known case where the female, through atrophy of her distinctive organs, degenerates into a male.

1905
DECOY FOR DESERTERS.

WASHINGTON, Sept. 20.

The War Department is efficiently served by Miss Edith King, an attractive girl of twenty-three, who makes it her business to round up deserters on behalf of the authorities. Yesterday she appeared at the headquarters of the army of the East, and handcuffed one soldier while two men who assisted her handcuffed another. The squad was then marched off, followed by a detective. Miss King collected 50 dollars payment for each captive, and then departed on other trails.

She is believed to have captured at least 500 deserters, flirtation being her only weapon.

Born of good family, Miss King was brought up in a convent, until reverses compelled her to seek work. She found man-hunting interesting, and became an army detective. Her prisoners do not appear to be angry, but look foolish at being trapped by a woman's wiles.—Laffan.

1913
CAGED WOMEN.

A REMARKABLE NOVEL OF HAREM LIFE.

"*We secluded women of the East are the guardians of the Mysteries of God Most High—the verities of life and death, of birth and growth and decay—of all those things that come directly from the hand of God. These are the sense of life, though much obscured by all the surface agitation which disturbs the life of men. We, in our calm retirement, always view them.*"

These words are supposed to be spoken by the principal wife of an Egyptian Pasha in a remarkable new novel by Mr. Marmaduke Pickthall, published to-day and entitled "Veiled Women" (Nash). She is addressing Mary Smith, the English governess, who has "islamed" and is giving to marry Yusuf, the Pasha's son. I put them at the head of my article, not because I commit myself to their doctrine, but because they are in such striking and amusing contrast with the chatter of certain of our western women here in England at the present moment. The venerable Murjanah Khanum thought our men's business—"the strife of tribes," she called it—mere nonsense, the froth upon the surface of the deep, a silly game that men will be playing; she and her sisters were the awful priestesses of the real things, of the "veracities," as Carlyle would have said.

East and West.

And here in London some women are ready to become criminals that they may have the vote"; that they may have a voice in choosing those to sit in the building that had become the Dung Market in William Morris's "News from Nowhere."

There are the two views; and the opposition between them is something to think about. I have just been putting them to a man who has seen the East and the world, and his opinion was that the Egyptian lady's philosophy was the true one; "only," he added, "it isn't carried out in the harim."

154 Women

1935
Eskimos—Ideal Race Says Red Emma

"The Ideal citizen!" World

BY A SPECIAL REPRESENTATIVE

HIGH Priestess of the anarchists, Red Emma Goldman has a soft spot in her heart for the Eskimos. Red Emma, who has been preaching anarchism for fifty years, has returned to England after a long globe trot. She does not agree with any state of society in the world. When I asked her which people came nearest to perfection, she said:—

"The Eskimos. They have an inner discipline, but no laws, no crime, and no bloodshed. Society should rest on the co-operative relations of man with man without interference of law and authority.

"Governments exist by violence. They are costly and unnecessary, so give me the Eskimos."

1932
PRINCESS CHANGES HER FAITH IN MID-AIR

From Our Own Correspondent

PARIS, Thursday.

THE English Princess of Sarawak, who was a Roman Catholic when she boarded a plane of Imperial Airways at Croydon to-day, landed a Mohammedan at Le Bourget, having changed her religion in mid-air.

The Princess, who is the wife of the heir-presumptive of Rajah Brook, her official title being the Dayang Muda, is 45, and the mother of four children.

She was accompanied by Dr. Khalid Sheldrake, president of the Western Islamic Association, who performed the ceremony on board the plane.

"TOO COMPLICATED"

"Why did you renounce Christianity?" I asked.

"My family are Quakers," the Princess replied. "I have been a Protestant, but I could not bear that religion. Then I became a Roman Catholic, and I came to the conclusion that this religion is far too complicated.

"I was received by the Holy Father two years ago. I wonder what he will say when he hears I have become a Mohammedan?"

Asked why she changed her religion while flying over the Channel, she replied: "It was because I love the sea."

The Princess was later greeted by leading Mohammedans of Paris, to whom she said: "I am happy to have found the path leading to light by accepting the teaching of the Prophet."

1938
HITLER FEARS THIS WOMAN

THE woman whom Hitler fears more than anyone in Europe has struck again. Two hundred agents of the Gestapo, Germany's dreaded secret police, have been rushed to Danzig to try once again to capture her. She will meet death by the axe twenty-four hours after her capture.

Last week people in Danzig twiddled their radio knobs. Suddenly they stopped twiddling, sat down and listened. A soft, slightly husky girl's voice began telling them the truth about Nazi Germany.

She said that 8,449 people from Danzig have been sent to concentration camps in the last year, and that nearly 3,000 people have vanished from Danzig without a trace.

Then she signed off—"Goodnight to the German people from the Freedom Station."

Hitler himself flashed urgent orders to Himmler, head of the Gestapo. And to-day the Gestapo rules in Danzig, seeking to track down this mysterious voice, the one voice in Germany which dares defy the Fuhrer.

Girl's Revenge

It belongs to a twenty-six-year-old girl from Bavaria. She broadcasts to avenge her lover's death in the notorious concentration camp of Dachau.

Two years ago the German Freedom Station began its regular broadcasts on a 29.8 wavelength.

The Gestapo know that the transmitting apparatus is mounted inside a van, that it never stays for more than three hours in any one spot.

The first broadcast came from the heart of the Black Forest. Night after night it continued. At the end of the first week three thousand police, led by thirty Gestapo agents, closed in on the small area where special detector apparatus revealed the van was situated.

They searched through the night —and found nothing. The Voice had vanished.

Broadcasts have come from every part of Germany. Any German giving information leading to her arrest will receive £5,000.

Bloodhounds Failed

Bloodhounds have been used to track her down, an army corps was once called on. The best radio brains in the Reich have devised special apparatus to locate her van. But so far she has escaped.

At the end of every week's broadcasting she announces: "I have spoken the truth for another week. Remember what you have heard. Next week the headsman's axe may fall!"

Her programmes have been jammed, but each time she has changed her wavelength. Her voice cannot be silenced.

And after the Gestapo has searched Danzig in vain a letter will be posted to Hitler. He has had one after every big drive he has launched against her. They are always the same thirteen words: **My lover was murdered; I shall live and speak until Germany is free.**

1904

WOMEN IN WAR.
Female Warriors of Ancient and Modern Times.

FROM time immemorial war has been considered almost exclusively as an affair of the sterner sex, says James Wilson, in the *Girl's Own Paper*. Yet in the profession of arms, as in nearly all other professions from which women are, or have been until lately, excluded, the softer sex have, from time to time, shown particular genius—not only as nurses braving death for the sake of the helpless wounded, but as combatants, fighting with spear, sword, or rifle against the enemies of their country, skilled in all the arts of destruction, and, in the majority of cases, exercising an encouraging and purifying influence upon their comrades in arms.

After referring to the well-known instances of Boadicea; Victoria, who controlled the fierce legions of Gaul A.D. 268; the Maid of Kent; the Maid of Saragosa, and Jeanne D'Arc, the writer goes on to mention some more recent instances of famous female warriors:

One of the best-known of English female warriors is Mary Ambrée, whose name should be familiar to readers of the works of the poet Butler. In one ballad he tells how she assisted in the attempt to regain Ghent from the Prince of Parma in 1584:

"When captains courageous, whom death did not daunt,
Did march to the siege of the city of Gaunt,
They mustered their soldiers by two and by three,
And the foremost in battle was Mary Ambrée."

The heroic Mary never tried to disguise her sex. As far as is known, she fought in ordinary female attire, armed with sword and target.

Determination to find a runaway husband is said to have been the reason for the notorious Christian Davies, or "Old Mother Ross," as she was nicknamed, turning soldier in 1700. She passed as a man throughout her career in the army, and eventually found her husband at an inn in Holland flirting with a waitress. It would be interesting to know what that worthy couple said to each other when they met.

The famous Hannah Snell became a soldier about 1750 for the same reason as "Old Mother Ross" did. She led a very adventurous life as a marine, and ended her career as the proprietress of a public-house at Wapping, called "The Widow in Masquerade," or "The Female Warrior:

The story of the Jewess Esther Manual, who, like Christian Davies, enlisted to find her husband, a private in the Uhlan Guards, has in it some very picturesque elements. She adopted men's clothes, entered the Königsberger 2nd Landwehr Uhlanen Regiment, and fought in all the battles of 1813 and 1814. She was wounded twice. At Jüterbock she received a bullet in the foot, and in the march through Holland, being in Bulow's corps, received the Iron Cross. She met her husband, who was serving in the Russian Army Corps, at Montmartre, on 29th March, 1814. He was shot dead by a cannon ball next day. Stricken with grief, she immediately quitted the army, resumed female attire, and returned home with her two children.

The eighteenth and nineteenth centuries were prolific in both heroes and heroines. In the insurrection in the Tyrol in 1809 women and children took part. The French Revolution, too, produced many female warriors.

By permission of]   *[The Girl's Own Paper.*
Hannah Snell, who joined the Marines in 1750, and served with them for many years.

1930

WOMEN STILL IN THE 'APE' STAGE

'THEIR REAL TROUBLE,' BY A NOVELIST.

NO GREAT ART.

156 Women

1930
CAN THEY RESIST FASHIONS?

I AM chuckling over the modern woman's predicament.
If she dresses in the fashion she is a slave.
If not, she is a frump. — MISOGYNIST.

1904
Intellect in Woman.

Intellect in woman has so dazzled us by its brilliance that we have failed to recognise it as a disease, like genius in man and the pearl in an oyster. But, nevertheless, it is a disease, and must inevitably be the death of a race in which it is fostered. — *Sydney Telegraph.*

1920
A NEW VIEW OF MARRIAGE.

Confessions of a Lady Novelist.

WHY MISS BURR IS NOW IN LONDON.

Miss Jane Burr, a young American novelist and poet, is now staying in London for reasons which she explained fully to a "Daily News" representative last night. They may be summarised thus:—

England seems to be the only place where there's any freedom.

I've got a book to bring out that they won't look at on the other side.

It's so restful over here.

Miss Burr has a remarkable personality. Although a member of the millionaire Guggenheim family, she dislikes money, and will only accept enough to enable her to write what she wants to write. In her own country she runs a country inn for authors, where only those who can afford to pay do so.

WHERE FREEDOM IS.

Miss Burr has herself written a book which is so extremely "feminist" that American publishers shied at it. She hopes to get it published in England—"because here you can say what you like." She declares that there is no freedom in America.

"Look at the way your young men and girls kiss each other in the parks. It's perfectly charming, and I simply love to see it; but in America they'd be arrested straight away."

But although Miss Burr is in favour of public love-making, she is not enthusiastic over marriage. "I've no use for it," she explained. "I can't take responsibility for any man's socks. What I want is romance—and marriage just knocks that on the head. I married at 18, and I was divorced at 24. Then I married again, and now I've left my second husband. I like men, but I can't stand having one in the house . . ."

HOME OF HIS OWN.

"Would you put up with one in the bicycle shed?"

"No, he'd have to be further away than that. He might have a home of his own where I could stay if I wanted to, and I wouldn't mind having him occasionally in my house as a guest. But it's impossible to have him always about the place. He interferes with one's work——"

"A husband should be a sort of week-end institution?"

"Well, yes, perhaps," said Miss Burr, "but a short week-end."

1918
THE BEST-HATED WOMAN IN JAPAN.

TOKIO, August 27.

Yone Suzuki, the Kobe woman millionaire, the most successful business woman in Japan, is at the present moment one of the best-hated persons in the country. Hated not because of her unusual business capacity, but for the large speculations of her company in rice, the staff of life in Japan, which has so risen in price as to be prohibitive to the poor and middle classes. The war profits of the Suzuki company are estimated at £10,000,000.

Fifteen years ago Yone Suzuki was an unassuming widow with a shrewd business sense who sat all day, Japanese fashion, on the mats, squatting before a diminutive desk, industriously figuring her losses and gains on the soroban, or abacus. To-day, the Suzuki Shoten commands all sorts of enterprises—steel works, camphor-refining, rice-importing, shipbuilding.

This unheard-of development by a woman was watched with sullen mutterings by the great mass of the people, who not only did not enjoy any of the blessings of war profits but also continued to bear the burden caused by the soaring cost of the necessities of life.

Then the storm broke; excited men and women surrounded the palatial offices of the Suzuki Shoten in Kobe, deliberately but very thoroughly burning it down. Yone Suzuki fled that night to Shizuoka, the great tea centre, but here the rice rioters were also most active, and when her identity was discovered the incensed people threatened to rise against her. She telegraphed to Tokio for rooms at an inn, but no hostelry would take her, fearing destruction. In vain did she send £100,000 to the Home Minister for the relief of the poor. The poor took no heed, and smashed and burned her company's factories.

Then, to escape with her life, she changed her name and in disguise sought refuge in a distant village, no one knowing where she is hidden.

A TOKIO HORATIUS.

In Tokio a mob charging over a bridge encountered a group of policemen armed with their regulation festive-looking paper lanterns—spheres of cream and scarlet. The police were scattered like chaff before a wind, and one guardian who dared draw his sword was thrown ingloriously into the canal.

Unchecked the mob ran, hurling stones at plate-glass windows, and poured through a business section to a quieter quarter where a lone policeman stood on the middle of a bridge. This was no obstacle to angry men, and on they came. But the policeman stood his ground, and holding aloft his paper lantern, addressed the rioters:—

"Honourable Gentlemen,—I have a wife and family, and suffer like yourselves because of the high cost of rice. But it is my duty to let no one pass over this bridge. Therefore, I request you please to take some other way."

A sudden calm came over the hasty-tempered, mercurial citizens of Tokio, for the policeman, as everyone knows, is the poorest-paid public servant in the capital.

Laughing and cheering, the crowd turned about, leaving him in undisputed possession of the bridge. — ZOE KINCAID.

1936
£112,000 Fortune of Woman Who Smoked Cigars

Miss A. Dillwyn

A WOMAN who smoked cigars, a pioneer among her sex in industry, politics and public affairs, has left £112,203.

She was Miss Elizabeth Amy Dillwyn, of Ty Gwyn, West Cross, Swansea. She died last December, aged ninety.

1923
"THAT AWFUL AMERICA!"

ISADORA DUNCAN KICKS OUT.

"Sunday Express" Correspondent.

PARIS, Saturday, March 31.

"Stupid, penurious, ignorant, intolerant America disgusts me—nauseates me — and I am going back to Russia, the most enlightened nation of the world to-day."

Isadora Duncan, the interpretative dancer, has stopped her American tour and left the country of her birth for the country of her adoption. But she had certain things to say about America before she left.

Isadora Duncan.

"You feed your children on canned peas and canned art, and wonder why they are not beautiful," she declared to America at large. "You will not let them grow up in freedom. You persecute your real artists. You put them under the heels of fat policemen like the ones who sat on the platform of my concert in Indianapolis. You drug their souls with matrimony. You import what art you have, which isn't much. And when any one tells you the truth you say, 'They are crazy!'"

Miss Duncan's tour in America was a stormy one. The audience laughed her off the stage in Brooklyn, the Mayor of Boston stopped her dancing, and told her to put on some clothes, and large prosaic policemen insisted on sitting on the stage when she was dancing in Indianapolis.

But now she has left for Russia, where there is peace—of a kind.

1930
WOMEN FOIL ITALIAN DICTATOR.

REVOLT AGAINST CAMPAIGN FOR BABIES

From a Special Correspondent lately in Italy.

ITALY is awaiting with intense interest the outcome of one of the strangest battles ever fought on a non-military field.

The struggle lies between Fascism and Feminism, and the issue—vital to Signor Mussolini's grandiose schemes for a greater Italy—involves half a million potential babies.

So far the Duce has admittedly been worsted, and Fascism is now facing, none too confidently, a new enemy, represented by the hosts of Italian women who resolutely refuse to fill any longer the subordinate rôle allotted to them in the Fascist social and economic scheme.

100,000 FEWER BABIES.

At the beginning of last year the Duce demanded a bigger quota of babies to realise a large scale emigration into Italian colonies, and extensive settlements on the land at home.

Yet Fascists now perceive that, instead of more, about 100,000 fewer children were born in 1929 than in previous post-war years.

Official statistics just issued show clearly that in Italy, as elsewhere, the birth rate is falling steadily. Even the extreme Fascist newspapers make no secret of the importance of this victory of women over the Dictator.

The defeat is all the more damaging since Mussolini has admitted that the future of Fascism lies with a younger generation, trained and moulded upon official lines.

I found convincing evidence of the consternation which Fascists experience over the revolt of womanhood.

It is clearly perceived that the Duce's policy—in which an energetic "back to the land" campaign is an all-important plank—cannot be carried out by the next generation if the birth rate does not rise swiftly.

PERIL TO FASCISM.

Unless the present decline is checked, and the women of Italy can be won over to his standpoint, the whole fabric of Fascism may be endangered.

The "virus" of independence, which has appeared unexpectedly in this vital section of society, must be eradicated at all costs unless Fascism is to be foiled by Feminism, and the Dictator beaten by the birth rate.

1906

IMPRISONED FOR PROPHESYING THE VIOLENT DEATH OF THE TSAR: AGAFYA PASTUKHIN.

The Kharkhoff gypsy woman whose portrait we give is a standing proof that a prophet has no honour in his own country. She was sentenced to twenty years' imprisonment for predicting that the Tsar would come to a violent end.

1917
FORCIBLE FEEDING.

New York's Interest in the First Case in America.

(From Our Correspondent.)
NEW YORK, Sunday.

America has her first case of the forcible feeding of a woman, and it is creating a great sensation both from its novelty and owing to the agitation of prominent women against the adoption of this method of prison treatment.

The case is that of Mrs. Ethel Byrne, who for some time past has been holding a clinic for poor women and distributing pamphlets on the subject of birth control. She was warned by the authorities, but continued her work, and was sentenced to thirty days' imprisonment.

She was arrested last Tuesday and taken to Blackwell's Island, New York's penitentiary in the East River. She at once began a hunger strike, refusing both food and drink. Up to yesterday afternoon for 103 hours she had touched nothing, and thereupon the officials began forcibly to feed her.

1927
HAREMS OF MEN.

TRIBE IN WHICH HUSBANDS ARE SLAVES.

Moscow, Saturday.

A tribe in which women practise polygamy and the inhabitants of the harem are men, and not women, has been discovered in Mongolia by M. Kasloff, a Russian scientist, who has just returned here from a journey in Tibet.

The tribe, says M. Kasloff, is ruled by women, and each woman has several husbands as her slaves.

M. Kasloff also relates how he braved "the demons" of Mongolian superstition by swimming across a sacred lake in the Gobi desert and was himself hailed as a demon when he came out of the water unscathed.—British United Press.

1905
LOUISE MICHEL DEAD.

Career of the Heroine of the Paris Commune.

MARSEILLES, Jan. 9.
Louise Michel died to-day.—Reuter.

According to our Paris Correspondent Louise Michel arrived in Marseilles on Thursday last, was taken ill at the station, and after she had been hurriedly conveyed to the Hotel de l'Oasis, a doctor was summoned, who found that she was suffering from pneumonia.

To the civilised world at large Louise Michel, the news of whose death comes from Marseilles, was the incarnation of anarchism among the weaker sex, and, to speak plainly, she was considered as nothing more than that. She was one of the most violent partisans of the Paris Commune, during which she donned male dress and risked her life—rifle in hand—in various encounters with the Versailles troops. She might have escaped when the capital fell into the latter's hands; the thought never came to her. Nor did she defend herself when tried by the 6th Council of War in December 1871. She frankly owned to having helped to set Paris on fire, and threatened to renew the attempt whenever she should have a chance, and wound up by asking her judges to sentence her to death. They sent her to New Caledonia instead, and while there she wrote a book for children, in which are some really charming tales, showing the big heart of the woman where the innocent and helpless were concerned. The proceeds of the publication went to the maintenance of her mother, whose comfort and peace, throughout the whole of her chequered career, Louise Michel never for a moment lost sight of. Seven years' stay at Nouméa neither curbed her refractory spirit nor caused her to forego her pretensions to reform society by her own particular system of pulling the foundations from under it rather than modify the superstructure itself by gradually applied and opportune improvements. In 1879 she refused a free pardon unless all those who had been transported for participation in the Commune should be accorded the same condonation. She clung to her decision until the general "amnesty" gave her satisfaction on that point; and in November 1880 she arrived in Paris.

LEADER OF RIOTS.

Ringleader of every riot, disturbance and political meeting that marked the second decade of the Third Republic, her reward was almost uninterrupted imprisonment and prosecution from the powers, cheap adulation from poor visionaries like herself, sham encouragement from those whose clamours for a social and political millennium but imperfectly concealed the chase after the loaves and fishes of office and which eventually came to their share, and derision from the rest of the world. She was branded as a virago and as a firebrand in petticoats, and those who saw her at the head of a mob in the streets of Paris, inciting them to arson, pillage, and worse, or heard her hysterically addressing such a mob from a platform, or read of those things, had reason for their epithets.

Yet this apparent virago, this firebrand in petticoats, had a heart of gold, responsive at the lightest touch to all the finer feelings of humanity, and almost divinely sympathetic with the sufferings and wretchedness of the disinherited of fortune. Her purse never contained either gold, silver or brass, for she gave it all. In the latter years of her life Louise Michel, while not abating one jot of her regenerating mission, had calmed down. The madness that was in her had spent itself.

'RED CLARA' AND 'GHETTO ROSE'

A "Cinderella" Romance

1933

Two women of world-wide fame died yesterday — Rose Pastor Stokes ("Rose of the Ghetto") and Clara Zetkin ("Red Clara"). According to Reuter, Mrs. Stokes died in Frankfurt-on-Main, and the Exchange says that Frau Zetkin died in Moscow.

NEW YORK, Tuesday.

Friends of Mrs. Rose Pastor Stokes asserted here to-day that her death was due to blows from a policeman's truncheon received in this city a few years ago during a demonstration against the occupation of Haiti by American Marines.

"Rose of the Ghetto" was struck while attempting to protect a young boy from a policeman.

This daughter of poor Russian immigrants who married the New York millionaire, Phelps Stokes, was a Communist at the time of her death, having run through the gamut of political opinions during her career.

After her divorce from Stokes eight years ago she declared: "We had become friendly enemies."

Her marriage to Stokes in 1905 was described at the time as a Cinderella romance of a beautiful factory girl who left her tenement home to live amid the splendours of a Long Island mansion.

A few years ago Rose married Isaac Romain, a Greenwich Village tutor.

Before going to New York, Rose's family lived in the East End of London, arriving from Russia when Rose was seven. She worked as a cigarette-maker in a Whitechapel factory, often being reduced to the greatest poverty and semi-starvation.

Rose Pastor Stokes.

Clara Zetkin.

FRAU ZETKIN

Moscow, Tuesday.

Frau Clara Zetkin, who passed away here to-day, was 76.

A former member of the German Reichstag, when the collapse of Communism came in Germany the Soviet Government gave her a pension.

"Red Clara" had led a stormy life as a revolutionary leader.

She had fought in street battles and led strikes. Last August, Frau Zetkin found herself the senior member of the German Reichstag, and by virtue of her age she opened the Reichstag when it assembled in that month.

She delivered a fiery address from the rostrum in which she particularly attacked Herr Hitler, not then in power.—Exchange.

1919

Dr. Mary Walker, whose death is reported from New York. Known as "the original suffragette," she had for years worn men's clothing, having special authority from Congress to do so.

KEY TO SOURCES

DC	Daily Chronicle
DCI	Daily Citizen
DE	Daily Express
DM	Daily Mirror
DMA	Daily Mail
DN	Daily News
DS	Daily Sketch
DT	Daily Telegraph
E	Echo
EN	Evening News
ES	Evening Standard
EST	Evening Star
ET	Evening Telegraph
F	Freethinker
G	Globe
GR	Graphic
IN	Illustrated London News
JG	St James's Gazette
MP	Morning Post
NA	Nation & Athenaeum
NC	News Chronicle
NW	News of the World
P	People
PG	Pall Mall Gazette
R	Reynolds's Illustrated Newspaper
ROR	Review of Reviews
RR	Rapid Review
S	Star
SC	Sunday Chronicle
SD	Sunday Dispatch
SE	Sunday Express
SH	Sunday Herald
SN	Sunday News
SR	Sunday Referee
SU	Sun
T	Times
TD	To-Day
TR	Truth
WD	Weekly Dispatch
WG	Westminster Gazette

Page 7 DM 18 Mar 1938
8 PG 7 Feb 1923
 16 May 1905
 _____ 1903
 MP 1 Jan 1936
 MP 22 Dec 1931
 DE 12 Jun 1934
 DN 31 Oct 1928
9 DM 11 Jan 1937
 DN 17 Sep 1921
 DM 11 Apr 1938
 _____ 1904
 MP 22 Dec 1931
 S 9 Jul 1948
 _____ 1905
 _____ 1916
10 DE 12 Nov 1928
 R 7 Jul 1929
 EN 19 Apr 1934
 WD 17 Jul 1927
 NC 4 Mar 1931
 NC 27 Jan 1931
11 EN 5 Sep 1934
 ES 7 Aug 1937
 DM 29 Jul 1929
 DN 9 Feb 1924
 EN 25 Sep 1920
 DM 23 Dec 1920
 DM 17 Feb 1940
 DM 24 Nov 1929
 EN 9 Apr 1921
 DN 31 Oct 1928
 DN 12 Dec 1921
12 DM 22 Jul 1936
13 DE 2 Sep 1920
 DN 18 Oct 1929
 R 12 Mar 1923
14 R 21 Dec 1924
 __ 19 Dec 1924
15 NW 24 Mar 1935
 NW 1 Apr 1934
 DT 12 Jan 1925
16 SD 25 Nov 1928
 DC 7 Apr 1906
 WD 9 Sep 1923
 DM 23 Apr 1942
 S 31 Mar 1925
 SE 29 Mar 1925
 DMA 25 May 1908
17 S 24 Jan 1905
 DC 13 Jun 1905
 _____ 1910
 DN 20 Mar 1922
 DE __ Jul 1908
18 EN 23 Feb 1920
 SP 9 Dec 1923
 DN 19 Mar 1928
 DN 7 Jul 1925
19 SD 21 Oct 1934
20 NC 16 Mar 1931
 _____ 1908
 MP 29 Aug 1934
21 DM 1 Apr 1929
 _____ 1906
 SD 21 Jun 1942
 WG 22 Apr 1903
 _____ Aug 1903
 _____ 1901
22 DM __ Jan 1904
 _____ 1906
 _____ 1900
 DE 23 Apr 1913
 DN 18 May 1921
 S 6 Feb 1932

DE 24 May 1908
DN 21 Jul 1930
EN 26 Oct 1938
23 WD __ Dec 1927
 R 21 Aug 1921
 R 4 Dec 1938
 EN 11 Mar 1921
 S 5 Mar 1935
24 DN 29 Jul 1927
 DC 10 Apr 1908
 _____ 1916
 MP 21 Jan 1932
25 DN 3 Feb 1914
 EN 17 Aug 1921
 R 14 Jan 1917
 _____ 1926
 S 22 Jan 1926
26 DC 1 Sep 1908
 WD 18 Sep 1927
 DN 26 Feb 1927
27 _____ 1905
28 ES 16 Aug 1947
 DC 12 Mar 1930
 _____ 1904
 _____ 1905
 DC 6 Aug 1903
 DM 19 Nov 1935
 DE 23 Dec 1903
 DN 26 Aug 1924
 DE 26 Jun 1927
29 NC 2 Feb 1939
 DT _____ 1943
 DN 29 Mar 1927
 SD 22 Oct 1933
 NW 23 Jun 1912
30 MP 31 Dec 1931
 R 18 Dec 1938
 MP _____ 1933
 MP 3 Jul 1934
 DM 8 Feb 1905
31 MP 22 Dec 1931
 __ 28 Sep 1927
 DM _____ 1945
 NC __ Mar 1931
32 DE 25 Jul 1909
 DE 13 Jul 1914
 IN _____ 1912
 R __ Mar 1912
33 DC 14 Dec 1910
 DM 9 Oct 1909
 DN 8 May 1928
34 SP 9 Sep 1940
35 SP 1 Sep 1940
 SP 9 Sep 1940
36 SD 19 Dec 1937
 ES 18 Apr 1941
 DE 16 Dec 1913
 DM 9 Dec 1940
 NC 9 May 1940
 SR 5 Mar 1939
 EN 30 Aug 1921
 SE 2 Apr 1922
37 SC 31 Mar 1929
38 _____ 1921
 _____ 1942
 NW 7 Feb 1932
 E _____ 1904
 EN 10 Mar 1936
 NW 16 Mar 1936
 NW 17 Apr 1927
 SD 18 Oct 1931
 NW 6 Dec 1936
 DM 20 Oct 1938
39 SD 10 Jun 1933

DM 9 Jun 1933
S 3 Apr 1933
DM 14 Apr 1934
__ 23 Mar 1909
DN 23 Jul 1924
40 DE 22 Dec 1908
 ES 27 Jul 1934
 WD 6 Aug 1922
 NW 2 Aug 1943
 EN 27 Apr 1936
41 NW 29 Jun 1924
 S 25 Aug 1939
 DM 7 Aug 1936
 __ 14 Mar 1908
42 WD 5 Feb 1928
 SR 16 Apr 1933
 DE __ Jul 1907
 NW 16 Nov 1924
43 NW 3 Apr 1938
44 DMA _____ 1903
 S 18 Oct 1915
 ET _____ 1919
 DT 8 Oct 1938
45 SP 6 Nov 1938
 _____ 1903
 JG 15 Feb 1905
46 DN 18 Apr 1929
 _____ 1913
 S 18 Jan 1929
 MP 19 Mar 1931
 _____ 1903
 SD 31 Mar 1929
47 S 8 Nov 1933
 DN 9 Jan 1928
 SE 18 Apr 1926
 DN 17 Jan 1930
48 NW 28 Mar 1926
 _____ 1916
 R 10 Apr 1921
 DN 25 Oct 1930
 S 16 May 1948
49 DM 24 Sep 1937
 _____ 1903
 MP 29 Aug 1930
 DM 11 Mar 1936
 R 2 Jun 1935
 ES 7 Oct 1929
 DN 8 Sep 1926
50 SR 19 Mar 1933
51 DM 26 Apr 1943
52 S 18 Jan 1924
 P 10 May 1903
 _____ 1913
 R 18 Apr 1937
 EN 26 Jul 1934
 DC 3 Aug 1911
53 S 12 Dec 1922
 DC 21 Feb 1905
 EN 8 Mar 1914
54 DC _____ 1916
55 SP 2 Sep 1934
 EN 27 Oct 1905
 MP 5 Jun 1931
 _____ 1934
56 PG 22 Jan 1913
57 NC 11 Aug 1931
 __ 10 Jun 1913
 DN 22 Jun 1927
58 _____ 1898
 R 5 May 1929
 DN 2 Feb 1915
 _____ 1918
 S 12 Feb 1926
59 TR _____ 1905

60 ES 15 Jul 1934
61 DN 9 Jul 1920
    DN 24 Aug 1923
    DM _____ 1947
    ES 17 Nov 1928
62 SP 17 Feb 1929
63 18 Apr 1926
    _____ 1903
    __ 20 Mar 1920
64 WG 5 Sep 1905
65 DM 21 Apr 1934
66 R 21 Aug 1938
    NC 27 May 1939
    SR 29 May 1938
    DE 2 Oct 1908
    NC 11 Jun 1931
    WD 23 Aug 1908
    _____ 1907
    DN 29 Jul 1927
67 NC 11 Oct 1936
    NC 9 May 1938
    EST 2 Jul 1906
    ES 21 May 1921
    DCI _____ 1914
    EN 18 Dec 1920
68 __ 4 Nov 1903
    EN 15 Jul 1940
    MP 17 Nov 1936
    SD 31 Jul 1938
69 ES 19 Jun 1939
    S 30 May 1905
    DM 28 Mar 1929
    NW 16 Sep 1934
    MP 29 Sep 1930
70 DN 23 Apr 1927
    EN 6 Nov 1944
    DN 28 Sep 1925
    R 18 Apr 1926
    RR __ Dec 1904
    SE 5 Jul 1925
    DN 2 Aug 1921
71 SD 18 Oct 1946
    DC 30 Apr 1907
    DM 22 Oct 1938
    DM 20 Jul 1945
    SC 1 Feb 1942
    _____ 1905
    MP 27 Aug 1937
    SR 23 Oct 1938
72 MP 30 Jul 1934
    SR 6 Nov 1938
73 SD 30 Oct 1938
74 DM 22 Jul 1938
    DM 26 Oct 1937
    R 24 Apr 1921
    R 1 Jun 1930
    DE 26 _____ 1903
    JG 15 Oct 1904
75 DM 6 Jul 1936
    DC 29 Oct 1906
    NW __ Oct 1926
76 DC 30 Sep 1904
    _____ 1912
    DC 8 Mar 1900
    SR 18 Mar 1934
    DE 12 Apr 1910
    SD 27 Aug 1933
77 _____ 1921
    EN 5 Dec 1921
    __ 16 Sep 1919
    WD 17 Aug 1924
    NW 4 Apr 1937
78 EN 7 Feb 1939
    S 3 Apr 1917
    _____ 1938

SP 15 Jul 1935
DT 23 Apr 1923
__ 12 Oct 1904
_____ 1919
NC 3 Jul 1936
79 DT 2 Mar 1938
    _____ 1907
    EN 14 May 1900
    NA 22 Feb 1930
80 DMA __ Sep 1907
81 DN 2 Sep 1927
    DE 11 Apr 1924
    _____ 1925
    NW 15 Nov 1936
82 DE __ Oct 1905
    JG 2 Dec 1904
    JG 15 Feb 1905
    ____ Mar 1904
    _____ 1908
83 DMA 22 Dec 1904
    DM 13 Feb 1905
84 DT 7 Feb 1925
    DN 30 May 1928
    DN 9 Apr 1923
85 DN 24 Mar 1928
    MP 24 Jun 1935
    R 1 May 1932
    S 12 Dec 1925
86 SD 11 Sep 1949
    DN 4 Jul 1921
    MP 10 Feb 1933
    MP 24 Sep 1937
87 DE 1 Nov 1928
    NC 31 Jul 1945
    DM 26 Jul 1940
    DE 23 Jun 1927
88 _____ 1905
89 DN 30 May 1921
    NC 2 Apr 1936
    _____ 1903
    DE 5 Jun 1903
90 R 21 Apr 1929
    SE __ Nov 1922
91 SE __ Nov 1922
    NC 4 Mar 1938
    __ 20 Oct 1909
92 TD 26 Nov 1902
93 SE 18 Nov 1934
94 DN 11 Mar 1927
    ES 22 Apr 1929
    ROR __ Jan 1905
    EN 6 Nov 1913
95 NC 3 Feb 1934
96 PG 17 Feb 1923
    MP 2 Feb 1935
    PG 9 Mar 1923
    DE 21 Dec 1928
97 DM 9 Sep 1904
    _____ 1904
    _____ 1903
    EN 26 Jan 1921
    EN 26 Jan 1904
98 DN 17 Feb 1930
    DN 18 Feb 1930
99 F 8 Dec 1940
    SD 28 Mar 1948
    SP 29 Jul 1934
    NC 27 Feb 1933
    EN 27 May 1915
100 T 23 Aug 1934
    S 4 Feb 1941
101 DC 19 Nov 1908
    MP 3 Oct 1933
    WG 5 Jun 1929
    MP 16 Jun 1934

102 JG 6 Jan 1908
103 DN 31 Jan 1923
    DN 3 Jan 1908
    DM 23 Nov 1933
104 SR 2 Oct 1938
    NC 29 Nov 1933
    _____ 1921
    DN 28 Jan 1924
    MP 3 Jun 1935
    NC 6 Jun 1934
105 NW 8 Dec 1936
    S 27 Aug 1924
    SP 16 Jan 1916
    DC 17 Jan 1905
    _____ 1903
    _____ 1924
    SC 27 Sep 1942
    SU 22 Mar 1906
106 DN 11 Apr 1928
    NC 26 Jun 1934
    DMA 5 Dec 1905
    R 6 Jul 1919
    DN 31 May 1929
    DN 26 Jun 1926
    __ 6 Sep 1901
    NW 30 Oct 1938
107 DM 19 Jun 1926
    MP 13 Jul 1934
    DM 23 Mar 1934
    _____ 1904
    SD 23 Mar 1941
    ES 14 Nov 1934
    17 Jun 1906
108 DN 20 Sep 1924
    _____ 1904
    DE __ Nov 1903
    SE 4 Jul 1923
    R 23 Sep 1923
    DN 13 Jul 1921
    SE 15 May 1927
    DN 25 Feb 1928
    EN 19 Apr 1934
109 DN 19 Feb 1923
110 DN 26 Mar 1919
    DC 18 Apr 1912
    SE 29 Nov 1925
    DE 11 Dec 1928
111 JG 11 Mar 1905
    DC 18 Sep 1908
    _____ 1898
    _____ 1904
    MP 15 Sep 1936
112 WG 25 Oct 1910
113 MP 31 May 1935
    __ 26 May 1905
    MP 19 Nov 1930
    _____ 1909
    G _____ 1902
    ES 14 Dec 1936
114 S 12 Oct 1931
    MP 3 Jul 1933
    S 6 Aug 1903
    DM 20 Jan 1937
    _____ 1906
115 F 11 Aug 1935
    SD 9 Dec 1928
    DE 10 Dec 1928
116 _____ 1898
117 GR 24 Aug 1929
    R __ Sep 1899
118 DN 25 Apr 1921
    DM 17 Dec 1940
    SE 25 May 1922
    EN 3 Sep 1913
119 R 7 Aug 1927

MP 9 Dec 1930
DN 8 Jul 1929
EN 22 Apr 1931
120 DC 1 Apr 1930
    MP 11 Oct 1930
    MP 30 Jun 1934
    R 6 Jul 1919
121 __ 7 Jul 1921
    NW 1 Sep 1913
    SP 10 Jul 1921
    _____ 1904
122 NA 17 Nov 1928
123 SP 5 Mar 1933
124 DMA 22 Sep 1921
    SC 21 Mar 1929
    DN 11 Dec 1918
    DMA 16 Aug 1910
125 R 4 Apr 1920
    SC 25 Jun 1939
    R 1 Jun 1913
126 NW 25 Mar 1937
    DE 2 Oct 1920
    DC __ Nov 1912
127 S 5 Mar 1929
    ____ Mar 1929
128 DM 12 Oct 1937
    EN 6 Apr 1906
    ES 13 Nov 1907
    EN 10 Apr 1915
    DMA 10 Dec 1906
129 DM 16 Jan 1907
    __ 27 Jun 1907
130 _____ 1905
    _____ 1906
    _____ 1906
    __ 29 Dec 1912
131 S 28 Jul 1928
132 WD 18 Jan 1925
    EN 3 Jul 1907
    DM 2 Jan 1941
    DM 11 Dec 1940
    _____ 1949
    DN 13 Apr 1927
133 EN 11 Aug 1933
    NW 20 Sep 1931
    _____ 1919
    EN 22 Jul 1948
    DT 3 Feb 1941
    G 13 Dec 1919
134 DN 15 Feb 1926
    EN 18 Oct 1930
    EN 2 Jan 1923
    SC 24 Oct 1926
135 __ 25 Jan 1913
    DN 11 Sep 1929
    DT 27 Oct 1938
    DN 19 Mar 1921
    SE 8 Mar 1925
136 DN 28 Jun 1930
    NW 20 Sep 1942
    SD 12 Nov 1947
    DT 21 Dec 1945
    NC 5 Mar 1936
    DC 11 Apr 1911
    DN 19 Jan 1923
    DE 4 Oct 1923
137 _____ 1907
    ES 1 Jan 1930
    _____ 1923
    _____ 1902
    DM 11 Apr 1930
    MP 4 Feb 1937
    ES 8 Apr 1936
138 NC 19 Jun 1936
139 F 18 Feb 1917

SP 2 Feb 1930
140 _____ 1920
    NW 5 Dec 1915
    DM 16 Apr 1941
    DN 7 Aug 1918
    DC 3 Sep 1915
141 DM 28 Jan 1938
    S 12 Dec 1931
    ES 9 Oct 1926
142 EN 26 Jan 1904
    SD 8 Dec 1928
    R 5 Mar 1922
    S 20 Nov 1929
    DM 13 Oct 1939
143 EN 27 Oct 1921
    DN 10 Sep 1918
    DM 23 Sep 1936
    _____ 1942
    DC 30 Oct 1929
    DC 19 Aug 1921
144 SP 3 Feb 1918
    DM 8 Oct 1917
    DN 11 Jul 1918
    _____ 1918
145 DM 26 Jul 1937
    S 16 Nov 1917
    DN 28 Jun 1918
    F 22 Sep 1918
    _____ 1904
    SH 29 Oct 1916
    DE 3 Jul 1928
146 DM 23 Jan 1909
147 R 10 Oct 1926
148 SN 30 Sep 1927
    NW 8 Apr 1945
    SR 8 Mar 1936
    R 7 Jul 1940
149 NC 18 Feb 1939
    PG 20 Oct 1917
    DM 1 Feb 1937
150 G 5 Aug 1920
    R 6 Sep 1931
    SD 16 Jun 1946
    NW 5 Mar 1944
    DT 31 May 1939
    DN 19 Nov 1920
151 DMA 30 Sep 1924
    _____ 1913
    DM 30 Mar 1940
    NW 13 Nov 1949
    NW 23 Jan 1928
    R 3 Sep 1916
152 _____ 1915
153 DM 13 May 1929
    ROR __ Apr 1905
    DC 21 Sep 1905
    EN 28 Jan 1913
154 NC 19 Feb 1932
    _____ 1935
    SR 14 Aug 1938
155 _____ Nov 1904
    DC 17 Jan 1930
156 DM 19 Feb 1930
    _____ 1904
    DN 10 Aug 1920
    DMA 11 Oct 1918
    DM 8 Feb 1936
    SE 1 Apr 1923
157 DN 19 Feb 1930
    DS 21 Feb 1906
    DN 29 Jan 1917
    WD 10 Apr 1927
    DC 18 Jan 1905
158 NC 21 Jun 1933
    _____ 1919